FIELDWORK AMONG THE MAYA

FIELDWORK AMONG THE MAYA

REFLECTIONS ON THE HARVARD CHIAPAS PROJECT

Evon Z. Vogt

UNIVERSITY OF NEW MEXICO PRESS
Albuquerque

Library of Congress Cataloging in Publication Data
Vogt, Evon Zartman, 1918–
    Fieldwork among the Maya : reflections on the Harvard Chiapas Project /
Evon Z. Vogt. — 1st ed.
        p.   cm.
    Includes bibliographical references.
    ISBN 0-8263-1502-X
    1. Harvard Chiapas Project—History.   2. Mayas—Antiquities.
3. Vogt, Evon Zartman, 1918–   .   4. Archaeologists—Mexico—Chiapas
Highlands—Biography.   5. Archaeologists—United States—Biography.
6. Excavations (Archaeology)—Mexico—Chiapas Highlands—History.
7. Tzotzil Indians—Social life and customs.   8. Chiapas Highlands
(Mexico)—Antiquities.   I. Title.
F1435.V732   1994   93-27203
972'.75016—dc20   CIP

Designed by Linda Mae Tratechaud

*To all who shared
the Chiapas experience with me
—the stimulating students and colleagues,
the loyal friends and family, and, above all,
the gracious and patient Tzotzil-Mayas.*

CONTENTS

PREFACE

Since the days that Malinowski spent some four years doing field research in the Trobriand Islands during World War I, there have probably been dozens of anthropologists whose total years devoted to fieldwork have exceeded that early record in the Southwest Pacific. I estimate that I have undertaken more than eight years of field research in the past fifty years. Yet in this age when books about fieldwork in anthropology are becoming fashionable and are being published at an astonishing rate, I have written little about field research per se. Indeed, the longest pieces I have published are "The Harvard Chiapas Project: 1957–1975" (Vogt 1979) and "Chapter 1: Field Research in Zinacantan," which I added to the second edition of *The Zinacantecos of Mexico: A Modern Maya Way of Life* (Vogt 1990).

I decided some years ago it was high time I wrote about field research and I began work on such a book, focusing it on the Harvard Chiapas Project, which was initiated in 1957 and has been in operation for some thirty-five years. The result is this personal chronicle of the project, which begins with my southwestern childhood and an account of how and why I became an anthropologist, describes the major features of the Harvard Chiapas Project, comments on changes in style and method of doing anthropology, and ends with my retirement dinner at the Harvard Club of Boston.

The field operations of the Harvard Chiapas Project were carried out in the Tzotzil-speaking Indian municipios of the Highlands of Chiapas located between the Isthmus of Tehuantepec and the Guatemalan border (See map p. 70). Tzotzil is one of the twenty-nine Mayan languages currently spoken by an estimated five million Indians—the descendants of the ancient Maya—who live in Chiapas and the Yucatan Peninsula in Mexico, the Highlands of Guatemala, and Belize.

The Chiapas Highlands rise to more than nine thousand feet, with fertile upland valleys at seven thousand feet, and are composed of rugged limestone and volcanic mountains. Like all of Mexico, Chiapas has marked wet and dry seasons. While the winters are dry, the heavy summer rains nourish the crops of maize, beans, and squash that feed the relatively dense populations of these contemporary Maya farmers. On the summit of the Highlands, the climate is cool and the scenery is beautiful, with the mountains cloaked in magnificent pine and oak forests—an ideal cultural and natural setting for a long-range anthropological field project.

The earlier chapters of this book intentionally provide more details about the field experience in Chiapas since the design and mode of operations of the project were slowly, and sometimes painfully, hammered out during these early years. Once the architecture of the project was shaped, it was possible to convey the essence of our operations in the later years in a more compressed style.

Although the volume is intended mainly for the anthropological profession, I have attempted to keep the style nontechnical enough so that others interested in anthropology and the cultures of the Southwest and southern Mexico can also enjoy the book.

ACKNOWLEDGMENTS

I am deeply indebted not only to the many students and colleagues in the United States and Mexico who worked with me on the Harvard Chiapas Project, but also to our Tzotzil-speaking Indian friends and colleagues who accepted us so gracefully in their home communities in the Chiapas Highlands over the years. Although I have not always followed their advice, the manuscript has benefited enormously from detailed comments and criticisms by Victoria R. Bricker, Frank Cancian, George A. Collier, John B. Haviland, Robert M. Laughlin, Joan Mark, and Nan Vogt. I also deeply appreciate the skilled editorial work of Dana Asbury and Anne R. Gibbons at the University of New Mexico Press. Finally, my apologies to those field researchers who do not appear in the photographs in the book; it was impossible to include everyone.

1 /
SOUTHWESTERN
PRELUDE:
1918-1953

 When my grandchildren talk about the Southwest (which they all cherish), they often ask me why I ever left our family ranch located under those azure blue skies among the pinyons and junipers in the mesa and canyon country of northwestern New Mexico. I probably never would have left except for a special concatenation of circumstances that made me into an anthropologist rather than a rancher.

I am one of the few anthropologists who was actually born in New Mexico, a state that has become famous for anthropological research. I made my appearance at St. Mary's Hospital in Gallup on 20 August 1918 and grew up on the Vogt Ranch located forty-five miles southeast of Gallup and ten miles west of El Morro National Monument at the foot of the Zuni Mountains. I was the eldest of four children with three younger sisters.

One can hardly imagine a more felicitous setting for the making of an anthropologist. Our closest neighbors were Navahos, who lived in scattered hogans and grazed their sheep less than a mile to the south and east of our ranch house, and Mormons, located in a verdant, irrigated valley with the small town of Ramah (population 250) a mile to the west. Twenty-five miles further west near the Arizona border was the pueblo of Zuni, which had been studied by a distinguished roster of anthropologists: Frank Cushing, Matilda Coxe Stevenson, A. L. Kroeber, Frederick Webb Hodge, to mention only a few whose books I remember vividly in the Vogt Ranch library. Other more distant, but also culturally distinct, neighbors included Spanish-American ranchers, clustered in the villages of Tinaja and San Rafael at the base of the Zuni Mountains and in Atarque in the mesa country to the south; and the most recent arrivals "the Texans," who came to grow pinto beans, settling near El Morro and also founding the community of Fence Lake. It was like a rural microcosm of the United Nations lying within forty miles of the Vogt Ranch.

The El Morro-Ramah-Zuni area was part of the Anasazi archaeological region that covers much of the Colorado Plateau country of New Mexico and Arizona. Not only was the immediate vicinity covered by Anasazi ruins, but their descendants in the contemporary pueblos of Zuni, Hopi, Acoma, Laguna, and the pueblos along the Rio Grande were all part of my early consciousness. This experience was especially meaningful since there is an Anasazi cliff dwelling in a sandstone canyon on our ranch, as well as dozens of Pueblo II sites. In fact, in 1915 when my father settled on the section of land that is now the Vogt Ranch, he used rocks from the nearest Anasazi ruin (one hundred yards away) to build the ranch house. My earliest formal anthropological research experience consisted of excavations in another nearby Pueblo II ruin at the age of eight. The excavating proved to be hard work on hot summer days, and my efforts were dilatory. But I did uncover some Anasazi pots and arrowheads that are still on display in the living room of the ranch house.

A key figure in this early experience was my father, who arrived in New Mexico in 1905 in time to make us "a territorial family," that is, a pioneer family that came before New Mexico achieved statehood in 1912. My father was born into a modest Swiss and German-American family in Upper Sandusky, Ohio, in 1880, the immigrant Vogt ancestor having come to America from Basel, Switzerland, in 1750. The Zartman side of the family (my father's mother's family) landed in Philadelphia in 1728. On my mother's side, the family histories are less complete, but most lines appear to have come to Illinois from Germany in the migrations of the 1840s.

My father's father was first a farmer and later owned a succession of small stores selling dry goods, groceries, and hardware in Ohio and Indiana. In 1892 the family moved to Dayton, where my grandfather worked until his retirement as a traveling salesman for the Souder Extract Company. In Dayton my father grew up speaking fluent English and German; he delivered morning newspapers to the Wright brothers while they were building their first airplane, learned to play tennis well, and purchased his first tailcoat in 1900—all facts that he never let us forget.

My father was the youngest of four siblings (two older brothers and an older sister), a family position that probably accounted for his ebullience

Evon Z. Vogt, Sr., during his early ranching days in New Mexico.

and optimism. He was also an obviously ambitious young man, imbued with the American success story, who managed to enroll at the University of Chicago as a member of the class of 1905, the first in his family line and the only one of his siblings to attend college. At Chicago his grades were not impressive, but he became something of a big man on campus: he was a member of Delta Upsilon Fraternity, a college marshall, and secretary of the Reynolds Club. He valued and kept in close touch with his fraternity brothers for the rest of his life; they included such prominent men as C. Arthur Bruce, president of the Bruce Lumber Company in Memphis, L. R. Smith, president of the A. O. Smith Corporation in Milwaukee, and William R. Wrather, former director of the United States Geological Survey in Washington.

In his senior year at the university my father contracted tuberculosis and was sent by his physician to the Southwest to recover. After some months of rest in the Albuquerque sun, the tuberculosis was arrested, and he enjoyed the Southwest so much he decided to remain in New Mexico. He engaged in various trading store and ranching enterprises between 1906 and 1913, when he sold his ranch north of San Mateo (near Grants) and spent a year in Europe, half in London and half in Paris. He had learned Spanish during his ranching experience in these early years; in Paris he improved his undergraduate French. I am still impressed that he was fluent in four European languages, especially since in my generation my three sisters and I learned only English and Spanish. (Growing up between World War I and World War II in New Mexico was certainly not a time to encourage the speaking of German, and unlike my father we did not study enough French to make us fluent.)

Returning from Europe, my father married Shirley Bergman of Chicago. My mother, born in 1894, the younger of two daughters, came from a well-placed German-American family in Freeport, Illinois, where her grandfather was the principal dealer in farm machinery and mayor of the town. After her father was killed in a train accident, the family moved to Chicago where my grandmother worked at Marshall Field and Company to support her two young daughters. Here my widowed grandmother met and married Charles W. Vogt, an elder brother of my father. When my father was at the University of Chicago he became acquainted with my mother when she was a child of seven; then returned to court and marry her when she was twenty-one, fourteen years younger than my father. (I have often wondered if some of my anthropological interests in kinship may have derived from having an uncle who was also my step-grandfather, a grandmother who was also an aunt by marriage, and two aunts—mother's sisters—who are also my first cousins.)

Following the wedding of my mother and father in Chicago, their honeymoon consisted of a two-week pack trip on the Upper Pecos River in the Sangre de Cristo Mountains east of Santa Fe. My mother had never been on a horse before her honeymoon, but she survived the experience and became an expert rider, continuing her riding on the ranch well into her eighties.

Unlike my father, my mother had only a high school education, and while she was a warm and effective person, she had limited intellectual interests and spoke only English. I was always astonished that my mother managed to live in the Vogt Ranch house for seventy-one years and never learned to speak more than a few simple phrases in Spanish, and only a few words of Navaho spoken by our closest neighbors.

The wedding of Evon Z.
Vogt, Sr., and Shirley
Bergman in Chicago, 1915.

My father stimulated my interests in other cultures as he reached out and engaged the neighbors around us in various and significant ways. Some of my earliest memories are of Navaho, Zuni, and Spanish-American neighbors coming to the ranch where they would invariably be greeted courteously by my father and invited into the house and fed, all in keeping with the manners and expectations of hospitality in early ranching life in the Southwest. I was always deeply impressed by his ability to engage these visitors easily in conversation and to make them feel at home. Since my mother had to feed all these visitors, and to put them up overnight if there had been a winter blizzard or summer cloudburst and the roads were impassable, she was obviously less enthusiastic about such visits. Not only couldn't she speak with these guests, but she also thought they were unwashed and left unpleasant smells in the ranch house.

I can also recall being taken on memorable trips by my father—to Zuni pueblo to see the summer kachina dances and the famous Shalako ceremony in late November or early December when the twelve-foot tall

Mr. and Mrs. Evon Z. Vogt, Sr., outside the Vogt ranch house constructed of rocks from a nearby Anasazi ruin in 1915.

Evon Z. Vogt, Jr., dressed in his Indian costume at age three.

masked Shalako gods came to visit in new or renovated Zuni houses and danced from midnight to sunrise; to Canyon de Chelly on my eighth birthday when we rode horseback up the canyon with a Navaho guide and encountered even less acculturated Navahos living in the canyon, and then on to a performance of the famous Hopi Snake Dance at Walpi, where the snake priests danced with live rattlesnakes in their mouths. Some years later, when I was sixteen, my father also took me along on an unforgettable pack trip with a Navaho guide from the southern base of Navaho Mountain (on the Arizona-Utah border) through almost impassable canyons to the foot of the beautiful Rainbow Bridge.

I was fascinated by these different languages and cultures, and would return to pore over books in the ranch library that described these cultures, especially the travel books of Charles F. Lummis, and the more technical Bureau of American Ethnology (BAE) annual reports, which included Matilda Coxe Stevenson's *Zuni Indians;* Frank Cushing's *Zuni Fetishes* and *Outline of Zuni Creation Myths; The Coronado Expedition of 1540–*

Anasazi cliff dwelling located in José Pino Canyon on the Vogt Ranch.

1542 by George Parker Winship; and *The Cliff Ruins of Canyon de Chelly* by Cosmos Mendeleff.

During these early years my father was appointed the first official custodian of El Morro National Monument, that impressive sandstone mesa containing the Spanish inscriptions of the conquerors and early governors of New Mexico, beginning with Gov. Juan de Oñate in 1605. There were also two prehistoric Zuni pueblos on top the mesa that yielded arrow points, fragments of pottery, and small beads (which could always be found on red anthills in the ruins when the ants picked them up with other small stones to build their homes). Because he was the custodian he was able to receive gratis the BAE reports and other government documents; he also became acquainted with and was visited at our ranch by a stream of famous writers such as Charles F. Lummis and Erna Ferguson.

Evon Z. Vogt, Jr., learning to ride at age five.

*Evon Z. Vogt, Jr., learning
the sheep ranching business
at age seven.*

Four Zuni Shalako performers at the edge of the Pueblo. (Photograph by Evon Z. Vogt, Sr., 1920)

At the height of our ranching operations my father controlled some two hundred thousand acres and ran more than twelve thousand head of sheep, as well as some cattle. These operations also significantly involved us with other cultures. Our employees were Spanish-Americans and Navahos, with an occasional Zuni being hired as a sheepherder. I was deeply involved in the operations, for, being the only son, I was thoroughly trained between the ages of seven and thirteen to assume command of the ranch. At our home ranch I learned to ride, rope, brand calves, butcher steers, build and maintain fences, chop wood, and milk and feed two cows morning and evening. I recall the greatest thrashing I ever received from my father was one morning when I paused to read the comic strip in the newspaper before proceeding to the corral to milk the cows.

My father also insisted that I join him on the range for the lambing season as soon as school was out in May. Here in sheep camp I worked on a daily basis with Navahos and Hispanics, speaking mainly Spanish with both groups, since the second language for Navahos in those days was Spanish rather than English. From the age of seven onward I was required to herd a small group of ewes and their lambs on the range all day. This was a sunrise to almost sunset regime, and I remember it as a very lonely, and often boring, experience. There were some exciting moments, especially when the play group of two-week old lambs began to gambol on their own while the ewes grazed quietly nearby. I also came to value the knowledge I acquired. For example, I learned how to persuade a ewe who has lost her lamb to accept another orphaned lamb. The ewe and the orphaned lamb (with the skin of the dead lamb tied on him securely) were placed together in a very small pen in which the ewe would smell the skin of her dead lamb and accept the orphan after a few days. I also learned how to feed orphaned lambs with baby bottles of cow's milk when no new mother could be found for them.

At the age of three to four weeks, the lambs all had to be earmarked and the males to be raised for the market had to be castrated. Both operations were bloody, especially the castration, for in those days the process was executed as follows: one herder held the lamb on his butt, securely keeping a grip on all four legs, while another cut the bottom off the scrotal sac and extracted the testicles with his teeth. While I did some of the earmarking and held lambs for the castration, the castrating itself was always done by my father who considered himself the expert. The lamb testicles were always saved and served fried for dinner, being considered a great delicacy and referred to as Rocky Mountain oysters. I remember them as a tasty addition to the monotonous sheep camp food, which ordinarily consisted of wheat flour tortillas, beans, and mutton stew, with rice pudding, containing raisins, for dessert.

I also learned to help one of the herders move camp, which consisted of moving not only the large canvas tents in which we slept, but also the provisions and the heavy cooking equipment, including enormous frying pans and Dutch ovens. The camp was transported on burros, which I discovered were one of the most stubborn and recalcitrant animals ever domesticated by man.

By June, hot weather arrived and it was time for shearing. The herds were assembled one by one in dusty corrals in the small settlement of Atarque. Here the sheep were sheared by seasonal Hispanic workers who started in southern New Mexico and worked their way north to Montana. One of these shearers was a wonderful, handsome Hispanic man, Andrés Martinez, from Ranchos de Taos who came by several seasons and courted and eventually married my mother's older sister, whom everyone had thought was destined to be an Old Maid. Aunt Dorothy and Uncle Andrés later moved to Ranchos de Taos, and after my aunt's death, Andrés became close friends with the writer John Nichols. Andrés became one of the protagonists in Nichols's famous book and film, *The Milagro Beanfield War*, and the book is dedicated to him.

My job during the shearing operations was either to tie up the fleeces and carry them to the large wool sack or to help pack the wool down in the large sack. I hated both tasks for it was hot and sticky from the weather, the machinery, the oily wool, and the body heat of sheep and shearers. During shearing season I discovered the pleasures of reading novels, and, when possible, I would slip off in the afternoon when my father was away and lie in my bunk and read novels by the hour.

I recall that for the most part my father seemed to get on well with his employees, in spite of the fact that they were working off debts they owed him and that, as at all other ranches, they were paid minimal wages, about one dollar a day and food. The Hispanics called my father Botas (Boots), not from the boots he wore, but from a Spanish corruption of Vogt, and I became Botitas (Little Boots). My father became quite portly in his later years, and the Navahos came to call him Pesoteaje (The Little Pig). I naturally became Pesoteaje Biye (The Son of the Little Pig).

On the other hand, my father never hesitated to use force if his position as the patrón (boss) were challenged in any way. I recall his telling us at the dinner table one evening how he had discovered a Navaho neighbor grazing his sheep on our land and had proceeded to whip the neighbor with his lariat. On another occasion, I remember an incident in sheep camp when a Hispanic herder had made an insulting remark about my father within earshot after my father had given him an order. My father turned, walked back to the herder, and knocked him flat with his fist. I was shaken by these displays of aggression, especially since I can recall only one real fistfight in my life—at the age of six, on my first day in school, I fought with a Mormon classmate for the affections of a pretty girl we both fancied. I do not remember who won.

Other early memories of other cultures included attending the all-night Squaw Dances of the neighboring Navahos. Here by the open campfires under the brilliant southwestern stars, the young Navaho men would pound on a drum and sing their incredible melodies that ranged over two octaves as their bodies swayed back and forth in the firelight. The young women of marriageable age would drag male partners into the firelight and dance with them until the men paid to be released. Even after I returned to the ranch and went to bed in the wee hours of the morning, the Navaho singing would continue to surge through my head, as would the wonderfully pungent odors of smoke from pinyon wood fires, roasting mutton ribs, and fried bread. It was only later, when I began my formal study of anthropology, that I learned the total purpose and meaning of the so-called Squaw Dances. They are part of Enemy Way, a ceremony performed to exorcise an alien ghost that has been bothering a Navaho patient; "alien" being defined as any non-Navaho.

I naturally had the most social contacts outside the family with the Mormon community of Ramah where I attended school from the first through the ninth grade. While I had many friends among the Mormons, both in school and in play groups outside of school, my father regarded them as very "clannish" and "different" from us. When he first settled at our ranch in 1915, the Mormon bishop and elders of the church had made it quite clear that he was not welcome at the Saturday night dances in Ramah. By the time I started to attend dances at the age of eleven, outsiders were welcome and I learned ballroom dancing, western style, at these affairs.

But I was much aware that while my classmates attended Sunday school and church on Sundays and belonged to age-graded groups that met at other times during the week, I was fundamentally an "outsider." Further, my father made it very clear that he did not wish his children to become Mormons. On the other hand, the nearest other churches we might have attended were in Gallup, forty-five miles away. While my father had had a fairly strict upbringing as a member of the Reformed Church in Ohio, he did little to indoctrinate us in Christian theology or practices. My mother was totally uninterested in formal religion, and her mother, Grandma Kate, who lived with us on the ranch for many years of her life after the death of her husband, was a professed atheist who drank Scotch, smoked cigarettes, and played poker and bridge. Before she died, I learned that her father had been born and reared in a strict Mennonite community in Illinois. At eighteen, according to my grandmother, he "escaped" from the Mennonites, and began to read the books on atheism by Robert Ingersoll. I finally understood why I had a grandmother who did all those worldly things that differentiated us from the nonsmoking, nondrinking Mormons I saw everyday in school.

Evon Z. Vogt, Sr., with Navaho neighbor Raphael Alonzo in 1924.

Once in a while there would be an event in our lives that brought a touch of Christian religion from the outside world. One such event was the arrival of Uncle Rufus Zartman, a pastor from the Reformed Church in Philadelphia, who discovered to his horror that my sisters and I had never been baptized. I remember distinctly how he lined us up under a pinyon tree outside the ranch house and performed the baptismal rite on all of us. (Fortunately, my mother kept the papers on this baptism so that some seventeen years later I could be properly married in the Episcopal Cathedral in Salina, Kansas.)

As a result of this childhood in the wilds of New Mexico my first encounter with the Christian Bible came when it appeared as required reading in the Humanities I survey course at the University of Chicago. To me there is nothing sacred about the Bible, and I believe this has been an advantage in my later studies of religion, ceremony, and ritual in various cultures.

As I grew older, I began to date the Mormon girls. These dates, especially after we learned to drive (I began driving by myself at eleven) and were permitted to take the car for the evening, were arrangements to pick up the girl and meet a group of six to ten couples at Marshmallow Roasts. These Roasts consisted of building a fire in the woods near Ramah, roasting marshmallows, and then "necking," either in the woods or in the car. In my experience, the Mormon girls were always well controlled, and definite limits were set as to how far the boys could go.

But even in these dating games, I was an "outsider." I recall vividly at the age of fifteen how one of my favorites announced firmly one evening that she could no longer go out with me because her parents had laid down the law about her dating a non-Mormon.

As I think back about the experiences that drew me into anthropology, I appear to share two fundamentals with other anthropologists. One was the early experience of "cultural differences" in a firsthand way as I lived among our interesting neighbors in western New Mexico. The second was a life-situation in which, apart from the small nuclear family, I was on the fringe, on the outside looking in, of the one neighboring community—the Mormon village—of which I might have been a genuine member, but was clearly not. I believe these two experiences prepared the way for an anthropological career in the sense that a burning curiosity about alien ways of life was generated early on, and a way of coping with those "others" developed: to study and try to understand them, even if you can't join them.

Over the years the social barriers that separated our family from the Mormon community became much more permeable. In fact, two of my sisters later married Jack Mormons (defined as Mormons who drink coffee and liquor, seldom attend church services, and do not take the official doctrine so seriously) and both Paul Davis and Paul Merrill have been exceptionally fine brothers-in-law. When my mother died in 1986, the funeral

Evon Z. Vogt, Jr., with sisters Barbara (now Mrs. Richard Mallery of Santa Fe), JoAnn (now Mrs. Paul Davis of Ramah, New Mexico), and Patti (now Mrs. Paul Merrill of Ramah, New Mexico), dressed for attending the Gallup Intertribal Indian Ceremonial.

was held in the Church of the Latter Day Saints in Ramah, with the eulogy delivered by a former Mormon bishop.

Another important influence that came to bear were the appearances of various scientists and scholars in the El Morro-Ramah-Zuni area. I recall that for years the Wintons from Texas Christian University came to the Vogt Ranch every summer, at first staying in one of our guest houses, but later bringing a house trailer (a kind of forerunner of the fancy recreational vehicles manufactured today). My father always let them park the house trailer at the ranch, and I went along on countless trips with them to visit Anasazi ruins and geological sites. Mr. Winton was a professor of geology, Mrs. Winton a professor of botany. In addition to teaching me about these subjects, they were also incredibly well informed about the archaeology and history of the Southwest, as well as the birds and mammals of the region.

My father was also acquainted with the early archaeologists who were engaged in pioneering studies of the prehistoric Anasazi culture. One was

Dr. Frederick Webb Hodge, who was excavating at Hawiku, the first of the six Zuni pueblos encountered by the Spanish conquistadores in 1540. Hodge was a close friend of my father's, and he often visited our ranch during the early period of his work at Hawiku (1917 to 1923). I barely remembered him from that period, but he later returned for work at Hawiku and visits to Zuni and I came to know him during my high school and college days as an incredibly bright and witty scholar. Dr. Neil M. Judd, who excavated at Chaco Canyon, and first worked out the sequence of construction of Pueblo Bonito and its relationship to the geological stratigraphy of the canyon (Schroeder 1979: 8), also knew my father and was the topic of many family conversations.

The famous Alfred Vincent Kidder, whose research focused on Pecos from 1915 through 1929, was likewise a friend of my father who came to know him from visits to the Pecos site. It is worth recalling that Kidder was the one who proposed prehistoric culture areas (Pueblo, Mogollon, Hohokam, etc.) to replace what were previously thought to be merely regional variations in the Southwest (Schroeder 1979: 9). He also started the famous Pecos Conference in 1927, the conference that proposed the eight prehistoric periods in the stratigraphic record, Basketmaker I-III and Pueblo I-V (Kidder 1927). At about the same time A. E. Douglas was working on the calendrical possibilities of tree rings, and announced the first date derived from a prehistoric timber in 1929 (Douglas 1929).

Meanwhile ethnologists were responding to the argument by John Wesley Powell (1891) and others that "nowhere in the United States was ethnographic fieldwork so badly needed and at the same time so eminently feasible as in the Southwest. And nowhere, for the same reasons, was it likely to yield more valuable results" (Basso 1979: 15).

The early ethnographers had focused on myths and migration legends to construct hypotheses about the origins and evolution of basic forms of social organization (e.g., Bandelier 1890–1892; Fewkes 1896, 1900; Mindeleff 1891). Franz Boas's opposition to prevailing theories of evolution led to more field ethnography and a more cautious interpretation of ethnographic facts. Indeed, from 1900 to about 1930 southwestern ethnologists treated culture as a number of discrete traits or elements, an approach exemplified in such works as Leslie Spier's (1928) *Havasupai Ethnography* and Elsie Clews Parsons' *Pueblo Indian Religion* (1939). Changes in concepts of culture, under the combined influence of Radcliffe-Brown (with his functionalist theory) and of Edward Sapir and Ruth Benedict (with their notions of cultural patterning and of culture as psychological phenomena) led to a shift in the 1930s to a view of culture as a system in which the elements or traits made a "contribution" to the whole (Basso 1979: 17).

Among the ethnologists in the mainstream of these heady developments in anthropological theory in the 1930s was Clyde Kluckhohn, who first came to the Vogt Ranch in 1922, having been sent out from Iowa to rest from a bout of rheumatic fever. Clyde was a first cousin once-removed by adoption of my mother. To explain: when Clyde's biological mother died, he was adopted by his mother's brother, George Kluckhohn, who was married to my mother's mother's niece. Although there was no gene-alogical kinship connection, my father and mother welcomed him to the Vogt Ranch.

My father proceeded to introduce Clyde to various living Indian com-munities and archaeological sites in the vicinity of the ranch. And it was from the Vogt Ranch that Clyde departed in June 1923 when he made his famous pack trip to the Rainbow Bridge, a journey that was later de-scribed in his book *To the Foot of the Rainbow* (Kluckhohn 1927). Clyde came to love the Southwest and returned again and again. On several occa-sions when he came, he would bring books for the Vogt Ranch library. I recall especially Homer's *Odyssey* and Alexander Dumas's *Three Mus-keteers*. Reading these books expanded my intellectual horizons from the Southwest to the larger world of literature and scholarship.

From 1932 to 1934 Clyde taught at the University of New Mexico and made a number of trips to the Ramah area. Beginning in 1936 he began his formal anthropological study of the Ramah Navaho. We not only saw Clyde each summer, but were also introduced to several talented students he brought to the field, especially David Aberle, John Adair, Flora Bailey, John Landgraf, and Harry Tschopik. Clyde himself combined a very char-ismatic personality with a powerful intellect. I particularly admired his ability to speak Navaho, one of the more difficult languages in the world for an Indo-European speaker to learn, and his skill in eliciting informa-tion from the Navahos. It was obvious that the Navahos also liked and appreciated Clyde, especially his fluency in their language; they all called him affectionately Hasteen Clyde (Mr. Clyde). When his wife, Florence, who was a brilliant sociologist, also joined him in New Mexico during the summer, there were intellectual fireworks whenever they stayed in one of the guest houses at the Vogt Ranch and ate most of their meals in the ranch kitchen with our family, or stayed at Mrs. Merrill's boarding house in Ramah and came to visit us.

It was a time when exciting work in ethnology was being done in various parts of the Southwest. While Kluckhohn and many others including Gladys Reichard were working on the Navaho, Morris Opler was busy with the Jicarilla, Mescalero, and Chiricahua Apache; Grenville Goodwin with the western Apache; Edward Spicer with the Yaqui; Leslie White with the Keresan-speaking Pueblos; Ruth Bunzel at Zuni; and Fred Eggan among the Hopi in field research that was ultimately published in his masterful *Social Organization of the Western Pueblos* (1950) that so successfully combined the functionalist approach of Radcliffe-Brown with the Americanist interest in culture areas and culture history.

It was during the late high school years when I returned from the Santa Fe High School, at the end of my sophomore year, or the Gallup High School, following my junior and senior years, that I began to learn much more about anthropology and anthropologists. On one memorable summer evening Clyde drove by the ranch in his aging Ford station wagon and invited me to attend a Squaw Dance at Two Wells, a Navaho community off the road leading to Gallup. We drove first to Zuni pueblo to pick up Ruth Bunzel, the foremost anthropological authority on Zuni religion (Bunzel 1932), and proceeded to the site of the Navaho Enemy Way only to discover that the patient had died and that the ceremony had been abruptly terminated. We decided to proceed to Gallup for a night on the town. Clyde produced a bottle of gin from the glove compartment and passed it around. My previous experience in drinking had been restricted to small samples of wine from the bottle I discovered that my grandmother kept secluded in a kitchen closet (my father was a teetotaler and disapproved of liquor of all kinds). So this was my first real brush with hard liquor, and by the time we reached Gallup I was feeling no pain. We made a round of bars, where I ordered only beer. At midnight we ended up in the basement of the White Cafe dancing La Raspa to a record on the jukebox. One of my most vivid memories was watching Clyde Kluckhohn and Ruth Bunzel doing this dance; for while they both loved to dance, neither had any sense of rhythm, and there was little coordination between their exuberant hops.

On the way home, Clyde wisely decided he was too intoxicated to drive and suggested that Ruth Bunzel take the wheel. Clyde was asleep in the back seat, but I recall how Ruth would speed up, rather than slow down, whenever she approached and crossed a bridge. After a few hair-raising near misses, I politely suggested that I drive. Ruth gratefully relinquished the wheel, and entertained me by reciting Zuni ritual poetry all the way back to the Pueblo where she was engaged in summer field research. After Clyde left me off at the ranch and returned to Merrill's boarding house, I discovered the results of too much hard liquor: the bed whirls in one direction and then the other and rolls and pitches and tries its best to toss you out.

Meanwhile my intensive training to take over the management of the ranch had continued until the Winter of the Big Snow. In November 1931, when I was thirteen, the Colorado Plateau had an unusually early blizzard that left three feet of snow on the ground. Since it was still early in the winter season, old timers assured us that the snow would melt in a few days. But instead, the weather turned bitterly cold, and three days later another blizzard added another three feet of snow and the nighttime temperatures dropped to forty degrees below zero. I can still remember vividly how the snow level reached well over my head. The country was gripped in a real crisis. Many Navahos, who were still in pinyon-picking camps away from their hogans, died of cold and hunger before they could be rescued. We were without our winter wood supply at the Vogt Ranch, and our livestock were dying of hunger. Since the snow level covered the grasses and even the sagebrush, the sheep could only browse on pinyon and juniper, plants that will only sustain them for a few days.

My father decided that he must try to move all of the twelve thousand sheep on the ranch into lower elevations toward the Saint Johns, Arizona, area to the west. He left the home ranch with all of the horses, except for one old grey mare that he turned over to me with these words about wood for our house, "Son, it's up to you to keep the ranch house warm." Since our house was heated only by fireplaces and a cookstove, forty degrees below zero required an enormous amount of wood. School was, of course, closed. Each morning for a period of two weeks I saddled up the grey mare and searched for dead pinyon and juniper trees in the woods. After chopping down the trees, I hauled the logs back to the ranch with a lariat attached to the saddle horn. After lunch, I spent the afternoon chopping up the juniper for the cookstove, the pinyon for the fireplaces. This wood supply lasted only through the cold night, and I had to begin all over again the next day. It was an experience with reality that made an indelible impression; it was through my daily hard work that the family survived at all. And I recall bursting with pride later on when my father praised my work and responsibility to some visitors at the ranch. I also felt that I had become a "grown up" in two weeks' time!

When weather conditions improved, we were able to hire a farmer in Ramah to bring the rest of our winter wood supply. But my father's efforts to save the livestock did not fare well. Paths were formed through the snow by dragging logs with horses, and baled alfalfa was strewn along these paths to entice the sheep to move toward lower elevations. But before the herds reached the lower Arizona country, about half the sheep had died. More importantly, when the rams were placed with the ewes in December to breed so that lambs would be born in May, the rams were exhausted from hunger and refused to copulate with the ewes in heat. My father returned to the home ranch at this point to report on the failure of the rams, and it was the only time I saw him break down and cry. It was a frightening experience since I had always regarded him as a pillar of strength. I knew that the sheep ranch was in deep trouble. We soon lost the large ranch at Atarque, where the land had been mortgaged, and were reduced ultimately from the original 200,000 acres to 640 acres, or one section (a square mile), contained in the home ranch. I sensed correctly that my life had been profoundly altered by the Winter of the Big Snow.

My father subsequently had a great deal of trouble even supporting his family. For a time he worked for a newly organized sheep company that had been formed from the ruins of the old company. He later became the publisher and editor of the *Gallup Gazette,* a weekly newspaper, which was lively but never really flourished. From 1936 he also spent some years working for the A. O. Smith Corporation of Milwaukee (owned by his fraternity brother, L. R. Smith) which was prospecting for gold in Colorado, Utah, Nevada, Arizona, and across the border in Mexico. At the time of his death in January 1943, he had been appointed an Indian agent with the United States Indian Service to supervise the affairs of the Ramah Navaho group.

During my high school years, I thought a great deal about my future career, knowing that it would certainly not be ranching. I was always ambitious in my aspirations for the future. At one point, I wanted to be a rear admiral in the Navy and explore the South Pole like Admiral Byrd; at

The Evon Z. Vogt family in front of the Vogt Ranch about 1935. Three sisters, left to right, are Patti, Barbara, and JoAnn.

a later stage I dreamed of becoming the mayor of San Francisco. Studies and extracurricular activities went well for me in high school, in spite of less than spectacular athletic skills. During my sophomore year in Santa Fe High School, I was deeply involved in the Boy Scouts and became an Eagle Scout, the badge being presented to me by Governor Hockenhull at a memorable ceremony at the Baptist church in Santa Fe, which sponsored the troop to which I belonged. In my final year at Gallup High School, I was elected president of the senior class, winning the election over the football captain, and I also edited the school newspaper and yearbook and gave the commencement address on the subject of Individualism versus Collectivism (I was strongly for Individualism). My grades, as I recall, were almost all A's, without doing any homework, and I shared valedictory honors with one other classmate in our class of sixty-four graduates in 1936.

All of this school activity was warmly supported by my father who held out the stars for all of his children and assumed confidently, in spite of economic reverses, we would all graduate from college. He sent me off to his alma mater, the University of Chicago; my eldest sister Barbara was sent to Stanford; my middle sister JoAnn to the University of New Mexico; and my youngest sister Patricia to the University of Chicago. As long as he

My first trip to the Rainbow Bridge, 1935.

lived, he assisted us in countless ways other than supplying us with money. He helped us secure jobs and made various arrangements for room and board through his network of college friends.

It was clear that I would need funds to attend the University of Chicago, so I decided to work for a year between high school and college. In the summer of 1936, I served as the ranger of El Morro National Monument where I lived in a small cabin and cooked for myself. I thoroughly enjoyed this duty, and especially enjoyed giving tours on the history, archaeology, geology, and botany to visitors. Tourist travel was often light, especially during periods of heavy summer rains, and I had much time to myself to read—I remember reading Tolstoy's *War and Peace* that summer—and reflect. It was the only time in my life that I have been completely alone, without even seeing another person, for four straight days. By the end of the four days, I was incredibly lonesome and practically fell all over the first group of visitors.

Serving as summer ranger at El Morro National Monument in 1936.

During 1936–37 my father arranged a job for me in Nevada, California, and Arizona with the A. O. Smith Corporation, which had set out to locate a mountain with low grade gold ore. The head of the corporation, L. R. Smith, was eager to try modern technological methods on ore that only produced something of the order of one dollar per ton in gold. Since I was considering mining engineering as a career at that point, it seemed like a plausible plan. I spent several months with the company at Round Mountain, Nevada, where I drove a water truck to service a drilling rig that was exploring to see if the mountain with low grade ore had been discovered. Most of the time I worked the graveyard shift (ten P.M. to six A.M.).

Later in the year I traveled with a field crew headed by a mining engineer as we explored several old gold mines at Rawhide, Nevada, and near Placerville, California, and Kingman, Arizona. My duty consisted of cutting samples of ore from the veins of the old mines. By the end of the year I discovered I was more interested in the Shoshone Indians who worked with me in the Nevada mines than I was in the technical process of extracting gold ore from the mountains. But, for those days, the job paid well. I made $150 a month, and lived on $50 a month. By the end of the year, I had more than one thousand dollars in a savings account and a two-year scholarship to the University of Chicago.

COLLEGE DAYS AT CHICAGO

In the fall of 1937 I arrived in Chicago by Greyhound bus and moved into the apartment of Nathan Plympton, the comptroller of the University of Chicago, located just south of the Midway and an easy walk from my classes. This room and board job had been arranged by John F. Moulds, the secretary of the board of trustees, and a fraternity brother of my father. My duties were to provide company for Uncle Nate Plympton at dinner in the evening, to wash and polish his car, and to drive him to the Baptist church on Sunday. After I picked him up at church, Uncle Nate would take me to the Quadrangle Club (the faculty club) for Sunday lunch. At home in the apartment, our meals were cooked and served by the Swedish housekeeper, Anna. The arrangement was confining for a nineteen-year-old freshman, but, along with my honor scholarship, it permitted me to attend college for which I was really appreciative.

It was also quiet for studying at Uncle Nate's apartment. And study was something that really occupied me during my freshman year. I discovered that I was surrounded by high school valedictorians who were incredibly bright and who were accustomed to homework. I have never worked so hard in my life as I did to make the enormous leap from the Gallup High School to the University of Chicago. The courses were exciting—Social Sciences I, Humanities I, Physical Sciences I, French I—and the very atmosphere was electric, sparking ideas and deep intellectual discussions in every encounter with faculty and with fellow students. I attribute a large part of this intellectual ambiance to the leadership of Chicago's president, Robert Maynard Hutchins, who was a very charismatic figure to undergraduates. We would literally get into an immediate, heated argument with one another about Aristotle or Plato just sitting over a cup of coffee in Hutchison Commons. In my sixty years of association with universities, I have never again encountered the kind of exhilarating intellectual electricity in the air that I enjoyed as an undergraduate at Chicago.

I worked hard and long on my courses, but at the end of the year when the six-hour examinations in each yearlong course were imminent, I was worried. So worried that I recall not being able to sleep before my first exam. I paced the streets of south Chicago for hours; finally returned home, had a cup of coffee, and walked to the examination room determined to do well. The results were gratifying: three A's and one B. I could keep my scholarship, after all, and continue in college!

My freshman adviser, Earl Johnson, took one look at my folder and announced: "You should be an anthropologist." But I did not take him seriously. I did concentrate in social science, rather than humanities or physical science, but I was really more interested in government and politics. This interest was stimulated by the presence of any number of student political groups and by violent arguments with student members of the Communist Party about Marxism. In my senior year I finally settled on geography as my major, which led me into a number of interesting courses in geography and geology.

In the spring of my freshman year I joined Delta Upsilon (where I was a legacy) and moved into the fraternity house during my last three years. I served as the steward during my sophomore and junior years, a post that involved planning the menu for the meals and supervising the cook. It was a job that paid for my board, and it had, in retrospect, some interesting moments. I recall that the future senator Charles Percy had the concession of selling the provisions to all of the fraternity houses. I would meet Chuck Percy each week at the back door of the DU House and place the order for the week. In my senior year, I was elected president of Delta Upsilon.

I also became involved in other extracurricular activities, especially the Chapel Union which was a student group organized by the dean of Rockefeller Chapel and his assistant. Given my early lack of indoctrination in religion, it is curious that I chose to participate in this religious organization, but I was attracted by their activities, especially their outings in the countryside. I was elected as president of Chapel Union in my senior year. This and other activities had made me prominent enough on campus to be elected to the sophomore honor society, Skull and Crescent, and to the junior honor society, Iron Mask. It was in the meetings of these Honor Societies that I became well acquainted with such notable members of our class as Charles Percy, later senator from Illinois and chairman of the Foreign Relations Committee, and John P. Stevens, now a Supreme Court justice. It was a shock for me when I did not make the senior honor society, Owl and Serpent, but I did become a marshall in my senior year, which took some of the sting away.

It was at a Chapel Union open house at Dean Gilkey's home on a Sunday evening that I met my future wife, when I was a junior and she was a freshman. In one of those fortunate quirks of fate we were introduced by my then current girlfriend, Margaret Hamilton, a Swedish countess with whom my relationship had suffered some ups and downs. I abandoned the Swedish countess and set out to capture the affections of Naneen Hiller of Salina, Kansas, with whom I had almost instantly fallen in love. It was a courtship and marriage that worked, having now endured happily for over fifty years.

During my college years, I needed to earn money during the summers. At the end of my freshman year I returned to Round Mountain, Nevada, where I had a job with the rock crew of a placer mine. My job, along with a crew of Shoshone Indians, was to lift rocks into an iron sledge that removed the rocks from the placer gravel pit. It was good, hard work in the open air: we once calculated that each of us lifted about ten tons of rhyolite rocks each day. After my sophomore year, I applied for and was fortunate enough to be employed as a summer ranger for the National Park Service during the next three summers. I served at El Morro National Monument in 1939, at Bandelier National Monument near Santa Fe in 1940, and at

Serving as summer ranger at Bandelier National Monument in 1940.

Montezuma National Monument in central Arizona in 1941. These were wonderful summers for me compared to the hard physical labor in the Nevada mines. I found that I enjoyed taking tours of visitors around the sites and giving campfire talks in the evening. My experience with other cultures was extended to Santa Clara Pueblo during the summer of 1940 when I came to know and admire the work of the noted artist, Pablita Velarde, who painted the fine murals for the museum in Bandelier National Monument.

Nineteen forty-one brought graduation from the University of Chicago and my marriage to Catherine Christine ("Naneen") Hiller in a formal wedding in the Episcopal Cathedral in Salina, Kansas. For a honeymoon, my wife and I went camping in the Southwest on a journey that included the Vogt Ranch, Sunset Crater, the Grand Canyon, the Hopi Mesas, Canyon de Chelly, and finally to Montezuma Castle National Monument where I finished my tour of summer duty. I have always been delighted that my wife enjoyed the life and scenery of the Southwest from the time of her first visit.

Our wedding in Salina, Kansas, with our parents in 1941.

Before graduation I had decided that geography was an intellectually sterile subject. While I enjoyed the maps and the investigation of spatial relationships, I discovered that the minute you asked more interesting questions of the geographic data, it took you into other fields such as anthropology, history, or political science. During my undergraduate years I had taken one course, Anthropology 201, from Professor Fay-Cooper Cole who was then chairman of the Department. It had been a fascinating course, so interesting in fact that I decided to speak to Professor Cole about my future.

I shall never forget the interview. Fay-Cooper ushered me into his large office, and as we sat down, he pointed to an elderly man with thick glasses sitting and reading a book at a small desk in the distant corner, and whispered to me: "That's Malinowski." I looked at the great man with awe, but was not introduced. Instead, Fay-Cooper asked about my business. I announced that I had decided to undertake graduate work in anthropology, and asked about fellowship support. Fay-Cooper was delighted in his enthusiastic way, and proceeded not only to assure me that I would be admitted as a graduate student, but proceeded to offer me the Charles R. Walgreen Fellowship for the Study of American Institutions. Those were the days when a chairman of a department had power to make decisions on the spot without the endless deliberations of admissions and fellowship committees we now cope with in all American universities. I was grateful for the fellowship, which made possible my first year of graduate work during 1941–42.

I worked assiduously on my graduate school courses with Fred Eggan, Robert Redfield, Sol Tax, and W. Lloyd Warner in social anthropology and ethnology, Abraham Halperin in linguistics, William Krogman in physical anthropology, and Robert Braidwood and Fay-Cooper Cole in archaeology. Chicago was a stimulating department in which to work in those days. Although I missed studying with A. R. Radcliffe-Brown, who taught at Chicago from 1932 to 1936 before he was called to the chair at Oxford, R-B's influence had had a profound impact on the department, and especially on Fred Eggan, who was one of his principal disciples, and on Robert Redfield, who brilliantly discussed the differences between British and American anthropology.

The debates among graduate students about Radcliffe-Brown's versus Malinowski's theories of "function," as well as the conceptual distinctions between "social structure" and "culture," went on day and night. We also considered the theoretical and methodological implications of British social anthropology compared to Boasian ethnology and the "scientific" versus the "humanistic" approaches to gathering and analyzing data that Redfield so cogently expounded in his classes. At the same time, W. Lloyd Warner was setting many of us on fire with his charismatic lectures on the six social class levels he and his colleagues were discovering in their field research on American communities such as the famous Yankee City (Newburyport, Massachusetts).

But these were troubled times, and when my wife and I awoke on the morning of December 7, 1941, to the news of Pearl Harbor, I knew that I had to make decisions soon about serving in the armed forces. I had been deferred while doing graduate work for one year, but it seemed unlikely that such a deferral could continue. My father also made it clear that he thought I should be serving in the armed forces rather than continuing graduate work.

In the spring quarter I made an appointment to see Fred Eggan who was

serving as my principal adviser. Fred felt that my graduate school performance was of such quality that I should continue in anthropology, and he
suggested that before I enlisted in the service, I take a crack at the examinations even though I had only been a graduate student for one academic
year. It was with some trepidation that I followed his advice. The examinations consisted of three-hour written exams in each of the five fields
of archaeology, ethnology, linguistics, physical anthropology, and social
anthropology. I sat for the examinations in May and was fortunate enough
to receive a High Pass in every field except for archaeology in which I
received a Low Pass.

Meanwhile, I explored various branches of the service in their recruiting
offices in downtown Chicago. I decided not to volunteer for the air force
because during my senior year I took a flying course offered at an airfield
nearby. While I managed to solo and pass the course, I remembered being
consistently graded 3 or 4, instead of 1 or 2, on my flying performance.
I did not seem to have a real knack for flying and could perceive myself
being killed in some operational accident. The marines put me off because
of their gaudy dress uniforms. I finally applied to the navy, which offered
an officer's training program for college graduates.

While I was awaiting orders from the navy, my wife, Naneen, or Nan, as
she is more commonly called, and I returned to the Vogt Ranch. It was during this summer of 1942 that I undertook my first formal field research in
anthropology. At the suggestion of Clyde Kluckhohn who was engaged in
research with the Ramah Navahos that season, I spent two months doing
fieldwork in the Zuni farming village of Pescado located six miles from
our ranch. Since I did not have an automobile, I rode horseback each day
from the ranch to Pescado for the field observations and interviews. Since
the time was necessarily short, I did not attempt to learn more than some
words of greeting in Zuni, but worked in English with the younger Zunis
and in Spanish with the older people.

Pescado was one of three summer farming villages, the others being
Hawiku (where Coronado first encountered the Zunis while searching
for the Seven Cities of Cibola) and Nutria, located at the base of the
Zuni Mountains. Pescado (meaning "fish" in Spanish) was named in the
chronicles of the early Spanish conquistadores who found fish in the local
spring. Since no formal ethnographic research had previously been done
in one of these Zuni farming villages, I focused on making a map of the

settlement pattern, including the houses and fields, and collected a village census. I also collected data on the interrelationships between Zunis and Navahos in this local area, a subject that greatly interested Kluckhohn, and he was kind enough to read and criticize my field notes. These critiques were useful for they pushed me in the direction of much more specific detail on behavioral sequences and on precisely what was said in each interview and what gestures and body language were being used by the informant. In August I attended the Gallup Inter-Tribal Indian Ceremonial and followed a Zuni family from Pescado through the four days of the Ceremonial. Afterward I arranged to ride from Gallup to Pescado in their wagon, and this gave me many leisurely hours of productive interviewing about their experiences in Gallup. I had attended the Gallup Ceremonial many times in my life; in fact, for many years my father served as the public announcer of events on the program. But seeing the ceremonial through Zuni eyes was an especially new and memorable experience.

Unfortunately, with navy duty imminent, the results of my first field research were never written up, but I have always considered the summer as a great experience in learning to establish rapport, make field observations, handle interviews, and, with Kluckhohn's help, produce detailed field notes, always with a copy, in case the originals are lost or destroyed.

NAVY DAYS: 1942 TO 1945

I received my training to become "an officer and a gentleman" at Dartmouth College in the autumn of 1942, and my first duty as an ensign was at the Naval Air Technical Training Center in Memphis, Tennessee, where I was in command of three barracks of 750 enlisted men.

Shortly after our arrival in Memphis, we received a telegram from my mother that my father had had a heart attack and was critically ill in the Indian Service Hospital in Blackrock, the agency headquarters for nearby Zuni Pueblo. My father had been pushing his car through the muddy New Mexican roads at the outskirts of Ramah when the attack occurred and he was rushed to the closest hospital some twenty miles away. Nan and I immediately took the train to Gallup, and it was a great shock to learn when we opened the *Albuquerque Journal* on the train passing through Albuquerque that my father had died in the hospital the night before, on 24 January 1943. He had been such a strong, but understanding and

Lt. Evon Z. Vogt, Jr., in dress uniform during
World War II.

compassionate, role model for me that his death was perhaps the greatest trauma of my life. It was extremely difficult for me to go through the
funeral in Gallup and his burial in the Sunset Cemetery in Albuquerque.

After a few months in Memphis, I realized that the experience was hardly
my expectation of joining the navy to see the world, and my duty, after
a time, was boring. I did learn some lessons about the application of authority when I became exasperated with the inability of the enlisted men to
keep their barracks shipshape. After finding several piles of clothes strewn
over bunks in one barracks, I canceled the weekend liberty in Memphis
for all 250 of them. Needless to say, I was not beloved by the men after
this; and although it did result in neatness in the barracks, it was a prime
example of a young, green ensign applying power way out of proportion to
the seriousness of the offense. With more experience, I learned about how
to make the punishment fit the crime.

After a few months of Memphis, I decided to apply for a transfer. Through the proper channels, I requested of the Chief of Naval Personnel that since I had majored in the geography of South America and spoke Spanish, I be stationed in that area of the world. In due course, orders arrived detaching me from the duty at Memphis and directing me to report to Patrol Squadron VP-94. I flew from Miami, and when I arrived at my new post I discovered that VP-94 was located in Belem, Brazil, the one country in South America that speaks Portuguese!

I served as administrative officer of the squadron of amphibious PBYs (or Catalinas), which were engaged in patrolling for and destroying, with depth charges, the German submarines off the northeastern coast of Brazil. I found the duty interesting and exciting. It was a new culture and new language for me, and I promptly engaged a teacher in Belem to give me intensive Portuguese lessons. For the most part, my duties involved handling personnel and paperwork problems for the squadron, but my Portuguese made enough progress in a few months for me to be of service as the squadron interpreter. Most of my fellow navy officers did not bother to learn more than a few words of "gook," a derogatory term commonly applied to the Portuguese language, as well as to the Brazilians who were called "gooks." This led me into a series of experiences that heightened my awareness of the cultural differences and of the systematic effort it took to learn about and understand a new culture. I had the honor of serving as the interpreter for Eleanor Roosevelt when she came by to visit the squadron and for Adm. Jonas Ingram, the Commander of the South Atlantic Fleet, when he and the local Brazilian admiral arrived to decorate each other's pilots in a formal ceremony.

I also met Carlos Lacerda at our base in Belem, and will never forget the details of our first encounter. The duty officer looked up and saw Lacerda approaching our command shack, and said: "Here comes a gook. Somebody call E.Z. because he is the only one who speaks gook." Luckily, Lacerda did not overhear the remark, and I stepped outside to meet the man who was, in the 1960s, to become the governor of Guanabara, the Brazilian state in which Rio de Janeiro is located, as well as being personally responsible for hastening the end of the Vargas dictatorship, and later pressuring Vargas to commit suicide after reelection as president.

I found Lacerda to be a very lively and learned young man (he spoke four languages fluently, Portuguese, Spanish, French, and English) who was serving as a newspaper reporter and had come to do a story on our navy operations in the South Atlantic. We spent more than a week together, including my first trip to the Island of Marajo, in the mouth of the Amazon, to visit the base where a navy blimp squadron was patrolling for submarines. One of the amusing measures of cultural difference came to light on the island of Marajo. Lacerda observed that the U.S. Navy always served peanut butter with our meals, and distributed peanuts for the men to eat during the movies shown on our bases. He found these practices mystifying, because Brazilians are convinced that peanuts and peanut butter are powerful aphrodisiacs, and, as he pointed out, "There were no women available for the sailors to visit on the Island of Marajo!"

I often flew along on coastal air journeys our patrol planes made to other bases in northeast Brazil and became acquainted with the interesting cities of Sao Luis, Joao Pessoa, Forteleza, Natal, and Recife. Great poverty, of course, was evident in all these cities, but I have never known a lovelier coastline.

Toward the end of my tour of duty in Brazil, our squadron moved south along the coast to Maceio, and from here I was privileged to have one weekend glimpse of Rio de Janeiro, which in 1944 was a beautiful, sparkling city without the smog, harbor pollution, and traffic jams that plague the city today.

As I think about my year in Brazil, it was an absorbingly interesting anthropological experience for me, especially the mastering of a new language and learning something of the customs of a new culture. It clearly reinforced my interests in pursuing further study in anthropology. While in Brazil I even attempted my first brief anthropological article. I wrote on Brazilian gestures and their meanings and sent the piece to Ralph Linton, then editor of the *American Anthropologist*. He never answered; I was never certain whether he did not receive the product or simply didn't like it.

By the end of the year I was desperately lonesome for my wife and it was time for another kind of experience. I applied and was accepted to Air Combat Intelligence School in Quonset Point, Rhode Island. My training at Quonset Point was very interesting; the instructors were first-rate and my fellow officers in training were very bright. I recall that one of my very best instructors was William Gurdon Saltonstall, who was later to become the principal of Phillips Exeter Academy at the time when two of my sons were enrolled at Exeter. We were trained in photographic interpretation, navigation, analysis of military targets, as well as in the history and geography of Japan.

My wife, who had returned to her studies at the University of Chicago while I was in Brazil, joined me at Quonset Point, and we had a wonderful seven months together after the year of separation.

Toward the end of Air Combat Intelligence School I again made a request to the navy about my future duty. I did not want to spend the rest of the war at some boring shore base doing nothing. This time I wrote to the former commanding officer of my PBY patrol squadron in Brazil, Captain Tibbetts, who was currently in the Office of the Chief of Naval Operations, requesting carrier duty. In due course my orders came and I was assigned as the Air Combat Intelligence Officer of VT(N)-91, a night torpedo squadron that would eventually board a carrier. The squadron was formed at Quonset Point, and, as luck would have it, the commanding officer proved to be the former executive officer of my PBY squadron in Brazil. Captain Robert Smith had been retrained to fly torpedo planes off a carrier. I had always liked him during our year together in Brazil, and this easy relationship continued during my duty with VT(N)-91.

The new torpedo squadron trained at Quonset Point, on Martha's Vineyard (in the middle of the winter!), and finally at Key West. We then received orders to report to Barber's Point on Oahu for further training. Since Nan was pregnant with our first child, she returned to her family home in Salina, Kansas, while I finished training with the squadron and then joined her for a final visit before rejoining VT(N)-91 in San Diego. We shipped out to Pearl Harbor on a seaplane tender, which sailed through gigantic swells in the aftermath of a Pacific storm. It was the roughest cruise I have ever experienced, but I discovered that I never have trouble with sea sickness even under extreme conditions, which in this case put 90 percent of the squadron as well as the crew of the tender in their bunks for days.

Honolulu was crowded with our armed forces in the spring of 1945, but our base at Barber's Point was comfortable and reasonably pleasant. In May our Air Group 91, composed of two squadrons, the other being fighter squadron VF(N)-91, went aboard the USS *Bonhomme Richard* for sea duty in the Pacific. The ensuing five months at sea were momentous ones for me. Our carrier joined the fleet during the aftermath of a typhoon in the middle of the Battle of Okinawa. I shall never forget going out on deck at sunrise that morning and looking across to two other carriers whose forward flight decks had been broken and pointed straight down toward the sea by the enormous weight of the waves during the typhoon they had sailed through two nights before.

Within a day or two, our carrier had launched its night planes and was deeply involved in the struggle. We had two principal concerns. The first was the operational hazard in taking off and landing aboard a rolling and pitching carrier after dark. We had highly skilled and superbly trained pilots at this point; those who could not measure up had been left behind, either at Quonset Point or at Barber's Point. But we still suffered far more casualties from night operations than we did in combat. Pilots would fly into the sea or into the island on the carrier, crash the planes, and be killed.

Our even greater concern were the Japanese kamikazes who were flying their planes straight into our carriers and causing many casualties during the Battle of Okinawa. Fortunately, the *Bonhomme Richard* was never hit, but we had a number of near misses with the kamikaze planes flying into the Pacific a few yards away. It was my most frightening World War II experience.

We spent the month of June anchored in Leyte Gulf in the Philippines while the fleet prepared for the final assault on Japan. The *Bonhomme Richard* sailed from the Philippines on 1 July, and we did not touch land again until 16 September—seventy-eight days at sea. This was the time when all of us began to think the world was made of ocean water. While our squadron engaged in some action over the Inland Sea and near Tokyo, we spent most of our time being idle aboard the carrier. For the operations were mainly hit-and-run at this point; that is, the fleet would steam in toward the coast of Japan and launch its day planes from carriers. By sunset the planes would return from their missions, and the fleet would steam far out to sea for the night. By the time it was dark enough to launch our night planes, the fleet would be out of range. Squadron VT(N)-91 spent most of its time either in the ready room playing bridge, or out on deck playing volley ball. We would lower the forward elevator on the carrier, and erect a net in a space that was a perfect size for the court. Playing volley ball on a rolling and pitching carrier required a good deal of agility, but I came to enjoy our almost daily matches when it was not a strike day.

It was a tense time since it was predicted that this final assault on Japan would eventually cost us more than one million casualties, and our fleet was in the front line of operations. Some members of the armed forces used to repeat the saying Golden Gate by Forty-Eight. But none of us in the fleet really expected to live through the war. But, suddenly, we were ordered to move more than a thousand miles off the coast and to engage in target practice. The two atomic bombs were dropped, and the war was over.

The *Bonhomme Richard* was ordered to remain at sea and launch its planes to locate and drop food at prisoner-of-war camps. Finally, we sailed into Tokyo Bay on 16 September, dropped anchor, and were given liberty to go ashore. It was a strange experience traveling unarmed on trains into Tokyo with people we had been fighting the month before. But all was peaceful as we visited the awful devastation (apart from the Emperor's Palace) in Tokyo. After returning to San Francisco on the *Bonhomme Richard*, I was mustered out of the navy in October 1945.

As I reflect on my navy experience, I realize that while I thought at the time I had lost almost four years of my career training and was angry about colleagues who had managed to sit out the war in various ways without leaving the United States, there were several positive aspects for my training as an anthropologist.

The year in Brazil immersed me in another culture with a new language to learn. The duty as an air combat intelligence officer in the Pacific was strikingly similar to much that I would do later as a professor of anthropology. Briefing the pilots in the ready room aboard the carrier using maps and a blackboard was a preview of lectures I would give later. Interviewing the pilots about their missions as soon as they returned to the carrier was not unlike the later interviewing of informants in the field. Writing reports on the missions, including presentation of the data and making interpretations at the end, was good training for professional articles that I would later write for the anthropological journals. So, all was not lost as I returned to Chicago with Nan and our first child, Shirley Naneen, who had been born in Salina, Kansas, on the day I reached Pearl Harbor, 6 March 1945. I did not meet her until I rejoined Nan at the Vogt Ranch in October and our lovely daughter was already six months old.

TRAINING FOR THE PH.D. IN ANTHROPOLOGY: 1946–1948

As soon as the war ended I wrote to Clyde Kluckhohn to seek his advice about graduate school. He replied that I should return to Chicago to finish my Ph.D. since with four social anthropologists in residence at Chicago, Robert Redfield, W. Lloyd Warner, Fred Eggan, and Sol Tax, the teaching staff was much stronger in the field that interested me most than it was at Harvard or elsewhere.

Correspondence with Lloyd Warner, with whom I had taken a number of courses focused on the study of social stratification in the United States, resulted in an offer of a job doing field research on his new project in Morris, Illinois. The social class system of this midwestern city and the surrounding Grundy County was being researched by an interdisciplinary team sponsored by the Committee on Human Development at the University of Chicago. My task was to study the social structure of the rural area of Grundy County and then utilize the data for my master's thesis for the Department of Anthropology.

In January 1946 we moved into an apartment in Morris, Illinois, and began to become acquainted with this pleasant prairie city. Fortunately, my wife had an introduction via her relatives to one of the upper-class families in town, and this contact immediately opened many of the events and social activities to us. We were invited to dinners and to sessions of "team bridge," which took many hours to play but introduced us to a wide range of professional families in the town.

As soon as the winter weather moderated, I bought a bicycle and undertook my research in the rural farm area. The rural area was interesting because it was divided into two basic ethnic groups: the Old Yankee Families and the Norwegians. From participant observation in work groups and church socials and from intensive interviewing of both the Yankee and Norwegian farmers, I discovered marked social class divisions in the Yankee population compared to a much more unified and cohesive structure among the Norwegians, who occupied a depressed position in the overall structure. While social class was an organizing principle for the Yankees, the Lutheran church was the core of the Norwegian community. These results were reported in my master's thesis and led to my first two publications: a 1947 article in *Rural Sociology* entitled "Social Stratification in the Rural Middlewest: A Structural Analysis" and a chapter entitled "Town and Country: The Structure of Rural Life" in *Democracy in Jonesville* (edited by W. Lloyd Warner) which was published in 1949. Since Lloyd Warner was away on leave during my participation in this Jonesville research, my field research and master's thesis were supervised more by the sociologist Everett C. Hughes and by the chairman of the Committee on Human Development, Robert J. Havighurst.

In the summer of 1946 we returned to Chicago, moved into one of the pre-fabricated graduate student houses next to Billings Hospital, and I settled into my scholarly work. My first task was to retake the examination in archaeology in which I had failed to receive a High Pass in the spring of 1942. I recall being so anxious about this examination that I spent most of the academic year 1946–47 reviewing archaeology. Then the night be-fore I sat for the exam, I developed a terrific case of diarrhea from the tension I felt. Thanks to a wonderful neighbor in the prefab community, a physician doing his residency at Billings, I received some pills to control my ailment and managed to pass the examination handily this second time around. I was then free to develop my interests in social anthropology and ethnology. But the positive side of this extra work in archaeology was that it reenforced my early interests in the field, and I have since always tried to keep abreast of major developments in archaeology, not only in theory but also in the substantive work in the Southwest and Mesoamerica.

The Department of Anthropology at Chicago continued to be an inspir-ing place in those days following World War II. Not only were the profes-sors stimulating and provocative, but I recall the absorbingly interesting conversations with my fellow graduate students that took place especially during the lunch hour and after hours in the large open room (where each of us was assigned a desk) on the third floor of the Social Science Building.

As my study of anthropology progressed, I prepared for my thesis re-search in social anthropology and for the special papers that were required in my two minor fields: ethnology and archaeology. I still remember dis-tinctly the topics given me for my special papers (they were like take-home examinations that were to be done in two weeks). The topic assigned by Fred Eggan in ethnology involved a critical assessment of the relation-ships between the Great Basin and the Plateau as two culture areas in North America. Kenneth Orr provided the assignment in archaeology: an evaluation of functional interpretation archaeology. Both proved to be stimulating topics.

I was concerned about support for my Ph.D. thesis research. The GI Bill paid $150.00 a month, but by now we had two children (our son, Evon Z. Vogt III, was born in Chicago on 29 August 1946) and finances were a genuine source of anxiety. Before the war I had planned to undertake field research in Guatemala under the supervision of Redfield and Tax. But now a more immediate prospect developed in the Southwest. Clyde Kluckhohn invited me to do research among the Ramah Navaho and suggested that I come to Harvard to examine field data in his Navaho files in the Peabody Museum. Since some funds were available to supplement the GI Bill payments and I had also received a Social Science Research Council Dissertation Fellowship, I decided to return to New Mexico for the Ph.D. field research.

On the visit to Cambridge, I shall never forget my shock in first seeing the famous Peabody Museum—it looked exactly like the ugly, red brick power plants I had known in small western towns. I have since become accustomed to the Peabody's external appearance and have become rather fond of its unimposing exterior.

After a look at the Ramah Navaho data, I had a discussion with Clyde in which two suggestions for a dissertation topic emerged. One was a study of Navaho polygyny, of which there were still several cases among the Ramah Navaho, a number of them being sororal polygyny. The other idea was to study the returning Navaho veterans from World War II to discover how they had been changed by their experiences in the armed forces and what effect they were having on cultural change among the Ramah Navaho. I chose to undertake the study of the veterans which, at the time, seemed both timely and natural for me to do since I was also a fellow veteran. But, in retrospect, the choice was probably an unfortunate one for my career in anthropology. I should have chosen to do the study of Navaho polygyny, which had never been systematically studied. It would have been a topic in the mainstream of anthropology as it unfolded in subsequent decades in which culture and personality studies (with a focus on individual case histories) fell out of favor and were little utilized as compared to social structural studies in the tradition of British social anthropology.

At the time, however, the study of the fifteen Navaho veterans among the Ramah Navaho proved to be exciting for me. We managed to buy, on a time-payment plan, our very first automobile, a 1947 two-door Ford sedan. After driving to New Mexico, we moved into quarters at the Vogt Ranch, which was my base of operations for the field study of the Navaho veterans during the ensuing nine months.

Headquartering at the Vogt Ranch had some major advantages for me. It was, of course, rent-free and it was located within a few miles of the hogans of the closest veterans. Furthermore, I was well-known among the Ramah Navaho as Pesoteaje Biye (The Son of the Little Pig) and hence had an immediate entree into Navaho families who were our neighbors. My visits in Navaho hogans, and overnight stays, especially when night ceremonials were being performed, could be reciprocated when Navaho families came to visit us at the ranch.

There were, of course, disadvantages. I was not placed in a setting in which I was forced to learn more Navaho. I could carry on an elementary conversation with non-English speaking Navahos, but could not interview in the language. I had to depend on either English, with the younger Navahos, or Spanish, which was spoken by the older generation. Some of the veterans were still essentially monolingual in Navaho (in spite of three or four years in the army), and with these I used interpreters. But, in my defense, I can report that Navaho is one of the most difficult languages in the world to learn fluently. It is a tonal language, and it has a very complex grammatical structure. Even Clyde Kluckhohn, who was gifted at languages and had worked on learning the language over a period of some thirty years, never spoke it fluently according to many Navahos I knew.

Another disadvantage was that when Navaho friends came to visit us, we could invite them for lunch or dinner and have them seated at the ranch table. But staying overnight presented some problems. Navahos in those days lived far from household water supplies, and if they bathed at all, apart from their sweat lodges, it was infrequent. Inviting a Navaho friend to sleep in a bed made up with my mother's freshly washed sheets proved to be difficult, if not impossible, and Navahos were relegated to outlying buildings on the ranch for the night. But, of course, when I visited Navaho hogans and spent the night, they did not furnish a bed for me; rather they would simply supply me with a sheepskin and I brought my own blankets or sleeping bag. In retrospect, my Navaho friends may not have been as upset about their sleeping arrangements at the Vogt Ranch as I was at the time.

During this 1947–48 field trip I was able to collect extensive life histories on each of the fifteen veterans; I also made detailed observations on their family life, as well as on their participation in the ceremonial and political life of the Ramah Navaho. Since there were no really usable portable tape recorders in those days, the life histories were recorded directly on my portable typewriter.

In December 1947 I had attended my first meetings of the American Anthropological Association in Albuquerque and presented a joint paper with John Adair, who was studying Zuni veterans at the same time I was doing research with the Navaho veterans. This proved to be a useful comparison, and both of us were able to present papers on different aspects of our comparative study.

John Adair proved to be a splendid colleague, and we met frequently at the Vogt Ranch or at the house he was renting in Zuni to discuss our data and our interpretations. These fruitful encounters led to the publication of our joint paper, which appeared in the *American Anthropologist* in 1949 as "Navaho and Zuni Veterans: A Study of Contrasting Modes of Culture Change."

A notable event occurred in early December when the celebrated literary critic, Edmund Wilson, appeared at Zuni to attend and write an article for the *New Yorker Magazine* on the Shalako ceremony that is performed each year. John Adair had the duty of escorting Edmund Wilson around Zuni Pueblo, which gave me an opportunity to meet and visit with Wilson when my wife and I attended the Shalako. Edmund Wilson also came with John for a brief visit of the Ramah Navaho and had lunch with us at the Vogt Ranch. Wilson's perceptive article on the Zuni Shalako later appeared in the *New Yorker* and in his lively book *Red, Black, Blonde and Olive* (1956). I have always considered the article a model of gracefully written ethnography; an edited version has appeared in four editions of the *Reader in Comparative Religion,* which I edited with William A. Lessa.

The other celebrity to appear during this 1947–48 field trip was Leonard McCombe, the noted *Life Magazine* photographer. McCombe had contacted Clyde Kluckhohn about doing a photographic essay on the contemporary Navaho. Clyde passed him along to various people in Navaho country, including Father Berard Haile and me. McCombe arrived in January and we made arrangements for his photography among the Ramah Navaho. The high point was my being able to arrange for the photographing of a Female Shooting Evil Way chant to rid a Navaho girl of the ghost of her grandmother, whose image had appeared repeatedly to her in dreams. In this case I participated in the ceremony and was included in the photographs along with the Navaho family. It was arduous duty since part of the ceremony included impossibly hot baths in the sweat lodge, followed by rolling in the winter snow dressed in only a breechcloth. Another part of

EZV participating in Navaho "Female Evil Shooting Way" ceremony in 1948. All the men, young and old, are in breechcloths and seated along the south wall of the ceremonial hogan. The pans are for the later drinking of the emetic and the piles of sand are for receiving the vomit—a ritual to rid all of the participants of the evil ghost. (Photo by Leonard McCombe, Life Magazine, © Time Warner)

the ceremony was the sweat and emetic ritual to drive the ghost from the outside and inside of the bodies of the participants. Again, the men were all in breechcloths, and the women topless, as the central fire in the hogan reached an intense heat for the sweating part of the rite. There followed the drinking of the emetic (composed of ritual plants in warm water) and the vomiting, induced with an eagle feather, into piles of sand which were later carried out to the north for safe disposal.

Life published an excellent article with McCombe's photographs on the Navaho in the spring of 1948. In 1951 Harvard University Press published *Navaho Means People,* which included a larger number of McCombe's photographs together with a text that I wrote jointly with Clyde Kluckhohn. While the book never became a best-seller, it did reasonably well and was a useful book on Navaho culture and the problems the tribe was having adapting to the world of the white people during the late 1940s.

The mother's brother of the patient vomits into a pile of sand. (Photo by Leonard McCombe)

After nine intensive months of field research on the veterans, I decided that I had exhausted the topic and that, with the corpus of data I had from the Ramah Navaho archives, I had sufficient data to write a dissertation. We returned to Chicago in April 1948, and I worked at fever pitch during the ensuing five months to analyze my field data and write my thesis. With a third child on the way, I was under heavy pressure to finish and locate a teaching position for the fall of 1948.

In the spring and summer of 1948 job offers began to come my way. My first offer was from the University of Wyoming in Laramie. I almost accepted, since we liked the mountain country of the West. But then I received a letter from Wilson D. Wallis at the University of Minnesota, offering a substantially better salary. I came within an ace of accepting Minnesota, when McGill University in Montreal called to offer a post there. The McGill offer was very appealing, especially since the summer vacation is five months long, enough time for a good field trip. Again, when I was about to accept the offer from McGill, I received a letter from Clyde informing me that an offer of an instructorship at Harvard was on its way. A few days later I received the formal offer from Talcott Parsons, the chairman of the Department of Social Relations. The offer was most intriguing because the Laboratory of Social Relations had just received a $100,000 grant from the Rockefeller Foundation to undertake a comparative study of values in five cultures in the Ramah area of New Mexico. I was slated to alternate with John M. Roberts as field director on an every other year basis; the alternate years being spent at Harvard teaching.

At this point I had been assigned a desk in the hallway just outside the office of Robert Redfield, the busy dean of the Social Sciences. With the Harvard offer pending, I made a formal appointment to see him, and I shall never forget his response, looking over the top of his reading glasses. "I do not see on my desk," he said, "any offers from universities superior to Harvard. I advise you to accept."

EARLY DAYS AT HARVARD AND THE VALUES STUDY PROJECT: 1948–1953

My wife and I and about-to-be-three children arrived at Harvard in our 1947 Ford in mid-September, just in time to move into an apartment and get ready for the first day of classes.

I vividly recall my first conversation with Clyde Kluckhohn, the senior anthropologist in the Department of Social Relations, about teaching duties. He first assured me that of course Harvard instructors were free to teach anything they chose to offer. Then he cleared his throat and mentioned that he had been teaching a course in Primitive Religion for some years. It was a course he had inherited from Alfred Tozzer, the famous Mayan archaeologist and ethnologist, but he was no longer able to offer it.

Then he cleared his throat again, and it was obvious that I was expected to offer Primitive Religion as my first lecture course at Harvard in the spring term. I accepted the duty with some trepidation since I had never had a course at Chicago on religion or ritual. My teaching duties were light during the fall term (since I was on halftime research support from the Laboratory of Social Relations); they included only duty as a section leader in one of the introductory courses. I recall spending many hours during the fall term reviewing anthropology books, both general surveys and ethnographic monographs, on religion.

The offices of the Department of Social Relations were principally in Emerson Hall where, being the junior member of the department, I was assigned an office up three long flights of stairs on the fourth floor. It was a large office shared with a visiting professor, Paul Lazersfeld, the sociologist from Columbia University. Lazersfeld was a very dynamic, but very nervous man. Puffing his cigar, he would often pace up and down our joint office, sometimes pausing to look at various ethnographic monographs on my desk. One morning when I had the various monumental volumes of Bogaras on the Chukchee of northeastern Siberia piled on my desk, he stopped and picked up a volume to peruse for several minutes. Before he strode off to pace back and forth once again, he said, "My God, you anthropologists know a lot. You don't know how you found it all out, but you certainly know a lot."

In those early years the Department of Social Relations was an exhilarating place. There were, of course, any number of stories about how the department had been formed by a group of disgruntled professors: Talcott Parsons, the sociologist who was fed up being dominated by Ptirim Sorokin; Gordon Allport and Henry Murray, two psychologists who had little in common with the so-called brass instrument psychologists located in the traditional Department of Psychology; and Clyde Kluckhohn who had had various political problems in the Department of Anthropology, especially those stemming from the intense competition with Carleton Coon.

This group moved to add Professor Samuel Stouffer from the University of Chicago to be the Director of the Laboratory of Social Relations, which was the research arm of the department. While there was a kernel of truth in these stories, this group of professors, with younger, lively appointments made in each field, had managed to create what I remember as a dynamic intellectual atmosphere. I recall sitting in each week on the interdisciplinary seminar taught by Parsons, Murray, and Kluckhohn that dealt with the efforts to bring various threads of each field together in a unified theory of social action. For someone trained in the Department of Anthropology at Chicago and who knew the ethnographic work of Elsie Clews Parsons, but had never heard about nor been exposed to the Weberian-derived theories of Talcott Parsons, the neo-Freudianism of Henry Murray, and the efforts of social psychologists to introduce some rigor into the methods for doing social surveys, including public opinion polls, I found my first years in Emerson Hall illuminating and fascinating.

The major integrative effort, edited by Talcott Parsons and Edward A. Shils, was published in 1952 under the title *Toward a General Theory of Action*. It has never had a major impact on anthropology, largely, I believe, because the theoretical system is so far from our empirical ethnographic data that it is virtually impossible to apply in any fruitful way.

These years in the Department of Social Relations were also stimulated by a number of visiting anthropologists who were invited to spend a term or more at Harvard while Clyde Kluckhohn was away or others were on leave. These visitors included A. L. Kroeber and Leslie White; they also included Ralph Linton and George Peter Murdock who came up from New Haven during a term on alternate weeks to lecture in Kluckhohn's course on the History of Anthropological Theory. I remember how in each lecture Linton, and then Murdock, would spend the first part of the period "correcting" what the other had to say the previous week.

The number of students, undergraduate and graduate, who were in social anthropology in the Department of Social Relations was always small, compared to those who specialized in the other fields. There were years when we had only ten or twelve applications to the graduate program in social anthropology in the Department of Social Relations. We would choose about half of them, and hold our breath, hoping they would be able scholars. In retrospect, we need not have been so anxious, for there was something about the interdisciplinary nature of the program that attracted interesting and creative students. Even though the numbers were small, we usually came out well. It was one of those years when we had only a handful of total applications that netted Clifford Geertz, now at the Institute for Advanced Study at Princeton, Hildred Geertz of the Department of Anthropology at Princeton, and A. Kimball Romney of the University of California at Irvine—all in the same class.

The Department of Anthropology continued with its offices in the Peabody Museum. When I arrived, Professor J. O. Brew was director of the Peabody Museum; Professors Ernest A. Hooton and Alfred Tozzer were still teaching; and the younger members of the department, along with Kluckhohn, were Carleton Coon, Alfred Kidder II, Hallam L. Movius, and Douglas Oliver. Clyde always kept his office in the Peabody Museum, rather than moving to Emerson Hall, in part, I am sure, to keep his relationship alive with the traditional department. Kluckhohn was especially busy in those years since he was also serving as the director of the Russian Research Center and had his principal office located in the center.

This first year at Harvard was hectic, but exciting and included the birth of our third child, Eric Edwards Vogt, on 22 October 1948 at Ayer, Massachusetts, and a visit by Carlos Lacerda and his wife, Leiticia. Carlos had come to the United States for his newspaper in Rio de Janeiro, the *Jornal do Brasil,* to cover the Dewey versus Truman election in November. I was especially pleased with what seemed to have been a successful lecture course in Primitive Religion.

The academic year 1949–50 was spent in the Southwest where I served as field director of the Comparative Study of Values in Five Cultures Project, or Values Study Project for short. In providing the funding grant to the Laboratory of Social Relations, the Rockefeller Foundation was interested in exploring the role of values in culture and in promoting an interdisciplinary approach to the study. The Ramah area of western New Mexico was an excellent field site for these objectives. Five quite different cultures (Zuni, Navaho, Spanish-American, Mormon, and Texan) lived here in the same ecological setting on the Colorado Plateau south of Gallup and to the west and southwest of the Zuni Mountain range (Vogt and Albert 1966).

The setting has some variations in the elevation and in annual precipitation, which averages 13.35 inches. Most of the communities are located at approximately seven thousand feet, except for Zuni Pueblo at sixty-three hundred feet. There is heavier average rainfall near the base of the Zuni

Field research in Fence Lake, New Mexico, in 1950. Texan homesteader Wilson Link cultivates his bean crop. (Photo by David DeHarport)

Mountains, which rise to more than eight thousand feet, than there is to the west and south, with Zuni, Atarque, and Fence Lake receiving at least an inch less. But, on the whole, a research design based upon five different cultures in the substantially same ecological niche was valid. Our task was to explore the extent to which differing cultural values had resulted in the persistence of five different cultures living here side-by-side in the Ramah area.

By the time of this post–World War II era in the Southwest it had become abundantly clear that the traditional cultures of the Native Americans were persisting in a way that would have astonished older generations of anthropologists who felt a sense of urgency to describe the old customs before they disappeared completely. To a degree, the same was true of the traditional Hispanic, as well as the two varieties of white American culture, Mormon and Texan, that we proposed to study. In all cases the central hypothesis was that certain core values in each culture probably accounted for the persistence of their varying ways of life.

Clyde Kluckhohn organized an Advisory Committee, consisting of himself, Talcott Parsons, and J. O. Brew, to advise on basic policies for the project. John ("Jack") M. Roberts served as coordinator, and I served as deputy coordinator from 1949 to 1953 and alternated as field director in the Southwest during those years. Ultimate responsibility for the Rockefeller Foundation grants ($100,000 for 1949 to 1952 followed by a renewal of another $100,000 for 1952 to 1955) was in the hands of the director (Samuel A. Stouffer) and associate director (Richard L. Solomon) of the Laboratory of Social Relations, who also provided needed advice for the two coordinators. In effect, Jack Roberts and I made policy decisions, but always in consultation with the advisory committee.

We had two basic research tasks. The first was to recruit effective fieldworkers to undertake basic research in each of the three cultures, other than the Navaho and Spanish-Americans. While Clyde Kluckhohn had been working with the Navaho in the region and his wife, Florence R. Kluckhohn, a sociologist by training, with the Spanish-Americans in Atarque since 1936, the other three cultures all required more basic ethnographic field research.

We persuaded Thomas F. O'Dea, and later Robert N. Bellah, two bright sociology students of Talcott Parsons, to undertake field research in the Mormon community of Ramah, which at that time was a compact village of some 250 inhabitants. From this research O'Dea published an excellent book (1957), and Bellah wrote the basic chapter on "Religious Systems" for Vogt and Albert (1966). Jack Roberts decided to work in Zuni Pueblo (population 2,500), which at that time was very sensitive to field research and opposed to having anthropologists live in the pueblo. The result was that Jack lived in Gallup and commuted to Zuni to do his research. Nonetheless, he was able to develop close contacts in the pueblo and to gather significant new data on Zuni culture. The notable publications stemming from this research were Smith and Roberts (1954), Roberts (1956), and Schneider and Roberts (1956).

What remained was the Texan community, which needed the basic ethnographic study, and being the junior member of the project staff this task fell to me. I was not very happy about this decision at the time. I had already done a stint of field research in Grundy County, Illinois, on the Lloyd Warner project, and while it had some interesting aspects, I never considered it "anthropological" enough. It was too much a part of my own culture to excite me, as had the work with the Navaho veterans and their families. For whatever it is that makes a good anthropologist, it is clear to me that a deep inner drive to make sense of a strange and alien culture is one of the most important aspects of that motivational complex. I did my best to try to talk Clyde Kluckhohn into expanding the Values Study Project to include the western Apache, not far away across the Arizona border, and letting me do my field research there. But he argued persuasively that this would weaken the overall tightness of design of the project. With my wife and three small children we began in the autumn of 1949, by moving into a rented farm house in the community of Fence Lake, population 232. I would have preferred to start the research during the summer, but I had to teach in the Harvard summer school in 1949 in order to pay back loans we had taken out to make the move from Chicago to Cambridge.

Our rented farmhouse had four rooms—kitchen, living room, and two bedrooms—and electricity, the Rural Electrification Authority power lines having just arrived in the community, but no running water. We hauled water in a project pickup or Jeep from the community well in the center of Fence Lake, a mile away. The cost was ten cents for a fifty-five-gallon barrel. The toilet facilities were an outhouse located by a juniper tree near the house. While the autumn weather was pleasant, the winter cold at seven thousand feet was something else again. We had only a fireplace, which burned pinyon logs, in the living room and a cookstove into which we stuffed juniper wood in the kitchen. Ice froze on the water bucket inside the kitchen during the night as outside temperatures reached twenty to thirty degrees below zero.

We soon became acquainted with our friendly Texan neighbors, especially Wilson and Ruth Link who rented us the farmhouse that had once been the home of his mother. The postmistress in the center of town was Virginia Bruton, a sister of Wilson Link, and she and her husband, Major (a given name, not a title) visited with us each day as we went to pick up the mail. Another neighbor, Fritz Jacoby, who I learned later was the village water dowser who used a Y-shaped stick, delivered two quarts of milk to us daily.

We also began to participate in the social life of the community: dances in the schoolhouse on Saturday night, poker games when it snowed and the men could not work outside, visiting in the local stores and in the saloon. By the time we had spent a total of eighteen months in this tiny community of 232 people, we knew every person in town, including the children, and we came to respect and to like the people very much. The basic ethnography on Fence Lake is included in my book *Modern Homesteaders: The Life of a Twentieth-Century Frontier Community* (1955b) and in various articles, including one comparing the social structure and values of the Mormon and Texan communities (Vogt and O'Dea 1953).

The second task Jack Roberts and I faced in the Values Study Project was to bring some interdisciplinary research to bear on the problem of describing and analyzing values, and by comparisons and replications across the five cultures to say something significant about the role of value systems in culture. We decided our best bet was to recruit a number of bright graduate students and young faculty members in a variety of fields and ask them to develop projects that would (a) involve "values," and (b) undertake research in two or more of the five cultures to give their designs a comparative dimension.

On the whole this approach was productive, if somewhat chaotic. Over the five years of active field research (1949 to 1954) the project managed to recruit anthropologists; sociologists; social, cognitive, and personality psychologists; philosophers; a political scientist; and a historian. Other than the staff anthropologists (Kluckhohn, Roberts, and Vogt), the major anthropological work was done by three colleagues, Katherine Spencer (1957), who published a fascinating monograph on Navaho values as reflected in Navaho chantway myths; John Landgraf (1954), who studied land-use patterns; and David P. McAllester (1954), who researched Navaho (especially Enemy Way) music, as well as by a number of talented graduate students, including Munro S. Edmonson (1957 on the institutional values of the Spanish-Americans), Tom F. S. McFeat (1960 on Zuni values as expressed in learning patterns), George Mills (1959 on Navaho art and culture), Robert N. Rapoport (1954 on the impact of Protestant missionaries on Navaho religious values), A. Kimball Romney (who collaborated with Florence Kluckhohn on a cross-cultural study of value-orientations), Wayne Untereiner (1952 on self and society in relation to cultural values), and Otto von Mering (1956 on individual and cultural patterns of valuation).

The major sociological thrust, other than the work done by O'Dea and Bellah, was the work of Florence Kluckhohn and Fred L. Strodtbeck on variations in value-orientations across the five cultures. This cross-cultural research was sophisticated and produced interesting results (Kluckhohn and Strodtbeck 1961), but I always had reservations about the validity of field research that depended on forcing responses on a schedule of questions and was more inclined to study values by examining how the different cultures responded to the common problems each faced in this ecological setting (see Vogt and Albert 1966).

The field research by psychologists involved some projects by cognitive psychologists, one by a clinical psychologist, and others by learning theory psychologists under the direction of my colleague John W. M. Whiting.

The psychoanalytically trained clinical psychologist, Bert Kaplan (1954), undertook to administer Rorschach tests to a sample of informants in four cultures (Zuni was not attempted), and the learning theory psychologists did extensive field research on child training patterns in the Texan, Mormon, and Zuni communities; their conclusions about the learning of cultural values are summarized in Whiting, Chasdi, Antonovsky, and Ayres (1966).

Two philosophers joined the project through the strong interests of Clyde Kluckhohn who always argued that if any of the disciplines should have something important to say about values, it should be philosophy. The first was John Ladd (1957) of Brown University whom Clyde persuaded to undertake a field study of the moral code of the Navahos. Most of his field data came from intensive interviewing of The Son of Many Beads, a noted Ramah Navaho headman and singer of Blessing Way, who was a thoughtful and profound Navaho philosopher. The second philosopher was Ethel M. Albert (1956) who joined us as a research associate and worked both at Harvard on the problems of describing and classifying values and in the field in the Southwest.

The political scientist, Guy J. Pauker, was recruited to do both library and field research on the various political systems in the Ramah area (1966). The historian who joined our project was Irving Telling who did research in the Southwest, where he gathered data during 1950 and 1951 for his Harvard Ph.D. dissertation on the social history of the Gallup, New Mexico, area (see Telling 1952, 1953, 1954).

On the whole the intensive field research phase of the project (1949 to

1953) went well. None of our field researchers were forced to leave any of the communities under investigation. The good people of the Ramah area had, of course, been irritated at times by having so many social scientists study them. But, interestingly enough, I discovered in later years that the feelings of deepest hurt were expressed not by the informants who were irritated by our research procedures, but rather by members of the various communities who had never been interviewed, who had never fallen into anybody's sample to answer a questionnaire. Several asked me with strong affect "Why didn't any of your Harvard people come around and ask me about things?" In the end, I decided, people everywhere feel themselves knowledgeable enough to be asked about their own culture, and are highly annoyed if they are NOT interviewed.

I found that the anthropologists managed to get along better in the various Ramah area communities than most of the field researchers from other disciplines; they should have, of course, since it is their major business to study and understand other customs. Some of the difficulties of adjustment to other customs were poignant. I recall the time when one of the sociologists with insufficient knowledge of Navaho culture arrived at a hogan one day shortly after a young Navaho had been killed by being bucked off a horse. The relatives of the deceased were in the process of building a coffin to dispose of the body as quickly as possible in order to avoid being in contact with the ghost of the dead rider. When the sociologist asked politely if he could help, the Navahos gladly handed him the hammer and nails, jumped into their pickup truck, and drove off, leaving our fieldworker with the heavy duty of finishing the coffin, digging the grave, and burying the body. Some of the incidents were amusing, such as the time when two of the learning theory psychologists were teaching a third to drive the project Chevrolet carryall on an isolated road in the countryside. The student driver encountered some soft sand on the road and the car began to skid dangerously back and forth whereupon her two colleagues simultaneously panicked and both reached across to grab the steering wheel. The carryall rolled over completely once, slightly injuring all three students who emerged in a dazed state from the car. One said immediately, "Somebody call a cab"—this in a remote area of the Zuni Reservation where the closest taxi was in Gallup, thirty miles away. Our Chevrolet carryall had an interesting "after life." We traded the wreck to the Ford agency in Gallup as partial payment for a pickup truck, and it was the Ford agency owner, Claire Gurley, who had the bright idea to saw off the top, equip it with balloon tires, and resell it to the Indian trader who ran tours over the quicksands in beautiful Canyon de Chelly in Arizona. Would that Jack Roberts and I had been bright enough to have the same idea and save funds for the project!

In 1953 Jack Roberts had completed his five years as assistant professor at Harvard and decided to accept an associate professorship at the University of Nebraska, where he had done his undergraduate work. I succeeded him as coordinator of the Values Study Project from 1953 to 1955, at a time when we were all much concerned with how we were going to produce a final report on the project that would pull together our diverse research results in some sensible fashion. We began by organizing a conference of the senior staff and advisory committee, which took place at the Museum of Northern Arizona in Flagstaff, Arizona, in the summer of 1954. We invited Professor Robert Redfield from the University of Chicago to attend as a discussant and commentator on our work on values. Flagstaff provided a lovely and cool summer setting, and the conference was very stimulating, leading to a general outline of a final report.

At the end of the Values Study Project I was a fellow at the Center for Behavioral Sciences at Stanford during 1956 and 1957; Ethel Albert served as a fellow there the following academic year. These fellowships gave us important free time to work on the earlier drafts of the final report. But, of course, like all joint ventures, some chapters were inevitably delayed. We were still working on the volume when Clyde Kluckhohn died suddenly (and prematurely at age fifty-five) of a heart attack in the summer of 1960. Ethel Albert and I finished and finally published the volume in 1966 under the title *People of Rimrock: A Study of Values in Five Cultures*. It would have been a more complete volume had Clyde lived to include more of his thinking in the final report. But, in retrospect, I believe we learned a great deal about the five cultures and their value systems and produced a significant series of publications. One of our major conceptual problems in the end, was to include too much territory under the rubric of "value"; it tended to lose its force and its clarity in analysis. I believe that this, in concert with the upsurge in British social anthropology, followed by the tremendous popularity of Levi-Straussian structuralism and by the Marxist theoretical thrust, accounts for the paucity of reference to the works of the Values Study Project over the years. In my experience, the British tend to avoid citing published works by Americans, unless those Americans have either been trained in England, or at least had some significant exposure to the British networks. As for Structuralism and Marxism, even British social anthropology was eclipsed by these intellectual tidal waves in the 1960s and 1970s.

I also often ask myself how successful interdisciplinary research was in the Social Relations and Values Study Project context. I can recall endless discussions, both before and after the publication of Talcott Parsons and Edward A. Shils's (editors) *Toward a General Theory of Action* (1951) in which Clyde Kluckhohn had produced a chapter on "Values and Value-Orientations in the Theory of Action," that focused on how in the world we should put all these disciplines together to provide a theoretical framework for significant empirical research. My own experience was that interdisciplinary research worked best when an investigator asked a concrete question and then proceeded to enlist collaborators from the fields that would be likely to answer the question. I regard my research on water dowsing to be my most successful effort in interdisciplinary research.

My interest in dowsing was first aroused when I visited with our neighbor in Fence Lake, Fritz Jacoby, who delivered our milk each morning. I had become bored with interviewing about patterns of family and social life that were generally familiar to me. But water dowsing was something that at least bordered on the exotic and the occult and about which I knew too little. I began to spend time in Fence Lake interviewing not only the dowser himself, but also the farmers in the community about the practice. I discovered that some were believers and never drilled a well without having the location specified by Fritz and his forked stick; others such as the well-driller, Lee Bell, were skeptics. I also kept careful track of the cases of drilling as to which were dowsed and which were not dowsed and checked to see which were successful and which were unsuccessful wells. Since my Fence Lake data indicated no consistent relationship between dowsing and the drilling of a successful well, I began to wonder why it was that people continued to believe in water witching.

Upon my return to Harvard I located some interesting books in Widener Library on the subject of dowsing and discovered that the practice could be traced back as far as 1551, when it was used in Germany to try to locate underground deposits of iron ore. From here the practice spread to England where it was used to dowse for water. It was carried by European colonists

A typical water dowser using a freshly cut forked stick to try to locate water.

to all parts of the world, but never used by indigenous peoples in Asia, Africa, Australia, or the New World before the Europeans arrived.

About this time I first encountered my colleague Ray Hyman, who was a young social psychologist in the Department of Social Relations. Quite by chance, at a cocktail party, I began to discuss my information about water divining with him and discovered that he had been a professional magician before he became a psychologist. He was well informed about palmistry, mind reading, table turning, and other occult practices. By the end of the party we had agreed to join forces and undertake a study of the empirical validity and the geographical distribution of dowsing, and, hopefully, the reasons why it was still practiced so widely in the modern world. We obtained a grant from the Hodgson Fund ("for the study of psychic phenomena") in the Department of Psychology, and employed two graduate student research assistants: the anthropologist Peggy Golde and the sociologist Elizabeth G. Cohen. We interviewed dowsers in New

England, West Virginia, and the Southwest. We mailed questionnaires to a sample of five hundred County Agricultural Extension agents in the United States, and we consulted with geologists in the Department of Geological Sciences at Harvard and in the United States Geological Survey.

The result was a genuinely interdisciplinary project that demonstrated (a) that water divining as an empirical technique does not work to locate underground water, and (b) that it is a technique of magical divination in American culture. Our book entitled *Water Witching USA* (1959; second edition 1979) has now been in print for more than thirty years. Because it is a "skeptical" book (two New York publishers turned the book down on the grounds that we came out on "the wrong side of the controversy"), it has never been a best-seller. But it has become the standard source for both social and natural scientists who wish to learn more about this curious practice.

In retrospect the Ramah Navaho Project, which sponsored my research on the Navaho veterans, and the later Values Study Project were rehearsals, in many significant ways, for my Harvard Chiapas Project. The emphasis on long-range research, the stress on fine-grained and penetrating ethnographic work, the training of students in a field situation, the involvement of several scientific disciplines, and the flexible organization that permitted individual researchers to design and carry out innovative projects were all features of my southwestern research experience in the decade from 1947 to 1957. These features were later incorporated, with appropriate modifications, into the design of the Harvard Chiapas Project.

2 /
THE ORIGINS OF THE HARVARD CHIAPAS PROJECT: 1954–1956

 In 1954 I was granted tenure at Harvard, and I was ready for a new chapter in field research. As much as I appreciated the Southwest and its people and cultures, I was bored with fieldwork in my native land. In this restive mood, I felt strongly that I wanted to work in another major ethnographic region, and the area to which I turned was Mexico.

My lifelong love affair with Mexico began in 1950 when my wife and I were able to leave our three children with my mother at the Vogt Ranch and fly to Mexico City for a ten-day vacation. My only previous experience with Mexico had been occasional forays across the border from El Paso into the frontier city of Ciudad Juarez. Now we landed in the heart of the Republic of Mexico, stayed at the Hotel Majestic on the Zocalo, and went sight-seeing—to the Cathedral and Palacio Nacional, to the Lomas de Chapultepec, to the floating gardens of Xochimilco, to Taxco, and to the Pyramids of the Sun and Moon at Teotihuacan. It was a mind-blowing ten days, and I was stimulated down to my nerve ends by the sights, sounds, and cultural encounters we had in Mexico. Among other things, I recall being astounded by the size and luxuriousness of the elite homes on the Lomas de Chapultepec, an experience that removed forever any lingering stereotype of Mexicans all living in small adobe houses in tiny villages such as the ones I knew in my youth in New Mexico.

SABBATICAL IN CHAPALA

In the spring of 1952 we took another vacation from fieldwork in the Ramah area and drove to Mexico in our station wagon with our three children and my mother. The purpose of the journey was to locate a tranquil Mexican town in which to spend a sabbatical leave and write up my field data on Fence Lake.

It was a fabulous journey from El Paso to Durango and across the Sierra Madre Occidental to Mazatlan. Some nights we camped out; other nights were spent in inexpensive motels or hotels. One night when we had to camp out occurred on the journey across the Sierra Madre, a trip so long and tortuous that dark caught us only at the halfway mark to Mazatlan. The curving, unpaved road was too dangerous to maneuver at night, so we found the only open space beside the road and laid out our sleeping bags under the stars. I recall that my mother asked me, just before I fell asleep, "Vogtie, did you bring a gun?" I had not brought any firearms, and felt perfectly safe in the Mexico countryside, as I have ever since, in spite of accounts about bandits and robberies, which circulate especially in isolated areas of Northwest Mexico.

From Mazatlan we continued on to Guadalajara, passing through Tepic where I first encountered colorfully costumed Huichols, an experience that quickened my interest in working eventually with some remote group of Mexican Indians. Finally, in the lovely town of Chapala, located on the north shore of Lake Chapala, we found the ideal site for my sabbatical and proceeded to rent a house located only a block from the lake.

In the autumn of 1952 we returned to our rented house in Chapala where Nan employed a cook and a maid to help with the housework while she became the teacher of our children, using the Calvert School system, and I settled down upstairs to write my book on Fence Lake. We returned to Harvard in time for my teaching duties during the spring term of 1953.

In the summer of 1953 I was not able to return to Mexico since I was one of the members of a summer interuniversity seminar on acculturation sponsored by the Social Science Research Council and held at Stanford. We camped across the United States arriving in Palo Alto just in advance of the birth of our fourth child, Charles Anthony Vogt, who was born on 27 July 1953 in San Mateo, California. This summer experience was important intellectually for me not only because of the stimulating seminar which included Homer Barnett, Leonard Broom, Bernard J. Siegel, and James B. Watson, but also because I encountered William A. Lessa, who was teaching summer school at Stanford, with whom I eventually published *Reader in Comparative Religion: An Anthropological Approach* (1958), now in its fourth edition.

Clyde and Florence Kluckhohn on fishing expedition off the West Coast of Mexico during the time they came to visit us in Chapala, Mexico, in 1952.

RECONNAISSANCE OF HUICHOL COUNTRY

I decided to spend part of the summer of 1954 making a reconnaissance of the Huichol area with the idea of organizing a long-range field project in this region of Mexico. I reviewed all I could locate in the Peabody Museum Library about the Huichol; especially the publications of Robert M. Zingg with his mystical ideas about the Huichol as he tried to apply the theories of Levy-Bruhl (Zingg 1938); the fascinating experiences of the great Norwegian explorer, Carl Lumholtz, who rode horseback along the summit of the Sierra Madre and spent eight months with the Huichol in 1895–96 (Lumholtz 1902). I decided the time was ripe for a more penetrating ethnographic study of the Huichol and an analysis of the processes of cultural change in this remote region of Mexico.

I flew first to Mexico City for a week to meet anthropological colleagues. Here I had the good fortune to meet Alfonso Villa Rojas, Roberto J. Weitlaner, and Barbro Dahlgren, as well as Alfonso Caso who was serving then as the director of the Instituto Nacional Indigenista (hereinafter INI), or National Indian Institute, and was clearly the leading anthropologist of Mexico. Although his technical work was in archaeology (he became famous for his excavation of Tomb 7 at Monte Alban in Oaxaca), Caso was widely knowledgeable about the field as a whole. I shall never forget our first meeting as I was ushered into his enormous office at 1279 Avenida Revolución. It was like being received by a contemporary Moctezuma, as one walked at least thirty paces to reach his huge, polished mahogany desk. Although I knew he was fluent in English, I greeted him in Spanish, and we carried on all of our forty-minute conversation in Spanish. (I had remembered how Clyde Kluckhohn had called upon him some years before and had made the mistake of speaking English during what had proved to be a quite perfunctory encounter. Only upon leaving did Clyde shift to some phrases in Spanish, which led Dr. Caso to comment favorably, but by this time the conference was over.) My visit had established good rapport with the number one Mexican anthropologist, and this later proved to be of crucial importance for my field operations in Mexico.

I also had long talks with Dr. Wigberto Jiménez Moreno in the Institute of Anthropology and History and he helped me secure a general letter of introduction from Dr. Ignacio Marquina, the director of the Institute. Jiménez Moreno also gave me a letter of introduction to Dr. Augustín Yáñez, the governor of Jalisco.

I likewise met and visited at length with Dr. Isabel Kelly, who had done archaeological and ethnographic field research in the Sierra Madre Occidental and was enormously helpful in providing guidance in the logistics of travel in this remote and rugged land.

My next stop was Guadalajara where I first visited old friends in Chapala and then spent a day back in Guadalajara where I called upon José Corona Núñez, the director of the Museum, whom I had met during our stay in Chapala. José took me almost immediately to arrange an appointment for me to see the governor in the afternoon. Gov. Augustín Yáñez, who was also a famous Mexican writer, received me cordially, discussed my research plans very intelligently, and promptly gave me two letters: one was a general letter of introduction, the other was a letter introducing me to José Limón Guzmán, the governor of Nayarit.

On to Tepic, the capital of Nayarit, where bearing the letter from Governor Yáñez of Jalisco, I called upon Gov. José Limón to request a letter of recommendation to be presented to local officials in Huichol communities in the Sierra Madre. Every governor of a Mexican state has a secretario particular, in essence a private or personal secretary, who manages the governor's daily operations. Since the governors do not keep appointment calendars, it is up to the secretario particular to make decisions as to who gets to see the governor and in what order, as well as deciding how many hours or days a visitor may be asked to wait.

In company with Dr. Peña Navarro, the director of the museum whom I had met on a trip to Tepic during the time we lived in Chapala, I met the secretario particular, one Licenciado Roberto Villalobos Sandoval, at the Palacio del Estado and presented my letters and my Harvard card. After a short wait, the governor received me. He was a rugged, handsome man who reminded me of many Spanish-American leaders I had known in New Mexico. I explained my purposes in visiting the Huichol communities in the Sierra as he looked me very directly and intently in the eyes to see if he could trust me. He promised a letter of recommendation, and the secretario reported that the letter would be ready in the afternoon. But when I returned for the letter, it had not been written. Instead the secretario was on the point of leaving for Santiago Compostela in the lowlands where there was to be a celebration inaugurating a Carta Blanca beer distributing agency. He invited me to go along with him. Off we went to the fiesta in his pickup. It was a glorious party with mariachis playing and with poetry being recited by the poet laureate of the state of Nayarit. After drinking endless Carta Blancas and eating *bíria* (roasted goat meat) and tortillas, we returned to Tepic some seven hours later.

I called at the office of the secretario during the two ensuing days. The promised letter was never ready. But I decided that I knew both the governor and the secretario particular personally and that I could proceed to the Sierra. This particular encounter was a crucial learning experience, for I had learned that what is important in Mexico is not the formal paperwork, but rather the face-to-face encounters between people that build relationships of confianza, that is, relationships of confidence and trust that mean much more than any number of written letters of recommendation.

From Isabel Kelly I had learned that the Sierra Madre region inhabited by the Huichol was also the ecological niche inhabited by a species of small deadly scorpions. A sting by these scorpions is fatal for children and paralytic for adults unless one receives an injection of the necessary antidote within thirty minutes after the encounter. Isabel Kelly insisted that to prevent being stung at night I needed to sleep on a cot covered by a mosquito netting for the scorpions not only crawl into sleeping bags, they also drop into beds from the ceilings of thatch-roofed houses. Further, I also needed to carry a kit containing the antidote and be prepared to inject the medicine myself into my hip in case I was stung by a scorpion in some remote area far from medical assistance. Needless to say, I arrived in Tepic equipped with the necessary cot, mosquito net, and injection kit, which I had purchased in Mexico City.

The western Sierra Madre, which I was about to enter, extends from Sonora and Chihuahua southward to Nayarit and Jalisco and is one of the most rugged, most impenetrable mountain masses on the North American continent. Viewed from the Central Plateau of Northern Mexico through which the highway leading south from El Paso passes, the Sierra seems to be quite insignificant, for it rises gradually above the surface of the plateau. But viewed from the Pacific Lowlands on the west, the mountain front rises as a magnificent escarpment to more than nine thousand feet. This escarpment is cut to depths of five thousand to six thousand feet by streams flowing into the Pacific, and many of these canyons rival the Grand Canyon of the Colorado in depth and grandeur.

Conferring with the local government officials and the protestant missionaries who were working in the Sierra Madre, I learned that the nearest Huichol communities could be reached either on horseback, which was at least a four-day journey up and down *barrancas* (steep canyons) thousands of feet deep, or by small plane, which flew from Tepic to the Mestizo town of Huajimíc, and thence by horseback. Since I only had a month for this summer reconnaissance, I decided upon the latter alternative and flew to Huajimíc where I managed to rent a room for fifty centavos a night in a house that had been occupied by a physician before he left for Guadalajara, leaving the village without any medical attention. I ate my meals for four pesos a day in Doña Lola Sanchez's house which served as the local *posada* (inn).

Huajimíc was a miserably poor rural community with homes that were as modest as the neighboring Huichol and lighted at night only by kerosene lamps. Here Doña Lola served not only as the innkeeper, but also as the local nurse. I recall one day when a terrified shout went up from the edge of town, whereupon Doña Lola immediately rushed out the door and ran with her hypodermic equipment to inject the antidote into a small child who had just been stung by a scorpion at the edge of a freshly ploughed field. Needless to say, I dutifully slept on the cot and pulled the mosquito netting over me each night.

From Huajimíc I was able to rent a horse and engage a knowledgeable guide to take me to the closest Huichol rancherías (extended family settlements), some four and a half hours away on horseback. Here I was struck immediately by the sensible Huichol architecture; the houses in which they stored their corn and in which they slept were built on stilts. When the notched pole ladder was pulled up at night, the maize was out of reach of rats and mice, and the people were safe from the deadly scorpions.

I was also deeply impressed with their strong sense of identity and pride in being Huichol. While the Mestizos in Huajimíc spent much of their time complaining about their isolated life in the Sierra and longed to be in Guadalajara or Mexico City, the even more isolated Huichol believed they were living in the very center of the universe and were glad to be there. I have often used this example in my lectures to explain the difference between a "peasant" and a "tribal" community. The Mestizos in Huajimíc were rural peasants living on what they regarded as the very edge of civilization and feeling deprived; the more remote (from our point of view) Huichols were tribesmen whose sacred landscape in this incredibly rugged and isolated mountain mass symbolized the very center of the cosmos.

On a second trip by plane into the mountains from Tepic I flew to San Juan Peyotán for another look at the Huichol settlements in that area.

This 1954 reconnaissance convinced me that the Huichol region was not a feasible site for a long-range project involving students, both graduates and undergraduates. The logistics were simply too difficult. I could see myself in the awkward role of constantly pushing students to get out of Tepic and into the field. Each journey into the Huichol communities would involve either flying in or organizing a pack trip. I was also deeply concerned about the genuine dangers posed by the small scorpions. It was more a field site for a young, unmarried ethnographer with camping and hiking experience in rugged terrain. Although I managed to publish one paper on the Huichol (Vogt 1955), I reluctantly abandoned the idea of working among them.

FIRST TRIP TO CHIAPAS: 1955

I still wanted desperately to work in Mexico, however, and was enormously pleased when I received a letter from Dr. Alfonso Caso inviting me to attend a two-week conference in Mexico City in the summer of 1955. The purpose of the meeting was to evaluate the programs of the Instituto Nacional Indigenista. My round-trip airfare and hotel and meal expenses were to be paid by the Instituto.

I flew to Mexico and attended these fascinating daily meetings. Professor George M. Foster of the University of California, Berkeley, also attended, as did Isabel Kelly, and many prominent Mexican anthropologists, including Manuel Gamio, Gonzalo Aguirre Beltrán, Alfonso Villa Rojas, and Julio de la Fuente. Each of the local directors of the coordinating centers of the Instituto reported on problems in his area; we also had reports by physicians, agronomists, and other specialists.

At the end of the meeting Dr. Caso organized a week-long field visit of the INI Centers in Chiapas and Veracruz. I went by INI automobile and my traveling companions were Dr. Manuel Gamio, the elder statesman of Mexican anthropology, who had taken his Ph.D. with Franz Boas at Columbia and was noted not only for his archaeological work in the Valley of Mexico, but also for his monumental study *La Población del Valle de Teotihuacan* (1922), which covered the pre-Hispanic, colonial, and contemporary cultures; Dr. Gonzalo Aguirre Beltrán, physician turned anthropologist, who was then serving as the director of the INI Center in the Highlands of Chiapas; and Dr. Luis Gomez Pimienta, the director of the Institute of Tuberculosis in Mexico City. They were all scintillating traveling companions, and it was a fabulous journey in totally new territory for me.

On the first day we left Mexico at six A.M., drove to Oaxaca for a five P.M. lunch, and arrived in Tehuantepec for a very late supper and overnight stay. This was a marathon journey, and I learned for the first time how famished a North American, accustomed to lunch at noon or one P.M., can get when Mexican *comidas* do not appear until five P.M.

The following day we traveled from Tehuantepec to Tuxtla Gutierrez, again for a late and leisurely comida, accompanied by rum daiquiris, at the Hotel Bonampak. Aguirre Beltrán decided at this point that we must see the *sumidero* (great canyon) before we proceeded on to San Cristobal Las

Casas and ordered the chauffeur of our INI car to take the winding, switch-back road to the top of the mountain ridge that lies just north of Tuxtla. We reached the summit just at sundown. From the viewpoint we walked to the edge of the chasm cut through the limestone by the mighty Rio Grijalva, which originates in the Cuchumatane mountain massif on the Guatema-lan border, flows south toward the Pacific, turns to the west through the Grijalva Lowlands, and finally flows northward through Tabasco into the Gulf of Mexico. From where we stood, we peered almost straight down for twenty-five hundred feet to the river below. Tuxtla, with an elevation of twelve hundred feet, had been hot, but here at thirty-seven hundred feet it was cool and pleasant.

Manuel Gamio produced a bottle of scotch whiskey that his niece had given him to keep warm in the Highlands of Chiapas. The chauffeur found cups and soda water, and we sat on the edge of the sumidero until dark, drinking whiskey, admiring the sunset, and engaging in spirited discussion of many topics: anthropology, politics, the relationship between the United States and Mexico. I shall never forget how these three Mexican intellec-tuals argued vociferously with me about birth control at that point. I had asserted that Mexico needed a birth control program. Their response, led by Aguirre Beltrán, was that Mexico needed a larger population for the economic and political development of the Republic; if there should be fewer inhabitants in North America, let the people of the United States control their population. I recall being astounded by their position, and it was indeed many years after this before Mexican intellectuals conceded that birth control was essential in their own country.

We arrived in San Cristobal after dark, ate a late supper at the Hotel Español, and tumbled exhausted into bed. The next morning I awoke at sunrise and went for an early walk along the streets of San Cristobal. It was a clear, sunny morning, quite cool and sparkling from the rain during the night. I could see that San Cristobal (elevation seven thousand feet) was surrounded by mountains covered with pine trees. There were only a handful of cars in those days, but the streets were full of Tzotzil and Tzeltal Maya Indians, carrying maize, wood, and charcoal with tumplines, headed for the market. Their dress styles, distinctive for each municipio, were incredible. There were Zinacantecos in short pants, pink-and-white striped chamarras, kerchiefs with pink pom-poms, high-backed sandals, and handwoven palm hats flowing with pink-and-red ribbons. Their bare-

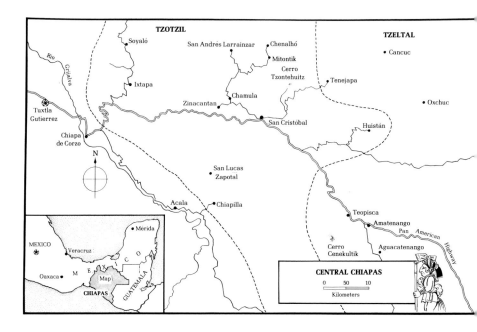

foot women in dark blue skirts and white blouses followed the men along
the hard paved street. The Chamulas, by contrast, wore white woolen chamarras, and white cowboy-style hats, while the women had coal-black
woolen skirts. Huisteco men proudly wore their characteristic white cotton pants that resembled diapers. With some briefing, one could tell at a
glance whence came each *indígena* family. These indígenas contrasted in
dress, language, and behavior with the Ladinos, the non-Indian families
who, with some admixture with Indians, were the descendants of the Spanish conquerors who founded San Cristobal Las Casas in 1528, named for
Saint Christopher, its patron saint, and for Bartolomé de las Casas, who
served as the first Roman Catholic bishop of Chiapas.

The ensuing three days were filled with visits to the INI Center on the
northern outskirts of San Cristobal, trips to communities such as Chamula
and Chilil (where INI had field projects), and long visits with such notables
as Don Manuel Castellanos, who was the head of Indian affairs for the
state government; Erastro Urbina, who began life as a Chamula, but was
now Ladinoized and owned a hardware store in San Cristobal; and Frans
and Gertrude Blom, whose home served as a gathering point for explorers
and European and North American tourists.

It was love at first sight. I knew by the end of our brief visit that the Highlands of Chiapas were where I wanted to spend the rest of my anthropological field career. Not only was I tremendously excited by the prospect of engaging in field research in the Maya communities, but I found I was intrigued by the patterns of life of the Ladinos in this old colonial town. Further, the ecological niche, with an altitude of seven thousand feet in the cool highlands covered with pine trees, was similar to the one in which I was reared, the Vogt Ranch in New Mexico.

My decision to work in the highlands was really underscored as we returned to Tehuantepec and drove northeastward to visit the INI Center in the Papaloapan River Valley of Veracruz. Here we had an interesting two days visiting with Ricardo and Isabel Pozas who had studied in Chamula (see Pozas 1959), after their initial field experience in Chiapas with Sol Tax in 1942–43.

Pozas was serving as the director of the INI Center that was working to organize new Mazatec communities that had been forced to leave their ancestral lands when a huge dam was built on the Rio Papaloapan. I also found the Mazatec people interesting, and being lowlanders, more open and friendly than the Highland Chiapas Maya. Over the years, I have discovered that, for a variety of reasons, lowland communities in *tierra caliente* in Mesoamerica are nearly always more hospitable and friendly to visitors than are the highland peoples living in *tierra fría*.

But here in Veracruz the hot lowlands were oppressive to me. The days and nights with temperatures in the eighties reminded me of the listless months I had spent on the Amazon in Brazil during my navy days. I have found over the years that although I enjoy visiting the lowlands and am always fascinated by visits to the famous Maya sites such as Palenque or Tikal, I would have been a failure as a Mayan archaeologist, for I am strictly a highlander when it comes to living and working.

SECOND TRIP TO CHIAPAS: 1956

During the summer of 1956 I participated in another SSRC seminar, this one on American Indian cultural change (Spicer 1961), at which I presented a paper on the Navaho. After the seminar in Albuquerque, we motored on to Palo Alto to take up my yearlong fellowship at the Center for Ad-

*Professor E. E. Evans-Pritchard of Oxford
University learns to grill chicken as EZV looks on.
At the beach at Santa Cruz, California, in 1958 when
we were both fellows at the Center for Advanced
Study in the Behavioral Sciences in Stanford,
California, and took our families to the
shore each Sunday.*

vanced Study in the Behavioral Sciences. The year was crucial for me since it gave me much needed time not only to complete a number of writing projects, such as the book on water witching, the *Reader in Comparative Religion,* and the chapter for the SSRC volume, but more importantly to design and to apply for the initial grants for the Harvard Chiapas Project. The 1956–57 year at the center was a banner year with amazingly stimulating fellows from various disciplines and a record twelve anthropologists. Many of the anthropologists were colleagues I had known before, such as John Whiting, Jack Roberts, Kim Romney, George Spindler, and Morris Opler. But some, such as E. E. Evans-Pritchard from Oxford University whose study at the center was next to mine, were totally new intellectual and personal acquaintances.

Over Christmas vacation, when the children could be taken out of school, the center was kind enough to give me permission and some travel expenses for another reconnaissance journey to Chiapas. I was particularly eager that Nan see the field site and get some sense of what life in Chiapas would be like before I committed myself to a long-range field effort. We proceeded to make the longest trip we have ever made by automobile in a four-week period (19 December to 14 January): Palo Alto to San Cristobal Las Casas and return, a distance of some sixty-four hundred miles. It was a long and strenuous journey in our 1950 Ford station wagon, but our four children (ages eleven, ten, eight, and three) were well behaved as we traveled down the Pacific coast of Mexico, stopping in Mazatlan and Tepic, and pausing for Christmas to visit Mexican friends in Chapala. Between Mexico City and San Cristobal the children amused themselves by counting the curves on the highway and announcing their results: approximately twenty-five hundred curves between Mexico and Oaxaca, another twenty-five hundred between Oaxaca and San Cristobal Las Casas.

We arrived at the Hotel Bonampak in Tuxtla Gutierrez just before midnight on 29 December. The hotel is modest by our standards, but luxurious by local standards, with its spacious dining rooms and outdoor pool fringed by coconut palms. My family was enchanted by the pool in this warm tropical setting, and over the next thirty years the Hotel Bonampak was destined to become a place of rest and recreation for us from the rigors of field research in the cold highlands. Compared to San Cristobal, Tuxtla was a swinging city and there has always been a rivalry between the two cities. Tuxtla Gutierrez was named from the Nahuatl words *tochtli* (rabbit) and *tlan* (abundance) and a former governor of Chiapas with the surname of Gutierrez. People born in Tuxtla Gutierrez are called *conejos* (rabbits), as contrasted with *coletos* (pigtails of bullfighters) who are the natives of San Cristobal Las Casas. Tuxtla became the capital of Chiapas in 1891 when the regime of Don Porfirio Diaz, who was president of Mexico from 1884 to 1911, decided San Cristobal Las Casas had an impossibly conservative elite that was unwilling to cooperate with the trends of change in the 1890s.

Leaving Tuxtla at noon the following day, the geographical tour of southeastern Mexico continued as we crossed the River Grijalva where it enters the great canyon called the sumidero and then passes through the old colonial city of Chiapa de Corzo where the Spanish conquerors first established their capital.

From the sweltering temperatures of Chiapa de Corzo located at about one thousand feet on the bank of the Grijalva, the Pan American highway ascends to eight thousand feet in twenty-seven miles as it climbs into the cool Highlands of Chiapas. The scenery on this section of the highway is spectacular as one looks down upon the Grijalva river valley and then across southwestward to the Sierra Madre on the Pacific Coast, where the highest mountain in Chiapas, Tacaná (elevation 12,688 feet), erupted in 1902 and buried much of the state in volcanic ash. Southeastward on the Guatemalan border is the equally impressive Cuchumatane massif, which reaches an elevation of more than ten thousand feet.

At eight thousand feet, not surprisingly called Yaleb Taiv (where the frost falls) in Tzotzil, on this stretch of road one reaches the cloud forest, which extends to the tops of the highest peaks at ninety-two hundred feet. The rugged terrain and the forests of evergreens are unbelievably beautiful.

Some fifteen miles from San Cristobal de Las Casas at an elevation of about five thousand feet we encountered the first Indian hamlets and began to pass Zinacantecos on the highway. Presently, one man, walking along the highway weaving a hat, waved an arm and we stopped to offer him a ride since I had long ago in Navaho country learned that this is one of the greatest favors an anthropologist can provide. I knew from my trip the previous year that it took Zinacantecos more than three or four hours of hard walking to reach the market in San Cristobal, and that a ride would be appreciated. His name was Gaspar Perez Hacienda and he lived in the *paraje* (hamlet) of Sek'emtik. It turned out that he was returning to his hamlet from working in his field. As the children stared curiously at this Tzotzil-Maya in his large hat with ribbons flowing, we visited in Spanish and I learned that he was fifty years old and had four children. I added in my field journal for 30 December 1956:

> He continued to weave, while riding in the car, whenever the conversation slacked off. He was carrying two petates and some dark palm strips for weaving hats that he had traded for in the lowlands. His *milpa* is on the right side of the road on the way up the mountain. He pointed it out to us with some pride. He did not initiate

any conversation, but in response to my questions, we learned that he goes hunting in May for deer. He also hunts and eats rabbits and badgers. His people eat corn in the form of tortillas, *pozol* [corn dough mixed with water], and *atole* [cooked corn gruel]. They have small herds of sheep, called *borregos* (in Spanish), which are herded by young girls. Sheep are never eaten, but the wool is used for weaving clothing. The officials will be changed in Zinacantan on New Year's Day. As we drove along, he seemed to enjoy having his friends and relatives see him in the car with us. He kept waving and greeting others. One man he greeted he said was his *suegro* [father-in-law]. One of his most characteristic expressions was *Pues* this, and *Pues* that. We let him out at the edge of his hamlet and proceeded on to San Cristobal.

In retrospect, my first informal interview with a Zinacanteco proved to be surprisingly productive, with bits of ethnographic information on weaving behavior, pride in cornfields, hunting, agriculture, animal husbandry, diet, and speech behavior.

Upon arrival in San Cristobal we checked in first with the administrative officer of INI about a suitable place for lodging. Since INI was expecting a delegation of important officials from Mexico, we were put up at the Hotel Español at INI expense for three nights.

The proprietor of the hotel, Don Valeriano Lobeira Castro, was very pro-Franco and kept a prominent photograph of the generalísimo hung on the wall of the hotel dining room. The opposite side of the Spanish Civil War was represented by the other small hotel that came to our attention, the Posada Maya, owned and managed by Don Antonio Palerm, an older brother of the anthropologist Angel Palerm. The Palerms had fought on the republican side in the war in Spain, and it was always ironic to see that the Spanish Civil War was still being played out in these remote Chiapas mountains.

On 31 December we drove out to Chamula to observe the change-of-office ceremony that occurs on the last day of the calendar year. I recorded in my field journal that

the road is now in reasonably good shape in dry weather, and can be driven in about 45 minutes. We arrived about 9:30 A.M. and stayed until noon. The ceremony of changing the Indian authorities was well under way when we arrived and there were several thousand Indians in the plaza of what is normally a "vacant-town" type of settlement pattern. The "ceremony" consists essentially of each new official being brought in from his home paraje, installed in the town center, and the outgoing official being taken home. The groups of 8 or 10 Chamulas bringing in the new officials leave their parajes early in the morning, but since the parajes are at variable walking distances from Chamula Center, they are in the process of arriving almost all day. When the group arrives at the edge of the Center, they all stop to pray in front of the large cross; then every few yards, the whole group of accompanying Indians gets down on knees and chants in unison—begging, in effect, the new official to come on in and serve them for a year. Then they all get up, go on a few yards, and repeat the performance. The final route is across the plaza, along a route bounded by treetops stuck in the ground. (It is probable that the "begging" performance also goes on before the groups reach the Center, but I am not sure, since I didn't see this). . . . Meanwhile, there is much other activity going on: an enormous market at the south edge of the plaza, with people selling foods of various kinds, tanned buckskin belts and bags, Zinacantecos selling salt, etc. Literally, hundreds of people, especially men drinking and getting drunk on aguardiente [sugar cane rum] and chicha [maize beer]. By noon, many men were out cold, lying in the plaza. A number of young men were wandering around with accordions and homemade guitars, playing tunes. There was much visiting of the church, where we noted that Chamula women do not cover their heads, as good Catholic women are supposed to in Ladino culture. Thousands of candles were lighted to and prayers said to San Juan who is the patron saint of Chamula.

Again, I was pleased to learn how much it was possible to learn of ceremonial life, of drinking habits, of contrasts between Tzotzil Maya and Navaho culture in a relaxed morning of field research. Many of these early bits of data, such as the weaving of hats while walking along the highway or while riding in a car when conversation lagged, or notes about the numbers of drunks, proved to be important later in the field research.

On New Year's Eve, we put the children to bed in the Hotel Español, tipped the night watchman to keep an eye on them, and proceeded to crash the Lion's Club dance where a lively marimba band was playing. When I explained at the door that we were staying at the Español and asked politely if we could join the party, we were charged a cover charge of twenty pesos and fifty pesos each for the midnight supper. We sat at a table, drank three shots of tequila each, and danced twice. With drinks, the total cost of this New Years celebration was only 129 pesos, or slightly over ten U.S. dollars, the exchange rate being 12.5 pesos to one dollar in those days. I cannot remember a less expensive New Year's Eve.

At midnight each of the fifty couples present came up to give us warm abrazos and wish us a Feliz Año. Then we moved to a long, horseshoe table for the midnight supper. It began with a glass of brandy, and was followed by soup, fish, meat, and dessert, accompanied by copious servings of wine and beer. The dancing patterns were conservative in the sense that each man danced only with his wife; only the young, unmarried generation danced with different partners. We stayed until 3:30 A.M. when we returned to the hotel full of New Year spirits; we learned later that the dance continued until 5:30 A.M.

This New Year's Eve experience was important for our relationship with the elite Ladino population of San Cristobal. During the evening we met Rodolfo Courstois, who was president of the Lion's Club and also the presidente municipal (mayor) of San Cristobal; Lucio Domñnguez, the local distributor of Carta Blanca beer and a son of Don Hernán Pedrero who was kind enough to purchase a glass of tequila for us during the supper. Don Hernán was a small businessman in San Cristobal who had had the good fortune to win 10 million pesos in the national Mexican lottery a few years before. He was reported as owning many *fincas* (plantations), several automobiles, and the monopoly on the distilling of sugarcane liquor for the state of Chiapas. We also learned that most of the important local Ladinos were present at the dance, for we would meet them later on the streets of San Cristobal and they would comment favorably about our being with them on New Year's Eve. It was also illuminating to discover that the INI officials lived in a different social world and were unaware the Lion's Club dance had occurred and were surprised that we attended.

On New Year's Day I spent most of the day locating a physician for our three-year-old son who had an inflammation of his tonsils and had been given medicine to suck and to take by spoon. He vomited up all the medicines, and eventually I was able to persuade Dr. Robles from INI to come and examine him. A shot of penicillin seemed to help, but an injection of aureomycin the following day helped even more and he rapidly recovered. I did have an interesting conference with Dr. Alfonso Caso and with Dr. Gonzalo Aguirre Beltrán, both of whom had arrived the previous evening. I learned that the large delegation of officials expected had not arrived with Dr. Caso after all—only Dr. Caso's wife, grandchild, and *pistolero* (bodyguard) who always travels with him. Dr. Caso suggested that we move from the Hotel Español to La Cabaña (the Cabin) as the INI headquarters was called after a log cabin that was the first structure built.

Aguirre Beltrán had just been appointed the rector of the University of Veracruz, a new position that pleased him very much. With Dr. Caso I had a long discussion about the difficulties that a blond, fair-skinned anthropologist might have working in Highland Chiapas, because the Indians would be likely to confuse me with one of the Evangelistas, the Evangelistic, protestant missionaries working in the region. We joked about how I would have to enter Indian communities with a carton of cigarettes in one hand and a bottle of tequila in the other to avoid being taken for a missionary.

On 2 January I drove out to Zinacantan Center for the first time, taking my son, Terry, with me. I noted that the ten-kilometer trip took about an hour, but that the road could be traversed by ordinary car in the dry season. I was immediately and deeply impressed with Zinacantan, both the natural and the cultural scene. As I noted in my field journal: "It's a perfectly lovely mountain valley, even more impressive than the setting of Chamula. . . . The church is even more beautiful than the church in Chamula, with fresh pine needles on the floor, women lighting candles, and praying to innumerable saints."

I also encountered some ethnographic puzzles that I found intriguing. Zinacanteco officials dressed in black robes and red turbans were sitting in a row in front of the town hall. They were being approached by various men who lifted their hats and bowed politely and were then touched on their foreheads by the officials who seemed to be releasing them from the bows. Who were these officials? What were their functions? What was this bowing-and-releasing behavior all about?

I was also intrigued by the Ladino who introduced himself as the secretario municipal (municipal secretary). What were his duties and powers? Why was he the first to greet us as we stopped and parked in front of the town hall?

After the visit to the church, we stopped at a small Ladino store across from the church to order a beer for me and a Coke for my son. Here we were served by an attractive Ladina, about forty-five years old, who proved to be a very articulate informant. She reported that she was a native of Zinacantan, and that she had three daughters and one son. When I asked about Evangelistas, she responded: "the people here won't let them come in . . . the Evangelistas have no god, or a different god. . . . We're all Catholics here."

This was a crucial encounter, for the attractive Ladina proved to be Doña Elisea Suárez, the dominant power in a large family of Ladinos that owned three stores in Zinacantan Center. Over the years since, I have always stopped to visit with her on journeys to Zinacantan Center and have never failed to come away with a small gold mine of information.

On our return to San Cristobal I stopped to offer a ride, for the first time in my experience, to an Indian couple who had never previously ridden in a motor vehicle. A young Chamula boy, dressed in Ladino clothes and carrying a metal suitcase, flagged us down and asked for a ride, asking me carefully how much I would charge. I replied "nothing," and he seemed relieved. Then I asked if the elderly couple in Chamula dress with him would also like a ride. The father climbed aboard after a few minutes of discussion, but there was much more discussion before his mother could be persuaded to get into the car. To continue from my field journal: "Then we set off slowly, at about 15 miles an hour. But while the father grinned and seemed to enjoy the experience, his wife held on to the seat, and looked terrified and dizzy. I asked her son how she liked it, and the reply was that she was frightened, having never been in a car before!"

In the afternoon we moved over to sleeping quarters at the INI Center, and I finally had a long visit with Alfonso Villa Rojas whom I had met in 1954 and 1955 in Mexico City and who was currently serving as the director of the INI Center in San Cristobal. Villa Rojas had just returned from the annual meetings of the American Anthropological Association in Los Angeles. His advice and assistance over the ensuing few years proved to be invaluable to me. I was fortunate indeed to begin a field project at a time when a professionally trained anthropologist was in command of the local governmental program involving the Indians.[1]

On January 3 I drove to the Tzeltal community of Aguacatenango where I knew that Duane Metzger, whom I had known as a junior fellow in the Society of Fellows at Harvard, was engaged in field research for a University of Chicago project. Metzger was not at his field house, but returned my call by driving to San Cristobal to have dinner with us at the Hotel Español. He arrived bearing a gift of *Comiteco*, the special bootleg sugarcane rum made in Comitan, and we had a long visit about fieldwork in Chiapas. Metzger reviewed the field research currently under way in Chiapas, including his own and that of Calixta Guiteras-Holmes (1961) who was studying world-view in the Tzotzil municipio of Chenalho on a grant from Robert Redfield. Calixta had attempted to work in the Tzeltal community of Cancuc, but was forced to leave when the Indians reacted against outsiders because they were being pressured by Evangelistic missionaries. Metzger also added that Ruth Bunzel had done some field research in Chamula (before she went on to Chichicastenango in Guatemala in 1930), but had had a rough time of it; she had some data and had published one article on Chamula (Bunzel 1940). Metzger had been helped enormously by Manuel Castellanos, who had placed him with an important Indian family in Aguacatenango.

It was obvious from the comments of Metzger that field research in Chiapas was going to be even more difficult than it was in the Southwest. The Tzotzil and Tzeltal communities were leery of outsiders in general, and who could blame them after the treatment they had had by the Spanish conquerors and their descendants living in the Ladino world of San Cristobal and other towns. The more recent arrival of the Evangelistic protestants from the United States had not only threatened the control of the Catholic church in the region, but applied pressures to alter many of the traditional religious beliefs and practices.

But I was determined to push on with plans for research and spent some time investigating logistic matters: Where could a base of operations be established in San Cristobal? What about transportation? For a headquarters, one possibility was the Casa Blom (also known as Na-Bolom, Tzotzil for House of the Jaguar). We visited with Frans and Gertrude Blom on a few occasions during this week in Chiapas in 1956 and found Na-Bolom to be an intriguing possibility. It was where the University of Chicago project personnel stayed when they came to San Cristobal. But in the end I decided that, at least for the ensuing summer of 1957, I would stay either at Don Antonio Palerm's Posada Maya, which was less expensive and provided more freedom of movement, that is, without rigidly scheduled meal hours, or in one of the rooms at La Cabaña, the INI headquarters, if I were lucky enough to be invited.

For transportation I discovered that Duane Metzger was pleased with the performance of the British-built Land Rover of the Chicago Project. I stopped and talked to the dealer in Tuxtla Gutierrez and found that I would need $2,754 to purchase a Land Rover with a canvas top; $3,015 for one with a metal top. Judging from experience with canvas tops falling apart in the Southwest, I knew that my first task was to raise funds for a Land Rover with a metal top.

On my return to the Center for Advanced Study in Behavioral Sciences, I began to write up a project proposal to submit to various foundations, including the Ford Foundation, the National Science Foundation, and the National Institute of Mental Health (NIMH). I first submitted the proposal to the Ford Foundation, where I knew Dr. Richard Sheldon who had taken his Ph.D. in anthropology at Harvard and was an executive associate of the Behavioral Sciences Program. My proposal was approved by the staff, but ultimately turned down by the newly appointed president of the Ford Foundation who had different ideas about research objectives.

I then submitted simultaneous applications to the National Science Foundation where I had come to know Dr. Harry Alpert, the director of the anthropology program, and to the Behavioral Sciences program in the National Institute of Mental Health, a program that was headed by Dr. Philip Sapir. Dr. Sapir was a psychiatrist by training, but being a son of the famous anthropological linguist, Edward Sapir, he had a deep interest in cross-cultural research. Furthermore, he was convinced of the long-range utility of *basic* research in the behavioral sciences. On a trip to Washington, where I was serving on a panel for fellowships in anthropology, I went to see Dr. Sapir and was encouraged to submit a five-year proposal to fund the field project in Chiapas.

THE DESIGN OF THE PROJECT

The design of the five-year project was ambitious, to say the least. It is worth quoting the essence of the five-year proposal that was submitted to the National Institute of Mental Health on 22 March 1957 and to the National Science Foundation on 15 July 1957.

> Mexican Cultural Change: Comparative analysis of the processes of cultural change in Tzotzil and Tzeltal Indian communities in Chiapas, Mexico.
> Research Plan
>   The aims of the project are to describe the changes currently occurring in the cultures of the Tzotzil and Tzeltal Indians in Chiapas, Mexico, as a result of the action program of the National Indian Institute of the Mexican government; and to utilize these data for an analysis of the determinants and processes of cultural change.
>   The field setting provides an unprecedented opportunity for controlled research on several aspects of cultural change. Within a radius of 30 miles of San Cristobal Las Casas, a Ladino town of 18,000 inhabitants, live an estimated 125,000 Tzotzil and Tzeltal Indians in scattered communities in the mountains. These closely related Maya-speaking Indians were first brought into contact with the Spanish in 1528 when the town of San Cristobal was founded by the ancestors of the present Ladino population. During the Colonial Period important changes occurred: political control was taken over by the Ladinos; the Indians were converted to Catholicism; new crops, domesticated animals, and iron tools were introduced. A pattern of intercultural life was developed in which the large rural population supplied the town with food supplies, cheap manual labor, wood for construction, and charcoal for fuel. In exchange, the Ladino town supplied the Indians with products and services for their religious ceremonies: fireworks, candles, incense, colored ribbons for their hats, Catholic priests to perform ceremonies in their churches, and aguardiente to drink on ritual occasions.
>   Within this framework of intercultural life, much of the aborigi-

nal culture remained unchanged: native religious beliefs and rituals continued underneath the Catholic veneer; concepts of disease and methods of curing were still largely indigenous; much of the ancient kinship and social organization remained intact; basic subsistence was still derived from crops of corn, beans, and squash tilled by ancient methods.

In the 1940s several Tzotzil and Tzeltal communities were studied by Professor Sol Tax (University of Chicago) and a group of Mexican students. These data provide a baseline for the investigation of recent changes.

In 1950 the National Indian Institute of Mexico established an operating center in San Cristobal and launched an elaborate program of changes that include health education and the establishment of clinics; formal school, especially to teach the Indians to speak, read, and write Spanish; the establishment of Indian-controlled stores in each village; the building, for the first time, of roads to many of the Indian settlements; and the improvement of crops and agricultural practices. With this program, the National Indian Institute has been a major force for change in the Indian culture of Chiapas—indeed, probably the most important event that has affected these cultures since the Spanish Conquest in the 1520s.

In brief, I propose to take advantage of this cultural laboratory situation to describe cultural changes that are currently occurring and can be observed firsthand. By using the Sol Tax data from the 1940s, by careful study of the new stimulus for change (i.e., the program of the National Indian Institute), and by continuing observations over the next five years, it will be possible to describe and trace the sequences and directions of cultural changes in detail.

The second aim of the project is to utilize the descriptive data for an analysis of the determinants and processes of cultural change. Anthropologists are now in substantial agreement that the crucial determinants of change in culture-contact situations fall into two major categories: (a) the properties of the two cultures that come into contact; and (b) the types of interrelationships established between them (Vogt 1957). The interaction between these two sets of determinants leads to a complex and varied set of processes of change that are just beginning to be understood adequately.

Among the properties of a culture that merit close consideration in accounting for the processes of change are the *value system* which appears to be extraordinarily persistent and to exercise certain controlling effects upon the rates and directions of change (Vogt 1955b); and the *social structure* which may (in rural Mexico) be tightly organized in a "closed" corporate community which grows crops primarily for its own use and controls its internal affairs with a political-religious subsystem that defines the boundaries of the community and acts as a rallying point and symbol of collective unity, and, hence, is resistant to change, or may be more loosely organized in an "open" community that emphasizes continuous interaction with the outside world, is more geared to the national market by selling cash crops, is more linked to Ladino influences, often having a Ladino population living in the town, and, hence, is more vulnerable to change (Wolf 1955). Preliminary data from Chiapas suggest that this contrast is a crucial variable in cultural change in Indian communities.

A crucial factor in the types of relationships established between cultures appears to be the extent to which the new program of change is "forced" or "permissive," the thesis being that changes backed by force or power are less likely to be accepted than are new patterns presented to an American Indian group under permissive conditions that allow for freedom to make choices and for a selective process of adaptation (Dozier 1955). Preliminary data from Chiapas also suggest that this variable is highly significant in accounting for variations in the adoption of or resistance to new patterns in Indian communities.

The processes in cultural change are of two major types: the *microscopic* comprising specific additions, subtractions, or replacements in *cultural content*—the replacement of stone by steel axes being a classic example; and the *macroscopic* comprising the more pervasive patterns of change which persist over long time spans and involve basic changes in *social structure*—the shift from bilateral to unilineal kinship organization being a good example (Vogt 1957).

The specific hypotheses to be investigated are

1. that more acceptance of the modernization program of the National Indian Institute (and hence

more cultural change) is likely to be found: (a) in "open" communities than in "closed" corporate communities; and (b) under conditions where the new patterns are presented in "permissive" rather than "forced" programs.

2. that in the "closed" corporate communities the process of change is more likely to be microscopic in character—simple additions to cultural content with little social structural change—while in the "open" communities the process of change is more likely to be macroscopic in character—with social structures undergoing important changes.

3. that the rates and directions of changes will be differentially affected by certain religious values—for example among the Tzotzil, sheep (which they herd in large numbers) are sacred animals because the first image of St. John presented to the Indians by the Catholic priests in the sixteenth century carried a lamb in his arms, and St. John was identified with one of their important native deities. The Tzotzil use the wool to weave clothing, but they never eat the sheep. If cows were introduced, it is likely that the Tzotzil would eat them, but it is doubtful if they could be persuaded to eat mutton as long as the current religious values persist.

Method of Procedure

Inasmuch as the Indian population is relatively large and their settlements numerous, the action programs of the National Indian Institute have reached the Indian communities in *varying* degrees and with *variable* results, a fact of importance for my research design, which will be based upon a series of comparative studies:

1. Indian communities which have been "progressive" in accepting the modernization program will be compared with those that have a record of marked "resistance" to change.

2. "Open" communities will be compared with "closed" communities.

3. More "permissive" programs will be compared with more "forced" programs of change.

4. Tzotzil communities will be compared with Tzeltal communities along the same dimensions. The two are very closely related linguistically and culturally, but it is possible that the differences which do exist (especially in the value system, as, for example, in the case of the sacred sheep) are important in the processes of change.

I shall also be able to take earlier "readings" on this cultural situation from the Sol Tax field notes of the 1940s, from the publications and notes of the National Indian Institute since 1950, and, farther back in time, from historical documents in archives in Mexico. This study in historical depth will provide data for comparisons between what has happened since the Institute began its operations with the earlier situation and permit me to describe and "track" the course of change in some detail.

More concrete operational strategy will involve the following procedures:

1. Headquarters for the field will be established near the operating center of the National Indian Institute in San Cristobal. The principal investigator will spend each summer in the field during the next five years and will place at least one graduate student assistant in the field for a full year during the duration of the project.

2. Actual research operations in the field will be carried out in a series of phases which will concentrate upon different aspects of the Indian cultures undergoing changes. The first year I plan to focus upon Indian concepts of disease and the ways in which these ideas and practices are changing under the impact of the health program of the Institute. The second year I plan to focus upon changes in agriculture and sheep husbandry patterns. A third

year will be devoted to changes that have been brought about by the building of roads for the first time to the Indian villages. A fourth year will focus upon the effects of the literacy program of the Institute. The fifth year will be devoted to synthesizing our data on changes in social and religious organization that have occurred in recent years. It should be emphasized that we shall be collecting some data on all of these problems each year, but that for maximum efficiency the research strategy will focus upon a special aspect each year, and I shall place a graduate student in the field who has had special preparation to work on that aspect of cultural change.

3. University headquarters for the project will be established at the Laboratory of Social Relations, Harvard University where I plan to have one 3/5 time graduate student research assistant working each year on the coding and analysis of field data and on the translation and analysis of historical data we collect from the archives in Mexico. We also plan to employ a secretarial assistant who will do a great deal of the routine typing, filing, and coding of data for us. At Harvard, the research will be planned and integrated through the medium of a Seminar in Middle American Ethnology that will be offered each year by the Principal Investigator. The graduate students serving in the field and at Harvard will be specialists in Middle American anthropology and will be using their research experience as a basis for Ph.D. dissertations.

Significance of This Research

In my judgment, the research findings should add significantly to our scientific knowledge of the conditions and processes of cultural change among American Indians and, more broadly, to other culture-contact situations in the world where indigenous peoples are in the process of becoming modernized and integrated into national societies and cultures. One of the most advantageous features of this program is that we shall be able to study cultural changes "on the hoof," and to control (by comparative analysis) the critical variables in these changes. Many of the earlier studies of cultural change among American Indians have involved an inferential reconstruction of what probably happened in the course of change; we shall be able to observe changes firsthand during the five-year period.

Since there was not sufficient time for this five-year proposal to be acted upon before the summer of 1957 when I hoped to begin, I had something of a struggle during the spring term at the Center for Advanced Study in Behavioral Sciences as I applied to several institutions for small grants: the Laboratory of Social Relations at Harvard, the American Philosophical Society, and the Small Grants Program of the NIMH. Professor Samuel A. Stouffer, director of the Laboratory of Social Relations, kindly gave me a grant of $500, and Professor David C. McClelland, who was interested in having some tests for achievement motivation administered in Chiapas, added $750. The NIMH Small Grants Program came through with $2,000, and the American Philosophical Society provided $450. With a grand total of $3,700 to pay for the Land Rover, my airfare, and food and lodging for a month in the field during August and September, the Harvard Chiapas Project was finally under way!

3 /
FIRST FIELD
RESEARCH IN
CHIAPAS:
1957

The Harvard Chiapas Project officially began when I met my first graduate student, Frank C. Miller, at the Hotel Geneve in Mexico City on 12 August 1957, a meeting that was not without a rocky start.

Frank was a bright student who came to Harvard from Carleton College in Minnesota. When I invited him to do field research in Chiapas, he enrolled in an intensive course in Spanish. But beyond some informal briefings I could give him about Mexico and Chiapas and some pointers about field research, he had little training for his year in Mexico. Frank had never traveled abroad before, and everything about Mexico was new and strange to him. To further complicate matters, his wife refused to come with him to Mexico with their two small children.

I had left Palo Alto with my family in late June, and we reached the Vogt Ranch in New Mexico where Nan and the children planned to remain while I spent the month in Chiapas. About three days before I was scheduled to meet Frank Miller in Mexico, I received a telegram from him reporting that he had decided he did not wish to become an anthropologist after all and had sold his portable typewriter and sleeping bag in the airport in Mexico City and returned to Minneapolis. I was in a dither. Here I was beginning a long-range project in Chiapas and scheduled to take delivery on the field vehicle in Tuxtla Gutierrez within a few days, and my first graduate student had panicked in Mexico City and returned to the United States.

Nan calmed me down and advised me to wait, for she was convinced Frank Miller would have second thoughts. Two days later he telephoned

My first graduate student on the Harvard Chiapas Project: Frank C. Miller standing by the project Land Rover on the road to Yalcuc in the municipio of Huistan in 1957.

me from Minneapolis with deep apologies and reported that he had purchased another typewriter and sleeping bag and would meet me at the
Hotel Geneve in Mexico City on schedule. It is a great tribute to Frank
Miller that he buckled down and stuck out the whole year in Chiapas,
collecting excellent data for his Ph.D. thesis.[1]

Before proceeding to Chiapas we stayed in Mexico City for two days
to introduce Frank to the anthropologists. We called upon and had good
visits with Alfonso Caso, Manuel Gamio, Roberto J. Weitlaner, Julio de la
Fuente, Miguel Leon-Portilla, and Ricardo Pozas.

On the second evening we took a taxi to the lively Plaza Garibaldi to
listen to mariachi music and drink tequila. These traditional Mexican musicians, with their enormous black sombreros and tight-fitting suits embroi-
dered with silver thread, provided music for weddings during the colonial
period; hence, their name from the French *mariage*. I recall with some

pride demonstrating to Frank how to drink tequila: lick left wrist and pour salt on the damp spot on the wrist, lick the salt on the wrist, pick up tequila with right hand, say a proper salud and down the shot in one gulp, and then grab and suck on a piece of lime as the aftermath burns like a hot flame.

ARRIVAL IN CHIAPAS

With hangovers from the tequila the night before, we caught the early morning plane to Tuxtla Gutierrez. The plane stopped in Veracruz and in Minatitlan and finally arrived at 12:45 P.M. The Land Rover agency was miraculously efficient; it dispatched our new vehicle with a driver to meet us at the airport and had all the papers ready for new license plates and insurance. After completing the negotiations with the agency, paying them 30,685.50 pesos (which equaled $3,086.83 U.S. at the exchange rate of 12.50 pesos to the dollar), and extracting a promise from the manager that locks for the two side doors and cushions for the backseat would be installed later, I invited the manager and his two salesmen to have a drink with us at the Hotel Bonampak where we were spending the night.

We sat at a table under the palm trees beside the pool and visited for more than two hours. Among the topics of conversation were the two Pedrero brothers, Hernán and Moctezuma. They had been named for Hernán Cortés, the Spanish conqueror of Mexico, and Moctezuma, the Aztec emperor. Don Hernán, who lived in San Cristobal, I already knew about, but now I learned that he was in business with his brother, Moctezuma, who lived in Tuxtla Gutierrez and was the owner of the Hotel Bonampak, as well as the producer and distributor of Bonampak rum. With sugar plantations and sugar mills, distilleries producing rum and aguardiente, and various cattle ranches, it was evident that the Pedreros were a powerful Chiapas family.

We spent a quiet and restful night at the Hotel Bonampak, reached San Cristobal the following morning (15 August) and drove immediately to La Cabaña where we found Alfonso Villa Rojas just outside his house. He graciously invited us in for a beer and introduced us to his lovely wife, Loly. We were then given a double room in the Casa de Solteros (House of the Bachelors) where we slept and worked on our field journals during the ensuing three weeks.

We later explained our plans in greater detail to Villa Rojas. The purpose of our field trip that summer was to make a reconnaissance of the

Tzotzil and Tzeltal area and to select field sites for Frank Miller and for me. Following the advice of Villa Rojas, we planned to visit virtually all the municipios that were reachable by road with our four-wheel drive Land Rover, and to ride horseback to visit Huistan and Oxchuc.

In the afternoon Villa Rojas invited us for comida at the Hotel Español and the conversation about Indians in Chiapas continued. We learned about a recent "delicate operation" that he had successfully carried out two months before. Don Hernán Pedrero had persuaded the state government to send soldiers into the area of Chamula where bootleg stills were making aguardiente. Since Pedrero was charging high prices for the cheap sugarcane rum, bootlegging became a popular economic activity among the Chamulas, who produced a better grade of liquor and sold it at lower prices. When the soldiers arrived, the Chamulas resisted and an open gunfight ensued in which the Indians killed the commander of the troops and the government soldiers killed one Chamula and wounded a second who later died.

Villa Rojas knew that quick action was required to avoid a major Indian-Ladino conflict in the Highlands of Chiapas, especially since only the year before, on 17 August 1956, a German-American painter, Arthur Silz, had been killed in the Chamula bootlegging settlement of Muken. As Frans Blom later described this event, Silz spoke no Spanish nor Tzotzil, but persisted in hiking alone to the indigenous communities where he would sit and sketch or paint Indians. On this occasion Silz had hiked alone into the bootlegging area, against the advice of friends in San Cristobal. When he reached Muken, he was tired and sat down on a rock to rest. Some Indian women saw him and started crying out that an angel had arrived. Some of the Chamula men, who had heard the Catholic priests fulminate against the Protestant missionaries, telling the Indians that they were devils and must be killed, came and asked him what he wanted and where he was going. Silz waved his hands, trying to explain that he spoke no Spanish nor Tzotzil. The men yelled that he was the devil and began to drive him away with sticks. Silz stumbled and fell, whereupon one of the Chamulas crushed his skull with a rock. The case was later investigated by INI and the Chamula authorities and the six Chamulas involved were arrested and jailed.

Villa Rojas called all the principales (traditional leaders) in Chamula together and explained during the meeting that they would have to bring all the stills into the ceremonial center and stop making the bootleg liquor or they would be in real trouble. The Indians agreed and brought in more than fifty stills, which were ingenious in design, using large Chamula pots and bamboo poles to do the distilling. Very simple in design, but effective in producing aguardiente.

Villa Rojas then went to see Don Hernán Pedrero to report that the Chamulas had brought in the stills and to extract a promise from him that he would produce and sell a better quality liquor at lower prices in the whole Indian area of Highland Chiapas.

I later discovered that while this was a good temporary solution to the conflict between the Pedreros and the bootleggers in Chamula, it did not last long. Within a week or so, the Chamulas, especially in the hamlet of Krus Ton on the southeastern slopes of Tsonte Vits (Spanish Moss Mountain), the highest and most sacred mountain in Chamula, were again busy producing bootleg liquor with their pots and bamboo pipes and have continued to do so ever since. Further, our fieldworkers in Chamula later discovered that the Indian authorities in the municipio give "official" permission to important cargoholders to set up stills and produce and sell this bootleg liquor in order to defray the high costs of serving in the cargos.

RECONNAISSANCE BY
LAND ROVER

Villa Rojas wisely suggested that we begin our reconnaissance by going to Chanal, at the end of a new road, while we were in a *canicula* (literally, dog days), a period of time during the summer when the heavy summer rains slack off and the unpaved roads are dry.

To assist in our reconnaissance, Frank and I had developed a field survey checklist for the Highland Tzotzil and Tzeltal municipios, which was focused on my interests in settlement patterns and religious acculturation and Frank's interests in patterns of health and disease. This checklist covered the following points:

Settlement Patterns (Make sketch maps when possible).
1. Size of the plaza—step off in yards
2. Buildings on plaza; directional orientation?
3. Dwellings in relation to plaza

4. Settlement patterns of parajes we pass through
5. Ask about comparative size of Ladino and Indian population, and what the Ladinos are doing in the Municipio.

Religious Acculturation

1. Size and description of the Catholic church
2. Number and type of *santos* (saints)
3. How often visited by Catholic priest and from where?
4. Protestant programs, if any?
5. Cemeteries?

Health and Disease

1. Disease profile
2. Clinic or only a *puesto* (a health post)?
3. How many people treated per week? Is the number changing?
4. When use doctor, when use *curandero*, when both?
5. Latrines?
6. *Agua potable* (potable water)?
7. What sort of DDT treatments?
8. What techniques are used: puppet shows, etc.?
9. Barbershop?
10. What health supplies in stores?

While this checklist was useful, it was obviously not possible to collect all these data during our brief visits, especially since some of the procedures, such as making sketch maps or counting the paces across a plaza, aroused immediate suspicion about our motives.

On 16 August we made the trip to Chilil and Chanal in the Land Rover. The drive took us eastward on the Pan American Highway toward Comitan for a few miles. Just over the pass east of San Cristobal the unpaved road to Chilil branched off to the north, climbing over a high saddle and through magnificent pine timber that is well above eight thousand feet and thence down through an open valley where we passed the Colonia de Los Llanos inhabited by Chamulas. We soon reached Chilil (meaning "black woolen *huipil*" in Tzotzil) and I remembered it was one of the hamlets I had visited in 1955 on my first journey to Chiapas.

Chilil was one of the hamlets of the Tzotzil municipio of Huistan, and it had become a showplace for INI, which had established a number of projects in this hamlet with its scattered houses and cornfields. There was an INI school, a clinic, and an agricultural station experimenting with fruit trees and new breeds of chickens. It was obviously a kind of beach-head for INI in a vast zone of contemporary Maya Indians, most of whom were unenthusiastic about relinquishing even a square meter of land for the building of clinics, schools, agricultural stations, or anything else. In later years during our field research in Chiapas, we noted that whenever a group of visitors arrived to observe what INI was doing for the Indians, they were inevitably taken to Chilil to visit the installations that were supposed to bring education, better health, and more productive agricultural items into the indigenous communities.

I later learned that Ricardo Pozas had lived in one of the INI buildings in Chilil and visited informants each day in the nearby Colonia de Los Llanos during much of the time that he was working in Chamula (Pozas 1959). When we later discovered how extraordinarily difficult it was to place students in Chamula center or in hamlets near the center, I understood why Pozas had chosen to work with a base in Chilil.

It took a long, backbreaking drive for another two hours beyond Chilil to reach Chanal which was actually only sixty-two kilometers from San Cristobal. I had previously thought the southwestern roads through Navaho country were among the worst roads in the world, but most of them were highways compared to the tortuous roads through the mountains of Chiapas in those days.

Chanal is a Tzeltal-speaking community, settled by families from Oxchuc. It is a recent community and has been laid out in a uniform grid pattern, with wide streets bounded by stake fences that surround the house compounds. These plots for the houses, most of them with wooden shingle roofs, called *tejamanil,* are all about fifty-by-fifty meters. The whole appearance is one of a well-planned community located on top a flat hill, rather than tucked into a valley as are many of the contemporary Indian centers.

While we were greeting and shaking hands with the Indian officials at the palacio municipal (town hall), the ever-present Ladino secretario appeared and took over the conversation. It had long been customary in the Indian municipios in Chiapas for the top offices (i.e., the presidente municipal, the *sindico,* and others) to be filled by bilingual Indians, but the state government always insisted that the post of secretario be filled by a Ladino. This pattern was justified by the argument that the indígenas could not read and write and therefore could not keep the official records of the municipio. While the secretary did indeed type official papers and carry on municipal correspondence in Spanish, he was always de facto a member of the PRI (Partido Revolucionario Institucional or "Institutional Revolutionary Party") party in good standing and hence part of the whole political apparatus designed to control the Indians. Most, if not all, Ladino secretaries had an ancient-looking telephone behind their desks by means of which, in case of emergencies, they could ring up the political leaders in San Cristobal or in the state capital in Tuxtla Gutierrez and ask that soldiers be sent to enforce law and order.

We had been told by Villa Rojas that some University of Chicago students were working in Chanal and we asked the secretary where they lived and worked. We were directed to the INI cooperative store where we encountered Mark Gumbiner who was collecting genealogies from a Chanal informant as part of his project to understand the social structure of the community. He invited us to accompany him to the old school building in which he lived with his wife, Kathy, and where he had been joined by Larry Kaplan, who was doing a study on ethnobotany.

From talking with the Gumbiners and Kaplan we learned more about the University of Chicago project, which was called the Man-in-Nature project and was funded by the National Science Foundation. It was directed by Professor Sol Tax with the assistance of the other principal investigators: Robert McC. Adams, Norman A. McQuown, Manning Nash, and Philip Wagner. The study area included a series of Tzeltal-speaking communities, as well as one Tzotzil municipio, San Bartolomé, running from the lowlands to the highlands. The design called for ethnographic studies of this series of communities followed by comparative analysis to determine the relationships of subsistence systems, settlement patterns, and agricultural practices, as well as social structures, to variations in the natural environment. There was also an interest in the degree of correlation between linguistic patterns and ecological zones (McQuown and Pitt-Rivers 1970).

We learned that the Gumbiners had been installed in the community with a letter of sponsorship from INI which had good relationships with Chanal. With this entry they had had no difficulty except that at first the indígenas always slammed the door of the church in their faces (probably thinking they were Protestant missionaries) and had been reticent to talk about religion and curing practices. We later tried to visit the church, but found it locked; but we did learn that the patron saint was San Pedro.

I concluded my field journal on the trip to Chanal with the following overall impression:

> In terms of my general hypothesis, Chanal would be considered a closed corporate community producing crops for its own use and controlled still by the civil-religious hierarchy and the clan-lineage system and with few Ladinos in town. Have there been changes or is the community fairly conservative? The religious, social, and economic structure seems strongly conservative, although there is some acceptance of INI medicine, and also, earlier in time, there was a shift to a very regular grid pattern of settlement, to the use of wooden shingles rather than grass thatch on roofs, and an overlay of Catholicism in the religion.

On 17 August Frank and I spent the morning typing our field journals at La Cabaña, and then set out for San Andrés Larrainzar at noon, taking along some tortillas and a can of Vienna sausages to eat for lunch along the road. San Andrés Larrainzar (Larrainzar being the name of a Mexican general in the nineteenth Century) is a Tzotzil-speaking municipio located north of Chamula; it was twenty-six kilometers and two hours by rough road from San Cristobal.

Here we found a quite different kind of ceremonial center located at a lower elevation (sixty-five hundred feet) than Chilil and with many more groves of oaks, rather than the pines we had encountered in the higher elevations in Chilil and Chanal. San Andrés Larrainzar contrasted both with Chanal, which was almost all Indian and compact in settlement pattern, and with Chamula, which was all Indian but dispersed in settlement pattern with a town center that was occupied mainly by officeholders. San Andrés center was occupied by eighty-four Ladino families who made their living as merchants and local ranchers. The Indian homes were not found in the center at all, but began in scattered clusters a few hundred yards from the plaza and were dispersed over the area from there.

In the conclusion to my journal I wrote: "In terms of my general hypothesis, San Andrés Larrainzar would be something of a mixed case. It has been penetrated strongly by Ladinos, but, on the other hand, the corporate character of the community, e.g., with subsistence milpa agriculture and a strong civil-religious hierarchy, is still intact."

As it turned out, our visit to San Andrés Larrainzar just preceded the first formal anthropological work in this municipio. In October 1957 William R. Holland, a student of Professor Edward H. Spicer of the University of Arizona, began his field research in Larrainzar and later published an interesting book entitled *Medicina Maya en Los Altos de Chiapas* (1963). I did not meet Holland until later, but Frank became acquainted with him as they were working on similar research problems.

The morning of 18 August proved to be an education for both of us. We awakened early and drove to the Posada Maya for breakfast. Here we encountered our first *mañanitas* celebration. It was Don Antonio Palerm's birthday and a marimba band was playing in the patio. For breakfast we were served full glasses of Bacardi rum and tamales stuffed with meat, raisins, almonds, and prunes and wrapped in banana leaves. While one does not always expect orange juice, toast, and fried eggs for breakfast, the shots of straight rum and the exotic tamales were something of a shock.

At least we were fortified for a trip to Zinacantan where I noted a number of features I had missed seeing in January. Zinacantan Center is located in a verdant valley at the western base of a volcanic crater which rises to more than eighty-five hundred feet. I added in my journal:

There is a large Ladino ranch in the southeastern (upper) part of the valley with many fences and pastures in evidence and many cows and horses grazing. A small stream runs out of the mountains here and passes through Zinacantan center. Streams are very rare in these mountains, apparently because the water disappears into cracks and fissures in the limestone formation; in fact, this is the first stream we have seen on this trip. There is an abandoned church across the stream to the north of the new church and plaza. There are many more Indian houses in the center than I had remembered, and many tiled roofs over Indian homes. Several Indian women were doing laundry in the small stream as we drove into town.

We drove to the cabildo where I presented my Harvard University business card and we introduced ourselves to the Ladino secretary, Don Belizario Lievano, as friends and colleagues of Professor Alfonso Villa Rojas. He immediately invited us into his office where we sat and visited for almost an hour. Both Frank and I were impressed with how friendly and intelligent he appeared to be. He was from a small ranch located in the valley between Chilil and Chanal and told us that he spoke both Tzotzil and Tzeltal. We later learned from Villa Rojas that Don Belizario had worked for years as a pistolero (bodyguard) for important politicians in Chiapas before he was appointed secretary of Zinacantan. He was paid two hundred pesos a month by INI to add to his meager salary as secretary with the understanding, according to Villa Rojas, that he would help promote INI programs in the municipio.

During our visit some fifty Zinacantecos were milling around the Indian authorities seated on the benches in front of the cabildo. Don Belizario explained that since it was Sunday these officials from the parajes had arrived to make their weekly reports to the town officials. There was also a group working on the accounts for the expenses of the recent fiesta for the patron saint (San Lorenzo) whose celebration occurs on 10 August.

Don Belizario reported that sixteen to eighteen Ladino families were living in Zinacantan center, all of them merchants with small stores doing business with the Zinacantecos. About four hundred Indian families lived in the immediate vicinity of the center, and there were eleven outlying parajes, located mainly to the west. The only problems with Protestant missionaries had occurred in the hamlet of Nabenchauk.

We asked Don Belizario about visiting the church and he said certainly. He stepped outside and asked one of the officials with a red turban wrapped around his head to take us over. The official agreed and led off at a fast impetuous pace that Frank and I had difficulty following. As we turned into the churchyard, someone inside the church spotted us coming and the doors were slammed shut and locked. I added in my journal:

> The official, as he saw the doors shutting, moved his right fore-
> finger vigorously back and forth, and spoke in Tzotzil. I gather this
> meant "No, don't shut the doors!" but it may have meant "Don't
> let these people in, despite what the Ladino secretary says." At any
> rate, we proceeded to the doors, and the official tried to open them.
> He, and one of the other young men standing nearby, shouted sev-
> eral times through the keyhole and looked inside. Finally, one of

the young men went around inside, and there was much conversation. But finally our guide announced that the doors were locked,
and that was that.

In spite of having the church doors slammed shut in our faces, I was
again much impressed with Zinacantan and began to think even more seriously about this municipio as a site for my own long-range field research.
Relatively few Ladino families lived in the municipio, so an ethnographer
working in Zinacantan would not be overwhelmed with Ladinos each time
he arrived in the ceremonial center—as would be the case in San Andrés
Larrainzar. Although Villa Rojas reported some tensions between the hamlets that were in the process of trying to break away from having to report to
the center on every matter, the central civil-religious hierarchy still seemed
strong enough to continue to function. Another advantage was that the
center and many of the hamlets could be reached by road or trail from the
Pan American highway. I also thought it would be relatively easy to rent or
buy horses for traveling in the municipio; for having been brought up on
the ranch in New Mexico, I naturally perceived riding horseback, rather
than hiking on foot, as being the way to travel if one could not get there by
automobile.

On 19 August we made our reconnaissance trip to the Tzeltal-speaking
municipio of Tenejapa (name derived from Nahuatl words meaning "river
with lime") located to the northeast of Chamula. The distance was about
the same as the journey to San Andrés Larrainzar, but the road was even
rougher. The road passes through Chamula territory along the eastern
slopes of Tsonte Vits where we encountered several pack-trains of horses
and mules carrying loads of *panela,* a type of brown sugar wrapped in
banana leaves, which the Chamulas were bringing from the lowlands in
great quantity. It was obvious that the amounts were more than enough to
sweeten their coffee and that they were importing the brown sugar for the
manufacture of bootleg liquor.

Tenejapa reminded us of San Andrés Larrainzar in that the center of
town was occupied by hundreds of Ladinos, with the Indians living on the
outskirts.

On the morning of 20 August we started to leave for a visit in Amatenango, but Manning and June Nash from the University of Chicago arrived
at La Cabaña and we spent most of the day visiting with them. In the

afternoon a former colleague from graduate school in Chicago, Professor John Murra, who was vacationing in Mexico that summer, also arrived, and I invited him to go along to *cena* with us and the Villa Rojases. Murra later went on to do his fundamental research in Peru and became noted for his theories concerning the importance of verticality (from the high Andes to the lowlands) in the ecological adaptations of the ancient Inca and the contemporary Quechua Indians.

Taking John Murra along to show him something of the back country, we made our trip to Mitontic, Chenalho, and Chamula on 21 August. It was a long journey, comparable to the one we had made to Chanal. We drove past the fork in the road that leads to Chamula, saving this ceremonial center until last in case of rain. The rough road, much of it built of limestone rocks that jar the back, kilometer after kilometer, leads toward San Andrés Larrainzar, then branches off to the northeast and descends into a beautiful, rugged valley. At the bottom of the valley, just off the road to the west, lay the small ceremonial center of Mitontic (meaning "conglomerated rocks" in Tzotzil), consisting of thirty-eight Indian families and six Ladino families, including the secretary, the schoolteacher, and four agronomists. San Miguel is the patron saint, whose day is celebrated on 8 May.

From Mitontic the land flattens as the road proceeds down the valley to Chenalho, which (like San Andrés Larrainzar and Tenejapa) has a very large Ladino population in the ceremonial center, with the Indians living around the outskirts and out in the hamlets. Since Chenalho (meaning "water from a rocky well" in Tzotzil) had been recently studied by Calixta Guiteras-Holmes (1961), we did not spend a great deal of time in the center.

On our return we stopped briefly in Chamula so that John Murra and Frank Miller could see this interesting ceremonial center. We parked in front of the INI cooperative store, located beside the cabildo, purchased Coca-Colas, and visited with the storekeeper. I assumed in these beginning days of field research in Chiapas that these cooperative stores were genuine cooperatives. Only later did I learn that most of them were cooperatives in name only. The very alert Indians would assemble two or more partners, receive a loan from INI's cooperative program, then proceed to set up a business with the profits being shared only by the partners who owned the enterprise.

ON HORSEBACK TO HUISTAN
AND OXCHUC

For our journey to Huistan and Oxchuc on 22 and 23 August we made arrangements through Villa Rojas to rent horses from one of the ranchers in the Valley of San Cristobal for eight pesos per horse per day (a modest sixty-four cents a day U.S.). The horses were ridden to Chilil the day before and were ready for us when we arrived there at eight A.M. with our guide, Francisco Gómez Sanchez, age seventeen, from the paraje of Tzopilja in the municipio of Oxchuc. Francisco was an *internado* (a boarding student in the INI school) and had been asked by Villa Rojas to serve as our guide.

We tied our gear, including sleeping bags, slickers, toilet articles, and some food for lunch, on the horses and set out at nine A.M. for Huistan Center. Frank was apprehensive, having never ridden before, but for me it was wonderful to be on a horse again. We passed through the hamlet of Chilil, noting that all of the Huistecos we met were in native costume; the men in their shirts open at the sides and with very short pants that resembled large cotton diapers; the women in blue skirts with loose blouses open at the sides, and showing no embarrassment whatever about exposing their breasts as they worked or nursed babies.

Our trail led around a large canyon and over a mountain before it descended to Huistan Center, which we reached about eleven A.M. Huistan is located on a knoll above the right bank of the Rio Huistan. Here we found a pleasant ceremonial center with seventy-five Ladino families and ten operating stores. Again, the Huistecos lived in thatch-roofed houses on the edges of the town. We tied up our horses at the cabildo and were greeted by the Ladino secretary, as well as by the Huisteco presidente municipal and a dozen other officials who arrived to shake hands with us. We also visited the church to pay our respects to the patron saint San Miguel (celebrated on 29 September) and to observe the groups of Huistecos lighting candles on the floor and praying to the various saints.

In a small Ladino store we were offered beer, but selected Coca-Colas. I then overheard the Ladina storekeeper asking our guide if we were headed for Corralitos (which we learned later is the headquarters of the Evangelical missionaries in Oxchuc). Francisco assured her that we were only going to Oxchuc center and that we were not Protestants. She looked skeptical.

It helped ease the tension somewhat when I lighted a cigarette, but I noted that in the future we should probably always drink beer to underscore that we were not Protestant missionaries out to preach against liquor.

From Huistan we crossed the river, which has a small flow this far upstream, and made the long climb to Oxchuc. We stopped for lunch at about two P.M. and finally reached Oxchuc about five P.M., making a total of approximately six hours of horse travel from Chilil, not counting our stops.

En route to Oxchuc we learned more about the Protestant missionary program from Francisco. The two largest concentrations of the Evangelicos, as the Evangelical protestants are called, were in Corralitos, northeast of Oxchuc Center, and in Rancho Conejo, east of the trail between Huistan and Oxchuc. In Corralitos the Protestants had a landing strip for a single-engine plane that flew in periodically from San Cristobal or Ixtapa. According to Francisco, this landing strip was necessary because the authorities in Oxchuc Center prohibited Protestants from passing through the town to reach Corralitos on horseback. The most active missionary has been Marianne Slocum who began her work in Yochib. Yochib is the hamlet of Oxchuc where Alfonso Villa Rojas had a field house built in 1942–43 while he was working for Professor Robert Redfield under the auspices of the Carnegie Institution of Washington project on the Maya. Villa Rojas once described the arrival of Marianne Slocum in Yochib. He and his wife were living in this field house on a second field visit in 1944 when one rainy late afternoon he looked out and was startled to see two blond North American women on mules approaching. He invited them to spend the night and became acquainted with them. Since he was to be leaving Yochib within a month or so, he wrote to Redfield and asked permission to turn over the field house to Marianne Slocum who was one of these two women. Redfield approved, and this transaction was the beginning of Slocum's missionary work in the municipio of Oxchuc.

However, Marianne Slocum had little luck in Yochib and soon shifted to Corralitos. The doctrines preached by these Protestant missionaries included the view that there is only one God; that there should be no worshipping of saints, nor should people even go into a Catholic church; no drinking of liquor, no smoking, no fiestas, no candles, no skyrockets or other fireworks. The conflict between the Catholics and the Protestants was most intense in 1954 when the Catholics stoned Marianne Slocum's house in Corralitos. Now, Francisco continued, the difficulties had been settled in Oxchuc, which had a Catholic presidente municipal, but a Protestant as sindico, the second in command in the civil-religious hierarchy.

Upon arrival in Oxchuc Center there was an ambiance that reminded me of the urban slums in which Evangelical Protestantism flourishes in our European and American cities. I wrote in my field diary:

> Our impressions of Oxchuc are of a miserable and dismal town made up of about 105 Ladino families, living in mud and grime and as poor as any I've seen in Mexico. No Indians live in the *cabecera*, except for some officials, although there is a paraje nearby on the trail to Tzopilja. The enormous church is by far the largest we've seen in the whole area. . . . Oxchuc is a hard 10 hours by horse from San Cristobal. The priest comes from San Cristobal only when there is an important fiesta. The mail comes through by horse on the way to Ocosingo every Saturday. Santo Tomas is the patron saint and his day is the 24th of December. Two of the newer Ladino houses have tile roofs—most of the Ladino houses here have thatched roofs and do not seem at all better than Indian houses we saw later—and have large white crosses painted on the roofs, to show they are Catholics we are told. This is, undoubtedly, a response to the Protestant program.

Francisco took us to the INI clinic, where we were put up in one of the rooms that had two beds, one with a mattress and one with boards, on which we put our sleeping bags. Frank graciously offered me the one with the mattress, which proved to be a good choice on his part. The mattress had fleas that proceeded to bite me all night! Our horses were cared for and taken to a nearby pasture to graze for the night.

At the clinic we had met Professor Otilio Vasquez, the INI inspector of schools, who was returning to San Cristobal after twelve days on the road. He took us under his wing and arranged supper and breakfast for us at Don Mariano's simple *fonda* (inn) on the plaza. It was here during the evening meal of beans and tortillas that I had one of the more embarrassing experiences of my field career. I decided to teach my graduate student how to consume chiles. I picked up one of the small, orange chiles on the table and said to Frank: "You dip it in salt, and then take a bite of the chile."

It was one of the most picante variety; not only did my eyes burn and ears ring, but I could not utter a word for at least a half hour. Needless to say, Frank wisely avoided following my instructions.

On our return trip we were accompanied part of the way by Professor Vasquez. It was a long and exhausting journey since we went by way of Tzopilja and a new Oxchuc hamlet called La Libertad and we were in the saddle for more than eight hours.

We reached the paraje of Tzopilja about 9:30 A.M. Here we visited the school being constructed and called on Francisco's family, which gave us an opportunity for the first time to see the inside of an Indian home. This was exciting for us and I recorded in my journal:

> The family owns three houses, one for cooking and eating, and two for sleeping; the younger brothers slept in one, the mother and father and baby sister in the other. I'm not sure where his married brother slept with his wife—but it was patrilocal residence. The beds were sleeping platforms of hewn boards covered with *petates* (reed mats) and then blankets over the sleepers—except for a magnificent yellow wood bed that Francisco proudly showed us and told us he had built for his mother and father. Other furniture included many pots, mano and metate, fireplace (no chimney), *comal,* gourd water containers—all in much disarray compared to the house of the teacher whose house was neat and included table and chairs for us to sit upon. Houses are placed right in cornfields, giving the impression of living right with the corn. The *temazcal* (sweat lodge) was nearby. Both here and at other parajes where we stopped, the whole student body, both boys and girls, came up to say "Buenos Dias, Professor" to me and to Frank. We must have shaken hands with a couple of hundred young Tzeltales altogether, but they were cute and had sparkling eyes, and you can never tell when you might be shaking hands with a future president of Mexico.

We were then invited for a late breakfast of tortillas, scrambled eggs, and sugared coffee at the house of the cultural promoter who is also the teacher.

Our next stop was La Libertad, which we reached at 12:30 P.M. Here we learned that the name derives from the fact that until three years earlier the Indians lived as peons on a Ladino ranch where they had to work three days a week for the Ladino and also give him some of the products from their fields. A loan of twenty-eight thousand pesos was arranged with INI with which the people purchased 150 hectares of good land and moved their town to the newly purchased land. According to Professor Otilio, the people have ten years to repay the loan and have already paid back some five thousand pesos by going off to earn wages on coffee fincas. The person who organized all this was the INI cultural promoter.

We found the town especially attractive, well laid out in a grid pattern and with a new INI school. I also asked to see a sweat house and we went to look at one deep in a cornfield behind a house. It was constructed of rock plastered with mud and was rectangular in shape. It had a flat roof, then above was a two-part pitched roof of thatch to keep the rain from washing away the mud plaster. Inside I noted a firepit at the back and a board floor. We were informed that the whole family go in, lie down with their feet to hot rocks, and put their heads on small blocks of hewn wood. They use water to wash with as they sweat. The custom was to take a sweat bath each evening right after sundown and before supper. I added in my journal: "Great contrast in all these Indian parajes who accept their situation with grace and dignity and work for better things compared to the utter misery in Oxchuc among Ladinos."

We finally arrived in Chilil, where we had left the Land Rover, about sundown, just in time to see an INI pickup arrive from San Cristobal and unload two attractive, young Huisteca women, each carrying nursing babies. We watched with fascination and enormous respect as they each loaded huge bags of maize, weighing at least 150 pounds, on their backs with tumplines. And with cheery smiles and their infants carried inside their rebozos in front to balance the loads of maize on their backs, headed off along a mountain trail toward their homes, God only knows how many miles away. I was somewhat stiff and Frank was suffering, having not had as much experience on horseback, but when we saw the two barefoot women carrying such heavy loads into the mountains, we forgot about our own aches and pains, climbed into the Land Rover and headed back to San Cristobal.

LATE SUMMER RECONNAISSANCE CONTINUES

On 24 August Frank and I were invited to have lunch with Roberta Montagu in the spacious colonial house that she owned near the Plaza Santo Domingo in San Cristobal. Bobbie, as she preferred to be called, was one of the more interesting members of the expatriate Euro-American colony who had purchased houses in San Cristobal and spent part or all of each year in Chiapas. She was from a well-to-do Sephardic Jewish family (her maiden name being Joughin) in New Orleans, and had studied anthropology at the University of California, Los Angeles, including some courses with my colleague Professor William A. Lessa. She had arrived in San Cristobal in the early 1950s and, through the Bloms, had met and married a Lord Montagu from England who later became ill and died on an expedition in the Lacandon rain forest of eastern Chiapas. She stayed on in San Cristobal and met Calixta Guiteras-Holmes who became a close friend; in fact, Calixta always stayed at Bobbie's house when she was in town. With the arrival of the University of Chicago project in 1956 Bobbie was recruited to help with the field research and worked especially with the Tojolabal Maya who were located to the east of the Tzeltal in the vicinity of Comitan.

Bobbie was always a gold mine of information, not all of it correct or in focus, but always interesting. She offered an explanation as to why the Protestant movement was so strong in Oxchuc. Oxchuc had too few cargos for the large population, and the cargos came to be controlled by a clique who passed them around among themselves. Corralitos, located over the mountain to the northeast, became increasingly left out, and hence were receptive to Marianne Slocum's missionary work.

At Villa Rojas's recommendation I returned to the Zinacanteco hamlet of Paste' to consider it further as a site for my own field research. Taking Professor Otilio Vasquez, our friend from the Oxchuc trip, with me in the Land Rover, I drove to the center of the hamlet, which has a corn-grinding mill operated by a Zinacanteca woman and an INI School in which the cultural promoter and teacher is Mariano Hernández Zárate whom Villa Rojas described as the most important principal (leader) in Zinacantan. Mariano was unfortunately not at the INI school when I visited, but I discovered that the hamlet lies six kilometers south of the Pan American highway at Nachih and overlooks the Grijalva Valley. I inquired of Professor Otilio about the cost of having a field house built for us in Paste' and he estimated it would cost about three thousand pesos to build an Indian-style house, but with a more permanent tile roof.

On 25 August we made our reconnaissance trip to Amatenango and Aguacatenango, which I had visited briefly before but wanted Frank to see. We did not consider field research in either community since Duane Metzger was already working in Aguacatenango, and Manning and June Nash were beginning their research in Amatenango. An interesting feature of both communities is how compact they were in settlement pattern with grid plans compared to Tzotzil municipios we had been visiting.

A journey to Ixtapa and Soyalo on 26 August finished our planned reconnaissance of Tzotzil and Tzeltal communities. We discovered that both of these municipios had very large populations of Ladinos in the cabeceras and were not where we wished to begin to do field research.

On 27, 28, and 29 August the University of Chicago Man-in-Nature project held a working conference at Na-Bolom to which Frank Miller and I were invited. It was chaired by Sol Tax, and was attended by his field researchers, including Professor Norman McQuown, June and Manning Nash, Mark Gumbiner, Bobbie Montagu, and Larry Kaplan, among others.

Joining forces with the University of Chicago group and driving Bobbie Montagu's Land Rover and our Harvard Land Rover, we traveled to Comitan and the Guatemalan border on 30 August to become acquainted with this southeastern Chiapas frontier.

In Comitan we stopped to eat breakfast, and picked up a handbill that exhorted all Catholics to come to a great demonstration for the Catholic faith and our Holy Mother, Guadalupe, the Queen of America, and against the Protestant propagandists. We thought little about it at the time, but proceeded on a paved section of the Pan American toward the Guatemalan border.

Returning to Comitan we drove into the center of the city to look in the local jail for linguistic informants from various Mayan-speaking municipios for Professor Norman McQuown, the linguist from Chicago. McQuown had discovered on earlier field trips in Mexico that the local jails always contained a number of Indian prisoners who, being bored, welcomed an opportunity to talk with him.

In Comitan we immediately noted that almost all the houses and places of business had signs on doors or windows reading *Este Hogar es Cató- lico. No Admitimos Protestantes!* (This place is Catholic. We do not admit Protestants!).

As we drove slowly down the streets, we were subjected to hostile glances and comments; it was obvious that the Comitecos thought our two Land Rovers were loaded with protestant missionaries. We stopped in front of the cabildo where Sol Tax, Norman McQuown, and others went into the jail to look for informants; others went for walks around the plaza. To continue from my journal:

> Just at this point a Jeep with a loudspeaker went by advertising the meeting against the Protestants, and adding a new point: that it was Gringo gold that was financing the Protestants. Shortly there- after a crowd of school children gathered around the two Land Rovers. We held off the crowd, smoked cigarettes, drank beer. Bobbie Montagu came back and smoked a cigarette, telling the crowd that Protestant missionaries don't wear lipstick or smoke. But . . . the kids were very forward and aggressive, pushing on each of our Land Rovers. There were also two rough-looking older men in the crowd, and I had the feeling that a rock thrown at one of the Land Rovers at this point could have set off a real riot. It was certainly not the place for a bunch of Gringos to be on the eve of a great Catholic demonstration against Protestant missionaries. We sent a runner in to alert Tax and McQuown in the jail, and very shortly thereafter gathered our group together and left Comitan immediately.

We were later informed that the demonstrators had descended on one of the houses of the protestant missionaries and broken all the windows by throwing stones. I learned that the Catholic-protestant conflict in Chiapas had real potential for violence and that the Catholic demonstrators did not pause to discriminate between Protestant missionaries and North Ameri- cans who were of other faiths and professions. In this instance the two Land Rover loads of anthropologists who were virtually forced to leave Comitan contained few Protestants; indeed, most of them were Jewish.

I am glad that Frank and I later took the trouble to pay a call upon Msgr. Eduardo Flores in San Cristobal who in those days was more closely in touch with the Catholic priests serving the various Indian municipios than was the local bishop. Monseigneur Flores graciously offered to explain to the priests in the diocese that Frank and I were anthropologists, not Protestant missionaries. We hoped this would help in our relationships with the Tzotzil and Tzeltal communities.

Since I was increasingly interested in Zinacantan as a field site, I spent the last few days in the field focusing on this municipio. I learned that the INI puppet show, called the Teatro Petul (Petul is Tzotzil for Pedro, one of the characters in the show), was planning to do performances in Paste' and in the neighboring hamlet of Elan Vo'. We had already visited the accessible hamlets of Nachih (the house of the sheep) and Navenchauk (lake of lightning) on the Pan American highway. I was glad to drive the puppeteers out in the Land Rover so that I could become better acquainted with these more remote hamlets. We made two trips to these hamlets (31 August and 2 September); on the first trip we took Mrs. Villa Rojas and some visiting friends along since the puppeteers were not ready to go on that date. On the second journey we transported the puppeteers, and I had my first opportunity to meet the INI cultural promoter in Paste', Mariano Hernández Zárate. I was told he was also the *comisariado ejidal* (the ejido commissar) who was in charge of distributing the ejido lands among families in the municipio.

I was especially enchanted by Paste' (meaning "chunk of wood" in Tzotzil), located an hour's walk or a half hour Land Rover ride south of the Pan American highway from Nachih. The hamlet could be conveniently reached on foot when the road was impassible after heavy rains, but was a completely Maya world, without the Ladinos who occupied houses and ran small stores in Zinacantan Center and, in even greater numbers, in most other cabeceras of the Tzotzil and Tzeltal municipios. The hamlet extends to the edge of the escarpment from which one looks south and six thousand feet down to the Grijalva River valley and southeastward across to the mountain ridges on the Guatemalan border—really breathtaking views!

As we reflected on our three weeks of field research, we thought about how our encounters with the Tzotzil and Tzeltal had been fascinating, novel, and sometimes frightening. On the whole the people were curious and friendly. But I recall a startling experience with a drunk Chamula, reeling about on the road leading into Chamula Center, who flagged us down. We stopped. He approached the Land Rover, babbling incoherently in Tzo-

Frank Miller (left) with his principal informant, Alonzo Vasquez, in Yalcuc in 1957.

tzil, and then began to push and rock our vehicle in a menacing way. We were terrified, not knowing how to respond nor how to gracefully detach him from the Land Rover. We finally managed to detach his hands from the rolled-down window and drive off leaving him again staggering on the road. We later discovered that intoxicated Tzotzil-Mayas were harmless, and we slowly learned how to cope with them.

Fundamental decisions had been made about the sites for field research. In a word, I had become fascinated by Zinacantan in the same way that I became emotionally attached to the Highlands of Chiapas on my first trip in 1955. Further, I was encouraged by Alfonso Villa Rojas who urged me to consider Zinacantan, and especially Paste', as a productive site for intensive and long-range ethnographic research.

For a field site for Frank Miller, Alfonso Villa Rojas urged that we consider the Municipio of Huistan, and especially the hamlet of Yalcuc ("water of the turkey"). We had passed through Huistan Center on horseback en route to Oxchuc and found it interesting. We had also been through Yalcuc on our way to Chanal. Professor Villa Rojas and Dr. Francisco Alarcón, the head of the INI Medical Program, went with us to Yalcuc to ask permission for the research (Miller 1989). Permission was granted through the assistance of Don Alonzo Vasquez who was the comisariado ejidal of Huistan and lived in Yalcuc. Arrangements were also made for Frank to sleep in a room in the INI clinic and to eat his meals at Don Alonzo's house nearby.

A year or so later I discovered how astute Alfonso Villa Rojas's advice had been. Mariano Hernández Zárate was the cacique (political boss) of Zinacantan with his power based on control of the distribution of ejido lands; Don Alonzo Vasquez was the cacique of Huistan with his power also based on control of the ejido. They were two caciques who were cooperating actively with the programs of INI. In working with them we were reenforcing the INI measures underway to modernize the Indians. But in suggesting Paste' and Yalcuc, Villa Rojas was doing more than merely promoting his own INI program. He was also placing Frank and me under the political protection of the leading caciques of Zinacantan and Huistan. We found this strategy to be important later in placing students, that is, to make certain that some important Indian, whether the head of a family or the presidente municipal, would be directly responsible for the welfare of the student.

During the three weeks I had also learned about many of the other intricate complexities involved in doing field research in Chiapas. In addition to the Catholic versus Protestant split and the bootleg liquor problem, I would have to cope with the local Ladinos, not only as the superordinate group living in San Cristobal, but also in the Indian municipios where, at minimum, there was always a Ladino secretary calling many of the shots, and at maximum a large population of Ladinos living in the cabeceras and exploiting the Indians from this vantage point. And there were the Indian caciques whose political power would have to be clearly recognized and respected. I also knew I would inevitably be drawn into the Euro-American colony, which was small but growing in San Cristobal in those days. Finally, I was convinced by the end of our reconnaissance that the members of my project would have to learn Tzotzil and Tzeltal, for although Spanish served well enough to get by in San Cristobal, good ethnographic work with the Indians was going to require control of these Mayan languages.

On 4 September Frank and I, accompanied by Arthur Rubel of the University of Chicago project, drove to Oaxaca to attend the meetings of the Sociedad Mexicana de Antropología's Mesa Redonda, a round table gathering of anthropologists specializing on Mexico. We reached Juchitan on the Isthmus of Tehuantepec the first night and discovered a fiesta in progress. After supper Arthur Rubel and I went out to drink beer in one of the open-air bars managed by the famous Tehuanas, the southern Zapotec women who are noted for their beauty and their business acumen. I recall that the bar we patronized was run by a very attractive young Tehuana who sold endless beers to twenty-two male customers and managed to flirt with all twenty-two of us!

In Oaxaca we stayed at the Hotel Monte Alban and I remember going to the first day of papers with great anticipation, especially since it was my first scientific meeting in Mexico. The papers were scheduled at hourly intervals, but the first paper, by Alfonso Caso, speaking on his archaeological finds in Tomb 7 at Monte Alban, lasted seven hours, four hours in the morning and three hours in the late afternoon following comida! He must have shown every Kodachrome slide that had ever been taken of Tomb 7 and its gold artifacts. Since Dr. Caso was the leading anthropologist in Mexico in those days, there was no way to contain him, and most of the Mexican anthropologists dutifully sat through the long seven hours. But along with many of my equally impatient fellow North Americans, I spent most of the rest of the conference time drinking mescal and visiting informally with anthropologists on the veranda of the Hotel Marques del Valle, which had a good view of the Oaxaca Zocalo and was a restful setting for quiet conversations.

While I flew to Boston from Oaxaca, Frank drove the Land Rover back to Chiapas to start his year of field research in Yalcuc for which he was well funded by a Doherty Foundation Fellowship. He focused his research on the impact of the INI development program, especially the diffusion of modern medicine, and regularly sent me copies of his field notes, which I read and commented on.

With my first-year field journal and with Frank Miller's field notes I started the Harvard Chiapas Project archives with a set of understandings that became project policy over the ensuing thirty-five years. Each field-worker has been asked to make a copy of his or her field data to be placed in the archives, which are kept alphabetically by last names and by the years each was in the field. Unpublished papers from all of my freshman and graduate seminars and from the field reports, as well as Ph.D. and A.B. theses, have been bound into volumes, one copy of which is kept in the Chiapas archives; a second copy has been given to the Tozzer Library at Harvard. It is firmly understood that field researchers have prior rights to the utilization and publication of their data, but may give permission to me or to any others on the project to utilize the field materials (including quotes). The members of the project have been very dutiful over the years about sending copies of their field journals to the archives, and I have vigilantly watched over these precious data to make certain that unauthorized scholars do not use the materials without the proper permissions. Surprisingly, we have had no serious difficulties among the members of the project with these basic policy rules, and, by now, we have a really substantial body of field data, extending from 1957 to 1990, stored in the Harvard project archives in my office in the Peabody Museum at Harvard.

As my first student on the project, Frank had the disadvantage of not knowing Tzotzil, beyond the few phrases he learned during his months in Yalcuc, and, therefore, having to work almost entirely in Spanish. Nonetheless, he wrote a fine Ph.D. thesis (Miller 1959) and published three excellent articles on his research in Huistan (Miller 1960, 1964, 1965).

To add a footnote on the logistic side, Frank Miller was noted for taking meticulous care of the project Land Rover. He not only drove carefully on the rough Chiapas roads, but after a trip to San Cristobal, he would personally crawl under the vehicle and grease the fittings, which lost grease from traveling through mud holes on the road. This proved to be an extraordinary performance; I later discovered that institutional automobiles are usually badly mistreated on anthropological field expeditions.

Back at Harvard I plunged into my teaching responsibilities as I anxiously awaited word from the National Institute of Mental Health and the National Science Foundation about the outcome of my five-year research proposal. Good news finally came in mid-December from the NIMH, which had approved a grant (Number M-2100) for five years in the amount of $63,000. I withdrew my application to the NSF and proceeded almost immediately to select the graduate student for the academic year 1958–59.

Since Frank Miller was at work in the field on changes in health concepts and practices, I wanted someone to work on the literacy programs of INI. I managed to recruit a very talented couple, Benjamin N. Colby and his wife, Lore M. Colby, for 1958–59. Colby, who is called Nick, from his middle name, was a Princeton graduate who had come to Harvard for his Ph.D. in anthropology. He had majored in Spanish literature at Princeton and spoke Spanish fluently. Lore was a German-born linguist working on her Ph.D. in the Department of Linguistics at Harvard. They were an ideal choice. Nick was interested in the problem of literacy. I knew we also had to start mastering Tzotzil and Tzeltal, and it was crucial for us to have a trained linguist. Lore was interested in working on Tzotzil for her Ph.D. dissertation in linguistics. During the spring term of 1957–58 Lore began to assemble what was known of Tzotzil—only two brief articles by Nadine Weathers (1947, 1950), the wife of a Protestant missionary who had worked briefly in the Zinacanteco hamlet of Nabenchauk in the 1940s.

For Tzeltal we were somewhat better off since Norman McQuown had kindly sent us copies of his Tzeltal lessons that had been used by his University of Chicago students in preparation for field research. Duane and Barbara Metzger had had the field experience in Aguacatenango and returned to duty in the Society of Fellows at Harvard. They served as our guides in a series of Tzeltal study sessions, and Nick also worked with me on field methods and Maya ethnology. By June 1958 I felt we were somewhat better prepared for Chiapas and was eager to get on with the field research.

4 /
THE FORMATIVE
YEARS:
1958-1959

The next two years were momentous ones for the Harvard Chiapas Project. It was during these formative years that the design of the project and our strategies for training and research were refined to fit the realities of Chiapas life.

The two features of our future research operations that concerned me the most during these years were (a) the need to move from Spanish to Tzotzil or Tzeltal in our communication with the Indians and (b) the necessity to deepen, as soon as possible, our ethnographic experience in the Indian cultures—something that would ultimately involve participant observation in the life of the indigenous communities. We made substantial progress on both fronts in these formative years.

THE 1958 FIELD SEASON

In the summer of 1958 the Colbys arrived in the field in June and were hard at work by the time my family and I reached San Cristobal. We traveled by Norwegian freighter, the *Bennestvet Brovig* out of Farsund, from New York to Veracruz, a voyage of nine leisurely days for reading and watching flying fish across the Gulf of Mexico. It was a welcome break after an exhausting academic year at Harvard, and an inexpensive mode of travel for a family of six. The freighter was utilitarian, but comfortable for our family, the only passengers, who occupied most of the passenger cabins aboard.

Upon arrival at the Port of Veracruz, we learned how ship captains deal with Mexican customs officials. The captain broke out a case of fine Scotch whiskey, some of which was served on the spot; the remaining bottles became gifts for the customs officials. All went smoothly as we arrived in the port and disembarked.

We flew from Veracruz to Tuxtla Gutierrez where Nick Colby met us with the Land Rover and drove us to the Hotel Bonampak for a swim and lunch. We arrived at the Casa Blom, where I had made reservations for lodging for our family, on 7 July in time for the end of Gertrude Blom's fifty-seventh birthday party, which was lively with marimbas playing, guests dancing in the patio, and cake and coffee being served.

I had decided to try the Casa Blom as our headquarters because Frank Miller had established his San Cristobal base there and had liked it. The next six weeks were interesting, but difficult ones at the Casa Blom. This renovated old house was presided over by the Danish explorer and archaeologist, Frans Blom, and his wife, Gertrude ("Trudi") Duby, a Swiss-born, German-speaking photographer.[1]

The Bloms purchased Casa Blom in 1950 and established Na-Bolom (House of the Jaguar), which has jaguars on tiles decorating the front of the house. The structure, constructed some years before by the Penagos family to serve as a Catholic seminary, had a large central patio, a chapel, and windowless rooms. It was rebuilt to provide a large dining room, a spacious library with fireplace, and a number of guest rooms. With a small archaeological museum and a growing library on Chiapas, Na-Bolom became a research center for anthropologists, as well as botanists, geologists, zoologists, and other specialists working in Chiapas. It also attracted writers, photographers, and artists, lured to San Cristobal by the exotic and colorful multicultural setting (Brunhouse 1976).

Trudi became especially noted for her photographs and studies of the Lacandons, a small group of fewer than three hundred Mayas who lived in the lowland rain forests of eastern Chiapas. The Lacandons, who had never been proselytized successfully by the Spanish friars, were believed to be the contemporary Maya group with a culture most similar to the ancient Maya. They had been studied by a number of anthropologists, including Alfred Marston Tozzer of Harvard University and Jacques Soustelle from the Sorbonne in Paris. Frans kept up his interest in Maya archaeology and ethnology and excavated one of the local archaeological sites, Moshviquil, located on a mountain ridge north of San Cristobal.

When I first knew them, Frans was a tall, commanding figure with a

Gertrude Duby de Blom and Frans Blom at Na-Bolom
in 1958.

great shock of white hair—both rugged and handsome in appearance—but given to bouts of heavy drinking. Trudi was a dashing, colorful, quite attractive woman with the most impressive collection of dresses, made from Mexican and Guatemalan textiles, and worn with as massive and exotic jewelry as I had ever seen. She was very active, typically taking a ride on her horse each morning. In the evenings before supper the two would take their places in heavy, wooden chairs, raised above the floor on platforms like thrones on each side of the fireplace in the library. Here each would regale the assembled guests with stories of adventure in the mountains of Chiapas and in the jungles of the Lacandons. Moving to the evening meal, Frans would sit at one end of the long table in the dining room; Trudi at the other end. And the sagas would continue, sometimes in English, but more often in Spanish, French, or German.

It was always a cosmopolitan collection of guests, all of whom paid fairly stiff daily rates at Na-Bolom, which had a sign on the front door saying casa particular (private home) to avoid paying taxes. But, in effect, it has always functioned as a hotel, charging not only for room and board, but also small fees to visit the museum.

The only guests who did not pay these daily rates were the visiting Lacandons who had flown up from the rain forest to spend time visiting Na-Bolom. With their long black hair and cotton gowns on both men and women, they present a striking contrast with the local Tzotzil-Maya who regard them not as distant Maya compatriots, but as savages. I remember a special evening that summer when Bor, one of Trudi's Lacandon friends, gave a remarkable performance at dinner that impressed us immensely. He imitated the calls of dozens of birds and animals that live in the Lacandon rain forest. I have never seen our four children's eyes grow any larger than when he imitated a howler monkey, a jaguar, a peccary, a coati, six species of parrots, and a harpy eagle.

Certain aspects of life at Na-Bolom made it less than a perfect place to stay. Our children, ages thirteen, twelve, ten, and five, were active and accustomed to the relaxed flow of life in an American suburban home. Na-Bolom, under Trudi, ran like a Swiss clock. Lunch, when the bell rang, promptly at 1:30 P.M.; dinner at 7:00 P.M. sharp. Latecomers were scolded as they crept to the dining room table. Nan felt that she had to keep the children "well-behaved" at all times, and managed quite well to do so. But it was a strain.

When Trudi took visiting guests off on trips to the Lacandon rain forest, Frans would fall off the wagon and start drinking again. As the days went by, he would become more morose, come to the dining table unshaven, and preside over the spare evening meal, consisting of only hard bread, sausage, and sliced pineapple. Needless to say, we were relieved at the end of six weeks when we were invited by Alfonso Villa Rojas to move to quarters at La Cabaña for the rest of the summer.

To keep our children interested and busy and provide what I thought would be ideal transportation for reaching remote Tzotzil hamlets, I decided to purchase four horses.

I finally acquired four reasonable looking horses for a total of 2,100 pesos ($168.00 U.S.); the saddles and bridles came to $48—for a total investment of $216.00 dollars. During the summer I took one or more children with me and we began to visit remote Indian hamlets on horseback.

Three of the four horses I purchased in the summer of 1958 to provide transportation to the Tzotzil-Maya hamlets and to keep the children entertained.

In the end, the grand plan of having our own horses for travel in Chiapas was a disaster. In the first place, two of the horses had been born and reared in tierra caliente where the grass is longer and there is more air to breathe. In the highlands at seven thousand feet, they were not only short of breath, but they had difficulty grazing on the short grasses of the valley of San Cristobal. I thought I knew a great deal about horses, but it never occurred to me to inquire whether the horses came from the highlands or lowlands when I bought them. Further, it was awkward when we arrived in hamlets and were stared at by Indians, especially since the Tzotzil Maya had horses and mules, but never rode them. They used them as pack animals to bring maize home from their distant fields. I soon realized that the image of "men on horseback" placed us immediately in the category of the Spanish conquering overlords, an image I certainly did not wish to portray.

The two lowland horses died the first winter after we acquired them; a third horse was stolen from the pasture at Bobbie Montagu's ranch where they were pastured; and I sold the fourth during he next field season and donated the saddles to Na-Bolom for them to use on their expeditions. Since that time, the members of the Harvard Chiapas Project have hiked on foot along the mountain trails to reach the remote hamlets—like the Tzotzil Maya do.

For their headquarters in San Cristobal, Nick and Lore Colby had rented a small, but attractive, third-floor apartment on a corner overlooking the central plaza of San Cristobal. The owner of the apartment was Don Leopoldo Velasco Robles from one of the old families in town. Known as Don Polo by everyone, he managed the local branch of the Banco de México whose offices occupied the first floor of the same building. By the time we arrived, the Colbys, with their fluent control of Spanish, had become friends of Don Polo and his family. We were introduced to the Velascos by the Colbys, and this proved to be an important event for us. Over the years Don Polo and his family were to become our closest friends in San Cristobal. They have visited us many times in the United States and have been guests at two of our family weddings.

Shortly after I first met Don Polo, he became the presidente municipal (mayor) of San Cristobal for a term of three years, and with his political connections, his wise advice and guidance over the years have been invaluable.

From our headquarters in San Cristobal I began to make journeys to the Tzotzil municipios to gather data and to develop rapport for the future. Often I worked with Nick Colby, who was getting acquainted with Zinacantan, and sometimes with Frank Miller. I made a special trip to Yalcuc early in the season to call on Don Alonzo, who had been so supportive of Frank Miller, and to present a gift of a sickle I had bought for him at Sears, Roebuck in Boston. He was enormously pleased and welcomed me warmly in Yalcuc.

We also revisited the INI facilities in Chilil about which Alfonso Villa Rojas, with his high sense of humor, later related a wonderful story concerning "the efficiency of applied anthropology." It seems that at a recent meeting in Chilil, the high command from the INI Center in San Cristobal urged all the Huistecos present to stop crimes, and, above all, the stealing that had been rampant in the hamlet. That very same night somebody stole all the chickens belonging to INI's agricultural station in Chilil!

Most of my field trips were focused on Paste', the hamlet I intended to

EZV with Don Leopoldo Velasco Robles (who was soon to be the presidente municipal, or mayor, of San Cristobal Las Casas) in 1958.

study in depth, and on Zinacantan Center itself. For our journeys to Paste' we would often take Lore and my whole family along and have a picnic lunch beside the road. On our first trips we noted how the Zinacantecos, and even their dogs, would all run and hide in the cornfields as the car drove along the INI road that led to the school and from there on to the edge of the rim overlooking the Grijalva River valley. After we stopped for our picnics, we would begin to see the dogs reappearing and then the dark eyes of Zinacantecos peering at us from the cornfields. Eventually, families would appear and we would share some of our food with them as we carried on conversations, partly in Spanish, which most of the Zinacantecos could speak only haltingly, or in our even sketchier Tzotzil.

Alfonso Villa Rojas had advised me to go repeatedly to Paste' and be seen as doing no harm to the people, and sometimes doing some good, such as offering rides in the Land Rover. This easy approach began to bring results by the end of the summer, when more and more Zinacantecos in the

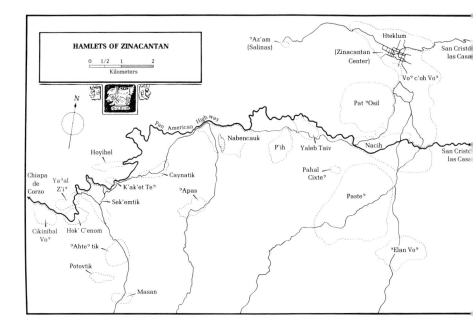

hamlet came to know us, and we came to know them, especially when we visited with them in the Land Rover on trips to and from San Cristobal.

These trips also brought more contact with the cultural promoter, Mariano Hernández Zárate, as we stopped at the INI school. I learned that he lived in Zinacantan Center with his wife and family of six children and always returned there on weekends, walking over the mountains from Paste'. On various occasions during the summer I began to interview him informally about Zinacanteco customs, including questions about sweat baths and curing practices. I used the strategy of describing some of our customs, as well as the customs of the Navahos I had studied in the Southwest. Mariano had an active curiosity about the outside world, and I sensed that being the busy cultural promoter in Paste' and the leading cacique of Zinacantan, he would be a good informant.

The second person with whom I became acquainted was Andrés Gómez Rodríguez who was president of the school committee in Paste'. His responsibilities, lasting a year until he was replaced by a successor, were to travel through the hamlet and round up children for school each morning, be on duty each day at the school to see that all went well and to greet visitors, especially when the teachers were absent, and to make certain that the chickens and the pig owned by Mariano were not stolen. I first met him in mid-July on a day when Mariano was away during one of my visits. He was an easygoing, soft-spoken, and quite handsome Zinacanteco who spoke Spanish well and, I learned later, was the leader of a group of twelve relatives who rented and worked fields together in the Grijalva River lowlands. I also began to engage in informal interviewing with Andrés and, especially, to collect Tzotzil words and phrases from him.

After a few weeks I was privileged to have my first inside view of two Zinacanteco houses. These were exciting episodes since my only previous glimpse inside a Maya house had been in the Tzeltal hamlet of Tzopilja in Oxchuc the year before. Not surprisingly, these houses were those of Mariano Hernández Zárate in Zinacantan Center and of Andrés Gómez Rodríguez in Paste'.

The visit in Mariano's house occurred one day when Nick and I had given Mariano and his wife and two children a ride to Zinacantan Center from the market in San Cristobal. On arriving in the center, Mariano asked that they be let off along the main road. Instead, I drove up the unpaved street to his house, having in mind that we might be able to visit inside. They thanked us very much as they unloaded their gear. Since we were near his home, I asked Mariano if we might visit him in his house. He responded "Bueno" and led us into the patio and on inside the house. To continue with a passage from my field journal:

> We found a son sick in bed in the corner to the right of the door, two teenage daughters grinding corn on metates beside the fire, and a daughter-in-law with a backstrap loom weaving a pair of short Zinacanteco pants. The whole family was really very gracious and hospitable, and I could detect no sense of strain at our being there. The daughter-in-law did stop weaving after a time and go outside, but I think this was because she was practically under our feet from where we sat on small chairs that were brought forward for us to sit upon. We stayed and had a wonderful visit for over an hour. The two daughters continued grinding all the time we were there—only giggling from time to time as Nick and I struggled to pronounce Tzotzil words. The daughter-in-law returned later and sat on the ground with her knees bent back under her body beside the fire. The mother sat by the fire on the other side from where

we were sitting. . . . For the first 20 minutes or so, Mariano stood in front of the fire facing us and talked—very much the way that Don Alonzo in Yalcuc had stood and talked to me the other day. Later Mariano found another small chair and sat down also. I kept the conversation going with questions and with joking about how our women didn't know how to grind corn or weave while both Nick and I looked carefully at the contents and construction of the house and patio. There are three houses—one of thatched roof and two with tile roofs—all with wattle-and-daub walls. The sweat house is attached to the side of the third house. Corn is growing in the house lot, along with apple trees. We saw two cats, a puppy, and a dog. The little daughter, Maria, threw sticks at the puppy to make it go out of the house. There were also chicks wandering in and out and a number of turkeys in the patio. There was a general impression of clutter of objects inside the house—apparently local housekeeping does not include the idea of keeping objects picked up and neatly arranged. The house had no windows, but two doors, made of two pieces of well-dressed lumber, which swung free— like old-fashioned saloon doors, one door on the east, one on the west. To the north of the center was the fireplace with a pot of corn being cooked. Another pot nearby had corn being soaked in lime.

The other visit occurred one day in Paste' when the motor on the corn-grinding mill beside the school would not start up. Andrés was on duty at the school as president of the school committee. We went together to inspect the grinding mill where I discovered that the points on the spark plug were completely closed. I adjusted the points with a pair of pliers and cleaned the plug with my knife. With the plug reinstalled, the motor started immediately. Following this small success, I told Andrés that I had brought a lunch and invited him to share it with me. I suggested we eat it at his house. According to my journal:

There was some slight hesitation, as he said his family was not there but had gone into the woods. But I said that didn't make any difference, and he responded "Bueno." So we drove to the rim and walked to his *sitio* (house site). He had to explain en route to a few people what we were doing, but we kept right on—noted that he let me walk behind—and the whole thing had the temper of a kind of lark. Arrived at the patio in front of his house and I started to sit down on a log, then he took the initiative and asked if it were all right out here or should we go inside. I said, let's go inside. . . . Andrés opened the doors of his house and we went in. Chairs were hauled out of the general clutter for Andrés, a brother-in-law who had come to visit from next door, and me. After about 15 minutes, a woman appeared, also very friendly, carrying about an 18-month-old baby girl. This was Andrés's wife, back from bringing water. She sat on the far side of the fire all the time, nursed the baby, and tended the fire on which maize was boiling. . . . I visited with them for about an hour before I brought out my lunch, taking down names of things in Tzotzil. Noted there was no tension at all on their part about writing things down. So for the rest of the stay, I freely took notes on all data. . . . I later shared my lunch with Andrés and his wife and brother-in-law. I only brought two beers and one Pepsi-Cola. The two men chose the beers and I drank the Pepsi. The brother-in-law shared his beer with his sister, Andrés's wife. They ate everything that was offered and the wife, Maria, passed bits of bread and cookies on to her baby.

These house visits were the beginning of a long, friendly relationship with Mariano and Andrés that extended over many years.

In August I also attended the Fiesta of San Lorenzo for the first time. This celebration for the patron saint—the municipio is officially called San Lorenzo Zinacantan—takes place in the ceremonial center in early August, the tenth being what the Ladinos term the *mero día* (real day). As I would discover later, the ceremonies actually commence on 8 August and do not finish until 11 August.

In retrospect my experiences and observations of the fiesta were quite superficial the first time I attended. I did, however, learn some crucial ethnographic facts and extend my contacts with Zinacantecos.

Accompanied by my family and the Colbys, I paid a call on Don Mariano Hernández Zárate on the morning of the first day of the fiesta (8 August) to deliver a gift of a bottle of sugarcane rum and a package of white candles. We found that Mariano's house shrine, a cross erected in the patio, was freshly decorated with pine tree tops and flowers and that copal incense had

The church of San Lorenzo in Zinacantan Center during the fiesta of San Lorenzo. (Photo by Frank Cancian)

San Lorenzo, the patron saint of Zinacantan, with
his necklaces of sacred coins, ribbons, and mirrors.
(Photo by John D. Early)

recently been burned in a censer in front of the shrine. Mariano came out
of his house to greet us and seemed to appreciate the gifts, but explained
that his atole (maize gruel) had not been made, or else we could taste it. It
was obvious that some kind of family ceremony was in progress, and we
were not invited into the house. I learned that a decorated cross shrine is a
reliable signal that family ritual of some kind is underway.

It is worth noting that by this time I was referring to Mariano as Don
Mariano because I sensed that this Spanish term of respect was due a Zinacanteco with his position as the most important cacique. Later I discovered
he should properly be called Totik Marian in Tzotzil. Totik is derived from
tot, which means "father," but the term is probably best translated as "sir."
Marian is the Tzotzil version of Mariano. As Mariano grew older, he was
more often called Mol Marian (Old Man Mariano), a term of even greater
respect among Zinacantecos.

I also noted in my field journal that I had explained to Don Mariano on this visit that my name in Spanish was Juan. He responded that this would be Shun in Tzotzil. I added that Nan's name in Spanish was Catalina, which Mariano translated as Katal. This transformation of names had been felicitously suggested a few days before by the linguist Norman McQuown, when I had complained to him that Zinacantecos were having difficulty understanding my name. McQuown thought that "Evon" was probably some eccentric family version of "Evan," which in turn was related to "John," a name that could be readily translated into both Spanish and Tzotzil. As a result I soon became Don Juan in Spanish or Totik Shun (Sir John) in Tzotzil. With advancing years, I was promoted to Mol Shun (Old Man John), a name of greater respect. Similarly, Vogt was usually pronounced Vo', the Tzotzil word for water, and my place of origin, Boston, as Posh Ton, literally Rum Liquor Rock. So I ultimately became Mol Shun Vo' and came from Posh Ton—Old Man John Water from Rum Liquor Rock—and was finally comprehensible to the Zinacantecos! (Vogt 1990:8).

Plunging into the crowds watching the fiesta, we discovered that saints from other Indian villages were being carried in procession into the ceremonial center and taken into the church of San Lorenzo where they would remain until 11 August. Because we had been warned by Don Mariano not to try to enter the church, we wandered about the enormous outdoor market beside the church and treated our children and five young boys I knew from Paste' to rides on the hand-operated merry-go-round. A Ladino band and a Zinacanteco drum-and-flute combo were alternately playing in front of the church.

A Zinacanteco acquaintance of Nick Colby appeared in the churchyard, elegantly dressed in full Zinacanteco regalia, including brand-new ribbons flowing from his hat. Nick introduced us to Domingo de la Torre Pérez who was a member of the staff of the Teatro Petul of INI. I gave Domingo a cigarette and bought him a piece of pineapple, and he reciprocated by inviting Nick and me to have a refresco (soda pop) with him in a nearby cantina (bar). We were offered our choice of beers. I chose Carta Blanca and the others followed suit. Little did I know at the time of this first encounter with Domingo de la Torre Pérez that he would become a crucial informant for our project over the ensuing eighteen years.

In the afternoon, Nick and I returned to Zinacantan to observe more of the fiesta, and I noted for the first time how Zinacantecos dance to marimba music that was being played in front of the church: "Various

Zinacanteco men were dancing with each other—either holding hands, or in some cases holding each other around the shoulders, or even assuming ballroom positions. . . . I noted the complete absence of drunks chasing women, which would certainly have happened at a Navaho ceremonial with as many drunk men as were present at this one." Meanwhile, the Zinacanteco women were sitting with their children around the edges of the churchyard, demurely watching the dancing.

On what is called in Spanish *la víspera del día San Lorenzo* (the eve of Saint Lawrence's Day, or 9 August) I observed that the number of people attending was much larger, probably reaching some five thousand in all. Nick and I had a good look at two painted-face performers called capitanes who danced by hopping on one foot and then the other. We had also observed them the day before in the processions that went out to greet the incoming visiting saints.

We later learned that Don Mariano was actually the incoming Alferez of Santo Domingo, one of the most important religious posts in Zinacantan. This is why all the ritual was going on at his home. But I would never have imagined at this point that these capitanes we observed, hopping on one foot and then the other, would later be featured in Eva Hunt's brilliant book *The Transformation of the Hummingbird: Cultural Roots of a Zinacantecan Mythical Poem.* Following my suggestion, Hunt concluded that these capitanes are indeed contemporary Zinacanteco manifestations of a centuries-old Mesoamerican image: the one-legged hummingbird god (Hunt 1977: 224–26).

In the evening we returned again to Zinacantan, bringing our families along, to observe the fireworks, which proved to be among the more spectacular ones I have seen anywhere. We arrived at sundown just as the new electric lights (from a generator installed by INI) were turned on at the Cabildo, in the church, and in some of the Ladino houses. We observed no lights in Indian homes. Some of the Zinacanteco men were carrying flashlights after dark, but groups of Indian women used pitch pine torches to light their way as they moved around in the dark night.

According to Alfonso Villa Rojas, there was considerable resistance in Zinacantan to the installation of these electric lights, especially in the church. The project was well along when one night the junior alcalde, whom we learned later is called the Bik'it Alkalte (Little Alcalde) in Tzotzil, had a dream that the saints would not like electric lights. As a result the electricians were forced to suspend their work on installing the lights in the church. But two weeks later, the higher-ranking senior alcalde, called the Muk'ta Alkalte (Big Alcalde), had a dream that the saints would be enchanted with electric lights—and the project was completed just in time for this fiesta!

The evening fireworks consisted of three *castillos* (castles) and five *toritos* (bulls). The castles were elaborate frameworks constructed of bamboo containing pinwheels and other types of exploding fireworks. One of the castles was ignited by a fireworks' airplane that descended on a rope from the top of the church to the castle. The bulls were frameworks of reed mats that had horns on the front and fit over the head and back of dancing Zinacantecos who whirled wildly as the fireworks exploded from the bulls just above them. Between these fireworks large, multicolored paper balloons were inflated with hot air generated by a flame from a ball of cotton soaked in gasoline and ignited in a wire rack at the base of the balloon. As the balloons rose and floated into the heavens, the band played wildly and the Zinacanteco men danced by the hundreds in the churchyard. Needless to say, our children were entranced, and so were we.

Among the dancers in the churchyard that wild night was my Paste' friend, Andrés Gómez Rodríguez, whom I treated to a beer. Afterward, I recorded:

> When we returned to the courtyard there was much dancing going on; I held Charlie and started in dancing to keep my feet warm. At this point, Andrés and his friend joined in and the three of us danced a couple of pieces. They seemed to enjoy dancing alongside me. At one point, the friend took my Ladino-style hat off and gave me his Zinacanteco hat, saying it was better this way, so I finished the piece with his hat and then gave it back to him.

Although the following day was another active one at the fiesta, I decided to wait until next summer to observe this phase of the fiesta. We joined the Velasco family for a picnic in the countryside to celebrate the birthday of their eldest son.

Since the University of Chicago anthropologists under the general direction of Sol Tax favored frequent meetings to discuss research results and strategies for further work, another meeting was convened at Na-

Bolom in mid-July. Along with Frank Miller and the Colbys, I attended some of the meetings, which included Alfonso Villa Rojas, Julio de la Fuente, Fernando Camara Barbachano, Calixta Guiteras-Holmes, Norman McQuown, June and Manning Nash, Duane and Barbara Metzger, Larry Kaplan, Joan Ablon, Eva Verbitsky Hunt, Juan Baroco, Esther Hermitte, Manuel Zabala, and Andrés Medina.

My most vivid memories of these meetings were of the fieldwork session on 15 July. Calixta Guiteras-Holmes related how she had been forced to leave the Tzeltal community of Cancuc in 1953. She reported that in spite of her smoking and painted lips, the people still thought she was "a Protestant in disguise."

Villa Rojas then described how only last year the word spread through San Cristobal that the Chamulas were about to start a rebellion. It seems that somebody reported a large group of Chamulas coming into San Cristo-bal with shotguns and heard shots at the edge of town. There ensued a general panic among the Ladinos, some of whom took refuge at the city hall, others sought shelter at INI. It was necessary for Villa Rojas to drive from barrio to barrio in the city and speak to the people, assuring them that there was no rebellion. Then Villa Rojas drove to Chamula to con-firm his opinion that there was no resurrection in the offing. In fact, he reported, "the Indians were asleep." I found it amazing that almost ninety years after the Chamula uprising in 1869–70 there was still continuing uneasiness among the Ladinos over the possibility of Indian uprisings.

The summer of 1958 also included my first journey to Maya country in the Highlands of Guatemala. Tucking our four children and travel gear into the Land Rover, Nan and I set out dauntlessly on the Pan American highway on 17 July for San José, Costa Rica, to attend the Thirty-third International Congress of Americanists. We were stopped at the Guatema-lan border by landslides that had covered the highway during the recent monsoon rains. Eventually, we had to travel to Guatemala by loading the Land Rover on a railroad flatcar headed for Tapachula.

From Tapachula we crossed into Guatemala and climbed from the coast up eight thousand feet to San Marcos, thence on to Quetzaltenango. After two nights in Guatemala City we reviewed our travel funds and looked again at the map—we were less than one-fourth of the way to San José. We promptly, and wisely, abandoned the idea of the International Congress and decided to focus our time on Guatemala.

In Guatemala City I telephoned Professor Richard N. Adams of the University of Texas who had married into one of the old German coffee plantation families and was then engaged in ongoing field research. Rick kindly took us out to dinner in Guatemala City; we also saw him again later in Panajachel. It was the beginning of a longtime friendship with Rick Adams who was becoming one of the leading specialists on Guatemala.

We spent more of our time based at the Hotel Tzanjuyu in Panajachel on Lake Atitlan—a beautiful natural setting that has been called the Switzerland of North America. At five thousand feet, Panajachel has a soft, comfortable climate, compared to cooler San Cristobal at seven thousand feet. We understood why this elevation is called tierra templada all through Central America. The clear, blue lake is surrounded by mountains, including three prominent volcanoes, the highest rising to more than eleven thousand feet. Around the shores and up on the mountain benches are more than twenty distinct Maya communities, each with its own interesting customs and colorful costumes. I could readily understand why my colleague Sol Tax, after an attempt to establish himself in Chichicastenango in 1934, chose Panajachel as a base for his field research in the Guatemalan Highlands.

We crossed Lake Atitlan by launch to visit Santiago Atitlan and San Pedro La Laguna, the latter community having been studied by my colleagues at Chicago Ben and Lois Paul. We also drove to Chichicastenango for a day visit in the fascinating municipio that had been studied by Ruth Bunzel in 1930–32. I was especially interested in the general similarities between Chichicastenango and Zinacantan—each with a dispersed settlement pattern comprising a ceremonial center and outlying hamlets. The pattern constituted a marked contrast to the very compact settlements, constrained by the local geography, around Lake Atitlan.

The journey had been a visual review of Sol Tax's classic article on the municipios of the midwestern highlands of Guatemala (1937). My thinking over the years about Maya settlement patterns was strongly influenced by my observations that summer in Highland Guatemala.

We regretfully left beautiful Panajachel and made the long return journey, again by railroad flatcar from Tapachula to Tonala. The trip had expanded my views of the Maya world, and it had provided a very pleasant setting for breaks from the rigors of fieldwork in the cold Highlands of Chiapas. In the years ahead I discovered that most students on the Harvard Chiapas

Project headed for Panajachel when granted their midsummer vacations of a week.

On 17 August Robert M. Laughlin, who was to succeed Nick and Lore Colby in the field during 1959–60, arrived to spend two weeks getting acquainted with the Highlands of Chiapas. Bob, like Nick Colby, was a Princeton man. He had a strong interest in ornithology, having spent a summer at the Smithsonian's Canal Zone Biological Area on Barro Colorado Island. After majoring in English literature at Princeton, he spent a year in Mexico, learning more Spanish, taking courses in Mexican folklore and Nahuatl at the University of Mexico, as well as studying anthropology for a semester at the Escuela Nacional de Antropología e Historia under Professors Jiménez Moreno, Miguel Covarrubias, and others. His training included a two-month field stint among the Mazatecs of the Papaloapan Basin that provided the basis for an article (Laughlin 1971).

Laughlin arrived at Harvard for graduate work in the fall term of 1957 and was the perfect choice to be tapped for the Harvard Chiapas Project. When I telephoned him in the early summer of 1958 I suggested that he make this preliminary reconnaissance trip to Chiapas. Nick Colby and I included him in our late summer journeys in the field.

Another very interesting research assistant who worked with us in Zinacantan during the summer and subsequent academic year was Manuel T. Zabala Cubillos, a student from Cali, Colombia, who was studying for his M.A. at the Escuela Nacional de Antropología e Historia in Mexico City. He and his wife had been students of Professor Fernando Camara Barbachano who taught social anthropology at the Escuela and had suggested the Zabalas come to Chiapas for field experience. I provided research funds from my grant to help Zabala finish his fieldwork, focused on the salt trade of the Zinacantecos, and his thesis, which was entitled "Sistema economica de la comunidad de Zinacantan" (1961a).[2]

During the summer I reached a solution to a pressing logistic problem: the construction of a small field house in the hamlet of Paste'. On 13 July I discussed the problem with Dr. Alarcón, the assistant director of INI. From my journal:

> Talked with Dr. Alarcón about building house in Paste'. He was all for going right ahead with the project—I pay for materials, the paraje furnishes the labor, then when we finish with house (which

could be built on the sitio where the school is), it could be used as an INI building for benefit of the paraje. But Villa Rojas later came in to advise proceeding more slowly; said I should go to Paste' each day for a week or two and let people get used to seeing me before we proposed the house plan to the people in the paraje. I'm sure Villa Rojas is right about this.

On 10 August the Villa Rojases and Colbys joined us for dinner at the Hotel Español, and we again discussed the house problem in Paste'. By this time I was concerned that a large public meeting at which INI asked for permission to build us a house in the hamlet would be likely to decide in the negative, especially if the residents of the hamlet were asked to contribute their labor for the project. My journal reads:

> I suggested that what we should do is simply pay from our budget for an INI house next to the school. In this way, it would not be necessary to have a large junta of people in Paste' to ask their permission. The house could simply be built as another INI project, used by cultural promoters and teachers when we were not there. Then we could move into it summers, while the Colbys and other students could use it at other times. This would avoid getting the Zinacantecos excited about a Gringo family moving into one of their parajes. Villa Rojas liked the idea very much and we will go to Paste' on Wednesday to see about it, and then talk to Sr. Leal [the administrative officer of INI] when he comes back from Mexico about specifications, prices, etc. Villa Rojas suggested we have a porch where Indians could sit and sleep and have shelter where we could visit with them.

I drove Villa Rojas and Leal to Paste' on 15 August to check on the site for the INI house we shall fund. The site selected was just to the southeast of the school and Don Mariano's small house. I added in my journal: "The house will be defined as a Casa de Visitantes (House of Visitors) of INI— for special people from INI to stay in. I talked with Leal later about the details—two rooms 4 × 4 meters—a kitchen 3 × 4 meters—porch 2 meters wide across the front—rock walls with windows on both sides—tile roof and tile floor." The cost for the house was 10,142 pesos, or $813.40 in U.S. dollars.

My family and I left Chiapas on 1 September, by air from Tuxtla Gutie-rrez to Villahermosa to Merida, for our first visit in Yucatan. I had yet to visit any Mayan archaeological sites and was eager to do so as soon as possible. We could only afford a day-trip to Chichen Itza on a pub-lic, unairconditioned bus. It was a long, hot, and uncomfortable trip, but very exciting and worth the effort. I was tremendously impressed with the architecture, sculpture, and scale of construction of this immense site.

All went well in Merida until we checked in at the airline office to con-firm our flight to New Orleans and Boston. One look at my Mexican tourist card and the Mexicana official asked, "But where is your automobile?" He showed me how my tourist card had been stamped by immigration officials at Tapachula when we returned from Guatemala *viajando por automovil* (traveling by automobile). I explained that the Land Rover had been pur-chased in Mexico and was permanently located in San Cristobal Las Casas. But to no avail. We were in deep trouble, and doubted we could catch our plane. It was my first serious encounter with Mexican immigration and custom officials who were following the ironclad regulation that if you bring an automobile to Mexico, you must take it out again, or pay heavy import duties. In desperation I went immediately to the American consul in Merida and explained my case. I have forgotten his name, but he was magnificent. He spent the next several hours on the problem, even coming to the airport with us to make certain all was in order. With a breath of relief, we flew off to New Orleans without even having to pay a bribe.

In retrospect, it had been a successful summer season. I had begun the process of getting acquainted both in Zinacantan and in San Cristobal. Plans were underway for a field house for us in the hamlet of Paste' for the following summer. Frank Miller had finished a year of solid research, and the Colbys were making progress on Nick's study of the effect of literacy programs and on Lore's study of Tzotzil. I had substantially expanded my view of Maya culture and Maya country with the interesting journeys to Highland Guatemala and to Yucatan.

As I celebrated my fortieth birthday at a wonderful party the Colbys organized with marimbas and dancing in the patio at Na-Bolom toward the end of the summer, I reflected on how fortunate I was to have shifted at the time that I did from one major ethnographic area to another. Had I waited any longer in my career, the shift would have been impossible. I was thrilled with the prospects of further research in Chiapas.

Our field house next to the school in the hamlet of Paste'.

THE 1959 FIELD SEASON

In the summer of 1959 we arrived in San Cristobal on 2 July and moved into Don Leopoldo Velasco's apartment building on the zocalo as a town headquarters for the summer. I agreed to keep the Colby apartment on the third floor for the year for project use, and also to rent the second floor apartment to accommodate my family for the summer. The rent for each apartment was a modest 300 pesos ($24.00) a month.

I drove at once to Paste' to see the field house, which had been finished during the year and occupied by the Colbys before our arrival. A week later, on 9 July, we moved to the field house in Paste' with all the family, Susan Tax, and Domingo de la Torre Pérez. It took two trips in the Land Rover to transport us all.

Susan Tax, the daughter of one of my University of Chicago professors, Sol Tax, had just started graduate work in anthropology at Harvard. Since she spoke Spanish fluently and had already had extensive experience in Mesoamerica, including time in Guatemala and a 1957 visit to Chiapas with her parents, I invited her to join us for the summer to see if she would like to continue to work in Mesoamerica. Her project was to study Zinacanteco weaving, which had never been systematically researched.

Domingo de la Torre Pérez had become the first Tzotzil Maya employee of the Harvard Chiapas Project. Feeling the necessity for a steady informant, Nick Colby discovered that Domingo was available when the INI Teatro Petul had run out of funds and laid off all their puppeteers. Nick moved immediately to employ Domingo at a salary of 80 pesos ($6.40) a week. I agreed to keep him on at that rate.

The field house had turned out well. I was pleased with the construction; the masonry walls were solid, the tile roof was rainproof, and the fireplace in the living room functioned. The windows on both sides of the long dimension of the house gave us magnificent views of Bankilal Muk'ta Vits (Senior Big Mountain) to the north and the Grijalva Valley lowlands to the south.

Because the living room and bedroom were only four-by-four meters and the kitchen three-by-four meters, it was a tight squeeze for four adults and four children. We had folding cots and sleeping bags for all. Susan Tax and our daughter, Skee, slept in the kitchen; Domingo de la Torre Pérez and our two older sons, Terry and Eric, slept in the bedroom; Nan, Charlie, and I had cots in the living room, which had the fireplace. Nan and I would build a cozy fire and sit in front of the fireplace and talk after the others went to sleep. It also helped having the long covered porch in front where the children could romp and play on rainy days and I could move out a table and do interviewing in the fresh air. Toilet facilities consisted of an old-fashioned outhouse behind our field house.

Lore Colby had put up curtains of unbleached muslin that were short and allowed the Zinacanteco schoolchildren to peer curiously through the windows, and awaken us about half past six each morning. Because the children had been up since dawn at home, their parents sent them to school early, and they had a couple of hours to play marbles in the schoolyard in front of our house before the teachers summoned them for school.

We soon learned that our field house had some unanticipated logistic problems and disadvantages. Because there was no running water, we had

Domingo de la Torre Perez (or Romin Teratol) whom Nick Colby first recruited to work on our project. (Photo by Frank Cancian)

to bring all our drinking water from San Cristobal in the five-gallon jugs in which purified water is bottled in Mexico. Water for cooking and washing was either drawn from barrels that collected rain water from the tile roof of our house, or during dry periods was hauled in twenty-gallon milk cans in the Land Rover from San Cristobal.

The tile floors were cold, especially in cool, rainy weather, compared to the warmer earthen floors in the Indian homes. The fireplace did not really keep the house warm, as did the open fires placed on the floor in Zinacanteco homes. The temperatures often dropped to the low fifties, even high forties, during the night at this elevation of seventy-five hundred feet.

During rainy weather the four children naturally tracked mud into the house and onto the tile floors. My wife was forever sweeping and mopping the tile floors to remove the mud. What a contrast to the floors of packed earth of our Zinacanteco neighbors. There tracking in mud simply added

Nick Colby (right) with Romin Teratol inside our field house in Paste'.

to the earthen floor, which only needed to be swept cursorily with branches daily to be kept clean.

I was aware during the summer of 1959 that we also erred by not performing the proper Zinacanteco house rituals for the Earth Lord. Since the Earth Lord owns the earth and all its products, he needs to be compensated for the materials taken from his domain to build a house. We should have buried chickens under the center of the floor as offerings to the Earth Lord; we should have erected a household cross out in the patio as a means of communicating not only with the Earth Lord but with the Ancestral Deities as well. Finally, to properly protect the house, we should have placed a small cross on the roof.

I tried through Don Mariano to assemble the requisite number of Zina-

Moving into our field house in Paste' in the summer of 1959. Romin Teratol on back of Land Rover; Susan Tax in right front seat; Nan in front; plus our three sons on the vehicle.

canteco shamans and to make the arrangements for a house ceremony. But my efforts were unsuccessful.

Meanwhile, Nick and Lore Colby with a year of experience in the field, had made some genuine progress on their research. Using Domingo as a linguistic informant, Lore was well along on her study of Tzotzil vocabulary and grammar.

Nick, with his interests in Konrad Lorenz's ethology and his experience in bird-watching, proved to be a very astute observer of Zinacanteco behavior. He was the first to notice, using his binoculars from the balcony of his third-floor apartment in San Cristobal, how a Zinacanteco woman with a small child would invariably use her shawl to brush the sidewalk space she had been sitting on in the zocalo. Later interviewing disclosed that the purpose of this sequence of behavior was to assemble the parts of the inner soul of her infant that had been lost by her sitting on the ground

Don Mariano Hernández Zárate (or Mol Marian Sarate), cultural promoter in Paste' in 1958, who became one of my principal informants in Zinacantan.

and restore these lost parts to the tiny body. This discovery in turn led to an inquiry into the rich domain of soul concepts, one of the ethnographic keys to understanding Zinacanteco culture.

Nick also introduced me to a number of Zinacanteco households, including those of Domingo de la Torre Pérez and of Antonio Montejo Cruz, a neighbor of Domingo in Zinacantan Center, and of Lorenzo Vasquez in Nabenchauk. The latter was a compadre of Nick's. It was in these households that I began to learn the proper etiquette for drinking rituals in Zinacantan. My journal records:

> We [Nick Colby, Susan Tax, and I] took the back road around the rear of the church to reach Domingo's house. Domingo was waiting on the street for us and had already been drinking—either, Nick thought, because he was sad about the Colby departure or nervous about my arrival. . . . We first passed Antonio's house, a very large and impressive structure. Antonio is a *bankilal h'ilol*

(senior shaman), and, according to Nick, the No. 2 man in the h'ilol organization. On to Domingo's house where his mother, Pascuala, and his wife, Matal, were grinding corn in preparation for our lunch. We visited inside the house for a time, then Domingo went after a case of beer. We moved outside in the patio, sat on small chairs, and began to drink the beer and a bottle of vino de frutas [sugarcane rum with a fruit flavor]. Later on, Domingo's mother's sister, who herds the sheep, joined us, as well as did Maruch [Tzotzil for "Maria"], who is Antonio's wife, and a widow from next door. We went through the etiquette of toasting, using a single shot glass to drink the vino de frutas. Domingo served the liquor in order of rank. One says *kich'ban!* (I drink) to each person in order of rank, then drinks the shot in one gulp, spitting out a little at the end, and making a face to indicate the liquor is strong! The response of the others when one says *kich'ban!* is *ich'o!* (drink then). Beer alternated with the sugarcane rum.

These toasts were accompanied by a highly patterned bowing-and-releasing behavior. A more junior person would bow toward a more senior person who in turn would release the bow with the back of the right hand. As I was included in the bowing-and-releasing, it soon became clear to me that age was the primary determinant of who bowed to whom. I noted, however, that in the liquor serving order, all the men were served first in order of their ages, then the women were served beginning with the eldest woman present.

For his study of literacy Nick Colby had designed a questionnaire that would provide some quantitative data on Zinacanteco views about formal schooling and literacy. The questionnaire was phrased and administered in Tzotzil; the answers were given in Spanish, if the informant were competently bilingual; more rarely in a combination of Tzotzil and Spanish. The questionnaire and some of the results were published in the appendix to Colby (1966). It was a beginning attempt to utilize Tzotzil in our research operations.

Bob Laughlin also began his year of field research in October 1959. His San Cristobal headquarters were established in the third-floor Velasco apartment, which I had agreed to retain for use by members of the Harvard Chiapas Project. His early field experience was focused on an all-out effort

Left to right: Robert M. Laughlin, EZV, and Nick Colby in Chilil in the summer of 1959.

to master Tzotzil—something that I strongly encouraged and that was reinforced by Clyde Kluckhohn. Laughlin (1975:3) writes of this experience: " 'Dumb as any stone,' " my eyes weeping from the smoke, I sat in Zinacantec huts recalling in misery Clyde Kluckhohn's injunction to commit to memory 75 words a day, as streams of unintelligible and unpronounceable sound swirled around my feet."

Meanwhile, I continued with my own research program, which focused on making a map and collecting a census of the hamlet of Paste'. I was convinced that we needed to understand the basic demography and social structure of one of the large hamlets in order to make any headway at all in grasping the elements of Zinacanteco culture. It would also, I thought, complement the work that first Colby and now Laughlin were doing in the ceremonial center.

Using Domingo de la Torre Pérez as my guide and interpreter, I proceeded to visit each area of the hamlet where I made sketch maps of houses to provide basic data for the study of the settlement patterns and social structure, as well as for discovering precisely who lived in these houses as I collected the census data. Whenever possible, I interviewed residents of each area of the hamlet, and also double-checked data with Andrés Gómez Rodríguez and Don Mariano. Andrés was, of course, more useful than either Domingo or Don Mariano since they both lived in the ceremonial center rather than in Paste'.

Early in the summer the Velasco family decided it was inappropriate and unsafe for our daughter Skee, age fourteen, to live in an Indian hamlet. They invited her to move to their home in San Cristobal, and we welcomed the opportunity she had to learn more about life in town and to improve her Spanish. While the two younger children, Eric and Charlie, spent time playing marbles with the Zinacantec schoolboys, I would take Terry, age thirteen, on field journeys with me. He became interested in these data-gathering expeditions and proceeded with a project on his own—to collect information on ethno-ornithology. Using my binoculars to spot the birds and interviewing Domingo, he collected a list of the twenty birds, with their Tzotzil names, that are commonly sighted in Paste'. It was the beginning of our ornithological research in Zinacantan.

In the late afternoon of 16 July I had a memorable encounter with Andrés Gómez Rodríguez who stopped on the road just below our field house and waved to me. To continue from my journal:

> He was looped to the gills coming back from San Cristobal. With him were his wife and infant daughter, who was born on June 20, and Manuel López Chiku' and his wife. He shouted for Don Juan and asked if I would come to visit him now. Domingo suggested they really wanted a ride home, so I went down to drive them out to the rim. Discovered that he had had the baby baptized in the cathedral in San Cristobal in the morning, with Manuel and his wife serving as godparents. Andrés kept calling Manuel *kumpale* (Tzotzil for "compadre"). Manuel was also drunk but not as far along as Andrés who was obviously celebrating this baptismal occasion. . . . At the end of the road, we left the Land Rover, Andrés put his arm around me, and we walked with arms over each others' shoulders all the way to the house. Upon arrival, I was im-

Andrés Gómez Rodríguez (or Telesh Lotrigo) in 1958;
he later became a shaman.

mediately ushered into the house and seated on a small chair near
the fire. Present were his father-in-law, Miguel López Chiku', and
his wife, and various small children. Women were making tortillas
and cooking chicken in pots. . . . Andrés said we were going to have
something to eat, and I responded that I would eat with them with
great pleasure. Pedro López Chiku' was summoned from across
the patio, and we all sat around a small table, which was covered
with a cloth. Hot water was served in a gourd to wash our hands,
then another gourd of hot water to rinse our mouths. Then came
a stack of tortillas and chicken stewed in spicy broth and served
in individual bowls. We all ate heartily, while Andrés leaned over
me and raved about how poor he was; how he had nobody to help
him; how he wanted to build his own house so he wouldn't have
to live in his father-in-law's house; and would I loan some money

for one year to pay for the house. I was cautious and noncommittal, but did ask how much it would cost to build a house. . . . He said about 500 pesos, but if I would loan him 200 pesos, it would help. Finally, he said "say yes or no," and I said I couldn't because of my own large family and our expenses. He understood, I think, but was really too drunk for me to really tell. After the meal, he said he was saving the bottle of wine I had brought him [on a previous occasion], and now we were going to finish it together. The bottle was brought out with a shot glass, and we went through the toasting and bowing-and-releasing behavior. . . . I then left, but Andrés and Manuel insisted on walking all the way back to the car with me (about half a mile), again Andrés and I walking with our arms around each other. Andrés hated to see me leave, tried to prolong the conversation as long as possible. At least, it was good white wine with the chicken!

I later realized that I had passed up a golden opportunity for closer rapport with Andrés during this encounter. The social event to which I was invited on that evening was not an ordinary Zinacanteco supper, but was an important ritual meal that always follows a baptism (Vogt 1990: 85–86). By Zinacanteco custom all of the adults invited to eat at the ceremonial table automatically become compadres and comadres with one another in the system of *compadrazgo* that is practiced in Zinacantan. Andrés had obviously tried to enter into a co-father relationship with me, and I had not been knowledgeable nor insightful enough to sense what was happening. Further, I had taken an unnecessarily hard line against loaning him money. He had only asked for sixteen dollars in our money to help him build his own home at a crucial time in his life when he was attempting to move out of his father-in-law's house and have more privacy and more independence. Fortunately, I overcame this gaffe with Andrés in succeeding years, but I am certain I would have learned the basic ethnography of Paste' more quickly had I been more perceptive on that July evening.

My mapping and census-taking procedures were proceeding apace, and I felt I was getting some comprehension of the various levels of social organization in the hamlet. I found that the patrilocally extended family was the most common arrangement for the basic domestic group. A series of these extended families composed a localized patrilineage, a unit that I call a *sna*.

For example, one patrilineage would be referred to by the Zinacantecos as Sna Akovetik (the houses of the Wasp Nests), another as Sna Ok'iletik (the houses of the Coyotes).

The snas, or patrilineages, were grouped around a sacred water hole whose name provided the social label for this group of patrilineages. For example, Bik'it Vo' (Little Water Hole) was the water hole group of three patrilineages called the Wasp Nests, The Coyotes, and the Liars, all of whom drew their water from this water hole. The next largest social unit was the hamlet, in this case Paste', containing six water hole groups (Vogt 1969: 176; 1990).

I was also attempting to acquire some comprehension of the patterns of shamanism and curing in Paste'. It was difficult even to determine the number of shamans practicing in the hamlet. Over the two summers of 1958 and 1959, the responses (when I asked) on the number of shamans in Paste' ranged from four to fourteen!

But serious trouble lay ahead for me in the paraje. On 23 July I recorded in my field journal:

This morning Andrés Gómez Rodríguez passed by our house on his way to San Cristobal, reporting that he would be back at 2 P.M. [to work with me]. I did not wait for him, but took Domingo and we went to the López Chiku' settlements confident that I could enlist someone to help me map the balance of the houses in the paraje this afternoon. But this is where the first trouble began. Pedro López Chiku', and his son, Manuel, were eating when we arrived. We greeted them, and after a few moments, Manuel brought out chairs for us to sit upon. After some preliminary chitchat, I had Domingo tell them I was making a map of the houses in the paraje in connection with my studies and wanted Manuel to help me map this part of the paraje. There ensued a long discussion, the gist of which was that people nearby were talking about how evil was going to fall on the community because I was gathering all the names of people to take back to my country, and that Pedro and his family were getting rich from the money I am paying them to disclose the names of people. While it was all right for me to visit in the sitio, nobody wanted to move outside to help me. It was clear that I had moved too fast in my mapmaking for this conservative paraje, and that

I would have to move much more cautiously from now on. There had even been talk about having a meeting in the paraje to find out what I was up to.

It was at this point that I remembered the advice of my colleague John M. Roberts, who had done extensive field research in the Pueblo of Zuni in the Southwest. Roberts found that when gossip built up against him in Zuni, the best procedure was to leave the Pueblo until the gossip died down. I decided we would spend more time in San Cristobal and less time in Paste' until the dust settled.

In the Velasco apartment in San Cristobal, I began a series of intensive daylong interviews with Domingo. The interviews proved to be enormously productive in a setting where we were not interrupted and in which Domingo could speak freely to me about the patterns of Zinacanteco culture. I could also record the interviews directly on my portable typewriter, which permitted me to collect nearly verbatim accounts.

These interviews were focused on the structure and function of the civil-religious hierarchy, called the cargo system, as well as on curing ceremonies and the Zinacanteco concepts of souls. I also collected a list of the Catholic saint images kept in the churches in Zinacantan.

By mid-July I had learned that the Zinacanteco cargo system was composed of fifty-seven positions in four ranks or levels (starting from the bottom): (1) twenty-four mayordomos and twelve mayores; (2) fourteen alfereces; (3) four regidores; (4) two alcaldes, plus one alcalde juez, a terminal cargo given an elderly man who was unlikely to make it any further in the system.

By the end of the summer I knew the names, costumes, ranks, and duties of each of the fifty-seven cargos. With Domingo's assistance I also managed to collect a complete list of the saint images and to map their locations in the three churches in Zinacantan Center: the Church of San Lorenzo, the Church of San Sebastian, and the Chapel of Esquipulas (Vogt 1969).

The interviews with Domingo on curing and other ceremonies performed by the shamans also went well. I learned that a shaman is called a h'ilol in Tzotzil, a term that means "seer" and refers to his or her ability to "see" into the mountains and communicate directly with a Totilme'il (literally, Sir Father-Madam Mother, or an androgynous ancestral deity). I also learned more about the concepts of souls, especially that every person

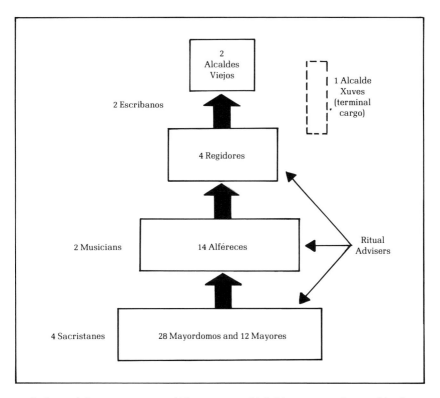

A chart of the cargo system of Zinacantan, which I began to understand in the summer of 1959.

has an inner soul of thirteen parts that is called a *ch'ulel*. This inner soul is shared with a wild animal, such as a jaguar, ocelot, coyote, or opossum. The wild animal soul, or animal spirit companion, is called a *chanul* and lives in a corral inside Bankilal Muk'ta Vits, where it is fed, watered, and generally cared for by the ancestral deities. If a person misbehaves, the ancestral deities will let his animal spirit out of the corral to wander desolately alone in the woods. Here it may be wounded or killed, thereby inflicting the same fate on its human companion (for further details see Vogt 1969b; 1976). It was evident by the end of the summer that, of all the interesting domains of Zinacanteco life, I was most intrigued by ritual and ceremony. Indeed, this became, along with an enduring interest in settlement patterns, the focus of my own research in Chiapas over the ensuing thirty years.

With the approach of the Fiesta of San Lorenzo in early August, we

The two alcaldes (top level in cargo system) standing, and the four regidores (second rank level) with black hats and staffs sitting on the bench in front of the town hall in Zinacantan Center. (Photo by Frank Cancian)

decided that it would be most efficient if Nan and the children returned to the Vogt Ranch in New Mexico for the rest of the summer while I immersed myself in the fiesta. After driving the family to Tuxtla Gutierrez to catch a 7 A.M. flight to Mexico City on 7 August, I moved into the house of Domingo de la Torre Pérez in Zinacantan Center for the duration of the fiesta. Since Domingo had been living with us in our field house in Paste', this proved to be a convenient reciprocal arrangement.

I was not the first anthropologist to live in an Indian home in Chiapas. That distinction belongs to Susan Tax Freeman who, with the assistance of the Colbys, had made close contact with Antonio Montejo Cruz's wife,

*The four regidores praying in front of Church of San Lorenzo in Zinacantan.
(Photo by Frank Cancian)*

Maruch, during her research on weaving, and was invited to move into
Antonio's house on 22 July. As Freeman (1989:90) describes her experience
in the household:

> I was invited to take up the loom myself. "You are so slow," ob-
> served Maruch, "that even your fleas are dancing with boredom."
> That every human being provides the residence for a number of
> fleas was to come true for me in that same house. At our first meet-
> ing, Maruch invited me to move in. The invitation was, I know, a
> product of the affection the couple felt for the Colbys.

During the fiesta that lasted from 7 August through 11 August while
I was living at Domingo's, just across the patio from Antonio's house, I
could keep a watchful eye on the flow of drunken activities that inevitably
accompany Chiapas fiestas and that I feared might endanger Susan.

The alfereces (third rank level in cargo system) dancing to violin and guitar music in front of Church of San Lorenzo in Zinacantan. (Photo by Frank Cancian)

Spending full time at this important summer ceremonial made an enormous difference in the level of my knowledge and understanding of the religious and social life of Zinacantan. I discovered that observations of the religious processions were an excellent check on Domingo's interview data on the cargo system. For when the cargoholders marched out to the edge of town to meet a visiting saint, the order of march displayed the ranks in the hierarchy in precise spatial terms. A cargoholder might be so drunk he could barely walk, but he NEVER marched out of order in a procession!

I also discovered a way to be certain of entering the church. From my journal on 10 August:

> At 4:15 P.M. I put another theory to an operational test. I reasoned that if I were to approach the church with a bundle of candles and go through the same ritual procedures as Zinacantecos, Chamulas, and Ladinos, I should be able to go in and right up to the altar. . . . I was tired of being discriminated against when any Cha-

mula or Ladino could freely enter. . . . I looked for the largest candles I could find, and purchased 5 of these one-peso candles in a Ladino store. I tucked them under my left arm and marched into the church, where I took off my hat, knelt and crossed myself three times on the way to the front where the candles were burning. I handed the candles to one of the Sacristans who was extremely gracious in thanking me. . . . This procedure worked so well I decided to repeat it for the Ermita of Esquipulas. . . . As a result, I had my first good look at the saints in the church of San Lorenzo and in the Ermita of Esquipulas.

I also deepened my knowledge of drinking etiquette and behavior in Zinacanteco society during the fiesta. Perhaps the most dramatic, and in some ways most frightening experience, occurred on 10 August when Antonio Montejo Cruz fell off the wagon and began to drink heavily. He struck his wife, Maruch, and terrorized the other people in his household, all of whom, including Susan Tax (Freeman 1989), were uncertain of what he might do next. After learning about these events, I recorded in my journal:

> I went to his house at 8 P.M. to take him to the fiesta. He had been drinking all day and was obviously in no mood to be told that he shouldn't drink. For the safety of Susan and others in the household, I decided the only possible strategy was to take him out, drink him under the table, and bring him home and put him to bed—which I proceeded to do. . . . Susan went with us and we also took along the two visiting Ixtapanecos—the Sacristan who had come to look after the visiting saint from Ixtapa, and the flute player. Fortunately, Antonio had not taken any money, a fact which gave me some control over what we drank, so we stuck to beer. We ordered the first round in Juan's store, and after we started drinking I told Susan to go on home and go to bed. . . . Antonio asked about her later, but I explained she was tired of walking around the fiesta all day and had gone to bed.

After the first round of beers, we made our way to the merry-go-round where Antonio decided he wanted to ride. We climbed on the horses and, at my insistence, rode twice to take up more time. Next came two more rounds of beers in another bar; then off to the Ladino dance that was being held on the front porch of the Cabildo to the music of a marimba. The only Zinacantecos present were dancing on the ground in front of the Cabildo, but Antonio boldly attempted to dance with a Ladina woman. He was completely rebuffed by both the men and the women, whereupon we went to yet another bar for two more rounds of beers. At this point, Antonio suggested we return home, but I insisted we have a third beer. After which Antonio wanted to return to the Ladino dance, but I responded that I was going to the church and pray, which I did for the salvation of Antonio! Fortunately, he followed me and also prayed. I was then finally in position to lead him home to his wife and we put him to bed. I later learned that before he went to sleep, Antonio had thrown around some more chairs, but fortunately no one had been hurt. It had been a wild night in Zinacantan that had all too clearly displayed the lines of tension between the Indians and Ladinos and the stress felt by an Indian like Antonio who had aspirations to participate socially in Ladino life (see Freeman 1989 for additional details on this episode).

On the following morning my drinking experiences continued. I was awakened at six by the compadres of Domingo and Matal who had been their guests during the Fiesta of San Lorenzo. The compadres were leaving the house next door in which they had stayed. I heard the compadre softly calling from outside: "Mi li'ote kumale?" (Are you there co-mother?), to which Matal, who was already baking tortillas, responded "Li'one kumpale" (I am here co-father). The woman of a household is always addressed first since it is assumed she is always at home. The compadre continued: "Mi li' li kumpale Romin?" (Is co-father Domingo there?), to which Matal responded "Li'e" (He is here) The compadre then addressed Domingo: "Mi li'ote kumpale?" to which Domingo, who was just awakening with a hangover, replied "Li'one. Ochan tal kumpale" (I am here. Come on in, co-father.)

At this point the compadres and their children entered the house; the husband was given a small chair by the fire, while the wife knelt near Matal. When the compadre presented a liter of *posh* (Tzotzil for sugarcane rum; literally, medicine) to Domingo, I knew I was in for an early morning drinking ritual. I climbed out of my sleeping bag and joined the men by the fire as Domingo began to pour and serve the liquor. One always hopes for coffee to begin the day in Zinacantan, but that morning it was very strong posh presented to express appreciation for the hospitality the compadres had received during the fiesta. Since I was the eldest male present, I had to go through the proper toasting and bowing-and-releasing behavior and down the first shot of liquor. The serving order went down the age hierarchy of males present, then Domingo served each of the women in rank order. As the younger bowed to and were released by the older participants, all dressed in their colorful Zinacanteco costumes, the scene began to resemble a flock of tropical birds engaging in exotic greeting behavior.

At the end of the first liter, which was carefully served in three rounds, following the proper etiquette, Domingo produced a second liter to present to his compadre. The toasting and bowing-and-releasing continued as the compadre served this bottle of the posh. Finally, about eight A.M. Matal served a breakfast of tortillas, beans, and coffee, after which I staggered out of the house to observe a procession of cargoholders marching by. As I watched them march in strict rank order toward Kalvaryo (loan word from Spanish "Calvary"), I looked up and saw the impressive sacred mountain called Sisil Vits (Santa Cecilia Mountain). Perhaps it was the influence of the sugarcane rum, but, for the first time, this sacred mountain above Kalvaryo, which I learned later is believed to be the meeting place of all the ancestral gods of Zinacantan, looked exactly like an ancient Maya pyramid. It occurred to me that there must be some conceptual relationship between these sacred mountains that are the homes of their ancestral deities and the steep-sided pyramids in the classic Mayan ceremonial centers of the ancestors of the contemporary Zinacantecos.

As the end of the field season approached, I reflected on the progress we had made, and I especially appreciated the work of the Colbys and of Susan Tax, the first to live with an Indian family.[3] From Lore Colby we had the first Tzotzil dictionary, which she had compiled during the year.[4]

Nick Colby not only broke new ground for us by employing our first steady informant, but also by establishing a warm working relationship with the families of Domingo de la Torre Pérez and of Antonio Montejo Cruz in Zinacantan and with the Leopoldo Velasco Robles family in San Cristobal. The results of his field research became a Ph.D. thesis (1960a) and a monograph (1966).[5]

It had been a good season, and as I returned to my fall term teaching duties at Harvard, I began to prepare for another field trip to Chiapas during the spring term of 1960.

5 /
FIELDWORK
SABBATICAL:
SPRING 1960

When McGeorge Bundy was dean of the faculty at Harvard, the late Clyde Kluckhohn persuaded him that anthropologists were different from other academics in that, for essential professional reasons, they needed a semester off between the normal sabbaticals, occurring every seven years, to go into the field. During the spring term of 1960 I was granted one of these fieldwork sabbaticals to return to Chiapas for another six months of research. Further, I had arranged to read term papers for my courses in advance of Christmas 1959 so that I did not have to be in residence at Harvard for the examination period in late January 1960.

Since the annual meetings of the American Anthropological Association were to take place in Mexico City at the end of December, I wrote my first article on the Chiapas research during the fall term and left for Mexico immediately after Christmas to present this paper. Entitled "Some Aspects of Zinacantan Settlement Patterns and Ceremonial Organization," the article laid out the basic settlement patterns of the municipio with its ceremonial center and its outlying hamlets, subdivided into patrilineages and water hole groups. I also described the movements of personnel and sacred objects from the hamlets into the center, and added the outrageous hypothesis that perhaps the classic Maya centers were organized to some extent along these same lines. The paper (Vogt 1961) stirred up a spirited controversy among Mayan archaeologists over the ensuing three decades about the nature of ancient Maya social and political organization. I had suggested that perhaps most of the ancient Maya also lived in outlying hamlets and that the ceremonial centers were used mainly for performances of rituals by rotating cargoholders. A few archaeologists thought my hypothesis had merit, but most argued that the Maya elite were permanently established in the ceremonial centers and that the hamlets were occupied by rural peasants who cultivated the maize and performed the manual labor necessary for building the centers. The debate still continues (see Vogt 1983; Vogt In press for details).

Upon arrival in Chiapas I moved into the home of Don Leopoldo Velasco Robles as a headquarters in San Cristobal. Since our children were in school, the family could not accompany me on this field trip. Further, Don Leopoldo's eldest daughter, María del Socorro, was living in our house in Weston, Massachusetts, for a six-month period to enroll in English classes at Harvard. It was a comfortable reciprocal arrangement for all concerned, as well as being excellent practice for my Spanish and learning more about the life of the Ladinos in San Cristobal. Don Leopoldo (hereinafter Don Polo as he is called by all who know him) had just finished his first of three years as the presidente municipal of San Cristobal and was a gold mine of information about local politics.

In the field I lived either in our field house in Paste' or, during fiestas in Zinacantan center, I stayed in Domingo de la Torre Pérez's home as I had in the previous summer. These arrangements significantly deepened my ethnographic experience in Zinacantan and added to my speaking control of Tzotzil.

Since I arrived in the field immediately after the anthropology meetings in Mexico City, the first few weeks brought a number of visitors (who had attended the meetings) on to Chiapas, including Professor John Adair, my former colleague from the Southwest, Professor Stephen F. de Borhegyi, and Professor Julian Pitt-Rivers and his first wife, Margot, who later did field research for the University of Chicago project in the lowland town of Chiapilla on the Grijalva River.

STUDYING THE WINTER CEREMONIALS IN ZINACANTAN

My own field research during January was focused on the winter ceremonials that occur annually in Zinacantan Center. The month following the winter solstice is, by all odds, the most complex ceremonial period during the entire year. Beginning with the period extending from before Christmas through the Day of Kings (6 January) and ending with the major winter fiesta of San Sebastian (20 January), more time and energy are devoted to ritual in Zinacantan than in any other month. When I think about all this ceremonial activity, I am always reminded of the complex ceremonies that cluster around and follow the winter solstice in the southwestern pueblos; for example, the Shalako and succeeding ritual activities in the pueblo of Zuni. There is no doubt in my mind about the crucial importance of the solstices in the ritual life of the American Indian.

For the Fiesta of the Day of Kings I moved into the house of Domingo de la Torre Pérez (hereinafter Romin Teratol, which he is always called in Tzotzil—Domingo equals Romin and de la Torre equals Teratol) in order to be present for all of the episodes of the ritual. The most distinctive ritual performance during this fiesta has been variously called a "ritual bullfight" (Vogt 1969), a "mock bullfight" (Bricker 1973), or a "drama of ritual aggression" (Vogt 1976) and consists of a humorous dance drama that clearly expresses many of the lines of tension in Zinacanteco life (such as the relation between husbands and wives, the relation between young and old, and the complex relationships between compadres). The bull appears to be a symbol of social disorder, which is eventually overcome and order restored as the bull is ritually killed (Vogt 1976).

During my first interviews about this dance drama in 1960 Romin Teratol denied any sexual symbolism except for women lifting their skirts to keep the bull from attacking their husbands. I added in my journal:

> but to my Freudian mind, the whole thing is full of sexual symbolism. The men [with their stick horses] look as if they are dancing with enormous penises, and stroking the penises with rattles, while the women hold them almost as if the penises were inserted in their vaginas. In addition, I noted from time to time the "husbands" danced with their arms around their "wives," and that sometimes they reached around and grabbed their "wives'" buttocks. . . . I could not unfortunately understand the jokes made by the dancers, but they were probably at least partly obscene sexually, judging from the hilarious response from the audience. . . . The whole thing must fit together in some kind of fertility rite or rite of rebirth at the beginning of the year.

From this first season of observation of this ritual I have been impressed by the natural manner in which Zinacanteco children gather to observe

The household of Romin Teratol where I lived during the winter ceremonials of 1960 in Zinacantan Center. Here Romin's wife, Matal (with her son Juan, or Shun, on her back), grinds maize for the morning meal of tortillas and beans. (Photo by Frank Cancian)

this sexually explicit dance drama. The audience is always full of hundreds of children, laughing uproariously at what would certainly be an X-rated performance in our society.

Shortly after this Fiesta of the Day of Kings, Romin Teratol arrived in San Cristobal for interviews and related a hair-raising experience with his wife's recent illness, which Bob Laughlin thought was probably an epileptic seizure. But Romin and his family interpreted the episode quite differently. As I wrote in my journal:

> About 10 P.M. Matal awoke shouting and then was stiff and quiet. Romin summoned his mother who came and shouted "Come back!" in both of her ears. According to Romin, she was actually dead for over half an hour. . . . Later they called the midwife to come and look at her. She pronounced that it had nothing to do

The performers in the ritual "bullfight" with their stick horses. (Photo by Frank Cancian)

with the imminent arrival of her baby. They then went to see an h'ilol, and he reported that it might have to do with the Earth Lord possessing her inner soul, the soul having been sold to the Earth Lord by people who are envious of Romin's family.

More than any other early event in my Chiapas experience this episode brought home the importance of inner souls and the ways in which the living interact with the dead. It became clear that the crucial interaction between Zinacantecos is not between personalities, as we view it, but between people's inner souls, and the concept extends to the interaction between people and deities, between people and objects (that also have souls), and between the living and the dead. I was also reminded of the institutionalized envy that permeates these Mayan communities.

For the Fiesta of San Sebastian I again lived with Romin's family. By this time Bob Laughlin, who was also present for the fiesta, appeared in full Zinacanteco regalia. I appeared partly dressed as a Zinacanteco, that is, with a chamarra and kerchief, but with blue jeans and Ladino style hat. We decided this was appropriate for each of us since Bob's Tzotzil was by this time far more fluent than mine.

With Romin's house as my base I had my first look at the day and night activities of this important winter ceremonial. San Sebastian's day in the Catholic calendar is 20 January, but this ceremony lasts nine days, from 17 January, when the mayordomos renew the flowers on their house altars, until 25 January, when the great alcalde transfers symbols of his authority to his successor. The ceremony has some unusual features, perhaps the most remarkable being that the major costumed performers are the cargoholders who have officially finished their year of service, but who must perform throughout this ceremony before they complete their duties. Sacred objects are brought into the center from various hamlets, including a highly sacred drum that symbolizes the New Year and is played for some of the dances, and a jousting target and a lance used for a jousting pantomime.

The ceremony appears to have some slight connection with the myth of the slaying of Saint Sebastian as told in Catholic theology, but it has obviously developed an accretion of many additional complex elements. It is an end-of-year ceremony with a riot of role reversals and inversions; it provides an annual commentary on the history and structure of ethnic conflict in the Chiapas Highlands, with the appearance of costumed fig-

The black-faced Black-Men with their stuffed squirrels and iguanas
performing at the Fiesta of San Sebastian in January. (Photo by
Frank Cancian)

The two K'uk'ulchon, or Feathered-Serpents, with ears of maize in the mouths of their headdresses, and other performers, at the Fiesta of San Sebastian. (Photo by Frank Cancian)

ures representing Feathered Serpents, Moctezumas, Spanish Conquerors, Lacandons, and Blackmen, as well as on the plant and animal world, with the appearance of Jaguars and Tree Mosses. I now think that some of the sequences may even derive from the activities of the twins in the famous *Popul Vuh* or its equivalent narrative told by the ancestors of the Zinacantecos. (For ethnographic details see Vogt 1969, 1976, 1990; Bricker 1973, 1983.)

Like most American Indian ceremonies, much of the ritual activity occurs at night during the Fiesta of San Sebastian. From Romin's house I proceeded to locate these nocturnal ceremonies. I was determined, among other things, to get my first look at the highly sacred drum called the T'en-T'en. I knew from Manuel Zabala's information that it was the most sacred object in all of Zinacantan and that it was a small slit drum of the type called a *teponaztle*. My journal adds:

Manuel Zabala had an invitation to accompany the group bringing the jousting target into the Center, so I decided to look for the

group connected with the T'en-T'en. After visiting several court-
yards on this dark night, I finally found a house with two Jaguars
and several black-faced dancers outside, and I knew this was it.
After walking by several times in the dark, I finally screwed up my
courage, and without an invitation, walked into the middle of the
patio as if I had been invited and belonged there. There was much
praying inside, and the group of assistants outside was very quiet. I
began to talk with two of the men on the outside of the group, and
displayed some knowledge that I already knew who the various
costumed figures were. The group was just on the point of leaving
this house to proceed to another one. One of the men invited me to
go along, and I was on my way to seeing the sacred T'en-T'en . . .
which was on an altar with an arch of pine tree tops and red geraniums . . . copal incense was thick in the air, white candles burned,
musicians played a violin and guitar, and many of the performers
danced in front of the altar. . . . As the liquor flowed, the dancing
became more spirited. . . . As the evening progressed, the music
was so compelling, especially the enchanting *Bolomchon,* I could
hardly keep myself from dancing.

Among the dancers were the Blackmen and Jaguars dancing with the
stuffed squirrels:

[They would] hold two [squirrels] up and simulate intercourse, or
would throw one over towards the fire where the women and children were and then come up and whip the squirrel with a whip,
making comments which made the audience roar. The Jaguars
used the "bull's penis" [carved from wood] on the squirrels after
they were tossed on the ground. One of these intromissions was
so damned realistic with the bull penis trembling as it entered the
squirrel!

Bricker (1973) later discovered that the squirrels being whipped represented delinquent cargoholders who stayed at home and had intercourse
with their wives instead of tending to their sacred ceremonial duties.
   In retrospect I am pleased with how much information we managed
to collect on the Fiesta of San Sebastian during this 1960 season. With
Bob Laughlin, Manuel Zabala, and I independently observing different

sequences of the ritual behavior, we were able to understand the basic outlines of the ceremony and to describe many of the episodes in some detail.
I also had some thoughts about the possible significance of the fiesta that
later became important in interpreting this ceremonial:

> It is worth noting that civil and religious officials become so com-
> pletely intertwined that it becomes impossible to differentiate the
> two—here we have the six policemen dancing as black-faced gods
> or phantoms for the sacred T'en-T'en drum in a completely reli-
> gious context! One possible line of explanation is to assume that
> this whole ceremony in some sense recapitulates Zinacantan cul-
> tural history (legendary and more factual). Could it be that the
> original Maya gods came in the form of Jaguars and Black-faced
> gods or phantoms of some kind? . . . Then comes later the Plumed
> Serpent who arrives from the Aztecs and brings the T'en-T'en; then
> come the Spaniards ushered in by the various costumed performers.
> But who are the White Heads, the Lacandons, and the Spanish-
> Moss Wearers—all purely fanciful perhaps, but what does it mean?
> (19 January 1960)

Our largest gap in the data was that we were still unable to understand
the spoken dialogue carried on by the costumed performers—a gap that
was later filled with the field research of Victoria Bricker (1973).

By February Bob and Mimi Laughlin had managed to rent a Zinacanteco house in the center and were becoming more and more embedded in
the flow of life, especially as Bob's control of Tzotzil improved.

FIELD EXPERIENCES WITH ARCHAEOLOGISTS

During the 1960 season the University of Chicago project was interested in
doing some archaeological work in Zinacantan. I assisted as best I could
with this plan, since I was also eager to know more about the prehistory
of the municipio. Professor Robert McC. Adams (now serving as secretary
of the Smithsonian Institution) arrived with one of his graduate students,
Edward Calnek, and I took them to visit Zinacantan Center and to Paste'
to observe the settlement patterns and to try to locate evidence of prehis-

toric sites. From all indications in the Spanish documents, it was probable that the prehistoric Zinacantan center was located where it is now. Calnek decided to try to obtain permission from the presidente municipal to under-take excavations in the center. Bob Laughlin and I advised him to spend some time at the Cabildo getting acquainted with the Zinacanteco officials before he asked for formal permission. Calnek dutifully spent many days informally talking with the officials, but when he finally presented his re-quest, the answer was "no." Furthermore, we discovered that gossip in the municipio about his plans to excavate had built up to such an extent that the shamans of Zinacantan held a special ceremony to block the vision of the archaeologist so that he would be unable to find anything. The ritual also included prayers to block the vision of the Laughlins who were living in Zinacantan Center at the time. Bob Laughlin reports that "somehow the blame was transferred to me. We could hear the shamans at San Kishto-val [mountain] praying to close our eyes! Romin notified us and fled. We holed up in our house for several days before daring to venture out and cross our neighbors' yards to reach the road" (Personal communication, 1 August 1991). It was obviously not a fruitful approach to obtaining an archaeological digging permit from the local Indian authorities, and it was more than a decade later before we managed to carry out an archaeological survey in Zinacantan (McVicker 1972). Calnek ultimately published his interesting thesis using historical sources (1988).

My other archaeological experience in the 1960 season was much more successful. My colleague Professor Gordon R. Willey and I had been col-laborating for some years at Harvard where we taught joint lecture courses on the peoples and cultures of North and South America and offered a graduate seminar on the Maya. We decided to exchange field visits dur-ing the spring of 1960 in order to learn more about each other's research operations.

In late March I drove our Land Rover to Guatemala City stopping in Quetzaltenango to spend a night with Munro Edmonson, whom I had known as a graduate student doing field research on Spanish-American culture in the Southwest. Edmonson had finished his Ph.D. at Harvard and was teaching anthropology at Tulane University. By 1960 he had shifted his interests to the Maya area and was becoming one of the leading authorities on the Quiche-Maya of Highland Guatemala. His classic translation of the Popul Vuh (Edmonson 1971) is known to all Maya scholars.

I met Gordon Willey in Guatemala City, and we flew together to Sayax-

Left to right: William R. Bullard, Jr., Mary Ricketson, and Gordon R. Willey arriving by small plane at Sayaxche en route to the archaeological site of Altar de Sacrificios in March 1960.

che in the Petén, and from here traveled by motorboat down the Rio Pasión to the famous site of Altar de Sacrificios, located near the junction of the Rio Pasión and the large Rio Usumacinta. Gordon had been excavating Altar de Sacrificios for a number of years, and I spent a week with him at his wonderful field camp which had been set up by his efficient and congenial field director, A. Ledyard Smith.

Each day we visited the archaeological site where a large crew of Guatemalans was excavating this Maya classic center. Work stopped in the late hot afternoons, and we would go for a swim in the river, or take one of the boats and go out fishing. At sundown, Ledyard would have one of his men

Gordon R. Willey (left) and
A. Ledyard Smith at the
Peabody Museum field
camp at Altar de Sacrificios
in 1960.

cut a heart of palm for hors d'oeuvres. Then Ledyard would break out a
bottle of S. S. Pierce whiskey. He always alternated between Scotch and
bourbon. When the bottle was empty, it would be time for dinner at the
camp. We would then fall into the cots, carefully covered with mosquito
nets, for a deep sleep, broken only by the cries of howler monkeys in the
tropical night.

It was a wonderful week. I was impressed with the quality of the meticulous archaeological work and by the well-organized daily schedule. However, I found the heat of the tropical selva enervating, and was again glad
I was doing my ethnological research in the cool highlands.

After we flew back to Guatemala City, Gordon and I drove to San Cristobal for a visit at my field site before continuing our joint travels back to
Boston. The Velascos kindly invited Gordon to stay in their house, so we
had comfortable headquarters in San Cristobal. I drove Gordon to Chamula, to Zinacantan Center, and to Paste' to observe our field operations.
I recall that Gordon, who was used to the systematic daily schedules of an

*Gordon R. Willey (left) and EZV at the field laboratory for the
excavations at Altar de Sacrificos in 1960.*

archaeological field camp, being rather uncomfortable with the constant
changes and demands of ethnological research in which one has to adapt
flexibly to, for example, a sudden evening request (just at dinner time) of
an informant for a ride to Zinacantan Center to locate a shaman to perform a curing ceremony for a sick child. Organized daily schedules are
simply not possible as they are in archaeological work. Gordon himself
recognized all this in a recent comment: "I would have made a poor ethnologist. I have often thought archaeologists and ethnologists have gone
on their different career ways because of their different temperaments. . . .
Nevertheless, ethnologists and archaeologists can learn from each other"
(Willey 1989: 30).

En route to Boston we stopped in Mexico City where we called upon
Dr. Ignacio Bernal. I recall a wonderful visit with him in his office at the
Instituto Nacional de Antropología e Historia, after which he took us to
his private club for lunch. I was delighted to see him again, especially as

he was such a lively and witty person. He later became Dr. Alfonso Caso's successor as the leading anthropologist in Mexico.

CONFERRING WITH NEW
GRADUATE STUDENTS

Back at Harvard I conferred at length with the two talented graduate students I had selected to replace Bob Laughlin in the field: Frank Cancian and Francesca Cancian. Frank was a student in social anthropology, Franzi (as she is called by all who knew her) a student in sociology. Both had taken courses with me, including a Maya seminar and were an ideal pair for Chiapas.

Frank had taken his A.B. in anthropology at Wesleyan University, where he studied with David McAllester, and had done summer fieldwork among the western Apache. He also spent a year on a Fulbright in Italy, where he did research in a southern Italian community. Frank spoke some Spanish, was a skilled photographer, and was interested in making a detailed study of the cargo system in Zinacantan, a subject I was most eager to have explored.

Franzi was an undergraduate at Reed College when I first met her in the spring of 1957, when my family and I spent the night in Portland with David and Kay French, Dave being professor of anthropology at Reed. Following dinner, Dave French suggested I might be interested in attending an evening seminar taught by his colleague Professor John Pock. He explained that two students just happened to be discussing my two works on Navaho veterans and modern homesteaders at the seminar! He suggested I leave on my travel clothes, sit with him in the rear of the room, and listen anonymously to the discussion. It was perhaps the most illuminating experience in my academic career—like looking through a one-way mirror at bright students taking my two books apart. At the end of the discussion, Professor Pock quietly announced that Dave French's guest in the rear of the room was none other than Evon Vogt from Harvard. The students did a doubletake, but quickly recovered, and over the homemade beer that used to be brewed at Reed College, the discussion went on until midnight. One of the bright students discussing my works was Franzi (the other was Volney Stefflre), and I, of course, urged them both to apply to Harvard for graduate work.

When Franzi arrived at Harvard she worked intensively with Talcott Par-

Robert M. Laughlin (left) and Gordon R. Willey beside the Harvard Chiapas Project Land Rover in the Highlands of Chiapas in April 1960.

sons on theory and with Robert F. Bales on studying interactions in small groups. Her project for Zinacantan would be an attempt to use the Bales approach to study families as small groups in a field setting.

I was somewhat concerned when I first selected Frank and Franzi that two unmarried students would be asked to share the same field headquarters apartment in San Cristobal. Fortunately, their friendship as graduate students grew into a romance and they were married on 30 October 1959; after one more year of course work they arrived in Chiapas to begin their field research in September 1960.

Unlike Frank, Franzi knew French and German, but no Spanish. We urged her to spend her time learning Tzotzil instead of Spanish, a decision that paid off handsomely, as she became quite fluent in Tzotzil after a few months in Chiapas. At first, Frank handled the Spanish for both of them.

Frank Cancian and Francesca M. Cancian (standing) with four of their Zinacanteco assistants and interviewers: (left to right) Guillermo Pérez Nuh, José Hernández Pérez (also called Chep Apas), José Hernández Nuh, and Manuel Pérez. (Photo by Frank Cancian)

Eventually she did learn sufficient Spanish to run their household in San Cristobal and to carry on visiting conversations, but over the years her control of Tzotzil continued to be impressive.

FIELD RESEARCH IN THE HAMLET OF PASTE'

After a few weeks at home with the family over Easter, I returned to Chiapas to continue field research, especially in the hamlet of Paste'. During May and June I spent most of my time living in the field house in Paste'. But I was able to make some arrangements that improved my rapport with the community and my potential for gathering ethnographic data. At the suggestion of Bob Laughlin, who had spent time with the Akov extended family, I approached Juan de la Cruz Akov (hereinafter Shun Akov) who was affiliated with Mariano Zárate as the secretary of the ejido committee and who lived near the school. By now I had learned to use the same strategy to ask for favors that the Zinacantecos use with one another. My journal records:

> I met him [Shun Akov] coming down to the school and suggested we return to his sitio and talk. . . . After we sat down, I pulled out a small bottle of posh and gave it to him. After he poured, and we drank the first shot, I told him that I needed somebody to work for me in Paste' and that Lol [Bob Laughlin] had recommended him. . . . I offered him 60 pesos a week during May, June, and July for the weeks that he works. It was understood that he might not always be able to hire somebody else to cultivate his corn and have to be away in hot country. . . . I said that when we worked in Paste', he would be eating at home, but that when we went to San Cristobal or elsewhere, then I would pay for his meals. . . . After some more shots of posh, I asked if I could get my meals in his father's house when I am living in Paste', and that I would pay 4 pesos a day for the food, 1 peso more than Lol paid, because I eat meat, and Lol doesn't. He said that was fine and he would tell his father about it.

The meals in Dionicio Akov's house were nutritious—beans and tortillas three times a day—but monotonous. I shall never forget the evening when, after ten days of the same menu, one of the women in the household came home with some delicious mushrooms she had gathered in the woods.

What was more important to me was the opportunity to interact with a Zinacanteco family each day in a context in which I could practice my Tzotzil and learn more about their everyday culture. When he was home Shun often joined me in his father's house while I was eating my evening meal and we would exchange information about our respective cultures. I remember one evening when I described hunting patterns in our society, and added that sometimes people in our society shoot cows or people by mistake on these hunting trips. As I wrote in my journal: "Shun found this hard to believe. He pointed out that you could even tell the difference among deer, rabbits, and sheep in the night by the color that is reflected from their eyes when a flashlight is shone on them—deer's eyes are blue, rabbit's red, and sheep's white. (These Zinacantecos are really sharp!)"

Shun Akov proved to be an excellent informant. He worked with me to complete the census of the hamlet and of each water hole group within the hamlet. By making walking trips together to different parts of the paraje, I quietly made a sketch map of the houses. Then, back at the field house, Shun would list for me the people who lived in each house. The total came to twelve hundred, a figure very close to that reported later in the official 1960 Mexican census.

This made me reflect about the problem of size in anthropology. Most of us are trained to work in small populations. My previous research had been focused on communities such as the Ramah Navaho (population 600) and Fence Lake, New Mexico, (population 232). Now I was dealing with a population of more than eight thousand in Zinacantan as a whole and where even the single hamlet of Paste' was double the population of the Ramah Navaho. One could never hope to become acquainted with the whole community in the same way.

PARTICIPATING IN LINEAGE AND WATER HOLE CEREMONIES

During the first part of May I spent most of my time attending and observing for the first time the ceremonials in Paste' that are called K'in Krus and that are performed on, or near, the Day of the Cross (3 May) in the Catholic calendar. K'in is a Tzotzil word that means "fiesta" to the contemporary Zinacantecos, but significantly it is derived from an ancient Maya word that means "Sun," "Day," "Time." These ceremonies are traditionally performed for lineages and for water hole groups in each hamlet.

I had originally thought there was only one Kalvaryo in Zinacantan, the one in the ceremonial center where the council of gods meets and which figures so prominently in ceremonies there. But that May I discovered there was a Kalvaryo for each water hole in Paste'. Later I found that there are hundreds of Kalvaryos in Zinacantan, one for each water hole and each sna (lineage). My journal adds on 17 May:

Today I discovered that even I have a Kalvaryo, and didn't know it before. The cross shrine on the hill just above the school is the Kalvaryo for the school, hence also for my house and for Don Mariano's house. Here is where our *totilme'iletik* (ancestors) have their meetings and where we must pray to them and offer candles through the good services of one or more shamans in K'in Krus ceremonies. It is interesting that the word *Calvario* (calvary) where Christ was crucified outside Jerusalem should have been selected to apply to the principal ancestral shrines of the Zinacantecos. I would like to know what the aboriginal word was for these shrines.

While most of the lineage shrines are erected on nearby mountains and designated as Kalvaryos, some are erected in caves and defined as means of communication with the Earth Lord.

Since the ceremony is repeated at the end of the rainy season in October, it appears to have little to do with the Christian concept of the cross. Christ and the crucifixion are not mentioned. The ceremonial appears to be a symbolic expression of the rights that members of the lineages have to the lands they inherited from their patrilineal ancestors. The rituals for these ancestral patrons not only pay respect to these deities, but also link together the descendants as common worshippers and members of the same sna, In this way the ceremony symbolizes the unity of the sna as a socially significant unit of Zinacanteco society.

I also learned that each water hole group maintains a series of cross shrines for its water hole. One of these shrines is at the side of the water hole; another is on a mountain or hill above the water hole and is designated as the Kalvaryo for the whole water hole group. At this Kalvaryo the water hole group's ancestors are believed to assemble and hold meetings to survey the affairs of their descendants and await the semiannual offerings in the K'in Krus for the water hole. The ceremony is performed by all of the shamans that live in the water hole group. It follows the same pattern as the ceremonies for the snas, except that before the opening ritual meal the men assemble to clean out the water hole, repair fences around the openings, and fix up the cross shrines. During the ceremonial circuit, ritual is performed at the water hole, at the houses of the mayordomos, and at the Kalvaryo where the ancestors are waiting for their gifts.

The ceremony appears to express the rights that members of the water hole group have to draw water from their water hole and their obligations to care for it properly. Control of rights to water is crucial for human and animal life in the Chiapas Highlands, especially during the long dry season from October to May when supplies of water are strictly limited. Just as the K'in Krus for the sna expresses rights in land, so the K'in Krus for the water hole group expresses rights in water. By including rituals for the deities associated with the water hole, the ceremony links together all the snas that compose the water hole group, and hence symbolizes the unity of the water hole group as another structurally significant unit in Zinacanteco society. (For details see Vogt 1969, 1976, 1990).

On 2 and 3 May I was invited to attend one of these K'in Krus ceremonies for the most important water hole in the hamlet. From my journal:

> My involvement . . . began at 9 A.M. on May 2 when I presented two dozen cohetes [skyrockets] and six 50-centavo candles at the house of the Senior Mayordomo, and ended at 1 A.M. on May 3. The ceremony was not over—I just couldn't take it any longer after 16 hours of posh, processions, and chilling cold. But during these 16 hours I had a deeper and more complete look at ceremonial life in Paste' than I have ever had before. As is by now usual for research in Zinacantan, things are more complex than I anticipated.

I was enormously pleased with my reception at the ceremony. To continue from my journal:

> Rapport could not have been better. During the entire time there was nothing but warmth, respect, and at times even gentleness in relations with me. I decided that the countless visits, Land Rover rides, and meals we had served to people had at last paid off. I am no longer a stranger in Paste'. . . . [When I arrived] I was offered a chair, and served atole. . . . I was included in all the rounds of drinks. . . . I was given a special chair and fed at the table with the h'iloletik and Mayordomos. When I looked cold during the night, Manuel Vasquez Shulhol brought me an extra chamarra to wear. . . . People sought me out to talk with me all during the night. I had never met the No. 1 h'ilol before, but he went out of his way to be friendly and include me in the proceedings.

During this long night there were a few memorable incidents that I shall never forget. One was the ritual episode at the Kalvaryo:

> Never have I seen a wilder scene, calculated to warm the heart and excite the interest of the most romantic anthropologist. The candles were burning, lighting up the cross with its pine and flower deco-

rations. Copal incense was thick in the air, the wind was blowing, and cohetes were being shot off periodically. The drums and flutes were playing, and the two kneeling shamans were praying like mad, periodically placing their foreheads flat on the ground. I tried to pick up the words to the prayer, but the only thing I heard clearly was Vashakmen—the third type of gods which we know virtually nothing about except that they miraculously built the church of San Sebastian in one night.

I also recall how the highest ranking shaman carried an ancient pocket watch and was forever checking his time with my watch. I was also continually asked by others what time it was. I noted in my journal that "I did not see that any of this was functional; i.e., that the ceremony went any faster or was in any way scheduled by the watches. But there does seem to be . . . a deep fascination with time as measured by the watches. I would suppose that this harks back to an ancient Maya concern with time."

At one point during the night the shamans took a long pause in the ceremonial proceedings and interrogated me about the nature of the oceans. They asked

about how wide the oceans are; are they wider or narrower than the land. When they found out that I had traveled across the Pacific, then they wanted to know if the sun is not close to the surface of the earth over there where it goes down and where it rises, for does it not seem to meet the earth? When I said no, it was just as high in the sky as it is here, they were amazed. Then they wanted to know what makes the ocean salty. How is salt born in the ocean? I tried a long geological and meteorological explanation of this, but I lost them, and they got bored and went back to performing the ceremony. But I must say they were all damned intelligent questions.

On the night of 4 May I was invited to attend the K'in Krus for the school. This ceremony had been instituted three years before when a man was struck by lightning and killed not far from the school. The residents of the hamlet decided then that they must hold this ceremony to avoid further difficulty from the Earth Lord who sends these lightning bolts to punish people. The ceremony begins at the schoolhouse with a prayer by the shamans. Then there is a ritual meal, and a visit to two crosses in a large cave nearby. The procession then returns to the Kalvaryo on the hill above the school, and ends with another ritual meal. It is funded and hosted by the three members of the school committee who collect one peso from each head of household in the hamlet.

Before the ceremony began I presented six fifty-centavo white wax candles to Don Mariano to be used in the rituals. During the beginning ritual meal in the schoolhouse, the senior shaman suggested that we use my candles to include my field house in the ceremony. I was, of course, delighted with this suggestion.

The procession went first to the cross shrines in the cave. It was here I learned that these shrines serve as channels of communication to Yahval Balamil (literally, Earth Owner), the Earth Lord who lives inside the earth and is the one who sends the lightning bolts up out of caves. The setting of the ritual performed in the cave was especially unforgettable that night. As I noted in my journal: "The situation was really beautiful, with moonlight shining down through the pines outside the cave, with the candles lighting up the crosses and the people inside the cave, and with the music playing, copal incense burning, and h'iloletik chanting their prayers."

After finishing their prayers at the Kalvaryo above the school, the shamans next proceeded to our field house. I was intensely curious as to where and how they would set up the household shrine for my house. There was no household cross outside in the patio; the floor was made of tiles, rather than of packed earth into which candles could be set in holes dug with knives in the floor. When the shamans reached the field house, they inspected the three rooms and decided to set up a shrine in the northwest corner of the dining room. Three pine tree tops were brought in and leaned against the wall, and fresh pine needles were spread on the floor. The president of the school committee, serving as a ritual helper, tied bundles of red geraniums on the pine tree tops. At the request of the shamans, I provided ten pesos to pay for two liters of posh, which Don Mariano sent a runner after. To continue from my journal:

When the first liter came, Don Mariano briefed me to give it to the senior h'ilol, saying "this is so you can see." I did so, it was graciously accepted, and placed by the crosses for a few minutes. Then the drink-pourer was summoned and he distributed the whole liter, but with great ceremony, bowing to everybody, including me to ask permission to pour, and then bowing again all around after he had poured. The h'iloletik then set up the three candles—with some difficulty because they had to stick them to the tile floor [with dripping wax]—and went through their long chant. Drums and flute played outside, the musicians [violin, harp, and guitar] sat on a wooden bench I provided and played. I felt the Harvard field house had at last been incorporated into Zinacanteco culture. It's true we don't have a rooster buried under the floor, and I don't have a small cross on top, nor a patio cross—but, at least we are making progress, little by little.

In Don Mariano's house which came next in the ritual circuit, I noted that the shamans set up the shrine in the very center, right over the rooster which had been buried under the floor. My comments on this ceremony from my journal:

It is extremely interesting how Zinacanteco culture has moved to encapsulate the school and its associated buildings—to ward off evil that might strike from Yahval Balamil, and perhaps other gods as well. . . . I began to wonder in the cave (and also in our field house where there were no crosses at all) if the aboriginal pattern was not simply puntas of juncia [pine tree tops] set up, decorated with flowers, and ocote [pitch pine] torches lighted in place of candles. In some respects, the cross is merely a solid structure on which to tie the pine and flowers! . . . Some time we must study and make a "flow chart" of posh as it flows through these ceremonies. If it were possible to measure and plot carefully the flow of posh, I will bet that some interesting regularities would emerge. I have a hunch that high status people are offered more posh but that the astute ones collect most of it in bottles and then use it to increase their status by passing it out later. Or perhaps in order for the flow to be equalized, it is necessary for high status people to collect and redistribute because they are offered it more often—not in the formal rounds, but in the informal exchanges, because on the formal rounds everybody gets a shot, including small boys.

Following these intensive days and nights of K'in Krus ceremonies, I interviewed Shun Akov about the ethnographic details of each type I had observed. In thinking about Shun's description of the ceremonies, it struck me that there is an interesting contrast in Zinacanteco culture between the relatively simple economic life, both with respect to what is produced and consumed, and especially with respect to the division of labor, and the complex ritual life. As soon as a ceremony begins, the division of labor becomes enormously complex. There are all kinds of specialists in a ceremony— nothing is left to chance, or done informally. Instead, there are shamans (all in rank order), there are one or more mayordomos serving as hosts. There is a candle-carrier, an incense-carrier, drink-pourer, cohete-shooter, drum and flute players, violin, harp, and guitar players. Special women make the atole (corn gruel) to drink. A young Zinacanteco is delegated to collect white roses; another one collects the pine tree tops. I speculated that this was a reflection of ancient Maya life in which the economic life was relatively simple, but the ritual life in the ceremonial center was enormously elaborated with all kinds of specialists, whether part-time or full-time with life tenure.

On 19 May a tragic event: the three-month old infant of Romin Teratol and Matal died of intestinal dysentery in Zinacantan Center. Romin had tried the INI clinic in Zinacantan for medicine, but the diarrhea continued. He then turned to a curing ceremony performed by Antonio Montejo Cruz; but the infant died during the ceremony. They came to see me in San Cristobal and report on the death. It was a sorrowful visit, and I offered to drive them home. To continue from my journal:

> Upon arrival, the first thing Matal did was to light a new candle for the place in the corner where the baby had died . . . she knelt and half-sobbed, half-prayed, as she pumped each of her still lactating breasts with her hands and then placed the milk on the ground in front of the burning candle, as an offering to the deceased infant. I was wondering what a nursing mother in this culture did about her milk when a baby dies, and we found out.

OTHER SUMMER EVENTS

I continued with field research in Paste' and Zinacantan Center through May, June, and early July. In early June Professor A. Kimball Romney, with whom I had worked in the Southwest and had spent a year at the Center for Advanced Study in the Behavioral Sciences at Stanford, arrived to initiate his own fieldwork in Chiapas. He had previously engaged in field research with the Mixtecs in Oaxaca, but was not acquainted with Chiapas. I devoted some days to showing him around, including driving him to Tenejapa (three and a half hours each way over muddy roads) for a look at that municipio. On another day we drove to Chilil, where we left my Land Rover and hiked into Huistan Center—two and a half hours each way—to explore that ceremonial center. He later decided to focus his research on Tenejapa where at least the municipio center was reachable by four-wheel drive vehicles.

During the summer Bob Laughlin finished his year of intensive field research. He had made enormous progress in learning Tzotzil and in how to behave in intricate situations in Zinacanteco life that required substantial knowledge of their complicated etiquette. I am not certain at what point he would describe himself as being fluent in the language, but I have always been impressed with his ability to converse freely in Tzotzil. At any rate, he reports that "after seven months of exposure to 'the boundless chaos of living speech' and with frequent recourse to Lore Colby's dictionary, I felt sufficient confidence to begin recording the folktales and myths that I hoped would reveal the wisdom of Zinacantec life" (Laughlin 1975: 3).[1]

MY FIRST JOURNEY TO EUROPE

In July I returned to Harvard to finish my paper for the International Congress of Ethnological and Anthropological Sciences that was to meet in Paris in August. It was my first trip to Europe, which may seem strange to many who have made repeated journeys there since college days. I have to confess that I was very anti-Europe in my early years; it always seemed like an oppressive, class-ridden society from which my German ancestors had successfully emigrated to a wonderful New World. I had seen parts of Latin America and parts of Asia well before this first journey to Europe.

My wife and I decided to take our four children and to spend some time traveling in Switzerland, Italy, and Spain, following the congress in Paris.

In Paris my paper, "Ancient Maya Concepts in Contemporary Zinacantan Religion," which had flowed directly out of my intensive field experience and reflections about this experience during the spring of 1960, went well, and we enjoyed our stay in Paris and in Switzerland and Rome. In Spain we went first to Barcelona, then out to Ibiza in the Balearic Islands, for a delightful stay on the Mediterranean. We traveled from Madrid to Granada and on to Sevilla.

By the end of our European journey I had completely changed my mind about Europe, and I realized what peculiar southwestern cultural lenses I had been wearing all those early years. Europe had proved to be an intensely interesting, civilized, and beautiful continent to which I have since returned repeatedly for travel and for international conferences.

On the other hand, any thoughts I had had about shifting my research operations from Chiapas to Spain were set aside. In Spain there was plenty of architectural and cultural evidence for the clash of cultures—Arabic and Spanish—but the contact had occurred centuries ago. In Chiapas the clash of cultures was still present, vivid and vibrant, for ethnologists to study on the hoof; and this contemporary encounter excited me much more.

The other decision I made by the summer of 1960, with four seasons of Chiapas fieldwork behind me, was that my original research design had been far too ambitious. There was no way I could adequately carry out the comparative studies between different types of Tzotzil and Tzeltal communities that I had projected during the five-year period ending in 1962. My subsequent yearly reports to the National Institute of Mental Health reflected this decision to proceed less ambitiously in terms of geographic scope and to concentrate our efforts on Zinacantan and, later, on the neighboring, Tzotzil-speaking municipio of Chamula.

6 /
UNDERGRADUATES
JOIN THE HARVARD
CHIAPAS PROJECT:
1960–1962

In the late summer of 1959 I received an interesting letter from Professor Charles Wagley at Columbia University informing me that he and Professor Marvin Harris had been in touch with the Carnegie Corporation of New York about an educational program of summer field research for undergraduates in Latin America. I was invited, along with Professors Alan R. Holmberg of Cornell and Joseph B. Casagrande of the University of Illinois, to attend a meeting at Columbia to plan an interuniversity field program that would involve undergraduate students from Columbia, Cornell, and Harvard. Casagrande was included since he had served for many years as a staff member of the Social Science Research Council in New York and had been instrumental in developing programs for anthropological field research.

A meeting on 23 September at the Faculty Club at Columbia set up the organization with Casagrande, Harris, Holmberg, Vogt, and Wagley serving on a board of directors. The plan was to invite undergraduates in the three universities to apply for a summer field research program, the field sites being Highland Ecuador, under the direction of Marvin Harris; the northern highlands of Peru, under the supervision of Alan Holmberg; and the Highlands of Chiapas, where I would provide the leadership. The purpose of the summer experience was (a) to expose college students to the realities of cultural contrasts and provide them with a deeper cross-cultural understanding, and (b) to encourage students to have a deeper appreciation of the goals and research procedures of the behavioral sciences. The undergraduates would be recruited from any field of study in the three universities, not just from anthropology majors alone. Six undergraduates

187

would be selected from among the applicants, and they then would be scrambled so that some Harvard students would go to Ecuador and Peru, as well as Chiapas; some Columbia students to Chiapas and Peru, as well as Ecuador, etc. Their basic transportation and living expenses would be paid by the grant from the Carnegie Corporation, which would also fund a salary for the experienced anthropologist who served as the field leader.

This was an exciting program that simply fell into my lap at just the right time, because I had wanted to include undergraduates in the field experience since the beginning of the Harvard Chiapas Project. It was hoped that the recruitment from all the fields in the universities would draw bright students into anthropology. I recall the comment of Harvard Dean McGeorge Bundy when I went to seek his approval for the program. As he signed the proposal, he commented: "Never have I seen a more cunning scheme to bend the careers of our bright undergraduates!"

Since I had plans to attend the Congress of International Anthropological and Ethnological Sciences in Paris in the summer of 1960, I persuaded Duane Metzger to serve as field leader for the first undergraduate students after I left Chiapas in mid-July. Metzger was an exceedingly bright and talented anthropologist who was a Junior Fellow in the Society of Fellows at Harvard and who already had solid field experience in Chiapas, beginning in 1956 with the University of Chicago Man-in-Nature project.

Both Metzger and I interviewed the twenty Harvard applicants and selected a number of top candidates to be recommended to the board of directors at the meeting at Columbia University in December. The final Harvard contingent consisted of seven students: George A. Collier, Jane H. Fishburne, James J. Fox, Stephen F. Gudeman, Alice Kasakoff, Naomi Quinn, and Martin G. Silverman. Of this talented group, Collier, Fishburne, and Gudeman were designated to go to Chiapas, and were joined there by William N. Binderman and Peggy Reeves from Columbia University and Henry E. York from Cornell University. Fox and Kasakoff went to Peru, and Quinn and Silverman to Ecuador.

For training during the spring term at Harvard, all of the Harvard students enrolled in a field training seminar (Social Relations 250: "Selected Problems and Methods in the Study of Latin American Ethnology") that I taught. The three headed for Chiapas were also enrolled in a Tzotzil course taught by Lore Colby. I decided not to try to struggle with the bureaucratic hurdles of obtaining official Harvard permission for this course on Tzotzil. Instead, I simply signed the three students up for "Independent Research"

The first undergraduates on the Harvard Chiapas Project, summer of 1960 at Na-Bolom. Standing (left to right): Henry York, EZV, Duane Metzger, Stephen Gudeman, William Binderman; seated (left to right): Jane Fishburne, Peggy Reeves, George Collier.

under my general supervision. This manner of handling the Tzotzil course was followed for many years, and the students always worked exceedingly hard on the language—the training included not only group sessions each week, but also individual drill, as well as work on tapes in the language laboratory. In addition, the students whose Spanish was not sufficiently fluent were required to enroll in an intensive Spanish course.

THE SUMMER OF 1960

The six undergraduates arrived in Chiapas in mid-June and moved into rooms at Na-Bolom, which was to serve as their San Cristobal headquarters. Duane Metzger and I immediately turned to the delicate operation of establishing each of them in a productive field situation in which they could work on their own research topic for the summer. I had already decided in this first year of the program that I would follow a policy of allowing the students a great deal of freedom in selecting their particular research topics. The only guide lines were that the topic had not been covered before and that the research was feasible in the field in Chiapas. Preliminary conversations with each of the students had established their general interests, but much needed to be done to make these research topics more specific and gear them to the realities of the field situations they were to encounter.

Bill Binderman from Columbia had expressed an interest in collecting oral history. His field arrangements included putting him in touch with a series of elderly Indian and Ladino political leaders who could provide their versions of the Mexican Revolution of 1910 to 1924, the topic of particular focus of his research. After a productive week of living with and interviewing Duane Metzger's principal informant, Juan Pérez, in the Tzeltal village of Aguacatenango, we took Bill to the Zinacanteco hamlet of Nabenchauk. Here, with the aid of Bob Laughlin, we had made arrangements to place him in the home of an important political leader and high-ranking shaman: Mol Shun Vaskis (Old Man Juan Vasquez). Mol Shun was a tall, stately Zinacanteco who had served as presidente municipal of Zinacantan and was one of the best-known shamans in the municipio. He was old enough to remember most of the important episodes in the Mexican Revolution as it was fought in Chiapas.

Metzger and I left Binderman at Mol Shun's house with his sleeping bag, his typewriter, and a canteen of purified water and expected him to remain in the hamlet for at least a week while he worked with the old shaman on his project. We were astonished to encounter Binderman at Na-Bolom the following day. What had happened? Mol Shun, it seems, behaved like a typical Zinacanteco. Not wishing to waste his time or Binderman's, he had insisted that Bill immediately set up his typewriter and go to work. Mol Shun started to speak in rapid-fire, broken Spanish about the revolution, and within a few hours had said all he wanted to say about the subject. In Binderman's words:

> Finally, just past noon, he said he had completed his account of the Revolution. Added that he thought he'd go back to his cornfields

tomorrow since there wouldn't be any more tale-telling. We chatted about odds and ends for a while longer, and I mentioned that I might go back to San Cristobal this afternoon. He said that was fine with him. Chatted some more and I noticed no one had shown any sign of offering me lunch. Time was 12:50 P.M. I took my cue and asked if there would be any buses passing soon. He answered that one would pass "in a little while." I said "Perhaps I'll go right now." He said that would be fine. His two granddaughters helped me carry my gear up to the road. . . . Got a ride on a truck right to the front door of Na-Bolom.

After this experience we realized we would need to keep placing Binderman with different informants who were likely to provide their accounts of the revolution in less time than we had anticipated. By the end of the summer Binderman had collected a respectable body of oral narratives and produced an interesting report on contemporary oral tradition of the Mexican Revolution.

George Collier, who had just finished his freshman year at Harvard, was fully intending to concentrate in physics before he enrolled in Clyde Kluckhohn's freshman seminar on the Navaho and later joined us for field research in Chiapas. George came from a family background that predisposed at least some of his developing interests in anthropology—his grandfather was John Collier, commissioner of Indian Affairs, during the Roosevelt years; one uncle, Donald Collier, became a noted archaeologist who specialized on Peru; a second uncle, John Collier, Jr., is a skilled photographer who has published books on American Indians.

George had expressed an interest in studying color categories among the Zinacantecos. We knew from preliminary data that the way in which Zinacantecos classify colors presented some interesting problems. For example, what we call "blue" and what we classify as "green" are labeled as one category, *yosh,* in Tzotzil; this is characteristic of all Maya speakers. But before George began his procedures to map the Tzotzil color categories, Duane Metzger and I felt he needed to immerse himself in Zinacanteco life and learn more Tzotzil. We placed him in Romin Teratol's house in Zinacantan Center where he spent a major part of the summer not only observing the daily flow of routine affairs, but also participating in curing ceremonies and experiencing the fiesta of San Lorenzo.

When he was ready to begin his work on the color categories, he was able to proceed in an effective and sophisticated manner using standardized procedures with seven informants. The result at the end of the summer was a remarkable paper on "Zinacantecan Color Categories." In retrospect, I am also impressed with the wisdom of his recommendations about recruiting informants for this kind of research:

> Targets for informants are relatives or friends of informants already worked. Possible workers are much more likely to consent to work if a pay incentive is offered. Husbands should be worked in the presence of their wives if the wife's work is to be requested. Women will only work with their husband's consent, but they should be paid for their work even if the husband has already been paid. In seeking an informant, it is best to present posh, and it is extremely helpful if a former informant is present to explain the nature of the work being done in his own terms (Collier 1960: 15).

When the undergraduate program was first discussed at Columbia, the board of directors, with much experience in Latin America, all thought that when women undergraduates were selected, at least two should be assigned to each field site so they could live together and chaperon each other in the dangerous macho world of Latin America. It took us only one season to discover this policy was a mistake. It unnecessarily restricted the freedom of movement of our women students, and we discovered that two women students, asked to live together in the field, were often likely to develop animosities toward each other. Further, if the research is done with Indians rather than with Ladinos, the dangers of unwanted macho advances are minimal, and it is always possible to ask the head of a family, and his wife, whether Indian or Ladino, to be responsible for the welfare of a student.

In the case of Chiapas, Duane Metzger and I learned the hard way about the folly of this original policy when we placed Jane Fishburne and Peggy Reeves together in one small house in the community of San Felipe. San Felipe is a small village, with a Ladinoized population derived from a Zinacanteco background, located on the western edge of the valley of San Cristobal. These two students were to spend the summer in San Felipe and undertake the first systematic study of this interesting community. The arrangement simply did not work. The strains were apparent from the beginning. Jane was only a sophomore, but already spoke fluent Spanish since she had gone to secondary school in Quito, Ecuador, where her father had been in the United States embassy. Peggy was a senior, but Spanish was still haltingly difficult for her. She seemed to have a perennial cold, and both women mentioned the rising tension they felt in the relationship.

Duane and I decided they had to be separated. We took a bouquet of roses and a bottle of wine to share with them one evening and announced that Jane would be taken to the hamlet of Paste' while Peggy would go to Aguacatenango—two of the most distant field sites in the study area. I took Jane to the Shun Akov family in Paste'. The road was impassable, and I can still recall walking to the hamlet, helping Jane carry her almost-too-large sleeping bag and transporting a bottle of posh to be presented to Shun Akov. The journey was successful and Jane was left for a week to cope with Zinacanteco life in the extended family of the Wasp Nests, as I reminded her of the great fieldwork of one of her predecessors: Margaret Mead.

We had made arrangements for Jane to have her meals with Shun's father and mother, as I had done earlier in the season, and to sleep in one of the houses. The food was fine, but Jane found that she was relegated to an abandoned house for sleeping at night. Later she discovered that the Earth Lord had shaken the ground underneath this house because he was offended by the paucity of offerings made to him at the time of its construction. Hence, the family had abandoned the house and sent the new Gringa to be exposed to the dangers of the Earth Lord! Jane survived it all, and spent the major part of the summer living with the 'Akovs and collecting data for a fascinating summer report, "Some Aspects of the Division of Labor in a Zinacantecan Household." From time to time, George Collier would visit her in Paste' where he slept in the Harvard field house and also took his meals at the 'Akovs. I later discovered that these journeys were more than looking for informants for his color category research; he and Jane developed a romance during that summer, which blossomed into marriage in 1962 at Christ Church in Cambridge. In the absence of Jane's father, who was in the U.S. embassy in Peru at that time, I was honored with the role of "giving away the bride."

Peggy Reeves, under the careful tutelage of Duane Metzger, went on to do excellent fieldwork in Aguacatenango and produced a first-rate paper on aspects of the compadrazgo system in a Mexican Indian village at the end of the summer. It is a tribute to both Peggy and Jane that they survived the traumas of their beginning experience in San Felipe that summer; further, after they were separated, they got on well together.[1]

Stephen Gudeman also had a problem with very limited Spanish. Duane Metzger and I decided to place him in the Huisteco hamlet of Chilil where arrangements could be made for him to sleep in a house belonging to the INI cultural promoter and to take his meals for seven pesos a day with a Huisteco family living nearby. Since his Spanish was limited at first, he wisely decided to focus on observations of the economic life, especially the agricultural system. He worked with the Huisteco men in their fields during the day, and played his saxophone to entertain his neighbors in the evening. His report at the end of the summer, "Some Aspects of the Economic System of Chilil," formed the basis for a longer study, "Toward a Model of the Highland Maya Economies" (1961), which became his A.B. honors thesis written under my supervision.[2]

Henry York from Cornell was also placed in Huistan, in the hamlet of Yalcuc where Frank Miller had worked three years before. Metzger and I arranged for him to sleep in the INI clinic and to eat his breakfast and lunch with the local schoolteacher and his family, and his dinner with Don Alonzo, the Huisteco cacique with whom Frank Miller had eaten his meals. In this setting he gathered ethnographic data and produced a good report on the kinship system of Yalcuc at the end of the summer.

Nineteen sixty was an eventful, and in some ways, stressful summer for the young married members of the project: Duane Metzger and Bob Laughlin. Both of their wives were imminently expecting babies. The Metzger baby (a son named John) was born prematurely in the hospital in Tuxtla and had to be flown to Mexico City in an incubator.

On 5 July Bob Laughlin's wife, Mimi, had broken her sac and labor pains had begun when Bob found me to borrow the Land Rover and make an emergency run to the hospital in Tuxtla Gutierrez where arrangements had been made for the birth. I delegated George Collier and Steve Gudeman to accompany the Laughlins on the wild dash down the mountains to the hospital—all the time with Bob still in full regalia as a Zinacanteco, having just returned to San Cristobal from a drinking ceremony in Hteklum, the ceremonial center. The Laughlins' first child, a daughter named Liana DeWolf Laughlin, was safely born two hours later.

About halfway through the summer, it was apparent that Na-Bolom was not the ideal headquarters for our students. They left for the field and re-turned to San Cristobal much too irregularly for the Swiss clockworklike management that Trudi Blom was always trying to impose at Na-Bolom. Further, they would come home late, long after the front door of Na-Bolom was securely locked and disturb the household by having to ring the front bell to be admitted when they forgot their keys. Duane Metzger moved them all to other headquarters, most of them to La Cabaña where Alfonso Villa Rojas was again gracious enough to provide INI rooms for them to live in while in San Cristobal. After this experience, we rarely placed a student at Na-Bolom, but instead found all of them housing in other locations in San Cristobal. This move proved to be advantageous for the students since it put each of them in contact with San Cristobal families and was a great help for improving their Spanish.

Remarkably, all of the Harvard students on the undergraduate summer studies program during this first season continued on to distinguished careers in anthropology.[3]

Casagrande, who was asked to travel to the three field stations during the summer and prepare an evaluative report, found that the program was generally a success. He wrote in part: "The intensity and excitement, both intellectual and emotional, of the experience of course varied from individual to individual, but it was a profoundly enriching summer for all concerned" (1960).

CHIAPAS 1961

Since we were assured of continuing support from the Carnegie Corporation for two more years and I was pleased with the procedures we had worked out for the Chiapas field station, I pushed ahead to select the students for the summer of 1961 when I was to serve as the field leader. Eight were selected from among the Harvard applicants. Four came with me to Chiapas: Donald Bahr, Adelaide Pirrotta, Jack Stauder, and Phillip Stubble-field. They were joined by Jordon P. Benderly from Cornell and Harvey E. Goldberg from Columbia. Two were sent to Ecuador: Susanna Ekholm and Renato I. Rosaldo; and two to Peru: Jane Fearer and Richard Price.

The Chiapas field party also included Eric Prokosch (1969), an under-graduate from Harvard who was highly qualified but could not be included among those selected for the Carnegie program; he served instead as a research assistant for Duane Metzger. The group also included George Collier and Jane Fishburne who were deeply interested in coming back to Chiapas and whose field research I supported from my NIMH grant, starting the precedent of inviting outstanding undergraduates to return for additional seasons of field experience.

Building on the experience of the previous summer, I encouraged the students to locate lodging in inexpensive hotels or rooming houses in San Cristobal instead of trying to place them all at Na-Bolom or other central locations.

George Collier continued his research on color categories, which formed the basis for his A.B. honors thesis in his senior year and his first technical article (1966). Jane Fishburne, who had by this time completed her junior year, collected data on the patterns of Zinacanteco courtship and marriage for her summa cum laude senior thesis, which was later published as a monograph (1968).[4]

Don Bahr came from a well-to-do family in Iowa who owned rich farmland. In Chiapas he was placed in the log cabin medical post in Yalcuc and took his meals with Don Alonzo Vasquez. An imaginative and insightful student, who painted when he was not doing anthropology, Don had developed some interesting ideas on the conceptual arrangements of space and work, which I encouraged him to explore in Yalcuc. He was stubborn, however, when it came to advice about health precautions; for example, he thought that our prohibitions against drinking the local water were simply ethnocentric beliefs on the part of North Americans. When he came down with a terrible case of dysentery, I had to bring him into San Cristobal in a dehydrated and emaciated condition and arrange for medical care by the INI physician. He not only required injections of antibiotics, but had to be placed on intravenous feeding of liquids to replace those lost by his body. Needless to say, he did not drink the local Yalcuc water again. He settled down to collect some of the more interesting ethnographic data of the summer. I recall his firsthand discovery that when a bull is purchased and butchered cooperatively by a group of men in Huistan, the sharing of the meat proceeds in a manner that would never occur in our culture. We would, for example, allot part or all of a hind quarter to one person, a front quarter to another, etc. In the case of the Huistecos, all parts of the bull, including the organs such as the liver, are cut into as many small pieces as there are men who purchased a share of the bull.

*Domingo de la Torre Pérez
and Jack Stauder in 1961.*

As the summer progressed Don came to like life in Chiapas more and more and did not really want to return to Winthrop House at Harvard. When he lost his tourist card (supposedly inadvertently, but I suspect it was unconsciously deliberate), I suggested he write immediately to his county courthouse in Iowa for a copy of his birth certificate so that we could proceed with the lengthy bureaucratic process of extracting a new tourist card. Then, after I had left for the States, Don lost the birth certificate. At this point, George Collier took over and created an official-looking birth certificate by photocopying a typed document and using his Harvard ring as a seal. It worked to secure another tourist card for Don, and I breathed a genuine sigh of relief when I finally received a telegram from Don informing me that he was safely back in the United States.

Adelaide ("Dili") Pirrotta was the daughter of an Italian-born professor of music at Harvard. She developed a close friendship with George Collier and Jane Fishburne and was invited to join them in a housekeeping arrangement in rented quarters on the edge of San Cristobal. Nearby was the village of San Felipe to which she was introduced by Jane, who had established some contacts in the community during the previous summer. Dili undertook a systematic study of the economic role of women in this marginal community, suspended between the Indian and Ladino worlds, between highlands and lowlands, which, for many generations, has supplied maids for San Cristobal, as well as middlewomen selling lowland products in its highland market.

During the summer a romance developed between Don Bahr and Dili Pirrotta. During the following year, they spent much time together on the third floor of Nine Bow Street, where my office was then located. I had assigned an office space to Don for the purpose of analyzing his Yalcuc data and writing his thesis. Here Don typed on his thesis, painted more pictures, and courted Dili. At the end of their senior year, Don and Dili were married, and Don continued to the Ph.D. at Harvard, after doing field research with the Papago.[5]

Jack Stauder came from New Mexico, having attended Las Cruces High School while his father was a professor at the State University of New Mexico. Since his grandparents were a ranching family in southern Colorado, I always felt a special bond with Jack. When he was selected for the undergraduate program, he was concentrating in English and American literature, and taking courses from Perry Miller and Alan Heimert. A strong, self-assured, and independent young man who knew Spanish well, he would, I decided, be an ideal candidate to undertake a field study of the lowland farming activities of the Zinacantecos. This was really rugged duty since it involved hiking down some seven thousand feet from the top of the escarpment into the valley of the Rio Grijalva south of the hamlet of Paste', hoeing corn for days in this sweltering setting, then hiking back up. Although a number of members of the project have hiked down to the Zinacanteco lowland fields, only two have hiked up: Jack Stauder on a number of trips, and Bob Laughlin on one occasion. Bob reports it nearly killed him.

Jack also prided himself on being able to live on very few pesos. He had a really modest room in the Posada San Cristobal, and he discovered how to eat a stand-up breakfast in the market for one peso: twenty centavos for a slice of pineapple, fifty for a hard-boiled egg, twenty for tortillas, and ten for a cup of coffee.

To facilitate his field research I introduced Jack to Shun Akov and to Telesh Komis Lotriko (as Andrés Gómez Rodríguez is called in Tzotzil) in

Paste'. He was able to accompany and to work with each of these groups during the summer. Jack produced a beautifully written and ethnographically significant report at the end of the summer entitled "Zinacantecos in Hot Country."

One night toward the end of the summer there was a quiet knock on my door; it was Jack Stauder wanting to talk about his future. He had become enamored of anthropology and wished to do graduate work after completing his A.B. at Harvard. I encouraged him. He received a Marshall Fellowship and went off to Cambridge to read social anthropology in St. John's College with Professor Jack Goody.[6]

Phillip Stubblefield came to Harvard from Wichita, Kansas, and was a very personable, hard-working student who planned to go on to medical school. Duane Metzger helped me place him in Aguacatenango, where he interviewed Tzeltal informants about their medical practices and produced a fascinating report at the end of the summer on medical beliefs and practices, and disease terminology in a Tzeltal village. Stubblefield also gathered some information in Zinacantan for comparative purposes and was able to write an honor's thesis on folk medicine in two Mayan towns during his senior year.[7]

The student from Columbia, Harvey Goldberg, experienced difficulties at first selecting a topic for his field research. The students from the other universities were given one opportunity during the spring term to visit Harvard (with travel expenses paid by the Carnegie Corporation grant) and confer with me about their research topics for Chiapas. The Columbia students usually arrived with grandiose topics in mind they thought could be researched during the summer. I recall asking Harvey about his principal research interests, and receiving the reply that he wished to study "cultural evolution" during the summer. When I pointed out that this topic was much too broad to tackle in a summer's fieldwork, he then suggested that he study "social structure." "Fine," I replied, "but precisely what about social structure are you going to investigate?" I finally suggested a manageable topic I had had in mind for some time—an investigation of cohete (skyrocket) manufacture in San Cristobal. Since San Cristobal and the surrounding Indian villages had the justified reputation of shooting off more cohetes than any other region of Mexico, I thought the topic could be an interesting one. Harvey was quite put off by this suggestion; he thought it was a trivial topic, but he eventually agreed to explore it.

With the good graces of Don Polo, we were able to introduce Harvey to one of his compadres who was a fireworks manufacturer in the barrio of Santa Lucia in San Cristobal, and the research began in this household. I shall never forget how Harvey came to me after two weeks to admit that skyrocket making was a very complicated topic. He had yet to master the details of the technology, much less to understand the social structure of the manufacturers and the symbolic importance of the skyrockets. By the end of the summer he had discovered that almost all of the coheteros were descended from, or were related by marriage to, two kinsmen with the surname of Martinez who started the business two generations before. Further, the network of coheteros was linked closely together by the ritual kinship system of compadrazgo, with godparents always being selected within the group. The tightly organized in-group living and working together predominantly in a single barrio resembled a Medieval guild. Harvey's summer paper, "The Coheteros of San Cristobal," is a fine example of what can be accomplished with a well-designed and focused summer project.[8]

The sixth new member of the field team, Jordan Benderly from Cornell, undertook a study of the division of labor in the production of panela on a cana ranch in Chiapas, panela being the brown sugar produced from sugarcane. The sugarcane ranch, located near Soyatitan in the lowlands to the southeast of San Cristobal, was Ladino-owned. Here Benderly could use Spanish in his interviewing. Again, the study was nicely focused and well executed.[9]

In reviewing the summer of 1961 I realize how important it was that I had a number of experienced field researchers to provide a support group for the new undergraduates. Duane Metzger was a great help, especially in taking the lead in placing and supervising Stubblefield and Benderly. Frank and Francesca Cancian had also spent a year in fieldwork in Zinacantan and were always at hand to provide advice. George Collier and Jane Fishburne were likewise of assistance, especially with Dili Pirrotta's project in San Felipe. We also made contact with Professor Henning Siverts from the University of Bergen in Norway who was working in the Tzeltal municipio of Oxchuc. Siverts had done his first field research in Oxchuc in 1953–54 and was making a second visit to Chiapas during 1961–62 (see Siverts 1969).

Beginning in 1960, and continuing in subsequent years, we established the custom of having a beginning conference, at which experienced students presented reports and led the discussion. Another conference was held in the middle of the season at which all students, graduate and undergraduate, were expected to present a progress report for discussion. Following the midsummer conference, all students were given a recess of a week to travel to the Pacific Coast beaches of Chiapas, or to Guatemala, where many of them went to spend time on Lake Atitlan, or to Yucatan and on to the beaches of Cozumel and Isla Mujeres.

In retrospect I also realize how much time and energy I invested in supervising the field research of the students in Chiapas, and how little time remained for my own research compared to earlier years. Moreover, I had promised the board of directors of the undergraduate program that I would visit the other field stations in Peru and Ecuador, a journey that lasted from 22 June to 3 July.

Returning to Chiapas, I devoted the time I had for my own research to interviewing Telesh Komis Lotriko about curing practices and sacred places. Through Telesh I was finally able to attend my *first* curing ceremony during the night of 20–21 July—it now being the fifth season since I had started my research in Paste'! To be sure, George Collier had witnessed curing ceremonies in Romin Teratol's house in Zinacantan Center in 1960. But Romin had already worked with Nick Colby, Bob Laughlin, Susan Tax, and me and was accustomed to an anthropological presence in his household. Frank Cancian had also been able to attend ceremonies performed by Mol Shun Vaskis when Mol Shun had requested rides for the curing parties in the Land Rover in the spring of 1961. Frank astutely agreed to furnish the transportation provided he could come along to the ceremonies, a bargain to which Mol Shun agreed. Again, Mol Shun had worked with Nick Colby, Bob Laughlin, and Bill Binderman. My attendance at Telesh's curing ceremony was our first experience with any curing ritual in the hamlet of Paste'.

When Telesh invited me to participate in the curing ceremony for his daughter, I quickly accepted. We set out for Telesh's house in the Land Rover at five P.M. An hour later we managed to become impossibly stuck in a mud hole on the road to Paste' and had to abandon the car and walk to the house, arriving about seven P.M.

The all-night ceremony took place first inside Telesh's house, then outside by the house cross in the patio, and ended inside. The ceremony con-

The famous shaman Juan Vasquez (called Mol Shun Vaskis in Tzotzil) of Nabenchauk, Zinacantan, with his bamboo staff of office on his way to perform a curing ceremony. His wife is seated on the right. (Photo by Frank Cancian)

Mol Shun Vaskis and the patient pray at mountain shrine to the ancestral gods while incense burns. Note shape of another sacred mountain (in the background) that resembles ancient Maya pyramid. (Photo by Frank Cancian)

The last sacred mountain to be visited during a curing ceremony is Kalvaryo (Calvary) where it is believed that the ancestral gods hold their meetings and eagerly await offerings from the living Zinacantecos. (Photo by Frank Cancian)

sisted of seven episodes, each punctuated by rounds of posh which kept us going through the night. (More details on this ceremony are provided in Vogt 1969: 643–66).

At the end I suggested that I return to my field house in Paste':

> but [as I recorded in my journal] Telesh suggested I sleep with them, saying it was only an hour or two before dawn. He moved the two drunk drink-pourers off a reed mat, spread it out for the two of us, gave me a wooden headrest covered with a clean cloth, and covered me with a black, woolen robe. It was very gentle and wonderful treatment. The next thing I knew it was broad daylight

and people were up and moving about the house. After a quick meal of tortillas and coffee, Telesh mustered six men to extract the Land Rover from the mud hole were we had abandoned it the night before and returned to San Cristobal in time to await the arrival of President López Mateos who was paying an official visit to the highlands of Chiapas.

A second landmark field experience during the summer consisted of my first walking trip from the Chiapas Highlands to the Rio Grijalva Lowlands. From my field journal for 25 July:

> Jack Stauder, my son Terry (age 15), and I walked today with Telesh and his in-laws in Sna Chiku'etik from the rim in Paste' to Chiapilla. We left the rim in heavy fog and light rain at 7:45 A.M. and reached Chiapilla on the river at 3 P.M. It was the hardest trip I've ever made in my life—with almost 7 steady hours on rough trails and almost all down hill. I got along well until the last drop of 2,000 feet when my knees and calves began to give trouble, so I had to fall behind. Jack, Terry, and Telesh stayed behind with me while the rest of the group went on ahead. It certainly gave me renewed admiration for the fortitude of the Zinacantecos, for the group contained old Mikel Lopis Chiku', who must be approaching 70, and a young boy not over 8 years old. By comparison with this trip Zinacantecos make to Tierra Caliente, the hikes they make between Paste' and Zinacantan Center and San Cristobal are nothing more than Sunday afternoon walks in the park!

While Jack Stauder and the Zinacantecos continued on to their lowland fields, Terry and I stopped in Chiapilla where we looked up Lilo Stern (now a professor of anthropology at Vassar College). Lilo was a Ph.D. candidate in social anthropology from Cambridge University who was engaged in a field study of the largely Ladinoized community of Chiapilla for the University of Chicago project under the guidance of Julian Pitt-Rivers. After an interesting evening visit about her research, Lilo graciously moved out of her rented room and slept in another house while the landlady fixed two beds for Terry and me in Lilo's room.

Terry and I left Chiapilla at half past eight the next morning on the truck (a four-wheel drive Chevrolet with chains on) that takes freight and passengers to Acala and Chiapa de Corzo. The trip to the Pan American highway near Chiapa de Corzo took more than five hours through the worst mud I have ever encountered either in the Southwest or Mexico. Once on the highway, we hitched a ride in a Jeep back to San Cristobal. Once again, I was glad to be working in the cool highlands instead of the sweltering lowlands.

THE SUMMER OF 1962

During the summer of 1962 I had planned another journey to Europe, this time to attend and chair an international symposium that I had organized on the cultural development of the Maya, sponsored by the Wenner-Gren Foundation for Anthropological Research and scheduled to take place at Burg Wartenstein in Austria from 6 to 13 September. With these plans in mind I persuaded Frank Cancian to serve as the field leader. The undergraduate field group consisted of five students, including three from Harvard (Nicholas A. Acheson, Susan E. Carey, and Matthew D. Edel), plus Allen Young from Columbia and Ronald J. Maduro from Cornell. George and Jane Collier also returned to Chiapas following their June marriage in Cambridge.

I devoted the months of June and July to preparing for the Conference at Burg Wartenstein, then flew to Chiapas in August to confer with Frank and Franzi Cancian, as well as to see how the undergraduates were progressing. As it turned out, Frank Cancian was handling the undergraduate student program adeptly, and I had time to collect shamans' prayers from Telesh Komis Lotriko on the tape recorder. Most of the data were collected at field headquarters in San Cristobal where we could work for long hours without interruption. These prayers were later transcribed by Romin Teratol in Tzotzil and translated line-by-line into Spanish. They have provided a basic corpus of data for understanding the six different types of ceremonies performed by the H'iloletik in Zinacantan: rituals for curing illness, dedicating new houses, protecting maize fields, lineages and water hole groups, year renewal, and rainmaking.

The undergraduates were deep into their various projects. Nicholas ("Nick") Acheson was a brilliant microbiologist working with Nobel Prize winner James Watson of DNA fame, but his hobby was birding and he had served as the president of the Harvard Birding Society. He was a natural for another project I had had in mind: a systematic study of the ethnozoology of Zinacantan. He produced a very sophisticated report at the end of the season which was later published (Acheson 1966). Among his interesting discoveries: Zinacantecos are better at recognizing birdcalls and songs then they are at identifying birds by sight. His explanation: Zinacantecos spend much of their time carrying loads with tumplines and watching their footing on rocky mountain paths; hence they look up at birds flying or perched on trees much less than they notice plants along the trails, which are more in their line of vision when carrying their loads.[10]

Susan Carey was placed in the home of the famous Doña Elisea in Zinacantan Center and undertook the first systematic study of its Ladino population (a core group of fifty in 1962). Her summer report on Zinacantan's Ladinos is a model of clarity (see Carey 1966), and is, I believe, still the only definitive study of the demography, social structure, and customs of the Ladino population in the *cabecera* of an Indian municipio in Chiapas.[11]

Our economist of the summer was Matthew Edel who Frank Cancian interested in doing a thorough study of the ejido of Zinacantan (Edel 1966). It is a fine study with an effective combination of historical information, data from government archives, and interview data from Zinacantecos.[12]

The undergraduate from Cornell, Ron Maduro, had expressed an interest in educational systems and was busily studying the various school systems of the Ladinos in San Cristobal. The Columbia undergraduate, Allen Young, devoted the summer to an investigation of Mexico's federal corn warehouses in Chiapas. It was a topic that strongly interested Frank Cancian, for it was a system to regulate the supplies and control the prices of maize.

In 1962 I recruited another graduate student to do field research in Chiapas: a talented Jesuit priest, John D. Early, who was studying for his Ph.D. in sociology under the supervision of the late Professor Talcott Parsons. Father Early was deeply interested in studying the details of the rituals of the cargoholders in Zinacantan Center. While Frank Cancian had done an admirable piece of scholarship in describing and analyzing the structure and economics of the cargo system, he was less interested in the details of the rituals. I can recall being in the field with Frank Cancian when we came to a Zinacanteco house with a freshly decorated household cross in the patio. I immediately began to think about and talk to Frank about the type of ritual plants attached to the cross and the copal incense burning in the censer and to speculate about what kind of ceremony was going on inside the house. Frank, on the other hand, immediately began to wonder out loud about "how did that man manage to pay for what looks like an expensive ceremony?"

With these considerations in mind, I was delighted to have a sociologist, whose special field was religion, express an interest in working in Chiapas. I also thought that a Jesuit priest would certainly have ready access to ceremonies going forward inside the two Catholic churches and the Chapel of Esquipulas in Zinacantan Center. John Early began his field research in December 1962 when Bob Laughlin introduced him to Zinacantan Center.

At the end of the 1962 season my first five-year grant from NIMH had reached its end, and it was time to take stock of what we had accomplished and to apply for a renewal for another five years. In my progress report I described candidly how I had been overly ambitious in my original research design. The plan to compare the responses of various Indian communities to the forces of modernization might have worked in a region such as the American Southwest in which there had already been more than a hundred years of accumulation of ethnographic data. But here in Chiapas we were beginning with almost no previous descriptions of the basic cultures, and, I realized later, they were cultures that were more complex than they seemed at first. During my first visits I had been overly impressed by meeting bilingually competent Zinacantecos and by observing all of the Catholic churches and icons. I had incorrectly perceived communities that appeared to be largely Catholic and peasant in organization and culture. While it was evident that the Maya language was still in use and that the people dressed in distinctive dress styles, the Indians appeared to be much like those described in the publications of Robert Redfield and Oscar Lewis on Tepoztlan. They grew maize and beans for food, they kept sheep for clothing, they went to mass in Catholic churches, and they had a political organization with familiar sounding Spanish positions: *gobernadores, jueces, alcaldes,* etc. Further, there were wooden crosses everywhere—on churches and houses, beside water holes, and on mountain tops—leading me to believe they were basically Catholic in outlook.

On the whole the native culture and social organization did not appear to be nearly so complex and intricate as those of tribes in the Southwest with whom I had previously worked—the Zuni, or even the Navaho. I had confidently expected that within a year or two of research we could have the basic outlines of the native culture well described and would have ample time to discover how these systems were changing in response to the contemporary modern world. I could not have been more mistaken.

It had become perfectly plain that we had underestimated the amount and complexity of ancient Maya social organization and culture that are still viable in these communities, and by focusing on various aspects of the Mexican government program and the ways the Indians responded to these we were only obtaining part of the data necessary for a penetrating study of the problems. We were, in a word, getting too much of an outside view and too little of an inside one.

By 1960 I had shifted strategy and we concentrated more on doing basic linguistic and ethnographic work that had to be covered before anything more than limited results could be achieved in the study of cultural change. This shift led us to concentrate heavily on mastery of the Tzotzil language, which is the key to solid ethnographic work. We also deliberately began detaching ourselves more and more from INI and other government programs and their technicians and identifying ourselves more with the conservative segments of the Indian communities. We started wearing items of Tzotzil clothing, rather than dressing as Ladinos, and we started living in Indian houses. Both of these moves were complex procedures. We found, for example, that it was appropriate in the Indian view to dress as Indians only insofar as we became fluent in Tzotzil. We had to engage in very complicated negotiations to rent Indian houses or to move in with Indian families. While living in Navaho hogans or Zuni houses in the Southwest had long been standard operating procedures for ethnographers in New Mexico and Arizona, living with indigenous families on a day and night basis had rarely, if ever, been done by anthropologists in Mexico or Guatemala. Our project members were pioneers on the Mesoamerican scene in this field strategy. As pioneers we were subjected to a certain amount of criticism from the Ladinos, as well as from some of the INI officials and members of the Euro-American colony in San Cristobal. We were crossing social boundaries that had never been traversed before, and the result was some tension in our relationships with non-Indians. But had we continued living and closely associating with INI officials and other Ladinos, our fieldworkers would have been fluent in Spanish, but halting in Tzotzil, and would have continued to view the Indian communities from the outside.

In distancing ourselves from INI, and other government agencies that came later in Chiapas, we were attempting to avoid being involved in the day-to-day action programs that occupied so much of the time and interest of most of the Mexican anthropologists. For while I deeply sympathized with the pressing problems of illiteracy, poverty, and disease that plagued the Tzotzil Maya communities (and, for that matter, most of rural Mexico), I felt strongly that *basic* research on the culture needed to be done. And I had observed how the Mexican anthropologists as employees of INI were understandably responding to the latest epidemic of disease or the most recent political crisis in the Indian communities and, as a result, were continually sidetracked from carrying out fundamental long-range research that would ultimately provide deeper understandings of this complex and intricate culture.

This led to a shift in our policy with respect to problem areas that were focal points for study each year. We abandoned (until later) the effort to understand directly the influence of government programs on the indigenous communities, and moved instead to study a number of basic areas of the culture: settlement pattern and social organization, economic patterns, mythology, the cargo system, curing rituals, the Tzotzil family, etc.

In particular, the research results of Bob Laughlin, which I have already described, and of Frank and Francesca Cancian had moved in this new direction. Frank devoted eighteen months of field time in Chiapas from September 1960 to August 1962 to the first intensive and systematic study we had had in Chiapas of a cargo system. Using a combination of observational and interview techniques to collect both qualitative and quantitative data he was able to describe the structure and dynamics of the cargo system of Zinacantan with precision, as well as to analyze its relationship to the economic and political structure of the municipio.[13]

During the same years Franzi Cancian's field research focused on adapting the Bales' methods of studying small groups in the laboratory to the field situation in Zinacanteco families. She was able to systematically score the types of interaction that occur in Zinacanteco families over a twenty-four-hour period.[14]

By 1961 the results of our research had become exciting. We knew we were dealing with Indian cultures that were far from being merely Catholic and peasant in nature; they were, instead, still basically Mayan and tribal in nature with a veneer of Catholic religion and Spanish political and social organization masking what lay beneath.

For my last year of the five-year grant, I made a move that I hoped would generate a quantum increase in close rapport with the Zinacantecos. I requested that ten thousand dollars be added to the original budget in order to purchase an extinct volcano for the community of Zinacantan. In this unusual proposal I pointed out:

> The political and ceremonial center of the community lies in a high mountain valley surrounded by a series of volcanic and limestone peaks that are highly sacred places. . . . The most important mountain peak is an extinct volcano known to the Indians as Bankilal Muk'ta Vits, or "Senior Large Mountain." The Indians believe that there exists in the interior of this volcano an enormous corral full of 7,600 *chanuletik,* or "animal spirit companions," one for each living member of the Zinacantan community. These animal spirit companions are believed to be jaguars and coyotes and other animals who have a special spiritual relationship to each Indian that is established at birth and continues throughout his life. . . . While all of the other sacred mountains around the ceremonial center are on Indian-owned land, this most important Senior Large Mountain with its supernatural corral full of animal spirit companions that are essential for the very life of the Indians is owned by a wealthy Ladino. . . . This Ladino rancher permits the Indians to make their pilgrimages to the top of the volcano, but a day never passes when the Indians do not look up at their important sacred mountain (which they used to own) and express feelings of deep anger that it is in the hands of a Ladino. Repeated attempts over the past several years have been made by the Indian leaders to acquire title to this property for the community under the provisions of the Mexican ejido laws. These attempts have all been blocked by the Ladino who is politically powerful in Chiapas.

My proposal was to purchase this real estate for ten thousand dollars—a price that Ladino friends indicated the rancher would be willing to accept—and turn it over to the community of Zinacantan. The title would have been vested in the ejido; hence, the community would benefit not only from the control of its sacred volcano but also from the grazing and farming land that would be added to its holdings.

The request was discussed with the Executive Committee of the Laboratory of Social Relations at Harvard and with Dean McGeorge Bundy before he left for his post with the Kennedy administration in Washington. Both the laboratory and Mr. Bundy felt the request was novel, but legitimate, and gave their approval to my including it in the NIMH budget for the year.

Unfortunately, the NIMH panel thought the request was too complicated and too risky and recommended disapproval. The ten thousand dollars for the volcano was removed from the approved budget. It was not until 1980 that the Zinacantecos were finally able to acquire their sacred mountain as part of a successful amplification of their ejido.

For my second five-year research strategy, I proposed to continue the basic ethnographic work in Zinacantan until we had reached what Geertz (1973) later called "thick description" and to expand our operations into the neighboring Tzotzil community of Chamula. We would also continue to collect data on the various government programs and on the relationship of Tzotzil communities with the Ladino world and the forces of modernization reaching into the Highlands of Chiapas, but this concern would be secondary to focusing on the basic ethnography of the indigenous culture.

I should add that the funding for the first five years of research operations were supplemented from a variety of sources. The NIMH grant was fundamental in keeping the Harvard Chiapas Project office at Harvard and the field project running—it paid my summer salary and my operating expenses in Chiapas, the salaries of a secretary and one or two research assistants in Cambridge, as well as basic stipends for some of the students. But the annual amounts of thirteen thousand to fourteen thousand dollars (not including indirect costs) would not have sufficed. The undergraduate program was funded by the Carnegie Corporation of New York. Some graduate students managed to receive individual field research fellowships—for example, Frank Miller had a Doherty, Francesca Cancian an NIMH fellowship—and this gave me leeway to fund others from my NIMH grant or to assist experienced undergraduates to return to the field for a second or third summer. The sensible rules about the allotting of funds, provided only that I did not run over budget, on the part of both the foundations and of Harvard, permitted me to involve many more talented researchers in the enterprise over the years.

I was delighted to receive word that my second five-year grant, running from 1963 through 1967, had been approved by the NIMH. I was now in position to take a longer-range view of the operations of the Harvard Chiapas Project, and Nan and I flew off to Vienna in early September and took the train to Gloggnitz where we were met by the car from the Wenner-Gren Foundation and transported into the mountains to that wonderful castle, complete with moat and drawbridge, where anthropologists have held so many productive international meetings. It was a perfect setting for a symposium on the cultural development of the Maya. The lodgings were spacious, with beautiful views of the mountains and evergreen forests; the meals and wines were delicious; and the large meeting room offered a setting for intensive discussion without interruption of telephones, traffic noise, or any interference from the outside world. Since Nan was the wife of the organizer, she was permitted to stay in the castle. It was a delightfully stimulating week, with discussions of papers by a group of Mayanists who came to be called by my students "the twelve apostles." They were Munro S. Edmonson, John Graham, Norman A. McQuown, Tatiana Proskouriakoff, Alberto Ruz, Henning Siverts, Terrence S. Kaufman, Sol Tax, Alfonso Villa Rojas, Evon Z. Vogt, Gordon R. Willey, and Günter Zimmerman. All attended the symposium except for Kaufman.

My two papers covered my first attempt to apply the "genetic model" to the Maya and the summary and appraisal. The papers by the participants were exciting enough to encourage us to plan a publication on *desarrollo cultural de los Mayas*, which Alberto Ruz agreed to publish as a special volume of his *Seminario de Cultura Maya* at the Universidad Nacional Autónoma de México.

7 /
THE HARVARD
RANCH:
1961–1981

 After the first four years of the Harvard Chiapas Project I decided we needed to change our living arrangements, both in the field and in San Cristobal, in order to increase rapport with the Indians and to deepen our ethnographic knowledge of Tzotzil culture. The field house in Paste' had been an essential first step to make significant long-range contacts in a Zinacanteco hamlet, but its disadvantages had become apparent. We were living as neighbors of Zinacanteco households, but it is not customary to call on neighbors without some business in mind—for example, to borrow an ax, to request the services of a shaman, or to petition a father for his daughter as a bride. We could never politely call upon a neighbor to pay a visit or "just to show our faces" as Romin Teratol explained. I realized that the only times we were able to interact with the Zinacantecos in the context of their flow of life was when we either arranged to take meals in their homes, or, better, when we lived in Indian homes in Paste' or in Zinacantan Center. Further, I discovered that formal interviews, either carried out in Indian houses or patios, or at the field house, *always* had curious onlookers present—sometimes family members, sometimes neighbors—as well as crying babies, barking dogs, and cackling chickens. The result: the Zinacantecos being interviewed were always distracted and guarded about what they had to say.

On the other hand, when we asked the Zinacantecos to come to San Cristobal for interviews, we had never found the ideal locations for these interviews. If I were staying at Don Polo's house there was always a certain tension—even on the part of this well-educated and liberal-minded Ladino family—when I tried to interview a Zinacanteco there. The various houses at INI never had enough rooms to provide privacy for one-on-one interviewing. The apartment of Don Polo in the center of San Cristobal was noisy, the rooms were small and cramped, and, as at INI, there were no fireplaces to warm them.

For those who think of sunny Mexico as a perennially warm setting, the cool temperatures of the Highlands of Chiapas at seven thousand feet, and often overcast with heavy clouds, come as a surprise. Without some source of heat in the room, long hours of interviewing and trying to type notes on a typewriter can chill one to the bone. The Indian homes always have open fires burning at the hearth and are comfortable. Most Ladino homes, constructed of masonry with tile floors and roofs and with high ceilings modeled on architecture appropriate for southern Spain, rather than the cloud forests of the Mexican highlands, lack fireplaces and are unpleasantly cold except on warm days at the end of the dry season. While the Maya Indians are warm and comfortable sitting by the open fires in their wattle-and-daub, thatched roof houses, the Ladinos put on sweaters and suffer in their large, dank living and dining rooms.

RENTING THE HARVARD RANCH

During the 1960 season Bobbie Montagu began to renovate the buildings on her *labor* (farm, or ranch), legally called El Labor San Juan de Dios Las Delicias, which she had purchased a short distance north of Na-Bolom on the outskirts of San Cristobal with the idea of establishing an anthropological field station.

The ranch contained some forty hectares of land, most of which were used for grazing cattle and horses. The horses belonged to Bobbie, but the cattle to Don Gustavo Hernández from the Barrio de Cerrillos who served as the mayordomo for Bobbie. The original buildings on the ranch, the oldest dating from 1610, included a large house (about fifty meters long), facing west, with adobe walls some two feet thick, encompassing four large rooms with high ceilings, and tile roofs, and along the front a covered porch. In recent years, two of these rooms had been used as milking rooms for Don Gustavo's cows and for keeping goats and chickens. North of the large house was a square threshing shed in which horses attached to a central pole were driven around and around to remove the wheat from its stalks, plus a *bodega*, or storage building, nearby.

Bobbie's plan for the anthropological field station envisioned living quarters for a large number of researchers and a communal kitchen and dining room where they would all eat their meals. She proceeded to convert the original large house into living quarters, the threshing shed into the communal cooking and dining area; across the courtyard to the west she constructed a new building that contained a series of bedrooms and small apartments. Bobbie asked the anthropologists from the various universities engaged in research in Chiapas if they would be interested in renting the buildings on the ranch as a field headquarters. We were all, indeed, very interested. It seemed to be an ideal long-range solution to the logistic problems we were encountering.

On 20 September 1960 the University of Chicago (represented by Norman A. McQuown), Harvard (which I was to represent), and Stanford (represented by Kim Romney), signed a five-year contract with Roberta J. Viuda de Montagu. The property was to be put in good order with five bathrooms, five fireplaces, new floors, new ceilings, interior plaster and paint. The three universities were to pay, in advance, the sum of $2,000 ($666.66 each), which would be considered as five years' rent in advance. The contract included an option to buy.

For this four hundred dollars a year from 1961 through 1965 we became the rental landlords of a spacious combination of old colonial buildings with newly constructed living quarters. In 1965, since Harvard had the most active research program at that time, I arranged a second five-year lease from 1966 through 1970 with an annual rent of eight hundred dollars a year, and an option to buy at the end of the contract. I took the lead in collecting the rent money from the various universities and paying the rent. It was during this period of time that Bobbie's ranch came to be called the Harvard Ranch or, in Spanish, El Rancho Harvard. The Harvard Chiapas Project continued to rent the ranch until 1981 for the same modest rental fee of eight hundred dollars a year.

Whereas the first lease was signed by Bobbie Montagu, the subsequent leases were arranged with Calixta Gutierrez-Holmes. Bobbie, who had moved from her home in the center of San Cristobal to the large two-story house just outside the entrance gate to our ranch compound, died suddenly of a heart attack on 31 August 1962. She had named Calixta, a close friend and colleague of many years' standing, as the heiress to her property, and as guardian of an Indian child named Tete whom Bobbie had adopted shortly before her death. Following Bobbie's death, the annual rent went to Calixta who had moved from Mexico to Havana to become an anthropological advisor for the Fidel Castro regime. Cali (as she was called by all who knew her well) had a Cuban father and an American mother, hence her surname of Gutierrez-Holmes. Her brother in Cuba, who was a noted opponent of the former dictator, Col. Fulgencio Batista, had been assassinated by the Batista regime; hence, Cali felt strongly in favor of the new revolutionary government of Fidel Castro. Cali appointed Dr. Johanna Faulhaber, an eminent physical anthropologist at the Instituto de Antropología e Historia in Mexico City, as her power of attorney. For fifteen years I dutifully sent the ranch rental funds (drawn largely from U.S. government sources) to Dr. Faulhaber, who in turn sent the money along to Cali in Havana. I gathered from talking with Faulhaber that Cali used these U.S. dollars to enable her to travel abroad, especially in eastern Europe, to visit other experiments with socialist societies. The arrangement permitted us to develop what proved to be an excellent base of operations in Chiapas.

The part of El Labor San Juan de Dios Las Delicias that we controlled contained not only the buildings I described, but also ample land for a large vegetable and flower garden on the north, a large lawn area to the south, all in a large courtyard within the compound, which had a ten-foot high adobe wall that ran between the various buildings to provide protection from the outside world.

EARLY YEARS AT THE HARVARD RANCH

Although I had inspected the ranch and become familiar with the general setting, especially during the 1958 season when our four riding horses and saddles were kept there, it was not until 2 August 1961 that my family and I moved to the ranch for the first time. We had been living at Don Polo's house during the early part of the summer when we were not in the field house in Paste'. While the Velasco family were most hospitable and it was a very pleasant San Cristobal headquarters, it was difficult for the children to adapt to the pattern and lateness of the meal hours. An enormous breakfast was served at nine or ten A.M., then no food until the late comida appeared sometime between two and five. Cena was also late, often at nine

P.M., and generally a lighter meal than our dinners at home. We were happy to be able to move to the more rustic buildings at the ranch. Our plan was to turn the Paste' field house over to the schoolteachers in that hamlet, and alternate our time between living in Indian homes out in the field and living and working at the new ranch headquarters in San Cristobal. The ranch had the immediate advantages of being quiet, providing privacy for one-on-one interviewing, and affording ample space for us to reciprocate the hospitality we received in Indian homes when our Tzotzil friends from Zinacantan or Chamula came to town to visit us.

I hauled the furniture from the Paste' field house to the ranch in the Land Rover, bought additional Chamula-made chairs in the market, and commissioned more tables to be constructed by Ladino carpenters in San Cristobal. Since the carpenters were always overbooked in their shops in those days, I soon learned from Duane Metzger how to ensure that a piece of furniture would be finished on schedule. The strategy was to bargain with the carpenter for the best possible price; then offer him 10 percent extra if he would finish the table in a week. It always worked.

My family and I moved into the large house, while other apartments across the courtyard were occupied by two smaller families affiliated with the University of Chicago project: the Duane Metzgers and the Roy d'Andrades. Roy had met Metzger while finishing his Ph.D. at Harvard and had developed an interest in the ethnoscience approach to eliciting ethnographic data in a rigorous manner, an approach that was highly popular in the 1960s and much used by Metzger and his colleagues.[1]

These 1961 living arrangements initiated a precedent that we continued for years. The living quarters at the ranch were reserved for the more senior members of the various projects—faculty members or senior graduate students—while the more junior graduate students and undergraduates were housed elsewhere when they came in from the field to write up their journals and rest in San Cristobal.

The large house into which we moved was spacious, but posed several problems. The two fireplaces perennially smoked, the chimney flues being inadequate to carry the volume of smoke produced by the pine firewood we burned. The tile floor of the large room on the northern end of the house reeked of the urine and manure from the livestock that had been kept there. My wife had to scrub the tiles repeatedly and order loads of fresh pine needles from the Chamula women who gathered them to form a better-smelling carpet on the floor. The walls had only a few small windows. When the large doors to each room were closed during days with heavy winds and rain, or at night to keep out the cold, the rooms became cold and dank.

We also soon discovered what must have been the most inefficient plumbing and water system that was ever installed. The town water lines did not reach the ranch; our water had to be pumped from wells in the courtyard. Hand pumps had been installed atop these two wells (one for each large structure) to raise the water from the wells and convey it to water tanks on top the houses. Problem: the pipes that ran from the pumps to the storage tanks were progressively smaller in diameter as they approached the storage tanks and would not carry a decent flow of water. After attempting to pump the water into the tanks ourselves, we discovered it was much more practical to hire a Chamula to do the laborious pumping. But the result was the most fitting commentary on the contrast between the developed and underdeveloped world I have ever encountered. If a student, in from the field, flushed a toilet, the Chamula would have to pump for over half an hour to replace the water in the tank of the toilet. If one of us took a shower, the Chamula would have to pump for almost two hours to replace the shower water. It was ludicrous!

By the summer of 1963 we had made some improvements in the water system. A gasoline-powered pump was purchased to convey the water to the tank of the large house and the tank of the former communal kitchen, which had been converted into an apartment. While Bobbie Montagu had envisioned communal dining with food prepared by a hired cook, we soon learned that individualistic Americans were much happier if they could maintain their own cooking and dining areas for their immediate families on a day-to-day basis.

I discovered that the former threshing shed was the best housing for our family. It was further from the front door in the wall of the compound; hence, those who lived in the large house would be the first to encounter visitors and to visit with them, thereby giving us more privacy. More importantly, this structure, which became known as Vogtie's House over the years, had a full wall of windows to the west of the large living room, and the afternoon sun would almost always warm and dry out this living space better than anywhere else on the ranch. Under the expert supervision of George Collier, a well-functioning fireplace had been constructed in the living room. Further, the view to the west, across the garden and the top of the compound wall, was of Bankilal Muk'ta Vits, called Huitepec in Spanish, the sacred volcano that contained the supernatural corrals of the animal spirit companions of the Zinacantecos. We could not have had a more beautiful or appropriate view, especially enchanting at sunset. The house had only one small bathroom, two bedrooms, a living room, and combination kitchen and dining room. But when our older three children reached the age of doing other things with their summers, we often had only our youngest son, Charlie, with us and the house was adequate. The house was rustic, with its stone floors and the barest of furnishings, but it had a certain charm. I always liked to point out the central pole (which helped support the roof) where the horses were tethered during the threshing process, and the circular stone surface of the threshing floor (called an *era* in Spanish), which was still clearly visible.

In that summer of 1963 Professor Kim Romney arrived from Stanford to work on his project in Tenejapa, and he and his family were installed in the large house, while my family lived immediately next door in the former threshing shed. I recall the hours that Kim and I worked together (whenever we were told by our wives that the water tanks were empty) in trying to start the gasoline pump. It proved to be a really frustrating motor that was continually stopping and had to be started again and again with a pull rope, like one starts the motor on a boat.

The lighting of the ranch in those early days was entirely by gasoline lamps and candles. By the mid-1960s propane-fed lanterns with mantles that gave a clear, strong light became available and replaced the more dangerous gasoline lanterns. Some years later, in 1968, I used project funds to have the city electric and water lines extended to the ranch. For the first time we enjoyed a relatively dependable supply of water and electricity. We could not, of course, drink the water, but could use it for showers, laundry, and house cleaning. For drinking water we continued to depend on the bottled water that was purified in the local plant by a twofold process. The water was first put through a process of electrolysis; then the twenty-liter glass jugs were placed in front of the household saint to add a supernatural purification. It was then sold for a very modest price; what was expensive was the deposit on the glass jug and the metal stand for the jug, permitting easy pouring of the water. These jugs were always in danger of disappearing into the Indian communities, for they were ideal containers for the bootleg cane liquor consumed at every Tzotzil ceremony; hence the elevated price of a deposit on these large *garrafones*, as they were called.

Most of the anthropological families living at the ranch hired at least one, and sometimes two, maids from the nearby barrios of San Cristobal. Full-time maids were quite inexpensive, being paid only a few dollars a week (and their meals), in the early days of the project. The level of poverty in Mexico has continued to be so miserable in the rural areas, and especially in the Indian villages, that a constant supply of domestic servants has always been available to the elite, as well as to the middle classes. Our policy was to pay them a somewhat higher salary than the going rate in the Ladino community. Not vastly more, a move that would have led to serious difficulties with our Ladino friends, but enough more to keep the pressure on for higher wages for the domestic servants who we always thought were underpaid. In any event, our maids were paid sufficient wages that they, in turn, were often able to hire cheaper servants to care for their small children at home when they were working for us.

Good maids would know how to help with or do all of the daily shopping in the large San Cristobal market. Since we had no refrigeration in the beginning years, it was essential to shop for fresh meats each day. The maids could also cook, wash dishes, clean house, do the laundry, and help tend the children. Since they were accustomed to carrying their own small children almost constantly in the first year or two of their lives, they were splendid nursemaids to comfort babies of busy anthropological mothers.

We had some wonderful maids over the years—all of whom were Mestizas, that is, part Spanish and part Indian—including Margarita from the Barrio of San Diego, who served as our principal maid during the early 1960s; María Luisa, a maid and compadre of George and Jane Collier, from the Colonia de Revolución, who also worked for us and later sent two different daughters to help in our household; María Elena and Teresita from the Barrio of Cerrillos. I believe the only time I behaved forcibly, like a typical Ladino patrón (boss), was one summer when I went to pick up Margarita at her home early in the morning and discovered that she had been employed by the Franklins who owned the Molino de Alborada Hotel on the southern edge of San Cristobal. In a rage, I drove at once to the Franklin's Hotel, asked for Margarita, ordered her to get her things and climb in the car, and took her to the ranch where she dutifully worked for us during the rest of the summer. Needless to say, Mrs. Franklin did not speak to me for several years!

We also had a permanently employed Chamula or Zinacanteco gardener to do the vegetable and flower gardening and to generally keep an eye on the ranch during the rare periods when no anthropological staff was in residence. In the early years our gardener, passed along to us by Trudi Blom, who no longer needed his services, was Salvador López Calixto, known as Mol Shalik (Elder Salvador). He lived in the Chamula hamlet of Peteh and had a large family, consisting of his wife and ten children. Like most Chamulas, he had small cornfields near his house, but they were insufficient to feed his family. Chamulas generally solved this problem by contracting to work on the coffee plantations in the lowlands of Chiapas. Mol Shalik's employment as a gardener at the ranch, where he served until his death, alleviated his need to leave home for long periods of time. Instead, he would return home on weekends, but live and do his own cooking in one of the rooms at the ranch during the week. He was an excellent gardener, tending both the flowers and the vegetables, except that he favored cabbage—which he liked to take home, with my approval, to his family—over other vegetables and had to be carefully supervised to keep the whole garden from turning into one large cabbage patch!

Mol Shalik also cut the grass in the courtyard with a machete, chopped firewood, split *ocote* (pitch pine for starting charcoal fires and fires in fireplaces) into smaller pieces, and carried the heavy garrafones of purified water from the cars into the various apartments. In his community of Peteh, he performed ceremonies as a shaman, and was highly knowledgeable about Chamula culture. He was steady, even-tempered, and a person of great poise and integrity. In later years we had various sons of Mol Shalik who served as gardeners; then, in the early seventies Andrés Pérez from the Zinacanteco hamlet of Ats'am became the gardener and served for almost a decade.

WORK AND PLAY AT THE HARVARD RANCH

Since one of the crucial priorities in renting Bobbie's ranch was to have a San Cristobal base for the more tranquil interviewing of our Indian colleagues, we always reserved spaces with simple wooden desks and chairs where a fieldworker could spend a day engaging in quiet one-on-one conversation. The most secluded location was the old bodega at the rear of the compound. In the early years this space continued to be used as storage space for belongings of the various anthropologists from the three universities that were renting the ranch. But it posed many problems. Like any institutional space, it tended to lapse into chaos as researchers left Chiapas and moved their gear into the bodega and others arrived to extract their belongings. Further, there were perennial arguments about which tables and chairs belonged to whom. Normally bright and mature scholars would fly into a rage if they arrived in San Cristobal and discovered that some colleague had appropriated their favorite bed or table in their absence. I would try to reason with them and point out that all of the furniture and cooking equipment was ultimately either the property of the university or of the foundation that had provided the funds for the research and living expenses of all of us. But this reasoning meant little, I am afraid, in the midst of the heated argument that ensued. I always found it amazing that individual researchers could become so proprietary about this institutional property, although I have to admit that often it wasn't the intrinsic value of the items so much as the effort involved in persuading a carpenter to build the furniture in the first place. In any event, my wife and I found that we spent considerable time mediating these recurring, petty disputes.

When a plan emerged to clean out the stored property and convert the bodega into four corner offices (leaving a middle room for storage), I warmly welcomed the idea. Frank Cancian deserves the major credit for having designed and funded (from one of his grants from the Ford Foundation) the renovation of the bodega. The four offices were all large enough to have large wooden tables and chairs and simple bookcases, as well as well-functioning fireplaces. These fireplaces were designed in such as way as to be elevated a foot or so above the floor and to provide warmth for people seated on chairs. I used by preference the office on the northeast corner, which had a view of the mountains rimming the Valley of San Cristobal on the north and also some early morning sunshine to help take the chill away. With a fire started by pitch pine and sustained by oak logs and charcoal, this office provided a wonderful setting for long interviews and for writing field notes as well as articles and books. I always brought my portable Olivetti typewriter with me (my original one was stolen one night by a thief who broke into the bodega via a window, but I purchased another one) to record interviews and to work on my latest article or book.

I soon discovered that on long periods in Chiapas—for example, six-month sabbaticals—I could devote more hours to writing, and still do my field research, than I could in Cambridge trying, usually impossibly, to allocate my time among teaching obligations, the endless department and committee meetings, and writing. At the ranch there was never a telephone to disturb us, and the gardener working with his machete just outside the bodega had explicit instructions to head off anyone who approached my office during the morning hours when I have always done my best interviewing and scholarly writing.

There were, of course, occasional times when I was interrupted by emergencies, such as the day when I was interviewing Mol Chep Nuh from the hamlet of Nachih and we heard loud shouts in the garden. Mol Shalik had just chased down and killed an opossum with his machete. When Chep Nuh heard the news, he turned as pale as I have ever seen a Zinacanteco face, and rushed out (with me tagging along) to closely examine the dead opossum. His animal spirit companion (of which he had had many dreams) was an opossum and he was frightened out of his wits that the one killed by Mol Shalik was his *chanul*. After detailed examination, the opossum proved not to have the identifying features of his animal spirit, and the color began to return to Chep's face. He knew he would live, and we could continue our interviewing session.

The other three office spaces were ordinarily assigned to other staff members or graduate students. But we would usually reserve one of them for undergraduates to use for their intensive interviews. For the most part, there was enough coming and going of personnel for there to be office space available whenever a researcher needed an office for working with an Indian colleague.

From the beginning of our headquartering at the ranch, I also maintained two large rooms in the newer building on the west side of the courtyard for research conferences and for parties. One of the rooms had a fireplace that provided necessary warmth and an atmosphere of good cheer for both conferences and parties. I considered the conferences crucial for good research performance and the parties essential for group rapport.

The conferences, which were held at Na-Bolom during the first few years, were now convened at the ranch where a long table provided seating for all in informal seminar style. We held these conferences at the beginning of the season to brief the students; midway through the summer to provide an opportunity for the students to present progress reports and receive feedback from the field leader, the more experienced students, and their fellow summer students; and at the end of the summer to hear an oral version of their final reports. The conferences would only last a day, or at most, two days. Longer conferences too closely resembled Harvard seminars and could become tedious and boring.

Beginning in the early years and evolving over time, my wife and I developed a style of dancing party that provided an opportunity for us to entertain the students, members of both the Euro-American and the Ladino population of San Cristobal, and our Tzotzil employees and colleagues. We would hire a marimba band for music, and for most of the years at the ranch the band was led by Don Timoteo, a *marimbista* from the Barrio of Cuxtitali, located on the northeastern periphery of San Cristobal Valley. It is reported that the original population of this barrio were Guatemalan Indians brought to San Cristobal by the Spanish conquerors during the colonial period. In physical type, Don Timoteo appeared to carry mainly Indian genes. He was illiterate, but a fine, dependable marimba band leader. He and his band would arrive on foot, carrying the marimba on their shoulders, and other instruments in their hands, at the appointed hour of nine P.M. For many years I paid him forty pesos an hour for his band, an amount equivalent to $3.20 an hour. We could afford to have him play until at least one A.M. and on many occasions, we would request, and pay him, to continue until three A.M. The instruments included the marimba, played by Don Timoteo and one other musician, a saxophone, and drums.

Preparations for the dance included placing dozens of *farolitos,* sometimes called *luminarios* (of the style used on top of adobe walls in Santa Fe, New Mexico, at Christmas time), along the edges of the porch in front of the party rooms and lining the path leading from the gate and crossing the courtyard. Farolitos consist of ordinary paper bags with the tops turned down about two inches from the top to provide stability. They are filled about one-third full of dry sand and a candle placed in the sand. When lighted, they provide soft, pleasing illumination and are relatively safe since if the wind blows the side of the bag into the candle and sets it on fire, it will only burn down as far as the level of the sand and then be extinguished. In the early years my children and I made the farolitos, but later we taught Mol Shalik, our remarkable Chamula gardener, to make them just in advance of each party.

The marimba band was placed in the smaller party room, which was lighted by candles for soft illumination for the dancing. The larger room was the bar and visiting room. Here the conference table became the bar. It was oriented East-West, like a Tzotzil ceremonial table, and a row of candles of the seven colors—always arranged with red on the east, black on the west, and blue-green in the center, replicating the Maya cosmos— was placed down the center. Drinks, especially rum and coke and beer, were served at this bar, as well as delicious tacos and fritos with various dips, prepared by Nan and the other wives with the assistance of the maids. Fresh pine needles were placed on the floor to make a carpet in this drinking room; extra pine needles and red geraniums decorated the center of the bar. The room was lighted with additional large candles in the corners and the light of the fireplace. The whole scene, especially on soft moonlit nights, was almost magical, and conducive to sparkling evenings.

Mol Shalik always came to the dance; he would tie a white bandanna around his head as a headband and sit on a bench near the doorway carefully watching the scene like the good Chamula shaman that he really was in his hamlet. He tended the fire, kept an eye on the candles in the farolitos, and appreciated the cokes I served him (he preferred not to drink alcohol) each time I served the musicians rum and coke. It was always the duty of the host at these parties in San Cristobal to keep the musicians properly fed and liquored up as they played away for endless hours. But I am sure that Mol Shalik considered himself to be the principal Totilme'il (Ritual Advisor) of the whole affair!

We would often have almost a hundred guests at these parties, including all the staff and students of the various university projects going on in Chiapas; the INI officials; many of our Ladino friends, especially the Velascos; members of the Euro-American colony, including Trudi Blom and all of her staff; and many Zinacantecos and Chamulas with whom we were working at the time.

The parties were always lively, with the drinking, eating, and visiting in the bar room, and, more especially, with the dancing in the other room. Since few students in the 1960s and 1970s had gone to dancing school, Nan and I undertook to teach them to dance, and they enjoyed learning. We emphasized the frequent changing of partners, by double-cutting, and by instituting dances in which a man could cut in by giving the large sombrero he was wearing to a dancing man and then dance off with his partner. Likewise, a woman would be given a broom with which she danced until locating a couple to cut by handing the female partner the broom and dancing off with her male partner. Even more spirited were the various line or snake dances done in Chiapas. These were formed by couples taking hands in long lines and then dancing either in circles or in snakelike lines that moved around both rooms and even out on the porch, picking up additional people until virtually all of the guests were included. With Don Timoteo picking up the spirit and playing a marathon of a lively *marcha* on the marimba, these dances reached almost a frenzy of communitas, which all enjoyed. I found that they really livened up the party; "it got off the deck" as we used to say in the Navy. Further, the evening-long dancing served to burn off the effects of the alcohol consumption, and we seldom had any problems with excessive intoxication. The students had not had much experience with handling alcohol, but with the spirited dancing, they had few problems. The Indians were used to heavy drinking; our mixed rum and coke drinks were mild compared to the straight posh they put away during their all-night ceremonies.

The dancing usually continued until about three A.M. when we would pay off Don Timoteo and send him home. Then with another round of drinks, one or more students would play the guitar and lead the group in singing by the fireplace. Often, this phase would last until 4:30 or 5:00, and we would feed the survivors breakfast in our house at sunrise. Sometimes, in the early years, I would join the students for a steam bath at Los Baños and then leave for a day in the field in Zinacantan. I always found it amazing that a good party gave me energy to work for a day without sleep.

Another feature that we added later, and especially on the eve of the Fourth of July, when we always gave a dancing party at the ranch to celebrate our own Día de Independencia, was the shooting off of cohetes (skyrockets) at midnight. At first, the Zinacantecos and Chamulas were in full charge of shooting off the rockets—a process that requires dexterity and a sense of timing. To set off a skyrocket, it must be held upside down while one ignites the gunpowder at the lower end of the cartridge with a lighted cigarette (a lighted match will not work). The rocket is then turned right side up and held for just the correct amount of time. If the rocket is released too soon—before there is sufficient thrust from the exploding powder to raise it into the sky—it will set off horizontally, and very likely injure some person standing nearby. If the rocket is held too long, it will explode in your hand, a fact that we were always forcibly reminded of when we went to purchase the rockets from one of the master coheteros who had only two fingers left on his right hand! Many of the students learned to fire off the cohetes, as did each of my three sons. To this day, I have never ignited a Chiapas skyrocket, nor do I intend to do so.

The firing of skyrockets created some problems for us at the ranch when it disturbed neighbors. For the most part our neighbors were several hundred meters away, but there was one exception: an attractive house located just outside the south wall of our ranch compound. This house was also owned by Bobbie Montagu at first, but it was later purchased by a retired engineer and his wife, Mr. and Mrs. Franklin, from Michigan (yes, the same Mrs. Franklin who later owned the Molino de Alborada Hotel and had hired our maid!). This couple were not party types, and they used to be annoyed by the loud din of our marimba parties. Relationships with them were often quite strained. One summer before a Fourth of July party, Nan and I decided to try to ameliorate the relationship with these neighbors. We invited them over for supper and extended a cordial invitation to attend the party. Late on the night of the party, one of the cohetes ignited by one of our Zinacanteco guests soared out of control and unfortunately exploded just over the bedroom of our neighbors' home! Needless to report, the pattern of strained avoidance returned to this relationship.

Marimba parties were not the only nocturnal activities at the ranch. For evening recreation we sometimes played bridge with couples such as George and Jane Collier. More commonly we would organize poker games that could be played by up to seven people if we stuck to "Stud" or a game that is called either "Toss" or "Grandma's Game" because it had been introduced to the Vogt Ranch in New Mexico by my late grandmother. "Toss" is played like five-card stud, except that the high and the low hands split the pot, and one can toss away and receive one extra card at the end of the deal. It is a simple, but fascinatingly sophisticated game if the stakes are high enough to permit credible bluffing. We never played for high stakes, but they were sometimes high enough to win or lose the equivalent of twenty U.S. dollars. The older members of the staff always undertook to teach the newly arrived graduate students and the summer undergraduates who were interested in the intricacies of poker. I remember that Kim Romney and Duane Metzger were especially skilled poker players, but many of the Harvard students, such as the Colliers, the Cancians, and later the John Havilands also became expert. In the early weeks of the arrival of new graduate students, the more experienced players would win substan-

The San Cristobal mariachis playing the Mexican birthday song, mañanitas, *for an early morning birthday at the Harvard Ranch.*

tial amounts of poker money from them. I recall that one season Duane Metzger and I managed to fund the everyday operating expenses for our respective projects from our poker winnings for several weeks. But the graduate students were all very bright—otherwise they would never have received their fellowships to do field research in Chiapas—and by the end of the season we had lost all these winnings to the students we had taught to play poker.

Since we soon discovered that these parties and games were crucial in creating group solidarity and in promoting good rapport among the research workers, we introduced more of them over the years. Nan and I lear .cd to celebrate birthdays in the Mexican way, and we attempted to provide a surprise celebration (modeled on the Mexican customs but with some embellishments of our own) of each of the student's birthdays that occurred while we were in Chiapas, whether during summers or during the academic year. The usual surprise episode of the birthday celebration occurred at six or seven A.M. when mariachis I had hired, along with other staff and students and invited guests, appeared at the door of the room in which the birthday person was sleeping. A *reja* (literally, grating), constructed

Student whose birthday is being celebrated at the Harvard Ranch breaks through the crepe paper reja *while the mariachis play* mañanitas.

of a latticework pattern of two-inch-wide strips of crepe paper, was held against the door by two members of the party, and fresh pine needles would be strewn in front of the door. Then, when all was in place, the mariachis would loudly play Las Mañanitas (The Little Mornings), a very touching and melodious piece traditionally played to awaken the birthday person. When the birthday person finally awakened (it would have been impossible to remain asleep with the mariachis blasting away outside the door), he or she would break through the crepe paper (obviously a symbolic recapitulation of birth) and be showered with confetti, then given an embrace by all present, and presented with a glass of rum. Some mighty sleepy looking, but always pleased, students came through the rejas. We would then move the scene to our house at the ranch where the floor had been covered with a carpet of fresh pine needles and the birthday person would be seated in a special chair decorated with pine tree tops and bundles of red geraniums like a Zinacanteco shrine. There would be dancing to the marimbas and a breakfast of the traditional festive tamales, made especially for birthdays, containing meat, nuts, and raisins, and wrapped in banana leaves.

If the student happened to be in the field and could not be surprised

*Dancing in our kitchen with floor covered
with fresh pine needles for an early
morning birthday celebration at the
Harvard Ranch.*

in his or her bedroom, then a surprise luncheon, with the mariachis playing the traditional tunes, and the birthday person sitting in the special
chair, would be given on the long front porch of the large house at the
ranch. I recall these wonderful birthdays being given for me during many
of our summers in Chiapas, and although I had to pretend to be surprised,
I always enjoyed them thoroughly and, from all reports, the students who
went through a Mexican birthday celebration always remember them. Traditionally, a Mexican took a holiday on his birthday, and so did I. After
the delicious breakfast, Nan and I ordinarily hired horses and went riding
into the mountains on my birthday, and I encouraged the students to do
the same. It was probably the only time that these busy North Americans
had ever taken a whole day off on a birthday.

In the 1970s we initiated square dancing at the Harvard Ranch, especially when John Haviland made a number of good tapes of records we
used in Cambridge for this type of dancing. Square dancing proved to be
a very appropriate form of recreation for the ranch since it only required
four men and four women for one square and was something that could be
organized on the spur of the moment using music provided by our tape recorders. Many of our colleagues and students became really adept at square
dancing; others had more difficulty, especially when they could not quickly
tell their right from their left hands. This style of dancing was unfortunately too complex for our Ladino and Indian friends who found the rapid
calls and synchronized movements impossible to understand, especially in
another language.

Over the years we also introduced various athletic games. One of the
tables in the large conference–party room at the ranch was a regulation
size Ping-Pong table that Duane Metzger had commissioned a carpenter to
construct of local pine lumber. The table tennis games played by most of
our staff and students became legendary over the years, even including a
"ladder" of competitors on the wall of the room. There were often spirited
singles and doubles matches, especially on rainy afternoons after the students who were in from the field had finished interviewing or typing their
field notes for the day. An innovative game called "around the world" was
later invented by John Haviland and his brother, Peter: a combination of
table tennis and squash in which the ball could either be played over the net
in the customary way or bounced off the walls of the room, as in squash.
I never attempted to play it, but it was wild to watch and was hard on the
paddles and on the Ping-Pong balls which were often broken in the fray.
For many years, I brought a new table tennis set and plenty of balls with
me from Cambridge to last out the season.

I do not recall who brought the first dart board to the ranch, but it
proved to be another intriguing game. It was installed on the covered front
porch of the bodega where it became an enjoyable form of recreation for
days that were too hot and sunny or rainy. We played especially over beers
just before lunch or over cocktails before dinner. The standard game was
the English pub form of 301 which I had learned from the eminent Oxford
Professor of sociology A. H. Halsey during our fellowship year together at
the Center for Advanced Study in the Behavioral Sciences. Although I have
no particular skill for such a game, I became skilled enough at 301 to take

on two students from Oxford in a local pub during our 1960 trip to Europe, and to win. They were astonished that I even knew how to play the game, which has some unusual features. Instead of winning by scoring points, you start with a score of 301 and must be the first to reduce it to zero. There are some further complications. You must "double in" to start reducing your score, and then you must "double out" precisely at zero to win. Many Americans, used to racking up points to win a game, were often troubled by these peculiar British rules. The games often went on for half an hour or more and could be played by several people. There were a number of formidable players during our years at the ranch. Kim Romney, who also learned the game from A. H. Halsey at the center, was my top competitor in the early years. Another skilled player was Dr. Dennis Breedlove of the California Academy of Sciences who became the world authority on the plants of Chiapas. I also acquired great admiration for the dart-throwing skill of Professor Thomas Crump (a Ph.D. student of Mary Douglas at the University of London and now a senior lecturer at the University of Amsterdam), who later joined our project to do field research in Chamula. Tom had a walleye, but always managed to see the dart board with sufficient precision to win, time after time.

I provided the first horseshoes for the ranch. They were purchased in the Ferreteria Nueva (New Hardware Store) in San Cristobal, which is one of the best hardware stores I have ever known. Every object for sale in the store is kept in systematic order, even the storerooms at the rear, which contain rolls of barbed wire, racks of pipe, and plumbing supplies. Behind the front counters are detachable display boards, showing each type of nail, each type of screw, each type of door handle, etc., for sale. Upon the arrival of a customer asking for a particular item, a clerk will promptly detach the appropriate display board and place it on the counter so that the customer can visually and manually select what is desired. The clerks know exactly where the stock is stored under the counter or in the wall behind the display boards and within seconds wraps up the desired item. Our American hardware stores are models of inefficiency by comparison—there is little logic in how items are displayed or stored, and you often have to search fruitlessly yourself for the desired object. They have always seemed to be examples of chaos to me. Dickson Hardware in Harvard Square immediately comes to mind as an illustration.

Since the usual Mexican store, as for example, for groceries, does not manifest this kind of order I wondered how Chiapas hardware stores managed to display such efficient order until I discovered that all of them were started by immigrant German families. Today these stores in San Cristobal are no longer owned by Germans, but the traditions established by their founders have been carried on by their contemporary Mexican proprietors.

The horseshoes I purchased were the ones used on the small horses of Chiapas—much smaller than regulation size. I like them for pitching horseshoes because I find I can barely pitch a regulation horseshoe from one pole to the other. The poles were pieces of metal pipes that we drove into the ground at the proper distance apart in the courtyard in front of the conference-party rooms. Horseshoes proved to be popular on dry days, and were frequently pitched just before lunch when the overhead sun provided the best illumination.

The game that proved to be the most popular, after it was introduced by George Collier and John Haviland, was volleyball, a game that could be played with from three to ten players, or more, on each side. The court was established in the cow pasture just outside the northeast corner of the ranch compound. To mark the line, gasoline would be poured in a line around the boundaries and then lighted. The burned line in the hard grass provided a visible boundary. The net, which required frequent repairs, came from the United States, as did the volleyballs and pumps to keep them inflated. George and John invented an ingenious system for keeping the poles upright in the ground, and at the same time permitting us to bring the net and poles into a sheltered location in the compound at the end of a game so that Don Gustavo's dairy cattle, which grazed on the court, would not damage the net and poles. There was also some chance that the net and poles might be stolen by people living across the pasture at Ojo del Agua, a village at the northern edge of the Valley of San Cristobal. We sank large pipes about a meter into the ground. The net poles, of suitably smaller pipe, with rings attached by welding to hold the net firmly in place could be placed into the larger pipes in the ground. At the end of a game, the net poles were removed and the net rolled up around them for safe storage.

Weather permitting, a volleyball game would be organized each afternoon at about four, with teams consisting of any of the staff or students who were present at the ranch or came down from San Cristobal center to join us. Everyone was encouraged to play, regardless of skill or previous experience. Teams would be chosen that were approximately matched for

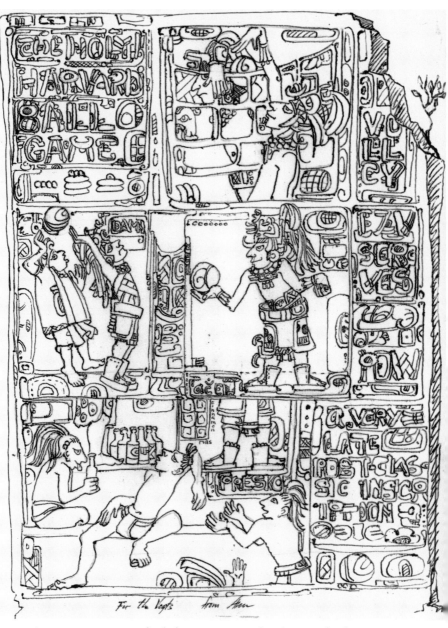

An imaginative pen-and-ink drawing presented to the Vogts by the artist, Ann Leggett. Utilizing the style of a classic Maya stela, the drawing depicts in glyphs various episodes in a typical afternoon volleyball game at the Harvard Ranch. Reading from left to right across the stela: (top row) "The Holy Harvard Ball Game," two players reaching over the net, "Volley"; (middle row) two players miss the ball and exclaim "Damn," player preparing to serve, "EZV Serves. Pow!"; (bottom row) the party at the Vogts' house following the game, including the cinnamon rolls baked by Nan and the word "Fresco," meaning "refresco"; finally (lower right) "A Very Late Post-Classic Inscription."

playing skills, and we would then play from four until past sunset and often into the twilight when it was no longer possible to see the ball. I remember several occasions when the game was lively enough to go on briefly into the full moonlight that followed the tropical twilight. Following the game, Nan would serve her freshly baked cinnamon rolls with soft or hard drinks. It was a refreshing and joyful daily experience as we played through the late afternoons and witnessed breathtaking sunsets filling the Chiapas sky over the Valley of San Cristobal.

PROJECT VEHICLES

The project vehicles parked just outside the wall of the ranch during the early years were the two Land Rovers belonging to Harvard and to the University of Chicago. Since the Chicago vehicle had been purchased first and had been subjected to severe punishment as multiple drivers of varying skill and knowledge about cars traveled to and from Tenejapa and Chanal over impossible roads, it gave out first. One summer I found it propped up on blocks at the ranch, someone having stolen all the tires and two of the wheels. I wrote to McQuown to see if I might purchase the remains to use for parts to keep the Harvard Land Rover in good repair. Mac was good enough to give it to me as a gift, and I have never forgotten that favor, especially since Land Rover parts were always in short supply in Chiapas.

Soon, however, our Land Rover with the Harvard logo and the words Museo Peabody de Antropología painted on the front door panels began to fall apart as well. I had learned during the Values Study Project in the Southwest how badly institutionally owned vehicles are treated by most fieldworkers. There were exceptions, of course, but many researchers seem to have an attitude that something belonging to Harvard, a rich institution, can simply be driven into the ground without accountability—a point of view I deplored, but could never do much about.

In June 1964 we purchased a second vehicle in Tuxtla Gutierrez, this time a sturdy Jeep. Although it was a backbreaker in which to ride, it served the project well until one unfortunate day in the autumn of 1964 when Bob Laughlin had parked the vehicle outside the house of one of his compadres on a slope on the edge of the escarpment in Paste'. A group of young, playful Zinacanteco boys climbed into the Jeep, which Bob had not troubled to lock in this remote hamlet, and managed to release the brake and take the vehicle out of gear. With the young Zinacantecos aboard, the Jeep began to roll off the edge of the escarpment, which lies six thousand feet above the Grijalva river valley. Fortunately, all of the agile Zinacantecos managed to jump out in the nick of time as the Jeep went over the edge. At the time, Bob Laughlin was seated next to a dying godchild being prayed for by a shaman. He heard shouts and later a loud crash. The shaman stopped in midverse and all rushed out of the house to find the Jeep stopped by a sturdy oak several hundred yards down the steep escarpment.

It took a wrecker truck with a winch to pull it back on top and haul the wreck to the Jeep agency in Tuxtla Gutierrez. It turned out that the insurance policy was a temporary one only covering such unlikely events as being struck by lightning or being damaged in a popular rebellion. Angel Robles, a good friend of Laughlin's, was able to convince the insurance company that there had been a popular rebellion and by this means the cost of repairs was covered. But completing the repairs was another matter. As I was about to arrive in the summer of 1965, Bob telephoned and told me that, after more than six months in the garage, the repairs had still not been done. I learned that these were the days in Mexico when the vehicles repaired were only those owned by friends of the garage owner or those who raised sufficient fuss to get action. I took a number of steps: I went to see the head office of the insurance company in Mexico City and I telephoned the agency warning them that I was arriving in Chiapas. By the time I reached Tuxtla Gutierrez six mechanics and body repair experts were working on our Jeep. But, even with this new attention, the Jeep was still not operable for some four weeks, and, in the meantime, the Land Rover had also broken down.

It was during this period that I made an interesting discovery. Without the vehicles the pace of life slowed down. Daily marketing for food and supplies had to be made on foot or by hired taxis, which never liked driving over the rough road to the Harvard Ranch. More importantly, I discovered how much time I had to talk to students as I traveled on foot with them to various locations. For example, on several occasions I walked from San Cristobal to Zinacantan Center with one or more students. It was a leisurely journey that took about two and a half hours. During the hike I could discuss their research problems and progress in more detail than I ever had in a vehicle that was rough and noisy and took only half an hour to make the trip. It was like having an ambulatory tutorial session, and I enjoyed the experience.

When the Jeep was finally ready, I went to Tuxtla Gutierrez to pick it up. All was finished, except that it did not have its lockable door handle on the driver's side. No problem, said the service manager. He took the same type of handle off a state government Jeep that had just reached the shop and would be there some days (or months!) for repairs. I was sure the same fate had befallen my door handle six months before. But then there was no key to fit the lock. Again, no problem. The service manager knew an expert who used to be an automobile thief, but now specialized in making keys for the garages in Tuxtla. The expert arrived with a set of wires he used to make measurements by probing inside the lock and within an hour produced the key that we used for the duration of the life of the vehicle. It was an object lesson about how easy it is to reproduce the average automobile key, and I reflected that, in the end, how much all of us depend on human trust in a world in which locks with keys may slow down, but never really prevent, theft.

LATER YEARS AT THE HARVARD RANCH

During the first decade of our occupancy of the Harvard Ranch I devoted considerable time and resources to the repair of the tile roofs, the extension of the town electric and water lines to the compound, the repair of the approach road, when it became impassable, and minimal painting of walls, usually done by whitewashing with lime. With the arrival of electric power, we acquired a small refrigerator and, for the first time, had ice (made with purified water) to put in drinks. (Before that time, I gather that Vogtie's warm martinis had become legendary among the field researchers.) The ranch was rustic, and minimally comfortable. I deliberately kept it this way during our first decade of occupancy, and resisted suggestions that we ought to purchase the ranch. Don Polo and others thought the property we were renting should and could be purchased for approximately ten thousand dollars in those days. But I had seen field stations that were owned by scientists. I particularly recall one owned by a botanist, whose name I have forgotten, in Panajachel on Lake Atitlan. It was very pleasant when we had cocktails with him compared to the rustic conditions under which we lived in Chiapas. But I noted that with ownership always comes what I call "nesting behavior," when too much of the effort of the researcher goes into improving the nest and too little is devoted to continuing scientific research. I was determined to keep the Harvard Ranch as it was—rented property and minimally comfortable—and instead to emphasize getting out into the field with the indigenous populations and continuing what I consider *real* anthropology. I believe that history will demonstrate I was correct.

I did, however, wonder after ten years of renting the ranch from Calixta whether we ought to explore the possibility of purchasing the property, especially since we could probably almost have paid for it with the amount we disbursed for rent during this time. I wrote to Calixta when the third five-year rental contract was being negotiated and asked if she would be willing to sell. She responded that she was saving the Chiapas ranch for her daughter, Tete, who might wish to return to the land of her ancestry when Cali died. However, she was happy to continue renting at the same rate of eight hundred dollars per annum.

The years at the Harvard Ranch brought many memorable experiences, including one that is indelibly imprinted on my brain: the Guatemalan earthquake of 4 February 1976 when twenty-five thousand Guatemalans lost their lives. The epicenter was only some 150 miles from San Cristobal. It struck in the middle of the night when Nan and I were soundly sleeping in our house at the ranch. I immediately realized what was happening, grabbed Nan's arm to awaken her, and we dashed out into the central courtyard in our pajamas to be clear of the tile roofs and heavy adobe walls. We watched in fear and horror as the walls visibly swayed back and forth and dust poured into the shaft of light from the single bulb on the front porch of the large house. The Zinacanteco gardener and his family were also out in the yard, each of them screaming their heads off. (I learned later that what Zinacantecos always do during earthquakes is to keep screaming at the Earth Lord under the ground until he stops shaking the earth!)

The whole ranch came within an ace of going down. But finally the shaking ceased, and, then, as we shivered from the night cold and wondered if another quake would occur, we heard the eerie swish, swish of the water sloshing back and forth in the old well in the courtyard. It was a night of terror I hope never to repeat!

But by and large life went on more routinely during the years my project was headquartered at the Harvard Ranch. On a typical day, I would awaken about sunrise and build a fire in the fireplace to take off the morning chill. Then I would either work on my field notes or, more frequently, especially in later years, drive to the San Cristobal market, located about

a mile away, to make some purchases, such as oranges for juice for breakfast or fresh meat for lunch or dinner, arriving in time to purchase the
better cuts.

The market was a typical Mexican arrangement, with some of the items,
such as meat, fish, and some of the vegetables and fruits, sold under a large
covered shed mainly by Ladinos. Outside, either in simple canvas shelters,
or in the open air, were hundreds of vendors, mainly Indians from most
of the thirty Tzotzil and Tzeltal municipios in the Highlands of Chiapas.
The market was departmentalized in the sense that one always knew where
to find charcoal, *juncia* (the newly cut pine needles), herbs, *cantaros* (jugs
for carrying water), meat, fish, or maize. There was less order in the arrangement of fresh fruits and vegetables, and the clothing stalls and small
restaurants were spread over a large area. I enjoyed these early morning
marketing trips as I appreciated the variety of colorful clothing styles and
languages being spoken, as well as the large number of Zinacanteco and
Chamula friends I would meet.

Following breakfast, the maid would arrive to wash the dishes, make
beds, sweep the floors, and wash clothes while Nan went marketing for the
rest of the daily groceries. Unlike Mexican families that usually had their
maids live in, Nan always preferred to have them arrive after breakfast
and, unless we were having guests for dinner, leave in the late afternoon. I
would spend the morning in my study in the bodega writing up field notes,
adding to my current book or article, or interviewing a Zinacanteco or
Chamula who would later have lunch with us. In the late morning, students
who were in from the field would arrive for consultations that would be
conducted in my study or over a game of darts or horseshoes, depending
on the weather. One or more students would often be invited to join us for
lunch about one P.M.

Following the midday meal, I usually took a siesta of an hour, a habit I
acquired many years before while stationed in the Navy in Belem, Brazil.
This nap refreshed me for productive afternoon and evening work, which
would consist of either more conferences with students or more interviewing. I have never been very productive trying to write (other than routine
field notes) after one P.M.; my peak hours have always been early in the day.
By 4:30 or 5:00 I would hear the sounds of the beginning of the volleyball
game and go out to join them on the court. If there was no party, poker, or
bridge in the evening, we usually read in front of the fireplace.

During these two decades (1961 to 1981) the Harvard Ranch served as effective San Cristobal headquarters. Field researchers could alternate between having a tranquil base that provided some of the amenities of their customary life while they were writing up field reports or were engaged in the intensive interviewing of Indian colleagues, and living directly in Zinacanteco or Chamula homes on a twenty-four-hour basis while they were in the field. In my judgement this latter experience accounted, more than anything else, for the depth of sophisticated understanding of Tzotzil culture we were able to achieve. Further, there is little doubt that the opportunities at the ranch for intensive interviewing likewise furthered this goal of reaching penetrating ethnographic knowledge. I am also certain that the capability we had to reciprocate hospitality by providing meals and overnight lodging for our Indian colleagues added immeasurably to our rapport with the indigenous communities. One time when Chep Apas arrived unexpectedly for a visit with his entire family of twelve, Nan managed, on the spur of the moment, to serve all of them lunch at our dining room table and to turn the occasion into a joyous party with balloons and jelly beans.

In 1980 Calixta Gutierrez-Holmes decided to sell the ranch. Her adopted daughter, Tete, had grown up and become an accomplished ballerina in Havana, and she had no desire to return to San Cristobal. Cali quite properly gave me first option to buy, and the price (for property we had been renting for eight hundred a year) was ninety thousand dollars. At the time, we were just finishing our eight-year tour of duty as masters of Kirkland House at Harvard and were faced with locating a place to live. As an old Harvard hand by now, I knew that Harvard per se would never be interested in acquiring a field station in Mexico if it had to be paid for by scarce, unrestricted funds from the Faculty of Arts and Sciences. I doubted that any foundation would provide this kind of money for a field base. Nan and I agonized over whether we should simply try to rent in Cambridge, or in the suburbs, and try to raise the ninety thousand to purchase the Harvard Ranch ourselves.

By this time, the city of San Cristobal had grown enormously, and especially from indigenous populations that had had to leave their traditional lands and move into the valley. This was especially true of a large group of converted protestants from Chamula who had been forced off their lands and had settled on the northern edge of the Harvard Ranch. Meanwhile, the Ladino population in the impoverished, and appropriately named, Colonia de Revolución that bordered the ranch on the southern edge had also exploded. I realized that anyone who owned the Harvard Ranch in the future would have to keep a steadily employed mayordomo on the scene to avoid the increased threats of theft and vandalism.

After much thought we decided to spend our scarce resources to purchase a condominium in Cambridge where we would spend most of our time, and to plan to rent other houses or stay in a hotel when we returned to Chiapas. In the spring of 1981 the ranch was purchased by Don Gustavo Armendariz, a wealthy sugarcane finca and cattle ranch owner from Comitan who had moved to San Cristobal. Soon the patio cross located beside the old well in the courtyard was gone, and there would be no further decorations or ceremonies with sacred ritual plants of this shrine (originally made by Thor Anderson and presented to me one summer by the students on my birthday) that came to symbolize the field center of the Harvard Chiapas Project.

Don Gustavo Armendariz has graciously invited us to stay at the ranch for short periods during more recent visits, but ultimately we discovered that it was more convenient to stay at the Hotel Parador Mexicanos, owned by a daughter of our old friend Don Fernando Hernández. This hotel has a tennis court and is located only a few blocks from the market where by now one can ride by Combi (a VW van) out to Zinacantan or Chamula for a few pesos. Thus, one longer needs to own or rent a field vehicle to engage in productive field research in Chiapas.

Interestingly enough, some of the official municipal maps of San Cristobal Las Casas still label the old Labor San Juan de Dios Las Delicias as the Rancho Harvard. I suppose I should have erected some kind of stela as we left, to record the twenty years the Harvard Chiapas Project headquartered in those lovely, rustic buildings.

8 /
USING AERIAL
PHOTOGRAPHY
IN CHIAPAS:
1964−1980

Shortly after I initiated the Harvard Chiapas Project I became interested in the potential uses of aerial photography for our ethnographic research. I knew something of the uses archaeologists had made of aerial photographs in locating and mapping their sites. I decided that in this rugged mountain terrain in the Chiapas Highlands, covered with tropical cloud forests, where travel was slow and difficult, especially during the rainy season with as much as sixty inches of rainfall between May and October, aerial photographs could aid us enormously in mapping settlement and land-use patterns. Since we were having difficulties with house-to-house census-taking, I also believed the same photographs could be shown to our Zinacanteco and Chamula informants who could be taught to view their communities from an aerial perspective and tell us precisely who lived in which houses.

I had used some aerial photos taken by the Compañia Mexicana Aerofoto in 1954 for the preliminary maps of the hamlet of Paste' that were included in my first paper on Zinacanteco settlement patterns presented at the American Anthropological Association Meetings in Mexico in 1959. By 1960 I had concluded that the Highlands of Chiapas would indeed be an excellent site for the exploration of a variety of uses of aerial photography in ethnographic research.

In the summer of 1962 fieldworkers from the Harvard and Stanford projects had hired a small plane at the airport in San Cristobal and taken aerial photographs of Aguacatenango and two hamlets of Zinacantan. Frank Cancian, who was an excellent photographer, took most of the photos, and they were used to prepare maps of houses for census-taking

245

operations. Although the results were useful, they had limitations. It was impossible, for example, to obtain controlled cartographic coverage needed for the production of maps of large areas, or to obtain the necessary controlled overlap of photos for stereoscopic examination in a study of the topography (Vogt 1974: 57).

In the autumn of 1962 Duane Metzger, then at Stanford University, called my attention to the astonishing advances in aerial photo technology being used by the Itek Corporation of Palo Alto to count grape-drying trays (two-by-three-feet in size) from photos taken at seventeen thousand to twenty thousand feet in altitude. These counts of the trays were used to estimate the size of the raisin crop in California. (I learned later that Itek had also been employed by the Internal Revenue Service to locate outdoor swimming pools in swanky California suburbs!).

It was evident that this new technology could be highly useful in solving many of our research problems in Chiapas. However, I knew from our previous experience that it would be less than productive for the members of the Harvard Chiapas Project to carry out the proposed aerial survey, that is, to hire a plane, take the photos, interpret them, and prepare the necessary maps. I concluded that we needed some kind of professional expertise in aerial photography and interpretation.

THE PHASES OF THE AERIAL PHOTOGRAPHY PROJECT

In consultation with Norman A. McQuown, University of Chicago, and A. Kimball Romney, Stanford University, both of whom were then also directing field projects in Chiapas, I decided we should enlist experts to carry out an aerial survey of the Highlands of Chiapas to interpret the photos, to train some of our graduate students in the techniques of photogrammetry, and to produce the necessary photomosaics and maps. Our investigation into this matter convinced us that the Itek Corporation was best equipped to carry out such an operation. Itek expressed strong interest in the project and agreed to work closely with us at each stage of the operation.

In the aerial photography and ensuing ethnographic research, I served as the principal investigator while McQuown and Romney served as co-investigators during the first two phases (1963 to 1967). I carried on alone as principal investigator during the last phase (1967 to 1969). The funds were provided by the National Science Foundation for each of the phases (GS-262, GS-976, GS-1524).

In our first proposal (approved by NSF for two years) we focused on the aerial survey and the use of the photos to study the natural and cultural determinants of the settlement patterns and land use of selected Tzotzil and Tzeltal communities, as well as to explore more specialized uses, such as the geographic orientation of ceremonial sites and sacred places in these communities. A second grant (for two years beginning 1 July 1965) focused on a system of information retrieval in the use of the aerial photographs at a Chiapas Project Aerial Photo Laboratory that I established in William James Hall at Harvard. The third grant (for two years beginning 1 July 1967) continued most of the work proposed in the second grant and permitted us to employ the Compania Mexicana Aerofoto to produce the required contour maps based on the aerial photos.

The intensive planning for the execution of the first phase of the project (the operational flying and photographing and the production of photo-mosaics and planimetric maps) took place during the summer and autumn of 1963. To plan this first phase, Richard Kroeck, who served so ably as the project engineer from Itek for this research, came to Chiapas for a week in August 1963 to survey the area we wished to cover, take ground photographs, and familiarize himself with the Indian communities. I remember what a joy he was to have in the field. He proved to be one of the quickest people to catch on to the intricacies of, for example, Zinacan-teco drinking rituals as we visited the various hamlets and called upon my Indian informants. In many respects Kroeck proved to be a keener observer and more adaptable field person than some anthropologists I have known, such as one of my Harvard colleagues who repeatedly released bowing Zinacantecos with his left hand, rather than the prescribed right hand.

Kroeck also began the delicate negotiations with the Mexican government to obtain permission for the operational flights, which would take off from Tuxtla Gutierrez and fly over terrain that was close to the Guatemalan border. The procedure proposed by Itek was to subcontract the flying and photography to the Compania Mexicana Aerofoto, using their plane, pilot, and Wild-Heerburg Reconnaissance Camera (RC-9) for the nine-by-nine-inch photo coverage, while using Itek's 70-mm High Acuity (HyAc) for the panoramic photography. This plan would involve an Itek photographer flying along in the plane to operate the HyAc camera.

In November 1963 I flew to California to consult with Itek personnel in Palo Alto and to attend the meetings of the American Anthropological Association in San Francisco. Bob Laughlin was also present at these meetings, accompanied by his two Zinacanteco collaborators, Romin Teratol and Anselmo Peres, who were spending some months in Santa Fe with Bob working on the Tzotzil dictionary. The two Zinacantecos, with their short pants, pink-and-white chamarras, and broad-brimmed hats trimmed with flowing ribbons, stopped the traffic at the annual meetings. I recall that I gave a party in my room to which I not only invited the members of the Harvard Chiapas Project, but also such notables as Margaret Mead. The Zinacantecos were playing Tzotzil tunes on the violin and guitar when Margaret Mead arrived in her usual commanding way, carrying the walking stick she always carried after she fell and broke an ankle. The two Zinacantecos immediately stopped playing and moved forward to bow to Margaret Mead, thinking that, with her staff, she must be a shaman. Not too far from the truth, actually!

While in San Francisco I spent one day conferring with Itek personnel at their headquarters in Palo Alto, and it was here, on 22 November, that I learned via a telex that President Kennedy had been slain in Dallas. Later, in San Francisco, the two Zinacantecos witnessed on television the shooting of Lee Harvey Oswald by Jack Ruby, and by the time these tragic days had ended, Romin and Anselmo were more than eager to return to the relative safety of the Highlands of Chiapas.

At the end of the meetings, I rode with Bob Laughlin and his Zinacanteco collaborators on the Santa Fe train from Oakland to Gallup, New Mexico, where we stopped to visit the Vogt Ranch, as well as various Navaho and Zuni friends of mine. I shall never forget the look of fright on the Zinacanteco faces as the train entered the long tunnel through the coastal range as we left Oakland. There were many understandable comments about the Earth Lord, this being the first time the Zinacantecos had been in a tunnel and thus entered the domain of this dangerous deity.

In New Mexico I found it strange to be serving as the interpreter between Zinacantecos and Southwestern Indians, especially since the friends we visited in Navaho and Zuni country spoke English, rather than Spanish, as a second language and hence had no language in common with these Chiapanecos. Not surprisingly, the Zinacantecos were astonished that Navahos and Zunis butchered sheep and relished the mutton, and that they lived in a matrilineal society in which the sons-in-law came to live with the wives' families. Romin Teratol also commented on Navaho log hogans that "their houses are like woodpiles" (Laughlin 1980: 18), while Anselmo Peres added that "the houses that they built looked like pigpens . . . instead of tiles, they just put dirt on top" (Laughlin 1980: 82).

To my Navaho and Zuni friends, the Zinacantecos were an equally weird spectacle, especially in their style of dress, for by this time all of the Navahos and Zunis were dressed in western-style cowboy outfits. It was obvious that Native Americans from distant parts of North America do not automatically feel a bond with one another.

Over the next several months the negotiations with the Mexican government concerning the aerial photography project became exceedingly complicated. I was told by my colleague Dr. Ignacio Bernal, director of the Instituto de Antropología e Historia in Mexico City, that the Mexican cabinet had set up a special committee of its members to study the Itek proposal and had rejected it twice. It seems that the territory next to the Guatemalan border was considered a military zone over which the Mexican department of defense exercised strict control of the air space. As I reconstructed the events from talking with Richard Kroeck, who had had previous experience in foreign countries and was well prepared for all procedures, a hefty bribe from Itek (I never knew the amount) was finally handed over to the Mexican general in command of this air zone who then "looked the other way" as the flights proceeded out of Tuxtla Gutierrez.

Some years later all of Chiapas was covered by excellent aerial photography by the Mexican government, and it is now possible to order aerial photographs of any region needed for research purposes. But in the 1960s we had nothing but the old nine-by-nine photos of the Compañia Mexicana Aerofoto from their 1954 flights.

During the months of February and March 1964, while the dry season was in progress but before the swidden farmers had set fire to their fields, a narrow window of opportunity in the annual calendar, the entire Tzotzil-Tzeltal habitat of 6,400 square miles was covered by the nine-by-nine-inch photography, as well as 985 square miles of selected areas with the HyAc photography and other selected targets with oblique photography (Vogt 1974: 60–61).

By the fall of 1964 we had in hand 1,226 exposures in the nine-by-nine-inch format covering the Tzotzil-Tzeltal habitat. Nominal flying height

Aerial oblique photo of Zinacantan Center in 1964. Note Church of San Lorenzo (center) and town hall (across the street to left of the church).

for this RC-9 photography was chosen at 11,600 feet above mean terrain. However, because of the large difference between the highlands and the Grijalva Valley in average elevation, the coverage was divided into two zones. The lower terrain (being 1,000 to 2,000 feet above sea level) was flown at 13,100 feet, the more mountainous terrain at 18,100 feet. Each exposure covered an area of approximately 30,000 square feet (a little over 1 square mile), providing a scale of 1:40,000 (1 inch = 3,333 feet) and with each nine-by-nine photograph covering an area of approximately 32 square miles. Flight lines were programmed to provide 80 percent overlap between successive photos and 50 percent sidelap between adjacent lines to give the potential for stereoscopic viewing. These cartographic photos proved to be excellent for large-scale mapping of both the highlands and lowlands.

Aerial view of the Zinacanteco hamlet of Apas in 1964, tucked between a mountain ridge (right) and a deep canyon.

The flights also produced 1,732 exposures, taken with Itek's HyAc panoramic camera, of the municipios of San Cristobal Las Casas, Zinacantan, Chamula, Tenejapa, and Aguacatenango in which the ethnographers from the three universities had focused their fieldwork. The HyAc was a direct scanning camera with a maximum scan of 120. It had a curved film plane and a high-quality narrow-angle lens, which scanned the flight path of the aircraft. As it swept back and forth, it photographed a wide swath of ground. By using only the center lens field over the total angle scanned, it photographed the entire swath of coverage in high resolution. However, the scanning action of the center lens produced distortion, occurring at both ends of the sweep. Consequently, much overlap was desirable, and flight lines were programmed to provide 40 percent forward overlap and 40 percent sidelap. The least distorted image was the one most directly be-

Chamula Center in 1964. Note Church of San Juan in center; the town hall is to the right and below the church. The houses that appear darker are roofed with thatch; the lighter roofs are constructed of more modern tile.

neath the flight line. Flying altitudes for the HyAc were 10,000 feet. At this altitude, the scale was approximately 1:10,000 (1 inch = 834 feet). Each exposure covered approximately 1,875 feet (about ⅓ mile) in the flight direction and a swath of 4.5 miles. At this scale, one can see all the individual houses, trees, and fields with clarity. As we discovered later, we could even distinguish between a thatched and a tile roof, using these high resolution photos.

Finally, we obtained 59 low-level oblique photos, taken with a handheld Fairchild K-3 camera, of selected targets in the research areas, especially of ceremonial centers, hamlets, and sacred mountains (Vogt 1974: 60).

Part of the contract with Itek during the first phase included the production of photomosaics of the municipio centers and of most of the hamlets

of Zinacantan, Tenejapa, and Aguacatenango, as well as a number of planimetric maps. We soon discovered that the maps were not as useful as the
photomosaics, because the Itek photo interpreters, being unfamiliar with
Chiapas, were unable to select geographically and culturally relevant details to place on the maps. We found that our field anthropologists, and
more especially our Indian collaborators, using the photomosaics were
better photo interpreters than the Itek specialists (Vogt 1974: 60).

Active research utilizing the aerial photography was begun in the spring
of 1964 and consisted of a number of ethnographic problems focused on
settlement patterns, land tenure, and sacred geography. I was able to present
a report entitled "The Use of Aerial Photographic Techniques in Maya
Ethnography" on our preliminary results at the Seventh International Congress of Anthropological and Ethnological Sciences in Moscow in August
1964 (Vogt and Romney 1971).

The second phase of the project focused on the establishment of a system of information retrieval and interpretation. It was supervised from
our Chiapas Project Aerial Photo Laboratory in William James Hall at
Harvard. We again turned to Itek Corporation to provide a system that included a set of graphics consisting of photo plot indexes for the RC-9 and
HyAc flight lines, which made it possible to easily locate any area covered
by the photos.

The viewing equipment for the retrieval system included an Itek Modi-
fied eighteen-by-twenty-four reader-printer and a Bausch and Lomb Zoom
70 stereoscope with a scanning stage. It was also necessary to have in-
dexed duplicate rolls of the seventy-millimeter negatives and to have some
of the RC-9 negatives reduced to seventy-millimeter size to fit them into
the reader-printer and Zoom 70 stereoscope.

Our aerial photo laboratory became fully operational during 1965–66,
and its facilities were made available not only to the coinvestigators at
Chicago and Stanford, but to other universities as well. George Collier
took a special interest in the aerial photography and began to apply his
recently learned computer skills to the solution of various demographic
and land tenure problems. In November 1965 Collier and I presented a
paper entitled "Aerial Photography and Computers in the Analysis of Zinacanteco Demography and Land Tenure" at the meetings of the American
Anthropological Association in Denver. A week's training program for
fieldworkers was provided by Itek in February 1966 at their laboratories

in Palo Alto; I attended this very productive training program along with Robert Mc. Adams, Frank Cancian, George Collier, Gary Gossen, Norman McQuown, Richard Price, Kim Romney, and Brent Berlin. In October 1966 Itek produced "A Manual for Users of Aerial Photography of the Highlands of Chiapas, Mexico" by Richard M. Kroeck, which was distributed to Chiapas fieldworkers.

During the third phase, while continuing to operate the aerial photo laboratory at Harvard, we obtained additional ground control surveys and photogrammetric work from the Compania Mexicana Aerofoto. They produced maps for us with a scale of 1:10,000 and with contour lines of ten-meter intervals for settled areas and fifty-meter intervals for farming areas, in order to test hypotheses concerning the influence of topography on land-use and settlement. The Compania Mexicana Aerofoto also asked to borrow the original film of our nine-by-nine coverage in order to complete a photomosaic of Chiapas that they were preparing for the Mexican government. We complied with their request and it soon became possible to purchase excellent copies of rectified aerial photomosaics of any part of Chiapas directly from the Compania Mexican Aerofoto (Vogt 1974: 62).

THE USES OF AERIAL PHOTOGRAPHY IN CHIAPAS

The use of aerial photography in the Harvard Chiapas Project turned out to have two major aspects. First, there were the uses that we anticipated and planned for in advance. Second were the unexpected uses, which emerged in the course of our project operations.

Five major uses of the aerial photography were planned for in the original research designs. I discuss each of them here briefly to provide a kind of inventory of the research.

ANALYSIS OF SETTLEMENT PATTERNS

The mapping and analysis of settlement patterns is in the long run perhaps the most fundamental use of aerial photography in ethnographic research. With aerial photos, the settlement patterns can be mapped with precision to provide a focus for the analysis of their ecological and cultural determinants. In the case of the Maya I hypothesized that the basic pattern was one of dispersed hamlets that sustain ceremonial centers either occupied by religious and administrative officials, or at least serving as the foci of ritual activity for the people living in the dispersed hamlets. I postulated that this settlement plan evolved early in Mayan cultural history and that the Mayas have tended to follow it in essence ever since (Vogt 1964). In the concept of ceremonial centers were included the large prehistoric centers containing pyramid temples, the minor ceremonial centers, the *cabeceras* of the modern municipios that now contain Catholic churches rather than pyramid temples, as well as a variety of water holes, caves, cenotes, and other sacred places that function as the foci for ritual activity for smaller units of Maya society.

A counterhypothesis argues that the observed settlement patterns reflect important ecological conditions and have little or nothing to do with the cultural patterns that have persisted from the prehistoric past. For the Maya area there had been a paucity of data on which to choose between these two extreme positions, a basic cultural hypothesis versus an ecological hypothesis, especially for contemporary communities. The efforts of the ethnographers had lagged behind those of the archaeologists, the ethnographers having produced little that compared with the precise and elegant maps drawn for the prehistoric sites in the Maya area (Vogt 1974: 63).

The data derived from the aerial survey combined with continuing ethnographic research were used to study selected municipios where the ecological and cultural conditions varied in specifiable ways. We soon discovered that the determinants of settlement patterns in any given municipio were an intricately interwoven set of ecological and cultural factors.

Some of the more interesting discoveries about the nature and determinants of settlement patterns in Zinacantan were made by Linnea Holmer Wren who began her research on the aerial photos in my freshman seminar on the Maya during the 1966–67 the academic year (Wren 1967) and continued the work during her undergraduate years culminating in her A.B. honors thesis (1970). Utilizing the aerial photos, Wren measured all the distances between houses *within* domestic groups and *between* localized lineages (snas) in three hamlets, which ranged from highly dispersed (Paste'), to intermediate (Nabenchauk), to compact (Apas) in settlement patterns. She discovered that the distances between houses within domestic groups (or patio groups) were remarkably constant. In each hamlet she studied, the mean of these distances lies within an eleven- to fifteen-meter range. However, the distances between the clusters of houses (forming the localized lineages) within the water hole groups varied in each of the hamlets. In Paste', the most dispersed hamlet, the mean was 550 meters; in Nabenchauk, the mean was 224 meters, in Apas, the most compact, the mean was 112 meters. These data indicated that Zinacantecos had a preference for keeping the houses of fathers and married sons all close together around the patios of their compounds. But the distances between these domestic group compounds located around their communal water holes varied significantly among the three hamlets (Wren 1974).[1]

The aerial photo data demonstrated that the crucial ecological constraints in Zinacanteco settlement patterns were the availability of household water during the dry season (during the rainy season ample water can be collected from runoff from house roofs)—that is, the more water available in the communal water hole, the more compact the settlement may be, and the microtopography, especially the degree of slope of the land. The critical cultural factors revolved around Tzotzil kin groups, that is, the preference for living in patrilocally extended families, which were the building blocks for patrilineages (Vogt 1974:63).

MAPPING LAND OWNERSHIP AND LAND-USE

The aerial photographs provided us with a wealth of data on land plots and land-use. We discovered that land-use can be determined quite exactly by ground checking sample areas with Indian informants. The land plots can be precisely mapped since each small plot always has some kind of border, such as a brush and pole fence, which shows up in the aerial photos. Present ownership and inheritance can be studied by presenting the photos and maps to Indian informants, who will describe in endless detail the transmission of land in the case of each plot used either for a house or a field.

Our studies of land tenure included the analysis of cemeteries in which previous owners were buried. The graves could be identified in ground photos and provided an excellent check on informants' memories about preceding generations, about how the plots were acquired, and about expectations as to who will acquire the plots in the future. The three steps were linked to a household census and a set of genealogical plates on each community, and the data were collected in a manner that permitted computer handling (Collier 1969; Vogt and Romney 1971; Vogt 1974: 67).

CENSUS-TAKING

In my early years in Chiapas I learned how difficult and time-consuming it is to take a precise census of a Tzotzil community by going house to house. Not only do ethnographic census-takers run into the usual suspicion in these closed communities as to what they plan to do with the census, but in traditional Tzotzil society it is customary to engage in ritual drinking when any kind of delegation goes from house to house, such as collecting contributions for the annual fiestas for the patron saints. Suffice it to say that even the most experienced drinkers are not likely to cover many houses in a day before they have been drunk under the table. These difficulties can be avoided by using a sample of informants to identify who lives in each house on a set of aerial photos. We found it was possible to reach nearly 100 percent accuracy in a fraction of the time and effort that is required for the traditional method of taking a census (Collier 1974; Vogt 1974: 67).

STUDY OF SACRED GEOGRAPHY

Another use of the aerial photographs that proved to have great potential concerned sacred geography. By this term I mean the location and mapping of sacred shrines that are visited by ritual processions performing ceremonies for curing illness, making rain, and worshipping the ancestral gods in the mountains and the earth god below the surface of the earth. The major mountaintop shrines show up clearly in the photographs, and with the aid of informants we were able to pinpoint the shrines at the foot of mountains, as well as the location of sacred caves that serve as channels of communication with the Earth Lord.

Two aspects of this sacred geography were of special interest. One concerned the precise location of the shrines with reference to the ceremonial centers and with reference to the cardinal or intercardinal directions. The second aspect of sacred geography we investigated was the relationship of social units to the ceremonial circuits made in ritual processions. The mapping of these ceremonial circuits performed by lineage and water hole groups pinpointed the size and structure of these social units in relation to the land and water holes they controlled.

Much more sophisticated use of the aerial photos was undertaken by Bob Laughlin who used them to elicit a complete inventory of place-names in the municipio of Zinacantan (Laughlin 1975: 573–86 plus maps).

INDICES OF CULTURAL CHANGE

From the aerial photography we also mapped certain kinds of data that would provide objective indices of cultural change. It would have been ideal to have a succession of aerial photos of the same municipios taken at intervals of five or ten years. But photos taken in 1954 by the Compania Mexicana Aerofoto compared to the same areas covered in 1964 provided useful comparative data on such matters as change in settlement pattern, demographic growth, and new roads.

Other evidences of change could be studied from the 1964 photos, especially from the large-scale HyAc coverage and the low-level oblique photos. For example, we discovered that the thatched peak of the steep traditional roofs reflected the light and appeared regularly as a white dot, something that was lacking on the tile roofs. Hence, we were able to count and map the distribution of the shift from traditional thatch roofs to the more modern Ladino-style tile roofs (Vogt 1974: 72).

In the course of our research operations, we also discovered five unanticipated uses of the aerial photography.

MORE PRECISE ETHNOGRAPHIC DATA

Although we anticipated that mapping of such features as settlement patterns from the aerial photos would result in much better information, we were startled by the extent to which this proved to be the case. A dramatic example was the settlement pattern map I drew in 1969 from the old 1954 photos and from my own fieldwork on the ground, and the settlement pattern map derived from the 1964 aerial coverage (see Vogt 1974: 73–74). Some of the difference is attributable to changes that occurred over the years, but more importantly the HyAc coverage permitted much clearer images for the location of houses in relation to water holes and to major hilly areas that are uninhabited. Further, the new photos provided for much more precise identification of lineage and water hole groups. With the better photos, the same informants I used in 1959 were forcibly reminded in 1964 of lineage groups and water hole affiliations they had previously overlooked. Paste' proved to have six water hole groups, rather than five, and the large water hole group in the southern part of the hamlet proved to have thirteen localized lineages (snas) rather than six.

A second example was the discovery that the municipio had fifteen rather than eleven outlying hamlets. This ethnographic error resulted from our having taken the Mexican census as the basis for the count. For purposes of census-taking the Mexican government grouped the hamlets into eleven units. Once we had the aerial photos it was possible to reexamine the whole municipio in detail, pick out clusters of houses in remote places, and ask informants about them. They would respond, for example, "Oh, yes, that's Potovtik, we forgot to tell you about that group before!" It became clear that from a Zinacanteco point of view, and judged by the operational presence of municipio officials representing the hamlets, Zinacantan had fifteen hamlets.

SAVING RESEARCH TIME

Although we had anticipated that the aerial photos would save us time in such matters as taking a census or mapping and land-use, we were again startled by their efficiency. A good example is Richard Price's (1974a) sophisticated study of land-use in Muk'tahok', a project on which he accomplished the fieldwork in less than a month. Price utilized print enlargements at an image scale of approximately 1:20,000 of the RC-9 photographic coverage and HyAc panoramic contact prints at a scale of approximately 1:1,250. After several days of familiarizing himself and a Muk'tahok' collaborator with photo analysis by walking large tracts of land with contact prints in hand, they sat down to chart the boundaries of the ejido and to make an estimate of the current state of each field—one year fallow, two years fallow, and so forth. Price estimates that comparable work without the aid of aerial photos would have required many months. I would judge at least six months, or a ratio of 1 to 6 in the saving of research time.

LARGE-SCALE ECOLOGICAL ANALYSIS

In conferences with George and Jane Collier the idea emerged to utilize the aerial photos for the analysis of macroscale problems. We asked ourselves, "What kinds of questions suggest themselves if one looks at the aerial photos of a large region, such as all of Chamula?" We began to scan our coverage of Chamula with a view to detecting things one does not notice either in looking at photos of smaller areas or in traveling over the country on foot or by Jeep. We began to notice that certain areas of Chamula, especially near the ceremonial center, appeared to be treeless and barren, and that other areas, which seemed inhabitable, were still almost completely devoid of houses. This led the Colliers to propose a detailed study using the RC-9 frames as samples running across the municipio, which would systematically classify each frame with respect to such features as tree cover, degree of erosion, presence or absence of houses and fields, and presence or absence of trails and roads. This kind of systematic analysis provided a series of hypotheses about long-range cycles in ecological relationships in the Chiapas Highlands that might otherwise have been missed. One example is the following hypothetical cycle in six stages (Vogt 1974: 76):

1. Pure swidden agriculture
2. Swidden farming with the beginnings of settlement
3. Diminished swidden; increased intensive horticulture, with pickaxe land preparation; introduction of sheep, requiring fencing of land parcels; increased settlement
4. Exhaustion of land for swidden agriculture; conversion of larger tracts to grazing of sheep
5. Abandonment of settlement; fences giving way to open grasslands for sheep grazing
6. Heavy erosion along trails, aggravated by sheep grazing, rendering the area unusable

This, and other cycles, have since been systematically researched, especially by George Collier (1975) who has continued to work with aerial photography. His most recent project (in collaboration with Ron Nigh) involves the use of satellite images to track the ecological and cultural trends in the Chiapas Highlands—an outgrowth of his original work with the Harvard Chiapas Project.

TRAIL PATTERNS IN A NONGRID WORLD

Another of Linnea Holmer Wren's novel research efforts focused on a study of communication networks in Zinacantan. She especially examined the networks of trails and roads that appeared on the aerial photos of the municipio. It was clear that one kind of pattern prevailed in Zinacantan center, which is laid out in a grid pattern, but that quite a different pattern characterized the network of trails in the nongrid world of the outlying hamlets. Her research disclosed that in Zinacanteco hamlets without grid patterns, the trails fork at an average of 60 degrees. The problem then became one of explaining this surprising regularity (see Wren 1974). Even with the appearance of the stimulating articles by G. William Skinner utilizing central place theory to analyze Chinese market areas (1964; 1965), I am confident it would never have occurred to us to explore this interesting problem in Highland Chiapas without the aerial photographic coverage.

GENERAL ETHNOGRAPHIC USE OF AERIAL PHOTOS

After the Chiapas Aerial Photo Laboratory was established, I would introduce new students to the photos and ask them to think of ways to use reader-printer prints, or other photos, on their particular field projects. The results were astonishingly productive over the years, much more than I anticipated. The aerial photos became as crucial to the majority of our students as notebooks and typewriters.

To provide some examples. In 1968 a graduate student, Gary H. Gossen, who had been collecting oral narratives and exploring what they revealed about the nature of Chamula society, decided to utilize aerial photographs to refine his description of the worldview of the Chamulas. He put together a photomosaic of the municipio utilizing RC-9 prints that were enlarged to twice the contact print size. Then with acetate overlays he set out to collect precise data on the location of some 110 Chamula hamlets, as well as data on more distant places to which the Chamulas travel. He also elicited detailed data on sacred geography by collecting all the geographic place-names in and around the ceremonial center. I shall never forget the day he set out to collect these place-names. He and his Chamula collaborator worked all day long and by late afternoon, after having collected more than a hundred place-names, they had only moved about one quarter of a mile from the church in the ceremonial center! The final result was a sophisticated article on the spatial aspects of Chamula cosmology (Gossen 1974a).

In 1967 Carolyn Pope, a Harvard sophomore, chose cemeteries and funerals as her summer research topic. Her goal was to study the social structure of Zinacanteco cemeteries and analyze the relationship of this social structure of the dead to the living social structure in hamlets. Carolyn focused on the cemetery of the hamlet of Apas for which she had a reader-printer print and a photograph taken by a fellow fieldworker, Mark Rosenberg, a junior who was a photographer on the *Harvard Crimson*, from the top of a nearby mountain. She experienced serious difficulties with the topic because only the women of Zinacantan go to the cemeteries each Sunday to take flowers, food, and candles for the dead. While the women are knowledgeable about the cemeteries as a whole, the men know only the graves of their immediate ancestors. But our Zinacanteco colleagues could not persuade the women to serve as informants for Carolyn. Finally, Chep Apas made the astute suggestion that a group of twelve men from Apas be brought into San Cristobal on the same day to serve as informants for Carolyn.

With Chep Apas serving as interpreter, Carolyn worked with the twelve informants, each drawn from different lineages in the hamlet, all sitting around a large table and peering at an enlargement of Mark's photo at the Harvard Ranch.

Although Carolyn was in something of a panic about committing most of her budget for informant fees to a single day of interviewing, the procedure worked beautifully. By the end of the day, she had complete data on who was buried in which graves in the entire cemetery. The informants all had an interesting and amusing time in providing the information and joking with one another. It was a wonderful example of an innovative interviewing technique that proved to be very productive (Pope 1967).

Although the results of the aerial photography project have appeared in numerous publications of the Harvard Chiapas Project, as well as in those emanating from Chicago and Stanford, the volume I edited entitled *Aerial Photography in Anthropological Field Research* (1974) provides the most comprehensive view.[2]

9 /
THE "EARLY CLASSIC" YEARS: 1963–1965

With the major components of the field operations in place, including our headquarters at the Harvard Ranch, and the aerial photography laboratory functioning in William James Hall, I added one more component to the Chiapas Project—a component that proved to be effective for recruiting able undergraduates. This was the freshman seminar at Harvard, which I offered twenty times, beginning in 1962–63 and ending in the fall of 1988–89.

At the outset I did not have the freshman seminar in mind as a means of recruiting bright, interesting students for Chiapas. I had known about the program because Clyde Kluckhohn offered a seminar on the Navaho the year the program was instituted at Harvard (1959–60), and I conferred with a number of the students in that seminar. It was in this connection I first met George Collier and was so impressed with his intellectual capacity that I encouraged him to apply for the Undergraduate Field Research Program at the end of his freshman year. Following Clyde's death in the summer of 1960, I made a point of calling in each of the other students and talking with them. This was how I met Richard Price who later also did such impressive field research in Chiapas.

I decided it would be interesting to work with Harvard freshmen and proceeded to offer my first yearlong seminar in 1962–63. One of the real stars in that seminar was Michelle Zimbalist whose brilliant work led me to invite her to apply for the undergraduate field program in her freshman year. Two other outstanding students in this 1962–63 seminar, Merida H. Blanco and John D. Strucker, were selected to go to Chiapas at the end of their sophomore year.

263

From my freshman seminar a total of fifteen exceptional Harvard undergraduates went on to do fieldwork in Chiapas, or elsewhere in the Maya area. Twelve of these students were members of the Harvard Chiapas Project; three others ultimately engaged in research in Chiapas or neighboring areas on other projects.[1]

During the 1960s and 1970s I continued to offer the freshman seminar on the Maya and the undergraduate field training seminar, "Selected Problems and Methods in the Study of Latin American Ethnology" (required for all students going to Chiapas), as well as the graduate student seminar. The graduate seminar began in 1956–57 and was entitled "Middle American Ethnology." During the academic year 1964–65 the title was changed to "Anthropology 260: The Maya" and the seminar was taught jointly with Gordon Willey for a number of years. Each year it served as a forum for students returning from the field and giving their reports, as well as for those in training to go into the field in the Maya area for the first time. Each of these seminars had its place in the recruitment and training of students for the Chiapas Project, but our most intensive effort became the course in spoken and written Tzotzil, offered each spring term, which met at least twice a week for two hours and also assigned individual work with tapes kept in the language laboratory in Boylston Hall. Over the years, with the help of many of the students, but especially the assistance of George Collier and John Haviland, several improvements were made in this informal course—informal because it never appeared in the Harvard catalogue. I decided not to fight the bureaucratic battle of convincing what was in those days a rather conservative Committee on Educational Policy that "Spoken Tzotzil" should be an approved course. I simply continued to sign up the students for Independent Research so they could receive credit.

One distinctive feature of that informal course is worth emphasizing: the teacher was, by common agreement, the member of the Harvard Chiapas Project in residence who knew the most Tzotzil. He or she was automatically appointed the teacher. Sometimes this instructor was a junior member of the faculty, often a graduate student, and at times an undergraduate who had mastered the most Tzotzil. I never had the distinction of serving as teacher, since there was always someone on the project who was more gifted linguistically and whose control of Tzotzil was superior to mine. Both my wife and I regularly attended this course and improved our Tzotzil by learning from these accomplished younger instructors. I became convinced that the best possible way to teach a language was following this procedure. I always made certain that the teacher was well paid; if he or she was not already receiving a salary from Harvard, I provided funds from my research grant.

A second innovation in this language course was instituted in 1965 when, following the suggestion of George Collier, we began to import either a Zinacanteco or a Chamula to spend a month to six weeks with us in Cambridge during the spring term. To engineer this procedure, I would have to go to Chiapas, or dispatch an experienced member of the project, to make certain the Zinacanteco or Chamula had all the proper papers for coming to the United States and then accompany him on the journey to Boston. Otherwise, we were always fearful that the informant would get lost or be stopped at the border. Our fears were well founded as there were usually difficulties at one border or another. On one occasion when I flew to Chiapas to accompany a Zinacanteco back to Cambridge, we were stopped by the immigration official as we were leaving Mexico City. I was certain all the papers were in proper order, but the official asked, "But where is the green paper?" I thought about this for a few moments, then took a twenty-dollar bill from my wallet, put it in a folded piece of stationery, and handed it to the official, asking "Could this be the required green paper?" The result was an immediate passage through migración and onto the waiting airplane for Boston! At the U.S. border, the immigration officials were always suspicious that we were importing a domestic servant of some kind.

While the informant was in Cambridge we provided lodging and meals for him in our own homes, taking turns for two or three weeks at a time. These were the years when little Spanish, and certainly *no* Tzotzil, was spoken in Cambridge or Boston, and we could not risk problems with our valuable friends and informants. At the end of the stay, we again sent someone to accompany the native Tzotzil teacher back to Chiapas to make certain he arrived safely.

During his stay with us the Zinacanteco or Chamula would attend the Tzotzil sessions each week and serve as a native speaker of the language, injecting an element of realism into the procedure. We also provided the informant with an office and a typewriter. Each student member of the training seminars was required to engage the informant in intensive interviewing about the research topic he or she was going to pursue the next summer in Chiapas. When the informant was not busy being interviewed, we would ask him to write texts in Tzotzil with interlinear translations in Spanish on topics for which we needed more ethnographic information.

By the mid-1960s we had taught a number of Zinacantecos and Chamulas to write in Tzotzil, utilizing Spanish letters plus appropriate symbols for glottalized consonants and the glottal stop. Several of them, including all of the ones who came to Boston, had also learned (during a time when they were receiving a steady salary from project funds), to touch-type so that the texts could be written with copies on the typewriter. The combination of language training, serving as an informant for interviews with students, and writing ethnographic texts kept the informant busy during his period at Harvard, and helped to prevent him from becoming homesick and lonely.

The three Tzotzil-speakers who came to Harvard in the spring term of six different years to help teach in this language course were José Hernández (known as Chep Apas) from the hamlet of Apas (1965, 1968, 1971); Domingo Pérez Pérez (known as Little Romin) from the hamlet of Nabenchauk (1969 and 1973); and Mariano López Calixto (known as Maryan) from the hamlet of Peteh in Chamula (1970)—he is the son of our former Harvard Ranch gardener, Mol Shalik.

With the freshman seminar and the graduate seminar on the Maya in operation to attract interested students, I was in position to channel really top students at both levels into the Harvard Chiapas Project, and with the combination of the field training seminar and the intensive course on Tzotzil, they had superb training for their Chiapas experiences. The result was a remarkable series of research seasons, which I consider to have been the "classic years" of the project.

THE FIELD SEASON OF 1963

In the spring of 1963, with our project Land Rover nearly out of commission, I decided to avoid the high prices being charged for Jeeps in Mexico by purchasing a new vehicle in Cambridge and getting official Mexican government permission to keep it at our field station in Chiapas. I had received a letter from Dr. Alfonso Caso, the director of INI, informing me that he would be glad to write to the secretaría de hacienda recommending that the vehicle be designated as one used for "scientific purposes" and allowed to be kept in Mexico.

EZV with our three sons on camping trip from Cambridge to San Cristobal in June 1963. This was the ill-fated jeep that I never received official permission to keep at the field station in Chiapas.

I purchased a Willys Jeep station wagon and drove the vehicle to Chiapas, accompanied by my three sons, Terry, Eric, and Charlie (ages seventeen, fourteen, and ten) and Nick Acheson, who was returning to Chiapas for an additional summer of research on his ethnozoological project. We took our sleeping bags and cooking equipment and camped in state parks almost all the way to Mexico City, taking refuge in motels in central Mexico when we hit heavy rains as we did not have a tent, but otherwise simply sleeping in the open under the stars. After a relaxed ten-day journey, with stops for rest in Texas, and at Tula and Teotihuacan, we arrived in Mexico City where we stayed for four days while I had good visits with Alfonso Caso, Ignacio Bernal, Alfonso Villa Rojas, and Alberto Ruz. We then met Nan who arrived by air (she had been taking our daughter, Shirley, to Montreal to board a ship for France for her freshman year at the University of Grenoble) and continued on to Chiapas, arriving on 6 July.

Three new graduate students were in Chiapas that year: John D. Early who had arrived in December 1962 and remained through 1963; Victoria Reifler Bricker, who came for a visit during the summer; and Daniel B. Silver, who arrived in the autumn.

As I predicted, John Early, as a Jesuit priest, had easy access to the churches in Zinacantan and was later invited by the local priest, Father Juan Bermudez, to perform Mass on occasional Sundays. From this advantageous position he could be present to observe the ceremonies of the cargoholders and of the shamans who came with their patients to pray to the saints, both before and after Mass. He was ultimately invited to attend the ceremonies of the cargoholders that were held in their houses in Zinacantan Center, and he also took a series of informative Kodachrome slides of these rituals. When the Church of San Lorenzo burnt down in 1976, John kindly sent copies of his beautiful pictures of the saints and altar to Bob Laughlin who presented them to the Presidente del Templo and the Sacristanes. Laughlin adds: "Tears came to the eyes of the president of the church and the sacristans when I entrusted the photographs to them. They exclaimed at how much more luxuriant the floral adornments used to be. With the aid of these photos the altar was faithfully reconstructed and San Lorenzo and several of his peers were reincarnated" (Personal communication, 1 August 1991).

John Early's Ph.D. thesis in sociology, "The Sons of San Lorenzo in Zinacantan," presented in 1965, provided exactly the kind of fine-grained ritual detail on the ceremonies of the cargoholders that I hoped he would gather. Although his thesis was never rewritten for publication, he did publish an excellent article on Zinacanteco ritual (Early 1966).[2]

Victoria Reifler came to Harvard from Stanford in 1962 and was a brilliant student in the graduate seminar on Middle American ethnology during her first year in Cambridge. During the course of the seminar I discovered that Vicki (as she is called by all who know her personally) was also gifted in languages and linguistics, in part, I am certain, because her father was a professor of linguistics at the University of Washington. I invited her to come to Chiapas for a visit in the summer of 1963 with the hope that she would choose to do her dissertation on Chiapas data. This first summer she set about learning about the field situation. She also later wrote a splendid piece entitled "Good Manners in Zinacantan: A Manual on Etiquette for Fieldworkers" (1963) which proved to be highly useful for several generations of students headed for Chiapas. The idea for this field manual emerged in discussion with the summer students, especially when I was told bluntly by one of the bright students: "You teach us a lot of nonessential guff in that field training seminar during the spring term at Harvard, but you never get around to teaching us how to behave in a well-mannered way in Zinacantan."

This preliminary experience interested Vicki in Chiapas. She returned for a year in 1965 to undertake fieldwork on ritual humor, an enterprise that called for a return trip to Chiapas in December and January 1968–69 to observe fiestas in Chamula and Chenalho.

Vicki proved to be a really gifted fieldworker. She not only mastered Tzotzil well, but also began, at the suggestion of Zinacantecos, the process of audio taping the ceremonial sequences that occurred during the ritual bullfight at the end of the year and during the fiesta of San Sebastian in January. For the first time we began to understand what was really going on in these performances.[3]

Daniel B. Silver arrived at Harvard from Berkeley, where he had been an outstanding student and prominent in undergraduate affairs, including serving as editor-in-chief of the Berkeley student newspaper. After his exceptional performance in my Middle American seminar for graduate students, I invited Dan to join the Harvard Chiapas Project. He developed an intense interest in studying shamans and curing ceremonies, a domain I knew needed more exploration.

After training in the Tzotzil course, Silver started for Chiapas in the late summer of 1963. When he reached Oaxaca, he suffered some kind of heart trouble in response to the altitude and flew back to California. In the late summer I learned that he had accepted a field position with Professor Robert F. Heizer from Berkeley who was doing an archaeological survey in the Sierra Nevada range at altitudes that exceeded the five thousand feet of the Valley of Oaxaca. I concluded that I had another case of a graduate student who had panicked in Mexico. I wrote Dan, pointing all this out. Within a week, he answered my letter, agreeing with me. He returned to Chiapas in the autumn and collected a systematic body of ethnographic data on the various types of rituals performed by the shamans in Zinacantan.[4]

In accordance with a policy of innovating new programs but not sponsoring them on a long-range basis, the Carnegie Corporation only provided support for the undergraduate program for three years. Beginning in 1963 the program was funded by the National Science Foundation. I also persuaded the Harvard summer school to list the summer field training as an official course so that the Harvard students could receive formal credit for their work and the field director's salary would be paid by the summer school. I appointed George Collier, by then a graduate student, as an assistant field director for the summer to help me with the large group of new students: four from Harvard, one from Columbia, and one from the University of Illinois, which had joined our interuniversity program, as well as one from Smith College and one from Paris, giving a total of eight new undergraduates to place in productive field situations.

Jane Collier had recently given birth to their first child, David, and the Colliers had moved to the Harvard Ranch in an apartment that came to be known as "the Collier apartment." They were a tremendous help in managing the summer students, but I nevertheless comment in my journal for July 18: "a field party of nine students [including Acheson] is too many to allow the field leader (or even two field leaders) to do much research of their own. Both George Collier and I have been spending most of our time during the past two weeks doing little else than supervising research and making various arrangements. I should keep the field party down to six in the future."

But the students were a talented lot who undertook fascinating research projects. Two from Harvard, Nicholas F. Bunnin and G. Carter Wilson, had coauthored the Hasty Pudding shows for two years in a row before they came to Chiapas. Nick Bunnin studied the flower industry of Zinacantan, that is, the commercial growing of flowers for sale in the markets of San Cristobal and Tuxtla Gutierrez (Bunnin 1966).[5] Carter Wilson undertook field research (our first undergraduate to work in Chamula) on drinking customs and has published an article on this research (Wilson 1973).[6]

Mary Lowenthal Felsteiner, a bright concentrator in History at Harvard, arrived in San Cristobal by bus with a handsome Mexican boyfriend she had met in Oaxaca. George Collier and I became concerned about this relationship, especially when we learned that there were gangs of young men in the plaza of Oaxaca who used to place bets with one another as to how speedily they could seduce a Gringa. After a week or so, we succeeded in persuading Mary to send her boyfriend back to Oaxaca, a move that later led Franzi Cancian to comment that sex within the Harvard Chiapas Project group was permitted, but that sex outside the group was prohibited. I had not thought about the policy in these bald and explicit terms, but on reflection agreed that Franzi was correct. I was, indeed, tolerant enough about what went on among the students, but dead set against intimate relations, and the ensuing emotional complications, that might develop with either Ladinos or Indians. I believe this was not prejudice on my part, but a cautious, realistic policy.

Mary expressed an interest in studying the elite families of San Cristobal and spent the summer interviewing extensively on this subject. She produced an excellent field report entitled "The Elite of San Cristobal" (1963).[7]

The fourth Harvard student was Michelle Zimbalist. Shelley (as she was called) was a brilliant young scholar who had not only produced a remarkable paper in my freshman seminar, but had also made great progress in learning Tzotzil. George and I placed Shelley in a household in the hamlet of Granadilla, where she thrived and spent most of the summer; her final report was so outstanding it was later published (Zimbalist 1966).

James P. Warfield was an undergraduate major in architecture from the University of Illinois, Urbana. He was a natural to undertake a detailed study of the architecture of Zinacanteco houses (Warfield 1966).[8]

The other student from the Carnegie program was David A. Zubin, an anthropology major from Columbia who focused his research on the corn market in San Cristobal. It was also a fine piece of research; one of his fundamental discoveries was that the bargaining between an Indian vendor and a Ladino buyer had little effect on the price of corn. Both the vendor and buyer knew the going price of corn at the beginning of the transaction, and repeatedly settled at this price at the end. The essence of the transaction was a recurring symbolic statement of the relationship between Indians and Ladinos, with the Ladinos expressing an arrogant attitude of superiority toward the Indians (Zubin 1963).

The Smith College student, Nancy Locke, was the daughter of a neighbor in Weston, Massachusetts, and urgently wished to do field research in Mexico. Since her major was history, she undertook partly archival, partly interviewing research in San Cristobal on why the state capital had moved to Tuxtla Gutierrez. Her final report, in the form of an A.B. honors thesis at Smith (Locke 1964), made the point that San Cristobal was too conservative for that famous right wing dictator of Mexico just before the Revolution, Don Porfirio Diaz, and he ordered that the capital be moved to the more progressive Tuxtla Gutierrez!

George S. Arbuz from Paris, where he had been a student of Georges Balandier and Claude Levi-Strauss, was another special case. He had come to America to do graduate work at Northwestern University and came highly recommended by Professor Paul Bohannan of Northwestern University. Arbuz proved to be a delightful young man who spent much of the summer with a craftsman who made guitars and violins in a hamlet in Chamula (Arbuz 1963).

The two most important field experiences I personally had during the summer were attending another curing ceremony at the home of Romin Teratol (for details see Vogt 1969: 666–71) and making a hiking trip to the summit of Its'inal Muk'ta Vits.

For several seasons I had been looking longingly from the Pan American highway at the remote mountain, east of Zinacantan and south of Teopisca, which the Zinacantecos described as Its'inal Muk'ta Vits (Junior Large Mountain). It was only visited by Zinacantecos when there was a prolonged drought and a specialized group of high-ranking shamans would organize a four-day pilgrimage to the summit to perform a ceremony for rain. I had learned that this pilgrimage started with a gathering of all the shamans for an all-night prayer session in the ceremonial center, after which the specialized group set out, stopping first to pray to the T'en-T'en drum at its shrine in the hamlet of Elan Vo'. From here it was an all-day and all-night journey to the summit, arriving at dawn. Facing east toward a shrine on the summit of Its'inal Muk'ta Vits, the shamans would then offer copal incense and candles and pray all day for rain. On the fourth day they would return to the house of the T'en-T'en and disperse from there.

By the summer of 1963 I was determined to make a journey to the top of this sacred mountain, called Cerro Chenekultik by the local Ladinos, to see what evidence could be found of this rainmaking shrine. John Hotchkiss of the University of Chicago project was then working in Teopisca, and he knew the political boss of the town, Don Chema (José María Alvarez), who owned a ranch called Rancho Chenekultik near the base of the mountain. Don Chema assured us that we would be able to hire a guide at his ranch to show us the trail to the summit.

In addition to Hotchkiss, I invited Nick Acheson and Shelley Zimbalist, who had expressed an interest in the expedition, to go along. On August 26 we drove by Jeep to Teopisca and left the vehicle at the end of the road by

*On the difficult hike to the summit of Cerro Chenekultik in the summer of 1963.
Left to right: John Hotchkiss, Nick Acheson, our local guide, Michelle Zimbalist.*

the cemetery at 8:30 A.M. From here the trail descended to the lowlands, crossing endless barrancas.

We did not reach the Rancho Chenekultik until 12:30 P.M. Here we hired a young man as a guide and set out to scale the mountain. The rough trail took us up a precipitous slope on the north face. En route to the top we encountered an Indian hunter carrying an ocelot that he had shot on the mountain. It was the first time I had seen an ocelot at close hand, and I wondered if it might be some unsuspecting Zinacanteco's animal spirit companion.

It was 3:00 P.M. before we reached the summit, approximately fifteen hundred feet above the ranch. Here, much to our delight, we found the shrine with a cross, decorated with pine tree tops and other ritual plants, as well as recently burned candles and copal incense. It was obvious that the shrine on the summit of this precipitous mountain was much used. But, even more exciting, the shrine is located on the western edge of a prehistoric platform, indicating that the current rainmaking ceremony must have had its pre-Columbian precursor.

Approaching the summit we began to notice terraces at least twenty to thirty meters wide, especially on the north and south sides. It became ap-

We reach the summit of Cerro Chenekultik (in Tzotzil, Its'inal Muk'ta Vits) where the Zinacantecos perform rainmaking ceremonies and look across to Cerro Mispia at the edge of the Grijalva River valley.

parent that the summit is an archaeological site of importance. There are at least six terraces on each side topped by two square rock platforms—one above the other—on the very summit. The ancient walls are exposed here and there, and the Zinacantecos had used rocks from the old ruin to build an enclosure around their cross. The enclosure was about four and a half feet high. There was only one wooden cross, but a relatively fresh pine tree top was tied to the cross, and others placed on each side to make the altar into the usual three crosses. There was a very plain censer with the base broken off lying in front of the altar. We also noted butts of green candles (probably about peso size) remaining on top of the wall enclosure, as well as some other color, probably yellow.

Shelley and Nick walked part way across the saddle toward Cerro Mispia and reported terraces on that summit also. We did not explore the other peak, toward Totolapa, but I would guess there are ruins also on that summit. At any rate, it was clear that Zinacantecos performed their rainmaking ritual at an ancient site and offered the prayers in the direction of the rising sun, the same direction that Bankilal Muk'ta Vits lies from Zinacantan Center! This site on the summit of Cerro Chenekultik appears on the archaeological map prepared by the University of Chicago project, but, to this day, it has not been excavated nor explored further.

It was almost sundown by the time we descended to the ranch. I had a painful knee, and the others were exhausted. We visited with the Ladina woman, one of Don Chema's mistresses, who was in charge of the ranch, and she graciously provided meals and lodging for us in the large ranch house. The food was very simple, and the accommodations consisted of cots and blankets. But we could have slept on bare stone floors that night.

After dinner the scene was flooded by light from a beautiful full moon, and we sat on the front porch of the ranch and talked of anthropology, life, Harvard, and other topics before falling into our assigned cots.

After thanking our hostess, we set out shortly after sunrise the next morning to make the long hike back to Teopisca. After about an hour of traversing barrancas, my bum knee threatened to give out altogether. Fortunately, a party of Ladinos on horseback headed for Teopisca overtook us on the trail. I was able to rent one of the saddle horses for the return trip, while its owner gladly accepted my twenty pesos and walked to Teopisca. By the time we reached the Jeep, I knew I had made the second most difficult hike I had done in Chiapas.

The other eventful journey I made during the summer of 1963 was my second trip (25 July to 9 August) to South America to visit the other field stations in Brazil and Ecuador run by our undergraduate program. My first destination was Sao Salvador, Brazil, where I was met by the director of the Columbia University field station, which was located along the magnificent beach north of the city at a small fishing community named Arembepe. The field director was the famous Carl Withers, a social anthropologist who had written a book I much admired: *Plainville, USA*, by James West (a pseudonym).

In Rio de Janeiro I visited my old friend, Carlos Lacerda, who was then serving in the prominent position of governor of Guanabara, the state in which Rio is located. I had not been in Brazil since 1943 and had not seen Carlos Lacerda since his trip to the United States in 1948. Nevertheless, I wrote him about my trip to Brazil and asked if he might have time to see me at the presidential palace in Rio. His response was a telegram saying he had never forgotten our hospitality in 1948 and to please come and stay with him in Rio de Janeiro.

It was an exciting few days for me. Carlos was busy when I arrived, but sent his official limousine with chauffeur to meet my plane. Upon arrival at Carlos's apartment, the television cameras were there doing a story on the governor.

I not only had wonderful visits with Carlos and his wife, Leiticia, but was also taken along with Carlos on one of his working days. I was fascinated by the manner in which he handled his business. Instead of sitting at his desk in the palace (he explained that you can always get caught at a desk and not be able to gracefully dispatch callers who overstay their appointments), he spent his time visiting various public works: new tunnels, new water and electricity installations, and state buildings under construction. He would take the appropriate cabinet minister along with us in his limousine and discuss problems while moving from one public work to the next. I always remembered this procedure and adopted it when I later served as chairman of the Department of Anthropology and as master of Kirkland House; that is, I made a point of not getting caught behind my desk with lengthy appointments. Instead, I either transacted business on the phone or suggested conferences over lunch or while walking from one part of the university to the other.

With Carlos Lacerda I was privileged to attend various social functions in Rio. One was a memorable dinner party at the Lacerdas' when I met V. V. Braga who came from the famous Brazilian family, the Nabucos. She later became a noted television star in Brazil. Another event began one morning when Carlos asked me at breakfast if I had brought my "smoking jacket," that is, my dinner jacket. Since anthropologists do not usually travel with tuxedos, I, of course, had not. "Never mind," replied Carlos and sent me off with his driver to visit a local tailor with dinner jackets for rent. None fit me, but measurements were made and by late afternoon I had a rented tux that fit reasonably well. The occasion: the twenty-fifth anniversary of Air France. It was a gala dinner and dance; I had never seen so many elegant women dressed in fur coats and dazzling jewels.

Seeing Rio de Janeiro again was wonderful, but compared to my visit there in 1943, the air pollution from the exhaust of cars and from the multiplying factories had already created a nasty-looking smog that obscured Sugar Loaf and Corcovado.

Leaving Brazil, I flew to Buenos Aires. Although we did not have field stations in Argentina and Chile, I had routed myself via these two countries in order to become acquainted with them for possible future field operations. In Buenos Aires, I also interviewed a candidate for secretary and administrative assistant on the Harvard Chiapas Project in William James Hall at Harvard. For some years, I had realized that I should have assistants in this post who were fluent in Spanish. As chance would have it, a young woman named Gloria Caetano from Buenos Aires was planning to come to the United States and had written Pres. Nathan Pusey, applying for a post at Harvard. This letter bounced around among a number of departments and finally landed on my desk, complete with Gloria's résumé. Since I was going to be in Buenos Aires during the summer, I wrote and made an appointment to meet her. I was impressed and hired her on the spot. She came with her husband, who found a job in an electronics firm, and served admirably in my office for more than two years. She, in turn, recruited another *Porteña* (a native of Buenos Aires) when she left, and for more than a decade I had a steady stream of either Argentineans or Chileans serving efficiently as my bilingual secretaries.

My last stop in South America was Quito, where I was met by Joe Casagrande of the University of Illinois, Urbana, who had taken over the responsibility for the Ecuadorian field station from Columbia when the latter moved their operations to the coast of Brazil. Joe met me at the Quito airport, provided a look at the capital city, and then drove me the next day south to the Salasaca region where he and his students were engaged in field research among these Quechua-speaking Indians.

Back at Harvard in the academic year 1963–64 we found ourselves more attuned to Latin American affairs than ever before. Gloria Caetano from Buenos Aires was the project secretary, and we also had two young Mexicans living with us in our house in Weston: Ignacio ("Nachito") Bernal, Jr., the son of Ignacio Bernal, Sr., and Jorge Ruz, the son of Alberto Ruz. Both had come to attend local schools and learn English. It was an interesting period, especially since Nachito and Jorge were poles apart in their political views and carried on long and complicated arguments in the bedroom they shared! Both have since gone on to successful careers in Mexico: Nachito as an economist, Jorge as a filmmaker.

1964: OAXACA, CHIAPAS, AND EUROPE

The spring and summer of 1964 was a totally different season for me. This was the year I worked intensively getting the aerial photography project underway, an experience described in chapter 8, and also the year when, with a spring-term sabbatical, Nan and I spent three months in Oaxaca. After Nachito Bernal had stayed with us for the fall semester in Massachusetts, the Bernals graciously offered us their lovely vacation home in San Felipe at the northern edge of the city of Oaxaca for the spring term. I was delighted to accept the offer for I was eager to get some fundamental work done on the articles and book I was writing on the ethnography of Zinacantan. I managed to accomplish a great deal until a freak accident that came close to killing me at the age of forty-five. Our son Charlie was flying a kite given him by an elderly Mexican neighbor. It was a glorious windy day for kite flying until the sun began to set and the wind died. The kite descended and became entangled on a tile roof on one of the service buildings behind the Rancho San Felipe, a resort hotel nearby. As a dutiful father, I went to help Charlie retrieve it. I managed to climb on top the building and slowly make my way across the sloped tile roof. Just as I was reaching for the kite, the whole tile roof collapsed beneath me and I fell six meters to the cement floor below as the tiles fell around me.

Miraculously, I was not killed, but I was knocked unconscious. Charlie ran home crying for help. His cries alerted one of the families who worked for the Rancho San Felipe, and they immediately found a car to take me to a doctor. The only physician they knew in Oaxaca was an obstetrician! But the good man examined me and managed to pull a very painful dislocated finger back in place; then sent me for X rays. There were no broken bones (except for a fracture in my right cheek bone that resulted in a swelling the size of a golf ball), but I was so badly bruised and shaken up that I could not walk.

Nan and the gardener, Eulogio, arrived with the Land Rover and managed to get me home and into bed. For almost six weeks, I required Eulogio's help to get in and out of bed, and we were grateful for his assistance. Recovery was slow, but it was a marvelously restful setting for recuperation. For years afterward, I kept hearing rumors that I had been killed in an accident in Oaxaca. I suppose such rumors always occur when one occupies a permanent post that others covet in a famous university like Harvard!

During the spring I was also coping with another irritating problem: what to do with the Jeep I had brought from the United States in the summer of 1963. In spite of the assurances of Alfonso Caso in advance and his later assistance in Mexico City, we were *never* able to receive official permission for the Jeep to remain in Chiapas as a scientific vehicle. Since my tourist card was officially stamped "Viajando con automovil" when I entered Mexico in the summer of 1963, I was forced to store the vehicle under bond in a secretaría de hacienda warehouse in San Cristobal before I could leave the country. By January 1964 the six-month permit had expired, and we were in even deeper bureaucratic trouble. I continued to work through INI to receive official permission to leave the vehicle in Mexico. On 17 April I wrote to Ned Spicer (who was helping me with the papers in Mexico City):

> I remember Licenciado Sergio Muñoz de Alba [the INI lawyer] 4*assuring* me that the whole affair would be straightened out "en la semana que entra" (next week)—this when I was in his office on February 1; to say nothing of Caso *assuring* me that I need not worry about the Jeep papers . . . just send them to Licenciado Salas Ortega [the previous INI lawyer] in mid-December and the affair would be arranged in plenty of time before the permit ran out on December 25—this when I was in Dr. Caso's office on June 28, 1963, just after I brought the Jeep into Mexico! Well, *ni modo,* I have learned . . . I will *never,* repeat *never,* try to bring in a vehicle under such conditions again. Instead, I'll buy a Mexican-made Jeep in Tuxtla.

For weeks I thought the Jeep would be confiscated by the Federal Registry of Vehicles. But with the help of Ned Spicer, who spent days working on the problem for me in Mexico City, visiting both the INI and the registry offices, we finally received official permission (by posting a bond that was secured by Alfonso Caso) for Professor Brent Berlin (who was in Chiapas and planning to return to California in late May) to remove the vehicle from Mexico. On 9 June I could write Spicer: "You will be happy I am sure to learn that I have just returned from Palo Alto where I rode in the Jeep with Brent Berlin. I considered this one of the miracles of the age, and I am eternally grateful to you and Brent." The Willys Jeep was sold in California shortly thereafter, and I have since carried out my pledge never to try to bring a project vehicle into Mexico with the notion that it could remain "for scientific purposes" in the country year after year.

In the summer of 1964 I planned to present papers on the Chiapas research at two important international meetings in Europe: the International Congress of Anthropological and Ethnological Sciences meeting in Moscow and the International Congress of Americanists convening in Spain. In preparation for the summer, I appointed George Collier as the field director and Carter Wilson as the assistant field director.

We restricted the number of new students going to Chiapas to six, five from Harvard and one from Cornell. George and Carter performed admirably in supervising their research, with good results at the end of the summer. Two of the Harvard students, Merida H. Blanco and Nancy J. Chodorow, undertook a fascinating field study of child training in Zinacantan. Their research report (1964) is one of the most-cited unpublished reports of the Chiapas Project.[9] Antonio Gilman engaged in important interviewing and archival research municipio organization (1965) and decided to continue in anthropology as a career[10]; Rand E. Rosenblatt was a pioneer in exploring law-ways in Chiapas (1964). John D. Strucker (1964) made interesting observations on the educational system of Chamula.[11]

The student from Cornell was Benedicte Fløystrup, who researched settlement patterns in relation to kinship in Zinacantan and focused primarily on the composition of snas in Nabenchauk and the ceremonial center (Fløystrup 1964).[12] Shelley Zimbalist also returned to Chiapas in the summer of 1964 to do a definitive study of Zinacanteco ethnoanatomy.[13]

The European journey took me first to Moscow for the meetings of the Seventh International Congress of Anthropological and Ethnological Sciences where I presented the paper, jointly authored by Kim Romney, entitled "The Use of Aerial Photographic Techniques in Maya Ethnography" (1971). The trip also provided an opportunity for me to meet the famous Yuri Knorozov of the Institute of Ethnography of the Academy of Sciences of the USSR in Leningrad for the first time. It was a key contact for me since I had become interested in Knorozov's attempt to decode the Maya glyphs, as well as his profound knowledge of the Maya codices.

I later traveled to Barcelona for the Thirty-sixth International Congress of Americanists. This congress, which alternates every two years between the Old World and the New World, was a moveable feast in 1964. It began in Barcelona, moved to Madrid, and then to Seville. My paper, "Ancestor Worship in Zinacantan Religion" (1966), was presented in Madrid.

In September 1964 I was appointed as Harvard's official representative to the ceremony for the inauguration of the new National Museum of Mexico, which was to open during the festivities 15–17 September celebrating Mexican Independence Day. It was another memorable experience, being the only time in my life I have been accorded "diplomatic treatment." The official representatives were given rooms in the elegant Hotel María Isabel at the expense of the Mexican government and invited to many events. We were always transported in official automobiles and given motorcycle escorts—the most efficient way to travel in overcrowded Mexico City.

The first official invitation was to attend the ceremony for the commemoration of Mexican independence on the evening of 15 September. We were invited to the reception that followed in the Comedor Presidencial (Presidential Dining Room) inside the National Palace at nine P.M. Dress was either dark suit or dinner jacket. This time I packed my dinner jacket, so I had suitable attire for the affair. We were all greeted by Pres. López Mateos as we arrived along with hundreds of other well-dressed guests in long gowns or dinner jackets. There was food and drink at the tables at which we gathered in the presidential dining room. Precisely at eleven P.M., the president carried the tricolor Mexican flag to a balcony overlooking the plaza packed with celebrating citizens and shouted what is called El Grito: "Viva La Independencia! Viva Hidalgo! Viva Morelos! Viva Juarez! Viva Mexico! Viva Mexico! Viva Mexico" the president shouted over the loudspeakers, while the amassed citizens answered "Viva!" (like an ancient Greek chorus) to each phrase in an affirming chorus. The president then rang the bell that is said to come from Dolores—where Father Hidalgo shouted the first Grito and led the call for independence from Spain at eleven P.M. on 15 September 1810—and then the bells pealed out from the tower of the National Cathedral. Fireworks, including colored skyrockets, were ignited, and the spectacle culminated with the setting off of a great castillo (castle) displaying the face of Father Hidalgo shouting out the original "Viva!" of 1810.

The same Grito is shouted from the balconies of all the gubernatorial palaces of every Mexican state and from the municipal palaces of every municipio in Mexico. Cabinet ministers are dispatched to shout the Grito to the Mexican populations in such cities as Los Angeles, San Antonio, Chicago, etc., and the Grito is even shouted to Mexican students at Harvard and MIT by the Mexican consul-general of Boston, with the ritual taking place on alternate years at the two universities. The effect of this simple but powerful ritual of reiteration is stunning. In one massive and simultaneous Grito throughout the Republic (and beyond), the independence from Spain is ceremonially reiterated on this most important holiday.

I had attended the ceremony before in the plaza in Mexico City with the masses, as well as in San Cristobal and Zinacantan, but had never before been inside the presidential rooms at the palace for the event. The contrast was remarkable, especially the rumors and gossip that circulated about which beautiful women were mistresses of which high government officials. The following day, 16 September, we attended the military parade in the plaza, witnessing the proceedings from seats in a grandstand. It was boring, compared to the liveliness of the ceremony the evening before.

On 17 September at 10:30 A.M. came the inauguration of the Museo Nacional de Antropología. Since the Museum was intended to become a tribute to and an eternal monument for Pres. López Mateos, the president himself came to the ceremony. The audience, seated on folding chairs in the patio of the Museum, near the fountain that spills down the massive central column holding up the roof, was comprised of high government officials, ambassadors, and representatives from universities in the front rows. Behind them sat the workers who had built the museum (and their families). All were in clean blue jeans and blue shirts and their wives in freshly laundered dresses. While Pres. López Mateos and other officials spoke, and the Mexican Symphony Orchestra played a special piece composed by the famous Mexican composer, Carlos Chavez, the workers listened quietly and intently. It was an impressive and emotional occasion, and I kept wondering if the workers on large public works in the United States would have been invited to such ceremonies and would have had the patience to sit through such a long program of speeches and classical music.

I was pleased that 1964 had been such a good year for the project and that my publications were beginning to appear. In addition to three articles (1964a, 1964b, and 1964c), our volume from the Burg Wartenstein symposium on Desarrollo Cultural de los Mayas was also published. The publishing arrangements of the volume were, however, something of a shock to me. I had organized and chaired the conference and assumed that I would be the sole editor of the volume. But when the bound copies arrived from Mexico, the front cover read that the volume was *Editado Por Evon Z. Vogt y Alberto Ruz L.!* To be sure, Ruz had done good work in seeing the volume through the press in Mexico, but there had been no mention of his becoming a joint editor. After my rage subsided, I decided that since the volume was already published, there was nothing I could do but accept a fait accompli. My colleague, Gordon Willey, helped soften the blow by reminding me that this kind of sharp procedure can be perpetrated by scholars of any nationality. He provided the example of the *Handbook of South American Indians of the Bureau of American Ethnology* at the Smithsonian Institution, which Alfred Metraux confidently expected to co-edit with Julian Steward, but when the volume appeared in print, Steward was the sole editor!

1965: CAMBRIDGE AND CHIAPAS

In 1965 Chep Apas, our first Zinacanteco collaborator on the Tzotzil course, arrived during the spring term, after having spent two weeks with George and Jane Collier at Tulane in New Orleans, two weeks with Bob Laughlin at the Smithsonian in Washington, and a week with Richard Price in New York City. Chep remained at Harvard for six weeks, assisting with the Tzotzil course and serving as an informant for interviews with me and with the students who were in training for summer fieldwork, as well as with the students in the freshman seminar.

Chep lived with us in our house in Weston, Massachusetts, and commuted with me to William James Hall each day. I shall never forget the day he arrived. We walked across Harvard Yard, and when we reached my office, his first question about the Harvard students who passed us in the Yard was "But, where are their cameras?" He had unconsciously assumed, from his experience in Chiapas, that most, if not all, Harvard students wore cameras around their necks as part of their standard dress!

Another observation I made was that whenever Chep and I proceeded together along the sidewalks of Harvard Yard, I could never convince him to walk abreast with me where we could easily carry on a conversation. Instead, it was *always* a two-man procession with Chep falling in a pace or two behind me. I was the ranking person, Chep was junior to me, there-

Field party in the summer of 1965. Standing (left to right): Stephen Young, Mary Anschuetz, Roger Dunwell, Elena Uribe, Renato Rosaldo, Todd Rakoff, Gwendoline Van Den Berghe, Richard Price, Sally Price, Gary Gossen, Claude de Chavigny. Kneeling (left to right): Gordon Gilbert, Dianne Scott, Barbara Strodt, EZV. (Missing: Patrick Menget)

fore he walked behind as he would have in an everyday journey along a mountain trail in Zinacantan.

During the summer of 1965 I served as field director of one of the largest groups of students we have ever had with us in Chiapas. It was a banner season for attracting graduate students to the project: Gary H. Gossen, Patrick J. Menget, Richard S. and Sally H. Price, Renato I. Rosaldo, and Elena Uribe all joined us. In addition, Frank and Franzi Cancian and Vicki Bricker had returned to Chiapas for further research.

Two of the new students, Gary Gossen and Patrick Menget, worked in Chamula; the others in Zinacantan. Gary came to Harvard after finishing his A.B. at the University of Kansas during which time he had developed a deep interest in folklore and mythology and had spent a year in Costa Rica. With his fluent control of Spanish—the most eloquent Spanish spoken by any member of the project—and rapidly developing control of Tzotzil, he set out to study the oral tradition and cosmology of Chamula.

Dressed for fieldwork in Zinacantan in 1965. Left to right: Victoria Reifler Bricker, Nan Vogt, EZV, Mary Anschuetz, Charles Vogt.

Beginning in 1965 and continuing in 1968 and 1969, Gary collected a large body of oral narratives in Tzotzil that formed the empirical base for his Ph.D. dissertation (1970), later published as the now classic work *Chamulas in the World of the Sun: Time and Space in a Maya Oral Tradition* (1974b).[14] Patrick Menget, a student from Paris, spent only one summer in Chiapas, but his fieldwork in Chamula was noted for its high quality (1968).[15]

Richard and Sally Price undertook a field study of the social organization of the Tzotzil-speaking community of Muk'tahok', which is located near the Pan American Highway above Chiapa de Corzo and is officially a hamlet of the municipio of Ixtapa. From this research came an article entitled "Aspects of Social Organization in a Maya Hamlet" (1970) and an article by Sally Price, "I Was Pashku and My Husband Was Telesh" (1966). The Prices returned to Muk'tahok' again in the summer of 1966 when they did the innovative work with the aerial photographs that I described in chapter 8.[16]

Following a summer of anthropological field experience in Ecuador on our undergraduate training program in 1961, Renato Rosaldo finished his

A.B. at Harvard in Spanish literature and spent a year on a fellowship in Spain pursuing his interests in that field. He finally decided to shift to anthropology and came to Harvard for his graduate work. After taking the graduate seminar on the Maya, he developed a strong interest in Chiapas. George and I persuaded him to undertake a difficult field topic: a study of the counting ritual performed with the sacred necklaces that are kept in the house altars of the mayordomo reyes, but taken at regular intervals to the Chapel of Esquipulas and placed on the saints. We had long been puzzled by the ritual counting routine (performed with kernels of maize), for it was reported that the number of coins on these necklaces increased or decreased depending upon whether the saints were pleased or displeased with the ceremonial performance of the mayordomo reyes (for details see Vogt 1976: 123–28).

Renato was placed in the house of a mayordomo rey so he could witness the rituals firsthand. During the first ritual counting, Renato was forced to drink so much posh that he passed out and was unable to observe the second half of the ceremony. He subsequently learned to control the consumption of liquor and make a series of observations that led to a solution of the puzzle. His brilliant article, "Metaphors of Hierarchy in a Mayan Ritual" (1968), provides the answers.

Elena Uribe came to Harvard from Mexico City College where she had been a student of Alfonso Villa Rojas. She was from a talented, upper-class family in Mexico. I had attempted on a number of previous occasions to recruit Mexican students to come to Harvard for graduate work in anthropology and then join me in the field research in Chiapas. These attempts never came to fruition, largely because the students did not speak sufficient English to cope with our courses at Harvard and came from families of modest means and were unable to pay their expenses, even if granted a partial scholarship for graduate work. I was delighted to have Elena since her English was fluent and her family was prosperous enough to fund her necessary expenses.

Elena expressed an interest in studying another one of the topics I knew needed much more research: the system of compadrazgo in the Tzotzil communities. Elena proved to be a fine field researcher. Since she came from an elite family in Mexico, she felt secure about her own cultural identity and did not have to maintain a distant and formal relationship with the Tzotzil Maya. She could easily live in Indian households and share beans and tortillas with indigenous families. She ultimately collected sufficient data in both Zinacantan and Chamula to do a comparative Ph.D. dissertation on compadrazgo (1979). INI later published the results in Mexico (Uribe-Wood 1982).[17]

The lively undergraduates in the summer of 1965 included four from Harvard, and one each from Barnard and Cornell. In addition, I agreed to accept two legacies, so to speak, both of whom did outstanding field research. One was Gwendoline van den Berghe, the younger sister of Pierre, the collaborator of Nick Colby, who was an undergraduate from the University of California, Berkeley. The second was Claude de Chavigny, a nephew of Alberto Ruz, from Paris.

One of the Harvard students, Roger Dunwell (1965), was placed in the hamlet of Nabenchauk where he undertook a fascinating study of the political factions that had threatened for many years to lead to a rupture in the social fabric of this hamlet. Todd Rakoff (1965) did a sophisticated survey of the ways in which men and women schedule their days in different settings in Zinacantan. Barbara Strodt's (1965) field research in the hamlet of Apas consisted of a detailed study of household economy. Steve Young spent most of the summer studying the behavior of the Zinacanteco officials in the town hall in the center and wrote an interesting report entitled "Their People's Servants" (1965).[18]

The Cornell undergraduate, Gordon Gilbert, undertook a study of the restaurants in San Cristobal (1965). The student from Barnard, Dianne Scott, was unfortunately ill prepared for field research and had difficulties adjusting to life in San Cristobal.

Claude de Chavigny from France added significantly to our ethnographic knowledge of San Cristobal by doing a detailed study of the professional weavers, who use archaic looms, in the Barrio Mexicanos (1965). Gwendoline van den Berghe from Berkeley also worked in San Cristobal, where she researched system of compadrazgo among the Ladinos (1965) and later published a joint article with her brother Pierre (1966).[19]

I recall receiving a magnificent gift from the students on my birthday that summer. It was a polished mahogany scepter (called a *bastón* in Spanish) with a silver tip and a copper base. On top it was inscribed with the word *síndico*, indicating that it had originally belonged to an official in some highland Guatemala community. It had been purchased by the students in a market in Guatemala City where they had gone on their midsummer vacation. This baston also had a silver ring that was inscribed, by the students, with Totik Mol Shun 1965 and was adorned with red ribbons. It was the type of staff carried by the highest ranking cargoholder, the Muk'ta 'Alkalte, of Zinacantan. I was delighted with the gift, and it has become the staff of office of the Harvard Chiapas Project. It has, I tell visitors, a strong inner soul placed in it by my anthropological ancestors, and commands power and authority. It hangs, with great pride, on the wall of my office, and is now removed only once a year when I use it as a baton to lead the Kirkland House seniors up to Harvard Yard following the traditional champagne breakfast and later to serve as an aide to the Harvard marshall during the annual Commencement Ceremonies. The baston always elicits many questions from students and returning alumni and is admired as an ongoing part of Harvard ritual life.

Another remarkable feature of the 1965 season was the presence of such a large number of graduate students. In retrospect, they not only added to the quality of the research by their own efforts, but also had a major impact on the undergraduate projects, which were of exceptional caliber. The graduate students had, of course, attended all the summer conferences and were often blunt and merciless in commenting on the undergraduate projects. I remember especially hearing Barbara Strodt say of Rich and Sally Price after they had sharply criticized Barbara's midsummer report, "The trouble is, there are two of them!" In the end, however, these comments served to upgrade the undergraduate research in a more effective manner than I could ever have achieved by myself.

10 /
THE "LATE
CLASSIC" YEARS:
1966–1969

The "late classic" years were a period during which we had our refined program of training in high gear; we were recruiting topflight
students at both the undergraduate and graduate level; the field
operations were going well, at least until the end of the period;
and project publications, including many of my own, were at last
coming to fruition. Although I regretted that I had little time during these
years for my own field research, I did allocate a major effort and many
hours to assisting students with their projects as well as to writing my own
articles and books, particularly the general ethnography on Zinacantan. I
had believed from the beginning that we ought to produce a general ethnography for each Tzotzil municipio we studied and decided to do the one
on Zinacantan myself. Little did I know, even with the help of the data collected and photographs taken by my students, how many years would be
required to finish the monograph. I came to have enormous respect for the
early anthropologists who wrote up general ethnographies of the cultures
they studied.

1966: CAMBRIDGE AND
ARGENTINA

During the 1966 season I planned to attend the Thirty-seventh International
Congress of Americanists in Buenos Aires in August and present a paper.
In preparation for this journey, and to further my work on the analysis
and write-up of field data, I decided to remain at Harvard during the early

289

EZV presents a copy of Los Zinacantecos *to the presidente municipal of Zinacantan, José Sanchez, in 1967.*

summer, and I again persuaded George Collier to serve as field director in Chiapas.

At Harvard I was working intensively on the writing of articles for, and editing, volumes 7 and 8 of the *Handbook of Middle American Indians* on the ethnology of Middle America, as well as drafting chapters for the general ethnography that was eventually published under the title *Zinacantan: A Maya Community in the Highlands of Chiapas* (1969). Although I had edited a volume entitled *Los Zinacantecos* published by the INI in Spanish in 1966, which reprinted six of my articles on Zinacantan, as well as seventeen articles by my students, I felt strongly that we needed a systematic general ethnogoraphy of the community as a base for further studies.[1]

On 31 July Nan and I flew to Brasilia for a day-visit, then on to Rio de Janeiro where we renewed our friendship with Carlos Lacerda, who had finished his duty as governor of Guanabara and was engaged in business. After Brazil we visited Buenos Aires, Bariloche, and then spent some time at Temuco in Chile to visit the Machupes who constitute the only large remaining indigenous population in Chile.

On 2 September we returned by plane to Argentina for the International

Congress of Americanists, which met in Buenos Aires and Mar del Plata. My paper, "Recurrent and Directional Processes in Zinacantan," was received well, and the meetings were generally very interesting.

Meanwhile, the field research in Chiapas had been very productive under the able direction of George Collier. The field party included two pediatricians, Drs. T. Berry Brazelton and John S. Robey, from the Harvard Medical School who were interested in doing a cross-cultural study of neonates and mother-infant interaction. The undergraduates included four new students from Harvard, plus Mary Anschuetz, who had been with us the summer before, as well as one from Sarah Lawrence and one from Barnard.

With the assistance of George Collier and Mary Anschuetz, the field study undertaken by the pediatricians had gone well. Collier was much interested in the program and provided Zinacanteco field settings in which the pediatricians could observe mother-infant interaction, as well as administer a set of tests, which had been used in American families, to the neonates.

Mary Anschuetz had been placed in the home of a midwife in Apas and thus had firsthand access to the procedures and rituals performed for births, *all* of which still occur at home in Zinacantan. She was the first ethnographer to witness a Zinacanteco birth, and her excellent summer report "To Be Born in Zinacantan" (Anschuetz 1966) has become the classic source on the process. She discovered, among other things, that the whole family is present for a Zinacanteco birth. When labor pains begin, the pregnant wife kneels on a reed mat on the earthen floor to give birth while her husband stands behind her, pulling her sash tight, and one of the older male relatives sits on a small chair facing her, seizing her by the shoulders to support her. With each labor pain, the family groans simultaneously with the birthing mother to ease her distress. The umbilical cord is cut with a heated machete, and within an hour a ritual is performed to symbolize the sex-identity of the new baby. The midwife holds the infant, and objects that will be used in the child's later life are placed in both of its tiny fists. A boy is presented with a digging stick, a hoe, and an axe. A girl is presented with a *mano* (which she will use to grind maize) and various parts of a backstrap loom.[2]

Brazelton and Robey returned to Chiapas to continue their research during two subsequent summers (1967 and 1969) and have been productive in publishing the results (see Brazelton 1972, 1973, 1974, 1975; Brazelton, Robey, and Collier 1969). One of their principal discoveries about Zinacanteco neonates is that they are constantly swaddled, carried in a shawl next to the mother's body, and nursed on demand. Their neonate tests showed the babies to be very passive and their motor development much slower than in American infants—for example, they walk much later than our babies do—all of which is adaptive for survival in a Zinacanteco house. A hyperactive American infant, walking before understanding language, would be likely to fall into the open fire, cut himself on a machete, or die of the cold as he kicked off the covers sleeping by himself in the middle of a cold Chiapas night (Greenfield, Brazelton, and Childs 1989).

In retrospect it is remarkable that the Chiapas Project could attract such eminent pediatricians and that they managed so well in Chiapas. Neither Brazelton nor Robey spoke more than a few words of Spanish, and no Tzotzil, but both had the kind of ebullient personalities that permitted them to reach out and favorably impress fathers and mothers of infants in a totally different culture. Berry Brazelton has since become the best-known pediatrician in America.

A second Harvard undergraduate, John B. Haviland, a concentrator in philosophy, proved to be a really remarkable new recruit for the project. George Collier and I soon discovered that John is an all-around genius. He was a very tall (six feet, four inches), well-coordinated young man who excelled in many sports, including basketball and table tennis, as well as in the complicated intricacies of square dancing. He played any string instrument placed in his hands: violin, guitar, banjo, and even a Chamula harp. He was a whiz at mathematics, statistics, and computers, and had the most impressive facility for learning languages of any member of our project. By the second season of fieldwork (1967), he had become fluent in Tzotzil. He continues to be one of two members of the project (the other being Bob Laughlin) whose command of Tzotzil, according to our Zinacanteco and Chamula informants, is flawless, practically on a par with native speakers of the language. George and I suggested, from his musical accomplishments, that he undertake a detailed study of Zinacanteco music. His splendid summer report, entitled "*Vob:* Traditional Music in Zinacantan" (1966), is the standard source on music in Zinacantan.

After a year pursuing his study of philosophy on a fellowship in Sweden, John decided to shift to anthropology and returned to Harvard to do his

The pediatrician, Dr. T. Berry Brazelton, doing research with Zinacanteco infants in 1967.

Zinacanteco mother shows concern as to what Dr. Brazelton may do to her baby.

Ph.D. I strongly encouraged this move since he was not only a talented scholar, but, with his skill in playing the Zinacanteco musical instruments, I knew that John would often be invited to perform as one of the musicians for the all-night ceremonies, placing him in an ideal position to collect ethnographic data as a participant observer par excellence. His field research in Zinacantan resulted in a distinguished Ph.D. dissertation on an intriguing topic. The title: "Gossip, Gossips, and Gossiping in Zinacantan: Gossip About Him Will Never Cease" (J. Haviland 1971).[3]

Haviland continues to engage in field research in Chiapas, especially in the hamlet of Nabenchauk where he has had a small house constructed in the compound of one of his compadres. Instead of headquartering in San Cristobal, as most of us continue to do, John Haviland *lives* in Nabenchauk, when he is in Chiapas, and travels into San Cristobal when he needs to shop for groceries in the market or visit colleagues. When I visit him in Nabenchauk, I never fail to admire his amazing command of Tzotzil, as well as his location in a setting in which he is gathering firsthand field data the minute he steps outside his door. John Haviland has reached the ultimate adaptation to Tzotzil culture, which I dreamed about when I first started field research in Chiapas. Even if I became sidetracked by other obligations, I am immensely proud that one of my students finally made it— without going native, but maintaining a balanced combination of intimacy with, but detachment from, the flow of Zinacanteco life.

Another of the Harvard undergraduates, Judy Merkel, was also an excellent field researcher. Her topic was Chamula curing patterns. By the end of the summer she managed to live in the home of a Chamula shaman in the remote hamlet of Yalichin. Here she could learn firsthand about their patterns of shamanism, which we knew little about at the time. Her summer report, "Chamula Curing" (1966), provided a preliminary view into the domain of curing practices in Chamula. I invited her to return to Chiapas in 1967 and she moved to the home of the same Chamula shaman, and by the end of this second season she obtained really penetrating ethnographic data.

A concentrator in English at Harvard, Judy wrote beautiful prose, as exemplified in the following passage from her 1967 field journal describing a night in a Chamula household:

> That night should have been a scene from the Theater of the Absurd: I, low person on the totem pole, slept closest to the door, and squirmed frigidly, inching closer and closer to the dying embers of the fire, where I finally nestled and dozed off with my arm around a still-slightly-warm beanpot. . . . SPHAT! I awoke from my jumbled dreams of candles and dried fish to the Harsh Reality of the h'ilol's guided missile of spit whizzing past my head. Unfor-

tunately, it was very dark and his aim very poor, and his spitting intended for the fire-bed had a wicked left-curve. . . . so for the rest of the night, whenever I heard the tell-tale snort, I would whisk my shawl over my head and instantaneously analyze the maximum security to be derived from dodging to the left or to the right (I usually lost). When I awoke the next morning, still curled up in a prenatal position with my head in the cold ashes, the old woman, thinking my head was a beanpot in the predawn dark, was about to pour a spoonful of red beans over my by-now-much-abused-head. "Vash elan! (For goodness sakes!) Has she slept here all night?" By then I thought it was pretty funny too, but I kept remembering the fairy tale, the Princess and the Pea, and wondering if my sleepless night, too, was a Test, and if the morning would bring a Handsome Chamula Prince and we would all Live Happily Ever After. . . . However, the curer merely mundanely pulsed the old man [a sick patient] again, as soon as they awoke.[4]

Another Harvard student, Ronald L. Trosper, was concentrating in economics, and Collier encouraged him to undertake a detailed study of the patterns of borrowing and lending money in Zinacantan. His summer research was of high quality (1966) and Ron was also invited to return to Chiapas in 1967 when he made a systematic study of schooling in Zinacantan (1967a). He also wrote his A.B. honors thesis for the Department of Economics on tradition and economic growth in Zinacantan, gradual change in a Mexican Indian community (1967b).[5]

Haven Logan from Barnard College broke new ground in studying one of the working-class communities, La Garrita, on the edge of the valley of San Cristobal. Since we knew that a constant process of Ladinoization (i.e., Indians becoming Ladinos by changing clothing and learning Spanish) was going on in San Cristobal, it was of great interest to our project to understand precisely how this process takes place at the lower lower-class level on the fringes of the city. Her summer report on "The Process of Ladinoization in San Cristobal" (1966) contains excellent data and a fascinating analysis. Lois Hinderlie from Sarah Lawrence College also collected ethnographic data on family life and Ladinoization.

Nineteen sixty-six was another very productive year for my publications on the results of our field research in Chiapas. Three articles appeared (Vogt

1966a, 1966b, 1966c), but, more importantly, a monograph *Los Zinacantecos: Un Pueblo Tzotzil de Los Altos de Chiapas* (1966d) that I edited was published in Spanish in the social anthropology series of INI in Mexico City. The volume reprinted five of my articles that had been previously published in English, as well as eighteen articles by my students who had done field research in Chiapas between 1958 and 1963. The monograph has proved to be useful, especially since it was published in Spanish, and is still in print (now in a paperback edition) in Mexico.

1967: CHIAPAS AGAIN

Beginning with the 1967 season the Harvard Chiapas Project was no longer part of the Undergraduate Summer Field Studies Program that had been running from 1960 through 1966. I did not discover until late in the 1966–67 academic year that Professor Marvin Harris at Columbia had decided to shift gears and start writing theoretical books instead of continuing field research in Brazil. He had not applied for renewal of the National Science Foundation grant that had been supporting the program. At Harvard we had assumed the program would continue and had already begun to solicit applications from students.

I was quite upset with my colleagues at Columbia who had failed to notify me about this change in plans. I later discovered that a bureaucratic flap had occurred: Marvin Harris had assumed that Professor Lambros Comitas, who had been managing the program for Columbia, had written me, while Comitas thought Harris had notified me.

In any event I was determined to carry on alone and, with some last minute scrambling, received enough funds from a combination of sources: the National Science Foundation, the Harvard summer school, and Abraham Lincoln Fellowships provided to two of my students by the Mexican government.

I served as field director and again appointed George Collier as the assistant field leader. In addition to Elena Uribe, John Haviland, Judy Merkel, and Ron Trosper, all returning for further research in Chiapas, we had two new graduate students and six new undergraduates.

The graduate students were Stephanie L. Krebs and Richard A. Shweder. During her undergraduate years Stephanie Krebs had worked with my Harvard colleague Professor Lawrence Wylie in a French village and had become interested in nonverbal communication and in filmmaking. Although she spent some time studying nonverbal communication during the summer, her principal efforts were focused on making a film that portrayed the life of a Zinacanteco wife and mother. Since Stephanie did not speak Spanish (her French did not help), nor more than a few words of Tzotzil, she needed help in the field. She brought along a colleague, Ana Montes de Gonzalez from Argentina, who was her interpreter in Spanish and had also had some experience in filmmaking. Ana was the wife of Professor Alberto Rex Gonzalez, the noted Argentine archaeologist. She was a delightful, mature person who was a help to all our staff in Chiapas that summer.

George Collier and I introduced Stephanie and Ana to Chep Nuh, an important political leader in the hamlet of Nachih, and the film was focused on Chep's wife, Shunka'. With suitable compensation, Chep Nuh had the bright idea of taking all the tiles off the roof of his house in order to provide ample light for filming indoors.

Chep Nuh's brother, Yermo Nuh, was serving a cargo position as an alferez in Zinacantan Center, and I tried to assist Stephanie with the complicated task of developing sufficient rapport with the alfereces to film their ritual activities. I recall the day that Stephanie was introduced to this group of cargoholders sitting on their long bench in front of the church of San Lorenzo. As part of the introduction, I offered posh to each of the alfereces; then discovered I was obligated to reciprocate by drinking a shot of posh from each of the fourteen cargoholders. At the end of this drinking ritual, I had to be led to the project vehicle where I passed out and did not come to until we reached San Cristobal.

In the end, filming the ritual activities of the alfereces did not work. Every time Stephanie tried filming, one cargoholder or another would become envious and upset, or one of the musicians would object. While it was possible to film all activities in the context of the domestic family group at home in Nachih, it was never possible to overcome the envy and the interpersonal tensions that exist among cargoholders, who come from many hamlets and many different lineages, in Zinacantan center. Nonetheless, the twenty-minute film called "Shunka's Story" (1967) successfully portrayed life for a woman in a Zinacanteco hamlet and has been well received.

Richard Shweder (called "Rick") likewise spoke little Spanish and less

Summer field party in 1967 at the Harvard Ranch. Back row (left to right): Daniel Silver, Fred Whelan, EZV, Ron Trosper, Charles Vogt, Mark Rosenberg, Carolyn Pope,George Collier, John Miyamoto, John Haviland, Judith Merkel, T. Berry Brazelton, Jane Collier. Middle row (left to right): Elena Uribe, Kitty Brazelton, Nan Vogt, Ana Montes de Gonzalez, Abigail Natelson. Seated (left to right): Shirley Vogt, Tom Brazelton, Cristina Brazelton, Stephanie Krebs, Candy Shweder, and Richard Shweder.

Tzotzil, but managed with the help of interpreters to carry out a fascinating experimental project during the summer. He worked with a matched sample of shamans and nonshamans with the idea in mind that the function of a shaman is to end bafflement for his patients. He presented the subjects with a graded series of photographs, beginning with one that was completely out of focus and ending with one that brought the object into sharp focus. He hypothesized that shamans, compared to nonshamans, would confidently name the object in the series of photographs much sooner than nonshamans, and thereby end bafflement for themselves and others by imposing form on diffuse sense data. The hypothesis was confirmed (Shweder 1972), providing us with the first solid finding on the psychological differences between shamans and nonshamans.[6]

The six new undergraduates worked on a variety of interesting problems in Zinacantan and Chamula. Leslie K. Haviland, recently married to John Haviland, focused on the social structure, especially the role of women, in the Zinacanteco domestic family.[7] John M. Miyamoto, a concentrator in psychology, undertook a study of the logistics involved in the making of sacred objects, especially the censers and candleholders, used in Zinacanteco ceremonies (1967). He later developed an interest in cognitive problems in Zinacantan, which he researched with an experimental design in the summer of 1968. The interesting results appeared in his senior honors thesis (1969). Abigail S. Natelson did field research on changes in clothing styles in Zinacantan and Chamula and produced an engaging final report entitled "Clothing Norms in Zinacantan and Chamula" (1967).[8]

Cemeteries in Zinacantan were the focus of Carolyn Pope's summer research. One of her goals was to understand the social structure of these burial grounds as reflected in the architecture and spatial arrangements of the graves. Carolyn was invited to return to Chiapas for a second summer to extend her research and her exceptional senior honors thesis was entitled "The Funeral Ceremonies in Zinacantan" (1969).[9]

Another talented undergraduate who had served as a photographer for the *Harvard Crimson*, Mark L. Rosenberg, was a premed student to whom we gave the difficult task of learning more about the lengthy curing rituals (which he dutifully photographed at each stage) and of studying the social bases for choices made between the shamans and the INI physicians in curing illnesses. I admired his stamina in staying with curing ceremonies for more than thirty-six hours in a stretch as the shaman proceeded from one sacred mountain shrine to another. His summer report (Rosenberg 1967) was outstanding as was his article in the *Harvard Medical Alumni Bulletin* entitled "Zinacantan: Which Doctor?" (1968). The sixth Harvard undergraduate, Fred G. Whelan, was a government concentrator who worked on calendars, dating, and concepts of time in Zinacantan and Chamula. It was a fine study, reported in his summer paper entitled "The Passing of the Years" (Whelan 1967).[10]

Nineteen sixty-seven had proved to be another productive season, something I could report with some pride in my request for renewal of the NIMH grant as the second five-year period was ending. Our control of Tzotzil had steadily improved. We had definitively added the large municipio of Chamula to our research operations and were beginning to make comparative studies of social and cultural patterns in Zinacantan and Chamula. In our research design to study cultural change we had also added field research in the central Ladino town of San Cristobal Las Casas. I was very gratified to learn that the third five-year grant for the years 1968 through 1972 had been approved.

1968: CHIAPAS, JAPAN, AND THE USSR

Nineteen sixty-eight was another interesting but complicated year for me. During the summer I again served as field director in Chiapas; during the fall term, on sabbatical from Harvard, I traveled to Japan, thence through southeastern and southern Asia and on to the Soviet Union, and returned to Cambridge by way of Europe.

In the spring term we again brought Chep Apas to Cambridge to serve as the native speaker in the Tzotzil course. His adventures at Harvard on this trip are recorded in a diary that he dutifully kept and that has been translated by John Haviland. An excerpt from one evening:

> Father John [EZV] arrived, but it was already past 6 P.M. It was already dark. "Well, Chep, we're going to the house of Doctor Thomas [Dr. T. Berry Brazelton]. But first we have to pass by another building to drink a little liquor," said Old John. "Okay," I told him. We went to another building where the old professors can drink [the Harvard Faculty Club]. Well, when we had drunk liquor, we went to the house of the man called Doctor Thomas, since we were going to have dinner there. We all drank together because lots of people had gathered. . . .
>
> Well, when we finished drinking liquor, we ate dinner. We ate chicken. Old Doctor Thomas offered us very good food. . . . When we finished eating, Doctor Thomas showed a movie. He had a little machine that was for looking at photographs, since he had stored away a great many photographs. There was one of the president

in Zinacantan Center. . . . There were pictures of all the students
of anthropology. There was a picture of all of Doctor Thomas's
children, and photographs of people from Nachih . . . and Nabenchauk, and from Apas. . . . Doctor Thomas had a very great many
photographs. (J. Haviland 1989: 46)

Chep Apas also had interesting visits with Dr. Ignacio Bernal's second
son, Carlos, who had come to live with us in Weston during the fall term to
learn English. Later Carlos Bernal moved to the nearby Cambridge School
of Weston where he became a boarding student, but still continued to
spend a great deal of time with our family. Carlos later went on to study
at Cambridge in England for a year before completing his law degree at
the Universidad Nacional Autónoma de México. He is now a practicing
attorney in Mexico City.

The newly recruited graduate students included Felisa M. Kazen and
Francesco Pellizzi. Kazen was a very bright graduate student in sociology
at Harvard who came from the border town of Laredo, Texas. Her father's
large family were Lebanese; they first settled in northern Mexico and later
crossed the border into Texas. Felisa was completely bilingual in Spanish and English and understood the subtleties of Mexican culture better
than any previous member of the Chiapas Project. At my suggestion, she
undertook a detailed study during the summer and subsequently during the
academic year 1969–70, of the introduction and operation of the textile
factory that Moctezuma Pedrero owned in San Cristobal.

Kazen's Ph.D. dissertation, "Sociocultural Aspects of Development: A
Case Study of the Introduction of a Textile Factory into a Community in
Southern Mexico" (1972), provided a detailed description and analysis of
this process. There were some surprising findings, at least for me. I had
predicted in advance that the arrival of the factory in San Cristobal would
involve significant employment for the Tzotzil Indians in the Highlands
of Chiapas and would become a significant force for change (Vogt 1967).
Kazen discovered that the factory owners had imported the most modern,
semiautomated machinery from Switzerland. These machines required few
workers, most of whom had to be very skilled in tending the machines. The
result: almost all of the laborers were drawn from the Ladino population
from San Cristobal and other cities in Mexico. The impact on the Tzotzil
communities was minimal.[11]

Arriving from Italy on a Harkness Fellowship, Francesco Pellizzi was a bright and attractive young man, and soon became one of the star graduate students in the Department of Anthropology. After training in anthropology in Italy, he had studied with the famous Claude Levi-Strauss in Paris and came to us with some of the latest word on structuralism. I was impressed and invited him to come to Chiapas. With his background in Italian and French, it was relatively easy for him to pick up Spanish—although, for a considerable period of time, I continued to hear piazza, rather than plaza, for a town square.

Francesco's first field research in Chiapas was focused on the organization and structural functions of Zinacanteco shamans (Pellizzi 1972). Francesco later developed an interest in witchcraft, a domain which had not yet been systematically studied in Zinacantan, and he proceeded to collect a vast number of cases of witchcraft over the subsequent years. Some of the cases he gathered directly in interviews, but many more were collected in the form of texts written on the typewriter by Zinacanteco informants, especially Romin Teratol, whom we had taught to read and write in Tzotzil. Part of this accumulation of witchcraft data was motivated by the need to keep Romin Teratol, who had been working for the project since 1958, steadily employed. This situation had become a problem for us since Romin did not like farming corn to begin with, and, as the years elapsed, he became even less inclined to cultivate corn and more dependent on our employment to support his family. Francesco was good enough to keep him employed through several years, and he now has more than three thousand pages of Tzotzil texts on Zinacanteco witchcraft (probably the richest collection of witchcraft data in the world), which has yet to be analyzed and published.[12]

Of the six undergraduates with the field party that summer, three undertook research in Chamula, two in Zinacantan, and one in San Cristobal. Maxine Warshauer chose to study the patterns of Chamula weddings, a topic I strongly encouraged to provide us with a case to compare with Jane Collier's excellent data on weddings in Zinacantan. While her report (1969) was not so detailed as that of Collier's, Maxine managed to break new ground and provided useful ethnographic information on Chamula. Another who worked in Chamula was a brilliant economics concentrator, Charles F. Sabel, who studied politics and land tenure history.[13]

More lasting and fundamental work in Chamula was undertaken by Jan

Rus III and his wife, Diane. This bright and attractive young couple moved into a house of a Chamula pottery-maker in the hamlet of Tsahal Te'tik and managed to get on well with the Chamulas and to collect the kind of ethnographic data on the flow of life that we had long since been recording on Zinacantan. Jan's A.B. honors thesis, entitled "Chamula Pottery Making" (1969), together with his high course grades, led to his summa cum laude graduation from Harvard.[14]

Carla P. Childs was one of the stars in learning the language; in fact, she was later selected as the teacher of our Tzotzil course. Carla undertook field research in Zinacantan and Chamula on animal spirit companions in 1968; in 1969 and 1970 she worked in the hamlet of Nabenchauk, assisting the psychologist Patricia Greenfield in a study of how girls learned to weave in this society. She was among the first of our women fieldworkers to learn to weave competently on a backstrap loom; it is a complicated process, as many of her predecessors in Chiapas discovered. Carla also became interested in the cognitive process of pattern representation in the weaving, which was the subject of her senior honors thesis (1970).[15]

Another Harvard undergraduate, Jonathan P. Hiatt, undertook a field study of Rancho San Nicolas, the Ladino-owned ranch located in the upper part of the Valley of Zinacantan. The ranch property included not only fertile land the Zinacantecos hoped to add to their ejido, but also Bankilal Muk'ta Vits, the volcano that is the mountain home of their most important ancestral deities. Hiatt's (1968) report describes the social structure and politics of this complicated enclave lying just east of Zinacantan Center.[16]

Susan P. Levine was a concentrator in psychology at Harvard, but had had some anthropology courses and was interested in field research on Mexican culture. At my suggestion she undertook a study of barrio organization in San Cristobal, a domain that had long interested me, especially since each barrio had its own church and patron saint, as well as special characteristics (weavers lived in one barrio, potters in another, etc.). Susan lived at the Baños. This was a privately owned public bathhouse that provided showers and steam baths and was also an inexpensive boarding house located in the barrio of La Merced. It was owned and run by Cresencio and Jovita Gonzalez who had a family of ten children.

I shall never forget the large horseshoe-shaped courtyard of Los Baños Mercedarios, where one encountered the huge steam engine, formerly used to power a sawmill, that produced the heat for the showers and baths. On the left were a row of shower stalls and steam baths, where for a modest few pesos one could have a steam bath, complete with fragrant odors from either eucalyptus or lime leaves.

At the back were the laundry tubs (for Doña Jovita also took in laundry) and the open-air dining room (with a large cage full of tropical birds nearby) where guests and the family were fed simple, but hearty meals. On the right were a row of Spartan bedrooms for family and guests, many of whom came from other towns and were enrolled in the local San Cristobal schools. There was only one small bathroom with toilet to serve all.

Duane Metzger first conceived the idea of placing students—who came in from fieldwork, discovered cold water for showers in their cheap hotels, and complained to the field leader—at Los Baños, where the living conditions were far from elegant, but there was always plenty of hot water. Subsequently, we had placed students there almost every summer, but we had never systematically studied the local barrio organization. It was a natural for Susan who managed to study not only the barrio of La Merced, but also the barrio called La Revolución, located adjacent to the Harvard Ranch. Susan produced an excellent description and analysis of the barrio organization of San Cristobal (Levine 1968).

A brilliant student who applied but was not selected to join the field party in 1968 should also be mentioned. Sarah C. Blaffer had just transferred from Wellesley to Harvard, was concentrating in anthropology, and wanted very much to go to Chiapas. But Sarah is over six feet tall, and I decided, mistakenly it turns out, that she would intimidate the short-statured Zinacantecos, especially the women who rarely measure as much as five feet. But Sarah was not to be put off by my decision. She later proceeded to visit Chiapas on her own and to write a remarkable summa cum laude senior honors thesis on Zinacantan under my supervision, which was later published as *The Black-man of Zinacantan: A Central American Legend* (1972). She went on to obtain her Ph.D. in anthropology at Harvard, specializing in primate behavior. Sarah Blaffer Hrdy is now a professor of anthropology at the University of California, Davis, and one of the outstanding anthropologists of her generation, having been elected to the National Academy of Sciences at the relatively young age of forty-four. I did not always make the right decisions!

My sabbatical journey to Asia and Europe began in Japan where Nan and I attended the meetings of the Eighth International Congress of Anthropological and Ethnological Sciences, held in Tokyo and Kyoto, and I presented a paper entitled "Penny Capitalism or Tribal Ritualists?—The Relationship of Market Behavior to Ceremonial Life in a Modern Maya Community" (1968a).

After visiting colleagues in Southeast Asia we proceeded to Moscow where I was an official guest of the Institute of Ethnography of the Academy of Sciences of the USSR for a month. My program divided our time among three cities: Moscow, Leningrad, and Tashkent. My Moscow program called for conferences with members of the Institute of Ethnography, including the director, Julian Bromley. Since I was an Americanist, my major contacts were restricted to members of the "American department" of the Institute. Many of them were of advanced age, and hardly an inspiring lot of scholars. I learned later that the more interesting and dynamic ethnologists in the USSR were the ones working in Siberia, where they could do firsthand field research. But in the rigid bureaucratic structure of the academy in those days, I was never scheduled to meet them. I did give one seminar on our uses of aerial photography in the Highlands of Chiapas. The Soviets seemed to be interested, but there was little discussion, and I suspected that some of them thought our aerial photographic project was part of a CIA effort in southern Mexico.

The Institute of Ethnography in Leningrad was much livelier. Our sponsors and principal hosts were the two Mayanists R. V. Kinzhalov, a specialist in ancient Maya art, and Yuri Knorozov, the famous expert on Mayan hieroglyphs and codices. This contact with the Soviets was much more interesting. I managed to confer at length with Knorozov. The latter was very excited with some of my contemporary Maya data on shamanism when I lectured on ancient Maya concepts in Zinacanteco culture at the Institute. We had some really stimulating discussions with Knorozov.

In Tashkent I wanted to see and understand some of the accomplishments, as well as the lines of tension, in the Soviet effort to include the large Central Asian populations, such as the Uzbeks, in the Soviet Union.

During January in England we spent time in London, Cambridge, and Oxford. At Cambridge our stay was graciously planned by my former student, Steve Gudeman, who was reading social anthropology under the supervision of Edmund Leach in King's College. I gave a seminar at King's College on Levi-Strauss among the Maya, in which I attempted to apply the structuralism of the great French master to an interpretation of the Zinacanteco Great Vision ceremony, their longest and most elaborate curing ritual. I was flattered that almost all of the staff attended, including Meyer Fortes, Edmund Leach, Jack Goody, and Audrey Richards, as well as my American colleagues Gordon Willey and Dell Hymes, both of whom were visiting in Cambridge. The performance seemed to go well, and Meyer Fortes encouraged me to write an article for *Man* on the subject, which I later did in collaboration with my wife (see E. Vogt and C. Vogt 1970). At Oxford I did not give a lecture or seminar, but we did have an opportunity to visit with two former students, Julie Taylor and Todd Rakoff, and to call on Evans-Pritchard and Rodney Needham.

1969: CAMBRIDGE AND CHIAPAS

Upon returning to Cambridge in the spring of 1969 I discovered that not only was Harvard in a turmoil of meetings and demonstrations that ultimately led to the occupation of University Hall by the SDS, but also that the members of the Department of Anthropology had quietly recommended to the dean that I be tapped to be the next chairman. At the time I was summoned to University Hall and asked to serve a tour of duty as chairman, the dean, Franklin Ford, had suffered a heart attack from the tensions of his job, and Professor Edward S. Mason had been appointed as acting dean of the faculty. I recall Dean Mason explaining to me that apart from one or two permanent members of any department who were too poorly organized to serve, every tenured professor of a department at Harvard ultimately had to put in a tour of duty as chairman. I also remembered Clyde Kluckhohn's warning that if I stayed on at Harvard, I would sooner or later have to assume heavy administrative duties. Furthermore, I felt that with the University in a state of turmoil, the least I could do was to accept the assignment and do what I could to restore some semblance of stability and order. I was appointed to serve for four years from 1 July 1969 to 1 July 1973, perhaps the most difficult years for university administrators in this century.

As a by-product of the Chiapas Project, and the close relationships developed in the field during the summer, I felt I was in touch with many students at a time when many members of the Harvard faculty felt thoroughly alienated from the student body. I remember some amusing moments, such as the day I responded to the plea that faculty members go to University Hall and talk with students who were occupying the faculty room on the second floor. I encountered Carolyn Pope, whom I had known well during her two years of association with the project, sitting cross-legged on top one of the large meeting tables. She quipped: "So this is the fancy place where you have your faculty meetings!" But then we went on to talk amicably about the Vietnam war, her senior thesis, and other project matters. It turned out to be an interesting afternoon.

In the spring term Domingo Pérez, or Bik'it Romin (Little Domingo), a son-in-law of Petul Vakis who was the son of the famous Mol Shun Vaskis, one of the grand old men of the hamlet of Nabenchauk, was brought to Cambridge during the month of April to serve as the native speaker in our Tzotzil course. Although the students were on strike and many classes had been suspended, we held our training sessions for fieldworkers in Chiapas without interruption through all the crises at Harvard. Bik'it Romin described his adventures in the United States in a text translated by Bob Laughlin (1989).

Assisted by the now very experienced George Collier, I again took on the duty as field director during the 1969 summer field season in Chiapas. The new graduate students included Benjamin S. Orlove, who had just graduated from Harvard, and was on his way to do graduate work in anthropology at Berkeley, and Ira Abrams, who had just finished his first year of graduate work in anthropology at Harvard.

Ben Orlove was placed in Chamula where, with the aid of aerial photographs, he conducted a first-rate study of land-use, settlement pattern, and transhumance in the hamlet of Bautista Chico (Orlove 1969).[17]

George Collier and I went to a great deal of trouble to place Ira Abrams in a Tzotzil-speaking home in the small community of Huitepec, located in the crater of the extinct volcano just to the west of the Valley of San Cristobal. It was an isolated settlement we had never studied and were eager to have more information about. Loaded with an appropriate liter of posh and with Ira Abrams in tow, George and I climbed up into the Huitepec crater and managed, after a great deal of explanation and pleading, to leave Ira Abrams and his sleeping bag in an Indian home.

To my astonishment Abrams was back in town within two days, and since he spoke Spanish fluently, had managed to place himself in living quarters at INI's La Cabaña headquarters. From this base, he caught a ride out to the cabecera of San Andrés Larrainzar, and the next thing I knew had undertaken a study of skyrocket-making in that community. I was busy with other students and did not protest too loudly to Ira. It was only after the summer had ended that I discovered Ira had taken along a movie camera and had intended to make a film of Tzotzil life during the summer. After all our trouble to place him in Huitepec, he had decided it was not colorful enough for the film he had in mind and had shifted to San Andrés Larrainzar where people still wore traditional clothing.[18]

We were glad to have Carla Childs, with her superior control of Tzotzil, for a second summer season, and Katherine Brazelton, the daughter of Dr. Berry Brazelton, who joined us to work on the meaning of the concept of *bats'i* in Zinacantan. This proved to be a complex concept meaning "real," "genuine," as, for example, in the Zinacanteco words for Tzotzil: *bats'i k'op* (the real or genuine language).

Of the new undergraduates, three worked in Zinacantan, two in Chamula, and one undertook a comparative project in Zinacantan and Chamula. Suzanne Abel worked with political leaders in Zinacantan and Chamula to collect systematic data on recent community events that had generated much controversy and political heat. Her illuminating report entitled "Patterns of Political Influence—Zinacantan and Chamula" (1969) made a notable contribution to our understanding of Tzotzil political structure. After her graduation, Suzanne held the post as the administrative and secretarial assistant for the Chiapas Project for two years.[19]

Carol J. Greenhouse had developed an interest in the anthropology of law during a freshman seminar with the late Klaus-Friedrich Koch. She decided to pursue some aspects of Zinacanteco law-ways that had not been thoroughly studied by Jane Collier, especially the strategy of litigants in choosing where to take their cases for settlement. Should they choose a local hamlet leader or the presidente in Zinacantan Center to resolve their problems? What is the role of shamans and curing ceremonies in conflict resolution? With good control of Tzotzil and a second summer in Chiapas, Carol produced not only a fine summer report (1970), but also an excellent A.B. honors thesis entitled "Litigant Choice: Non-Secular and Secular Sanctions in Zinacanteco Conflict Resolution" (1971).[20]

Timothy N. Rush was placed in Nabenchauk to undertake our first systematic study of the political factions that were threatening to split the hamlet apart. These factions were an important factor in cultural change because one faction favored modernization, and the other was conservative and strongly opposed to change. The factions were spatially discernible, especially at night. The faction favoring modernization had newly installed electric lights in their houses. Tim was an excellent fieldworker, had good control of Tzotzil, and produced a first-rate report and later a senior honors thesis on Navenchauk politics (1969a, 1971).

Tim also studied a most intriguing event that occurred in the hamlet during the summer. A young man (age thirty) had three dreams about seeing a bell buried in the ground on top of a small hill south of Nabenchauk. After he related his dreams the hamlet became very excited because there had been earlier stories about the bell having been put in the hill eighty to one hundred years before by the ancestral deities. Within days, the hamlet organized what can only be described as a ritual or sacred expedition, preceded by prayers to the saints in the church in Nabenchauk and a ritual meal, to dig up the bell. Rush wrote in his journal:

> Finally, about midnight, we started the long leave-taking [from the house in which the ritual banquet took place]. . . . Heading up the trail, some beautiful touches of starry sky open right above us, I felt like an anthropologist on the way to the mine with the Seven Dwarfs. Most of the men were carrying tools over their shoulders. . . . The last stop was a cross where . . . the green cross we had brought along was put in the ground, the dahlia blossoms tied to it. . . . We struggled to light the three candles. . . . each of these prayer stops had taken about 45 minutes . . . so it was about 2 A.M. that Manvel [a shaman] started blessing the tools, two at a time; and everybody startled the sleep out of their eyes to begin the real night's work. . . . After about an hour's work it was noticed, with great excitement, that some rocks seem to be giving off light. This is taken as a sign that they are digging in the right place.

The digging continued almost continuously for days, eventually involving as many as eighty men (the women were never permitted to come close to the sacred site). After eight days, the shafts had gone down more than twenty-five feet into solid limestone—all excavated during early July at the busiest time of the maize-growing cycle, when the fields are being hoed free of weeds. The bell was never discovered, and the effort was abandoned, but I was especially interested in this event because of an earlier "myth" we had collected concerning a sacred mountain in Zinacantan Center. It seems that in earlier times the Zinacantecos had messages in three shamans' dreams from the ancestors that a bell was to be found on top of the mountain called Mushul Vits. They dug for the bell and found it, but then a Catholic priest visited the site with a young girl along. Since it was taboo for women to come close to the diggings, the bell sailed away in the air and disappeared (Laughlin and Karasik 1988: 185).

Intriguingly, when one climbs to the summit of Mushul Vits today, there is an enormous hole, apparently man-made, on top of the mountain, behind the cross shrine! It appears that history was repeating itself in Nabenchauk in the summer of 1969 and that at least some of the myths we were collecting were reworked versions of historical reality. More details are reported in Rush's "Digging for Bells in the Highlands of Chiapas" (1969b).[21]

A fourth undergraduate, Joshua Smith, engaged in linguistic research during the summer, working mainly in Chamula. Another, Lars C. Smith, an interesting student from Denmark, proved to be one of the most self-sufficient and independent fieldworkers on the Chiapas Project. We placed him in the Chamula hamlet of Lomo, which was noted for the production of clay metates for the cooking of tortillas over the open fires in Tzotzil houses and sold widely in the Highlands of Chiapas. Lars's senior honors thesis, entitled "Making a Living in Lomo: The Consequences of Economic Change in a Maya Community" (1970), has a fine analysis of the processes of change in a Chamula hamlet.[22]

The sixth undergraduate, Robert F. Wasserstrom, was a brash, brilliant young man, whom I placed in the very remote Zinacanteco hamlet of Ats'am (Salinas), which had an ancient salt well from which, with a great deal of ceremony, salt was extracted and brought to Zinacantan Center. I knew that elaborate ceremonies took place around the salt well during the Fiesta of the Virgen del Rosário in October. John Early had attended these ceremonies and provided some information, but there were many ethnographic details still to be explained. But Rob did not remain long in the hamlet. He kept coming back to San Cristobal, and I sensed after a time that he was less interested in the symbolic details of ritual than I was. He did, however, collect sufficient data to write a first-rate senior honor's thesis the Lady of the Salt (1970), and he made good progress in learning Tzotzil.

While doing graduate work in anthropology at Harvard, Rob became more and more interested in Marxist theory and in historical research. With his wife, Janice, he returned to Chiapas for his Ph.D. research. While Rob continued to do some interviewing of Tzotzil informants and spent some time living in the hamlet of Petztoh near Ats'am, he later spent less time doing firsthand ethnographic research in the field and more time with historical sources and archives, particularly those produced by the Catholic clergy. His thesis, "White Fathers and Red Souls: Indian-Ladino Relations in Highland Chiapas, 1528–1973" (1977), was the basis of his later book (1983).[23]

Even with all the burdens of assisting the students with their projects, I did have some time for my own field research during the summer. Having completed my general ethnography on Zinacantan, I decided to focus my future efforts on their complex ritual life, a domain which clearly interested me the most. Perhaps my most important fieldwork during the summer was an interview with Mol Shun Lopis Chiku, the present owner of the T'en-T'en, the small slit drum that is the single most sacred object in Zinacantan. I learned that the drum is believed to have been found "sitting on its end, under the arm of San Sebastian in the cave in the side of Jaguar Rock, that is, the cave in which the [impersonated] Jaguars [during the Fiesta of San Sebastian] lie down and 'die.'. . . It is *only* played at San Sebastian; it *cannot* be played at any other fiesta." I also learned that the drum has been in this Lopis Chiku lineage for at least four generations.

I likewise had time for some leisurely visits with an interesting German ethnologist, Dr. Ulrich Köhler, now with the Institut fur Volkerkunde in Freiburg University, who was then working in the municipio of San Pablo Chalchihuitan (see Kohler 1977).

The fall term was busy as I took the reins of the chairmanship of the Department of Anthropology, but not without its more rewarding happenings. My large ethnography, *Zinacantan: A Maya Community in the Highlands of Chiapas,* appeared and won the Faculty Prize "for the best work of scholarship written by a Harvard faculty member and published by the Harvard University Press." It also won the Fray Bernardino de Sahagun Prize for the year 1969 from the Instituto Nacional de Antropología e Historia, in the branch of anthropology, judged to be the best work of the year by a foreign investigator. The latter prize included a beautiful gold medal with a portrait of Sahagun on one side and a Teotihuacan jaguar motif on the other. Needless to say, I was immensely pleased that all my efforts on the Harvard Chiapas Project were being recognized. I was also gratified that the two volumes on the ethnology of Middle America of the *Handbook of Middle American Indians* on which I had been working for almost ten years were also published in 1969.

In December I received ominous news that cast a pall over these more joyful incidents. An event occurred in Chiapas that nearly resulted in the permanent termination of the project. Some still-unidentified thieves broke into the Church of San Lorenzo in Zinacantan Center and stole a silver cross from the wall and the golden chalice from the main altar. The silver cross was believed to have been found in remote antiquity by a Zinacanteco who visited the Earth Lord in a cave in the hamlet of Paste'. When the Zinacanteco, the story goes, came out of the cave with the silver cross and some bags of money, he encountered a Ladino with mules packed with bags of money. The Ladino challenged the Zinacanteco to a contest to see which had the most money. The Zinacanteco won, but only because he had the silver cross, which was believed to have the power to make money. The cross was later placed on the wall of the church in Zinacantan Center where it continued to have the power to manufacture money and was the only reason the Zinacantecos had as much money as they did in the contemporary world. The crucifix was carried as an icon in processions of the mayordomos in the ceremonial center. The Zinacantecos were understandably more upset by the loss of the silver cross than they were about the golden chalice.

The Zinacanteco officials had discovered tracks of tennis shoes (which were often worn by anthropologists) outside the church, and within hours word had spread throughout the municipio that anthropologists must have stolen the sacred objects. We discovered that two other churches had also been broken into the same night (one in San Cristobal and one in San Felipe at the edge of San Cristobal) and colonial art pieces removed.

Fortunately, the Harvard Chiapas Project had two very experienced and gifted fieldworkers, John Haviland and Francesco Pellizzi, in Chiapas at the time. They managed to ride out the immediate political storm with the aid of the Mexican government authorities and the Catholic bishop and various priests, all of whom helped reassure the Zinacantecos that we were not the thieves. John Haviland even took Chep Apas to Mexico City to search through a government warehouse filled with colonial art objects that were confiscated from thieves. But all to no avail. Since the thieves have never been apprehended, we have concluded that they were probably agents of some international mafia dealing in art objects and that the stolen items are now probably in New York, London, Paris, or Tokyo. It took at least five years for us to reestablish the warm rapport we had in Zinacantan before this unfortunate event occurred.

11 /
THE "POST
CLASSIC" YEARS:
1970–1980

Although I continued to engage in periodic field research in Chiapas through the 1980s and into the 1990s, the years from 1970 to 1980 were the last in which I had research grants and took students to Chiapas. As the decade unfolded I found myself becoming more involved with administrative duties at Harvard as well as more eager to focus my project efforts on the analysis of ethnographic data and the publication of books and articles, which I felt were overdue. Hence, I designate this period as the "post classic" years of the project.

1970: CHIAPAS

The spring of 1970 brought the first visit of a Chamula to Cambridge: the bright and talented Mariano López Calixto, the son of Mol Shalik, our elderly gardener at the Harvard Ranch. Mariano, or Maryan as he is called in Tzotzil, had been Gary Gossen's principal informant and was one of the first Chamulas our project taught to read and write in Tzotzil. Maryan served admirably as the native Tzotzil speaker for our Tzotzil course at Harvard.

During the summer in Chiapas, I served as field director with George Collier, who by then was an assistant professor at Stanford, as my experienced assistant. The season was characterized by a large number of returning students bringing a high degree of expertise to our field research, something we needed after the unfortunate theft of the sacred objects from the church in Zinacantan Center. The returnees included Carla Childs,

315

Mariano López Calixto, who came to Harvard in 1970 to assist in the teaching of the Tzotzil course, having a coke in Cambridge with EZV.

Carol Greenhouse, Tim Rush, Lars Smith, and Rob Wasserstrom, as well as the two graduate students, John Haviland and Francesco Pellizzi, who had spent the academic year in the field.

An important collaborative piece of research that summer was the innovative "Who's Who in Zinacantan" produced by George Collier and John Haviland, using panels of informants. Collier was interested in hamlet political structure, whereas Haviland was studying the patterns of gossip. Haviland (1977: 13–14) describes the methods used to elicit the "Who's Who":

We reasoned that panels of Zinacantecos, selected to be representative and knowledgeable, could produce lists of the well-known people in each hamlet and then supplement these lists with basic identifying information about each person. We found that it was indeed possible to elicit lists of names for each hamlet. The work had two stages. First our panelists (of three to five Zinacanteco men) would respond to the question . . . "Who is best known in each of the hamlets?" When we had exhausted this question, we asked the panel to name people from the hamlet who fell into various categories (e.g., curers, moneylenders). . . . For each name we elicited a cargo history, a record in civil office, age, and some rudimentary genealogical information, and we noted short descriptions which occurred while the men on the panel tried to identify the individuals among themselves. We realized that we had captured the skeletal forms of reputation—that we were dealing with incipient gossip, as the men on the panel discussed each man at length, argued over his past performance, and joked about his nickname. The format of the Who's Who eliciting sessions was amenable to gossip as well as to the census-taking we were doing. Therefore, I used the same panel of Zinacantecos to generate stories of the people on the Who's Who lists for three hamlets. The stories were tape-recorded. . . . This by far was the richest source of gossip: I recorded and transcribed more than forty hours of such gossip sessions, replete with wild laughter, joking, and mocking as the panel considered the reputations and exploits of Who's Who notables. Losing its initial inhibition, the panel gradually warmed up to the task. Professor Collier and I frequently withdrew from the conversation completely and let the men talk naturally. Conversations continued long after we had left the work room and turned off the tape recorder.

The new graduate student recruits for the summer were Jeffrey C. Howry and Priscilla Rachun Linn. Howry did field research on the ecological and economic aspects of ceramics, focusing on Chamula, one of the two Indian municipios in the Chiapas Highlands that continued to make pottery. His interesting Ph.D. dissertation was entitled "Fires on the Mountain: Ceramic Traditions and Marketing in the Highlands of Chiapas" (1976).[1]

After graduating from Cornell, where she worked with the late Victor Turner, Priscilla Rachun went to Oxford for her D.Phil. with Professor

The 1970 field party. Standing (left to right): Carla Childs, Lars Smith, Carol Greenhouse, Peter Guarnaccia, Kenneth Carson, EZV, John Haviland, Nan Vogt, Tim Rush. Kneeling (left to right): Lauren Bardrick, Susan Epstein, Priscilla Rachun Linn, Lisa Wiesner, Patricia Greenfield. (Missing: Jeffrey C. Howry)

Rodney Needham. When she became interested in Mesoamerica, Needham suggested she write to me about field research opportunities. I was delighted to have her as a member of the Harvard Chiapas Project.

After spending a year at Harvard working in the project archives and learning Tzotzil, Priscilla chose to work on the intricate details of the cargoholders' rituals in Chamula. She soon learned enough Tzotzil to carry on conversations and to interview in the language, and she spent a great deal of time living in the houses of incumbent cargoholders. Her field research nicely complemented that of Gary Gossen, who had focused more on the oral narratives than on the structure of the cargo system and the symbolism of the cargoholders ceremonies. Priscilla's two-volume dissertation for Oxford University, entitled "The Religious Office-Holders in Chamula: A Study of Gods, Ritual, and Sacrifice" (1977) is both a gold mine of information about Chamula and a brilliant interpretation of their ceremonies. It makes the ethnographic data on rituals equal, if not superior, to the corpus collected on Zinacantan.[2]

Of the five new undergraduates, three worked in Zinacantan and two in Chamula. Lauren Bardrick had been the star member of my freshman seminar during 1969–70 and had developed a deep interest in the symbolic aspects of Zinacanteco ritual. She was one of only six freshmen ever selected for the project, the other five being George Collier, Shelley Zimbalist Rosaldo, Emily S. Apter, Peter J. Haviland, and Cynthia McVay. In spite of stern warnings that she should not travel alone in Mexico, Lauren, who was an attractive young woman, chose to take Mexican busses from Texas to Chiapas to save money. She arrived in San Cristobal a total wreck, having been unable to sleep on her journey as she was constantly beating off amorous males during the nights. Her body was also racked with dysentery. Nan put her to bed in our house at the Harvard Ranch and nursed her back to health.

George Collier and I placed Lauren in a hamlet called Yaleb Taiv (Where the Frost Falls) in which no field research had been done previously. It was the highest hamlet in Zinacantan, located at eight thousand feet on a pine-covered, windswept mountain top in the cloud forest. The house in which she lived, belonging to a compadre of George, had a sick infant with a rash who was constantly crying. In spite of all these difficulties Lauren collected superb data on the relation of cultural boundaries to social order as she examined the domains of houses, churches, crosses, graveyards, and mountains. The data were analyzed, using especially the concepts of Mary Douglas, in her summer report entitled "Face to Face with the Gods: A Study of Ritual Order and Holiness in Zinacantan" (1970), which was one of the most insightful of the summer.[3]

Peter Guarnaccia also worked in Zinacantan, doing a first-rate study on land-holding patterns in Zinacantan Center (1970). After a second summer, in 1971, when he extended his research on land-reform efforts of the Zinacantecos, he wrote his senior honors thesis that was entitled "Land and Tortillas: Land Reform in a Maya Indian Village in Chiapas" (1972). The third student to work in Zinacantan was Lisa Wiesner, the daughter of MIT president Jerome Wiesner, who undertook a fascinating study of the function of dreams (1970).[4]

The two students who worked in Chamula were Ken L. Carson and

Susan E. Epstein. Ken focused his field research on the hamlet of Peteh (in which we were able to place him with the assistance of our gardener, Mol Shalik) where he studied symbols and beliefs from maize agriculture (1970). I gave Susan Epstein an even more difficult task, that of describing the structure and operation of the Chamula cargo system. At the outset of our field research in Chamula, I assumed the structure of the cargo system was similar to Zinacantan where the cargoholders pass through four ranked levels. Susan began with the Zinacanteco model in mind, and was frustrated for the first part of the summer trying to conceptualize the Chamula system in these terms. By the end of the summer she discovered that the Chamula cargo system was quite different and did not follow the Zinacanteco model, as she made clear in her report entitled "Civil and Religious Officials in Chamula" (1970). Susan's work helped provide a basis for later research by Priscilla Rachun Linn that finally cleared up the ambiguities.[5]

By the summer of 1970 I had finally learned how to handle a field party of students and also seize some time for my own research. Having published the general ethnography, I was focusing my work on a detailed study of ritual symbolism and interviews with Anselmo Peres, a Zinacanteco shaman, who had collaborated extensively with Bob Laughlin on his dictionary. I developed a special method of interviewing by accompanying Anselmo into the woods to collect all the plants needed for a curing ceremony. We would then bring the plants back to my study at the Harvard Ranch and I would ask him to teach me how to arrange and manipulate the plants for a particular ceremony. Not only did I learn a great deal about manipulating the paraphernalia, but in the process of gathering the plants and teaching me how to manipulate them, Anselmo himself would remember other details to tell me. The very feel and smell and colors of the sacred plants set up a very productive eliciting situation.

It was in this manner I learned for the first time that Zinacantecos believe the inner souls of the sacred plants have distinctive temperatures (hot, medium, cold) and strengths (strong, medium, weak). Now, in attempting Levi-Straussian structural analyses, there were even more chips to play with than before! Some of these results were published in an article in a festschrift for Levi-Strauss (Vogt 1970a); more appeared later in *Tortillas for the Gods: A Symbolic Analysis of Zinacanteco Rituals* (1976).

My other notable field experience was an all-night experience when Nan and I attended the house-entering episode of Mariano López Calixto's marriage on 9–10 July. Quoting from my field journal:

> Ever since Maryan, the 4th son of Mol Shalik (our Chamula gardener), saw his first copy of *Playboy* in the Leverett House Senior Common while he was serving as a Tzotzil teacher at Harvard, he seems to have one major goal in mind—to consummate his marriage to one of the belles of Peteh, Losha Bakbolom (Rosa Thin-Jaguar). Nan and I were privileged to be the only invited guests at this third, and last, formal petition made by the Lopisetik to the Thin-Jaguars for the bride. . . . It was the last episode before Maryan was to bring Losha to live in the house of his father.

Upon our arrival at Mol Shalik's home the gifts that would be taken to the Thin-Jaguars were being assembled: a net bag full of overripe bananas, a five-gallon jug of posh, a carton of cigarettes and twelve cigars, two rolls of brown sugar, two kilos of beef, and two cases of Coca-Cola. With Mol Shalik as the petitioner leading the way, we marched in procession, carrying the gifts, to the house of the Thin-Jaguars, arriving at sundown. After a long petitioning process, consisting of the long oral pleas by Mol Shalik and Mateo, both of whom were on their knees, and an exchange of drinks between the wife-receivers and the wife-givers, lasting almost an hour, we entered the house. The father and mother and eldest brother of Maryan all entered crawling on their hands and knees and placed their foreheads on the ground, to ask the father and mother of the bride to relinquish her. I recorded in my journal:

> Inside, the house was jammed with people, but arranged in such a way as to warm Gary Gossen's heart: men sat along the north side, women along the south side, with all the wife-givers on the east, the wife-receivers on the west. The men were all on benches and small chairs, with Mol Shalik placed next to Shun Thin-Jaguar, putting the two fathers side by side. The bride was kneeling on the floor with her mother and grandmother and other women relatives; Maryan's mother was placed beside the mother of the bride.

The ritual sequence that followed was executed by Maryan serving superbly as the drink-pourer. There was first a round of posh, then tortillas and beans, then another round of posh. We also washed mouths and hands both before and after the meal.

> Then there occurred an utterly fascinating ritual sequence I have not noted before. . . . Under the direction of Shun Thin-Jaguar and his assistant, Maryan served a full glass of posh to the entire assembled group, i.e., he passed the posh in rank order among the men and then among the women with each person taking a sip in a genuinely communal drink. Then he poured a glass for himself and, with Shun Thin-Jaguar inspecting, drank exactly half, then passed the other half to his bride, who drank it. [All through the sequence there was very formal bowing-and-releasing among all participants]. Another communally shared glass followed; then a glass served first to his bride, who sipped it and passed it back to Maryan who drank exactly half; it was then served to his bride who finished it. A sequence of actions that was clearly a symbolic expression of bringing the two groups together, followed by a liquid one-to-one relationship between the groom and the bride.

About ten P.M. all of the wife-receivers said goodbye and left Maryan to continue to serve as a drink-pourer for the Thin-Jaguars. Back at Mol Shalik's house we drank and ate, awaiting Maryan's return, which occurred at two A.M., to give his father a detailed account of what went on at the Thin-Jaguar's house. At 3 : 30 a large meal of beef and cabbage was served to all, and at 4 : 30 A.M. we left Peteh to be greeted on our way back to San Cristobal by a spectacular sunrise. To continue in my journal: "I reflected as we drove to San Cristobal . . . that had the residents of Peteh never heard of the Catholic church nor of the Mexican government, they still had plenty of ritual to more than seal a lifetime marriage. In fact, the amount of ritual behavior in just one night of the "house entering" was as long, and twice as complex, as the formal Connecticut wedding we had attended in June."

1971: AN AUTUMN SABBATICAL IN CHIAPAS

Since I had served as field leader in Chiapas for five consecutive summers, I decided to spend the summer of 1971 at home where I could devote more time to writing, and then spend the autumn term doing field research in Chiapas. I persuaded John Haviland, who by now was a very experienced Chiapas researcher, to take the duty as the field leader. During the spring we again had Chep Apas at Harvard to help teach the Tzotzil course. Chep also spent some weeks with the Colliers at Stanford and had this to say about his journey:

> On the third trip I got to know much more. I went to San Francisco, California, to Palo Alto, to Stanford University. . . . This was the last trip I took. But I thought it was the best, since there wasn't snow. It was good and warm. That's how I got to know how they eat there. No tortillas, just Bimbo bread in place of tortillas. That's how the third trip ended. Thanks to Mr. John Vogtie, and all the students who let me get to know their country. (Laughlin 1989: 71).

In Chiapas the field party included an interesting new graduate student, Thomas Crump, whose work was being supervised by Professor Mary Douglas at the University of London. Crump was a bright, older person who had already experienced two previous careers. He had served as a Church of England rector for seven years before he became a barrister. He practiced law for another seven years before deciding to become an anthropologist. Because he came highly recommended by Mary Douglas, whose work I greatly admired, I decided to accept him as a member of the Chiapas Project.

On this first trip to Chiapas, Crump engaged in field research in Chenalho and Chamula and was especially interested in economic organization and more particularly in the function and symbolism of money. After accepting a teaching post at the University of Amsterdam, he married the departmental secretary and returned to Chiapas with his wife and child to pursue his research. Crump had the imagination to ask novel questions and come up with significant results. His thesis, entitled "Boundaries in the Function of Money: Internal and External Debt in Selected Mexican Communities" was submitted to the University of London in 1977.[6]

Of the undergraduates that Haviland supervised that summer, four worked in Zinacantan, and one in Chamula. Jason W. Clay undertook a study of the new eight-kilometer pipeline that runs from a spring at the foot of Huitepec Mountain to the hamlet of Paste', bringing running water to this settlement of Zinacantecos for the first time. His report (1971) also analyzes the changes in water hole groups and K'in Krus ceremonies resulting from the arrival of the new pipeline. Rachel Z. Ritvo became interested in the psychological meanings in Zinacanteco mythology and, after collecting more myths during the summer, wrote an excellent senior honors thesis entitled " 'Christ and his Brothers' as Reflections of the Developing Child" (1972). Patricia E. Lynch studied gender roles in Zinacantan and her sophisticated final paper, 144 pages, was the longest undergraduate summer report ever submitted on the project (1971). Elizabeth A. Werby recorded cargoholders' prayers and produced an interesting summer report entitled "Tzotzil Speech and Couplet Pair Formation in Zinacantan" (1971).[7]

Roger H. Reed, undertook a study of Chamulas who worked in the lowland coffee plantations and did field research both in Chamula and in the coffee fincas. After spending a second summer in the field, he wrote a fine senior honors thesis entitled "Chamula and the Coffee Industry of Chiapas" (1973), containing some of the best information we have on the role of the coffee plantations in Chamula life.[8]

Once the students had departed I had a very productive fall term for research and writing. My major project was to forge ahead on my book, *Tortillas for the Gods,* in which I planned to provide detailed descriptions, episode-by-episode (as these were classified by the Zinacantecos), of a large sample of Zinacanteco rituals and then proceed to decode their symbolic meanings. I found it very productive to analyze data and write in Chiapas. When a question arose I could arrange for another interview with an appropriate Zinacanteco informant to answer the question before I proceeded. I worked intensively with my experienced informants from Paste', Shun Akov and Telesh Komis Lotriko, both of whom I had now known well for more than twelve years, as well as with Anselmo Peres from the hamlet of Pat Osil, and Chep Nuh from Nachih.

I was also fortunate that Dr. Dennis Breedlove, who by now had become the foremost authority on the plants of Chiapas, was in Chiapas in 1971.

After the Zinacanteco shamans had named and classified the sacred plants they used in rituals, I would save the collection and show it to Dennis, who was kind enough to identify all the plants and give me the scientific names used in our botanical classification.

Assisting me with the analysis, the illustrating, and the editing was Elizabeth M. Dodd, a Harvard undergraduate majoring in biology, who had come to Chiapas on a year off and was eager to be involved in research. I set up some interviews for her to carry out and also arranged some field trips in various hamlets. Betsy proved to be a skilled pen-and-ink artist and drew the informative illustrations of the sacred plants used in Zinacanteco ceremonies (see especially Vogt 1976: 68–69). She also did splendid editorial work on the manuscript, both in Chiapas and during the following academic year in Cambridge.

One of Betsy Dodd's field trips consisted of joining a Zinacanteco petitioning group in the hamlet of Pat Osil one night. She was taken along as the group, consisting of two petitioners and the prospective groom, carrying a five-gallon jug of posh with a tumpline, all quietly approached the house of the prospective bride. After the petitioners made the excuse that they would like to borrow an axe, the door was opened and they rushed inside to fall on their knees and start asking the girl's father for the hand of his daughter. At the first house, where the first choice of the groom lived, the father steadfastly refused to accept the first shot of liquor—even after a solid hour of pleading on the part of the petitioners, who eventually had to leave this house without any success whatsoever.

Betsy then recorded in her field journal how the petitioning party built a fire in the woods and discussed at length what they would do next. Because it is always difficult and very expensive to assemble the petitioners with their gifts, it was finally decided to approach the home of the prospective groom's *second* choice, whose house was nearby. Here the petitioners were successful, and the young man later married his second choice! Although we had been told by our informants that grooms-to-be sometimes had to settle for their second choices as brides, I did not think it actually happened until Betsy Dodd observed the whole improbable scene unfolding on top the mountain in the hamlet of Pat Osil.[9]

1972: CHIAPAS, HAWAII, AND JAPAN

In 1972 I received the fourth five-year grant (which ran from 1972 through 1976) from NIMH. We had now reached the point where we finally had solid, in-depth ethnographic data on both Zinacantan and Chamula, and we were beginning to make controlled comparisons between the two cultures and to track, with some precision, the ongoing trends of change in these two Tzotzil communities, as well as to engage in more subtle studies of various domains of the indigenous culture.

Because I had been invited to teach summer school at the University of Hawaii and could only spend part of the summer season in Chiapas, I persuaded Priscilla Rachun Linn to serve as field leader. Although I assisted with the students for the first month of the season, Priscilla was an experienced fieldworker with many contacts in the Indian communities, especially in Chamula, and was in a position to carry on with expertise and success after my departure.

The field party consisted of five students from Harvard and two from Tufts University who were added when the National Science Foundation specified that our funds would be contingent on our considering undergraduate applicants from other universities in the Boston area. Three of the students worked in Zinacantan, three in Chamula, and one in San Andrés Larrainzar.

Jane B. Baird spent the summer learning about the various social pressures that are brought to bear on men in Zinacantan to serve in the religious cargo system (Baird 1971), while William S. Freeman studied problems and problem areas in Zinacanteco married life (1971). Freeman returned the following summer and wrote his senior honors thesis on the lawyers of Zinacantan (1974), a very sophisticated study of the men who play the roles of mediating disputes and of representing plaintiffs or defendants before the native Zinacanteco court.[10]

Eliot Gelwan was the only concentrator in astronomy who ever applied for the Chiapas Project, and I was delighted when he was selected, especially since I had always wanted someone to do more research on the ethnoastronomy. Eliot was armed with a map of the early night sky for the latitude of the Tzotzil region, and looked forward to many nights of viewing with informants. Unfortunately, the night sky proved to be overcast so often during the rainy season, that he was only able to elicit data on five nights during the entire summer. There were also some difficulties in communication. While in English we distinguish clearly between "a star" and "a constellation," in Tzotzil the same word is used for both, a constellation being multiple stars. Nonetheless, his final report, entitled "Some Considerations of Tzotzil-Tzeltal Ethnoastronomy" (1972), was a significant piece of research that still needs to be repeated in the dry season.[11]

Of the three undergraduates who worked in Chamula, Suzanne E. Siskel had perhaps the most significant field experience. She was placed in the household of Mol Pancho in the hamlet of Ichin Ton (Owl Rock). This small hamlet is located on the road that leads from San Cristobal to Chamula and Zinacantan. I first became acquainted with Mol Pancho because he had a distillery and made bootleg posh, which our Zinacanteco informants frequently stopped to purchase when we offered them rides to Zinacantan Center in a project vehicle. I also started making my purchases of cane liquor from Mol Pancho, and we frequently took students to his outdoor patio for late afternoon cocktails. It was an easy drive from San Cristobal, and the view of the Valley of San Cristobal and surrounding mountains at sunset was breathtakingly beautiful. Further, one could throw a cocktail party for ten to twenty people and never have to spend more than fifty pesos. Mol Pancho's liquor was not only good tasting, but was strong enough to impress even the most experienced drinker. His household became known among us as "the Chamula Bar."

Over the years, we developed a closer and closer relationship with Mol Pancho and his wife and daughters and were able to persuade him to accept Suzanne into his household. Although there were some disadvantages for Suzanne, especially drunken parties that ensued when Chamulas and Zinacantecos stopped by to purchase liquor, there were advantages in that Mol Pancho had served in important cargos and his daughter, Pashku, was a charismatic and highly respected shaman. Using his household as a base, Suzanne made a study of the Chamula system of schooling during the summer of 1972, then returned for a second summer, in 1973. to focus on shamanism. Her senior honors thesis, "With the Spirit of a Jaguar: A Study of Shamanism in "Ichin Ton, Chamula" (1974) is an excellent example of the subtle and sophisticated research that we were finally prepared to undertake in Tzotzil communities.[12]

A second student working in Chamula, Mary E. Scott, had been a member of my freshman seminar. She proved to be highly gifted in learning Tzotzil and in getting along well in Chamula households where she collected first-rate ethnographic data during her two summers in Chiapas.[13]

Ricardo D. Sutton, one of the undergraduates from Tufts University, did research on the highland agricultural situation in Chamula (1972). Although he spent only one summer doing the research, the results, including some recommendations for practical improvement of Chamula agriculture, were interesting.

The second Tufts undergraduate was Marta D. Turok from Mexico City, who had the advantage of fluent Spanish. Marta focused her research on weaving and did field research in San Andrés Larrainzar, whose women weavers are noted for the beauty and quality of their fabrics with complex designs. Her summer report entitled "Handicrafts: A Case Study of Weaving in the Highlands" (1972) was followed, with more field research, by "Symbolic Analysis of Contemporary Mayan Textiles: The Ceremonial *Huipil* from Magdalenas, Chiapas, Mexico" (1974).[14]

Having made no attempt to do archaeology in Zinacantan since Edward Calnek's request was refused by the indigenous officials in 1960, we decided to make another attempt in this season of 1972. I recruited Professor Donald E. McVicker, who had worked with Robert McC. Adams on the University of Chicago archaeological project in Chiapas in 1961–62, to undertake an archaeological survey of Zinacantan. We knew that the chances of receiving permission from the Indian officials to excavate in the municipio were nil, especially after the theft of the sacred objects from the Church of San Lorenzo a scant three years before. Instead, McVicker did a surface survey of particular areas of the municipio that were probable prehistoric sites, including locations in Zinacantan Center and along the ancient trail that led into the Center from Ixtapa and Ats'am (Salinas) to the west. This survey proved to be productive, especially as it indicated, from exposed ancient walls, that the pre-Columbian center was most probably located where the Church of San Lorenzo now sits, and that the ancient trail into the community from the Lowlands has probably been used for centuries. Of particular interest is a location on the trail to Ats'am called Ch'ivit Krus (Market Cross) where the concentration of shards suggests that it was indeed a marketplace for the exchange of highland and lowland products in pre-Columbian times (McVicker 1972; 1974).[15]

It was late July when I turned the Chiapas field station over to Priscilla

Linn, and Nan, our youngest son, Charlie, and I flew to Honolulu where I taught an introductory course on cultural anthropology at the University of Hawaii. It was the first time I had spent any time in Hawaii since my Navy days in 1945, and it proved to be an interesting six weeks. At the end of the summer school session, Nan and I flew on to Japan for two weeks, this time to visit Hokkaido and northern Honshu.

1973 AND 1974: CHIAPAS

The summers of 1973 and 1974 were the last seasons when we had large numbers of students in the field parties in Chiapas. I took the duty as field leader both summers, which proved to be busy and productive. As was usual by now, I was fortunate to have both experienced graduate and undergraduate students in the field to help with the placement and ongoing management of the new students. In 1973 John and Leslie Haviland and Jan and Diane Rus were with me, as well as Bill Freeman, Tim Rush, Mary Scott, and Suzanne Siskel as returning undergraduates. That same spring we again brought Bik'it Romin of Nabenchauk to Cambridge to serve as a teacher and native informant in the Tzotzil training class, and all of the students were well prepared for the field.

During the 1972–73 academic year I had been approached by Wolper Films with the proposal that an educational ethnographic film be made on Zinacantan. I was, of course, delighted. I had seen a number of such films that contained excellent photography, but since the filmmakers had too little ethnographic understanding of the culture, much of the action was incomprehensible. We had been studying the Zinacantan culture for fifteen years and felt we knew enough to provide an illuminating commentary. I decided that John Haviland, with his masterful control of Tzotzil and his close contacts in the hamlet of Nabenchauk, would be the ideal person to serve as the major anthropological consultant for the film and to assist Wolper in the field.

A grant was received from the National Geographic Society to fund the film and all seemed promising. But the enterprise fell apart, largely because of the difference in perspective between the professional filmmaker and the ethnologist. I managed to mediate one quarrel over details before the group flew to Chiapas. But in Chiapas an irreconcilable dispute arose. The field party was filming family life in Nabenchauk, which had several local bars with a loudspeakers on poles that beamed out Mexican ranchera songs for the whole hamlet to hear. The film director from Wolper wanted John Haviland to have all this loud music stopped while he was filming. He argued that it was jarring for the main theme of the film, which was emphasizing the traditional life of a Maya family and that discontinuities in the music would make final cut and paste editing just about impossible. Haviland felt that the loud music from the bar was a fact of life in contemporary Mayan communities and an authentic part of the ethnography. Besides, it would have been impossible for Haviland to persuade all the bars to shut off the loud music.

It proved to be impossible to settle this kind of dispute, and we cancelled the project and returned the funds to the National Geographic Society. Since that time Haviland has taken some excellent coverage on film in Nabenchauk, especially of the ceremonies performed during Holy Week. I guess the major lesson for me in this experience was that ethnographic films are best made by anthropologists themselves, rather than trying to compromise the views of a strong-willed film director from Hollywood and an equally strong-willed ethnographer.

George Collier, who by this time was teaching at Stanford, had his own summer Chiapas project, made up of Stanford students including our son Terry and our daughter-in-law, Mary Anschuetz, who was just finishing a graduate degree in the School of Communications at Stanford.

Of the new Harvard students, four of them did superb field research and ultimately wrote senior honors theses on their Chiapas experience. One was Thor R. Anderson, an interesting Winthrop House undergraduate who had had a falling out with his wealthy father in Illinois (where the father served as Master of Fox Hounds for the local hunt). Thor took up carpentry to earn money for his Harvard education so he would not have to depend on funds from home. He soon become a skilled carpenter. Tall and rugged, he was a natural for field research in the remote back country of Chamula on which we needed additional ethnographic data.

We decided to place Thor in the hamlet of Krus Ton (Cross Rock) on the eastern slopes of Tsonte' Vits (Spanish Moss Mountain), the highest elevation in central Chiapas. This was the hamlet that specialized in bootleg rum liquor and the hamlet in which the German-American painter, Arthur Silz, had been slain in 1956. The Chiapas Project had developed a contact with one of the major bootleggers over the past decade as various of our fieldworkers had obliged Zinacanteco cargoholders by providing for the transport of jugs of the liquor from Krus Ton to Zinacantan Center. With John Haviland along to assist with his fluent Tzotzil, I took Thor to Krus Ton in the project Jeep and we presented a liter of posh to our bootlegger friend and pleaded with him to let this new student live in his house so that he could learn Tzotzil and Chamula customs. It was, by far, the most difficult placement (for understandable reasons!) that we have ever made in a Tzotzil household. It took at least two hours of pleading and explanation to enable us to leave Thor and his sleeping bag in the house of the bootlegger.

The Chamula bootleggers took one look at the tall, rugged Thor and immediately put him to work carrying wood on a tumpline to fuel the distillery. For days Thor did little else but carry heavy wood. But little by little he learned more Tzotzil and was accepted by the household and then by the larger community. He adapted so well that he was eventually given a piece of land on which to build his own Chamula-style thatch-roofed house. After writing his senior honors thesis, "Krus Ton: A Study of House and Home in a Maya Village" (1975), Thor returned to Chiapas for more field research and developed even closer rapport with the Chamulas in Krus Ton and in the municipio at large. He was later able to obtain official Chamula permission to film the major Chamula ceremonies performed at Carnaval, in advance of Lent. This award-winning film, *Sacred Games: Ritual Warfare in a Maya Village* (1988) provides rich ethnographic coverage of Chamula ritual life.[16]

Another student who worked in Chamula, Thomas L. Paradise, had a field project focused on the patterns of land tenure and inheritance in the Chamula hamlet of Peteh. Utilizing our aerial photographs of Chamula and our close contacts with the family of Mol Shalik, our Chamula gardener, Tom produced a first-rate undergraduate thesis entitled "Land Tenure in Peteh" (1974).[17]

John N. Burstein focused his field research on collecting Zinacanteco oral narratives that are related about Indian kings. His senior thesis, "The King Tales in Translation" (1975), is also outstanding. John is another student who returned to Chiapas to spend some years working with a nongovernment organization and finally with the Mexican Secretariat of Public Education on various programs designed to aid the Tzotzil in becoming literate in their own language.[18]

The second student to work in Zinacantan was Alaka Wali who had a strong interest in the position of women in the society of Zinacantan and wrote an excellent senior thesis entitled "Dependence and Dominance: The Status of Women in Zinacantan" (1974).[19]

Two other students who did interesting field research in Zinacantan were Emily S. Apter and Rowena I. Frazer. Emily had enrolled in my freshman seminar on the Maya and had produced such remarkable research papers both terms that she was selected to do fieldwork focused on the symbolism of the saints. Rowena Frazier, the daughter of an American father and Peruvian mother, knew Spanish and had had experience in Latin America. Her Chiapas research involved the first systematic study of ritual foods.[20]

My youngest son, Charlie, also assisted me with field research in the summer of 1973. I had set out to discover whether the contemporary ceremonial centers of the Indian municipios in the Highlands of Chiapas were laid out by our compass directions (i.e., with streets that ran north, south, east, west) or whether they conformed to the prehistoric Mesoamerican tilt. Archaeologists had repeatedly reported that a high percentage of the archaeological sites in Mesoamerica were oriented with a tilt that is east of north, or south of east. We knew from the aerial photos that the ceremonial centers, unlike the hamlets, were laid out in a grid pattern, but the question was, How does this grid fit with our compass directions? I decided to use the line between the front door of the principal church and the image of the patron saint located in center position behind the altar as the operational measure of the orientation.

Since the aerial photos were not precise enough to make this measure accurately, I needed a research assistant to reach the cabeceras of all of the Tzotzil and Tzeltal municipios in the Highlands of Chiapas and take compass readings on the orientation of the churches. Many of these cabeceras could be reached by Jeep or truck, but several were still only accessible by foot or on horseback. Charlie had had much experience backpacking in mountain country and was able to reach each ceremonial center and take the required compass readings. The results were fascinating. While the town of San Cristobal is laid out precisely according to our compass directions, twenty-six of the thirty-seven Indian ceremonial centers conformed to the Mesoamerican tilt, that is, they were oriented south of east, like their pre-Columbian precursors (see Vogt 1978a). In 1973 Alain Breton from the University of Paris initiated his ethnological investigation of the

Tzeltal community of Bachajon. He returned to Chiapas in 1974–75 (when I had an opportunity of meet him) and again in 1976 (Breton 1979).

At the end of the summer, the Highlands of Chiapas were subjected to persistent tropical downpours from passing hurricanes emanating from the Gulf of Mexico. Since the valley of San Cristobal is completely surrounded by mountains, the only drainage into the Grijalva River in the lowlands was through a subterranean cavern called a *sumidero*. The sumidero proved to be inadequate to carry off the floodwater that year, and soon large parts of San Cristobal, including the Pan American Highway were under water. We had a frightening week as we watched the water level rise several inches each day and wondered if even the Harvard Ranch would be inundated. Finally the rains stopped and the flood waters subsided, after what was described as the second worst flooding since the Spanish conquest. This incident led me to reflect that the pre-Columbian Tzotzil had built all of their settlements either on high ridges surrounding the Valley of San Cristobal, or in other valleys that had adequate drainage. This placed all the Indian settlements above the dense fog that settles in the valley and above the dangers of flood waters. The pre-Columbian Indians used the valley bottom for farming and for gathering the grass for thatching the roofs of their houses—another example of how the Native Americans made wiser use of their ecological settings.

During the academic year 1973–74, an event occurred at Harvard that profoundly altered our lives for the ensuing eight years. One day my secretary had a telephone call from Massachusetts Hall informing me that President Bok would like to see me in his office on Friday afternoon. When a call comes from the President's Office, one always wonders "Now, what have I done?" and I arrived at the appointed hour in a state of some apprehension. But the president greeted me warmly, ushered me into his office, and told me he would like me to become the next Master of Kirkland House.

The twelve residential houses at Harvard are modeled on the Oxford and Cambridge colleges and the appointment as master is one of the signal honors at Harvard. Each master is provided with an elegant master's lodgings—really a small mansion—in which to live rent-free as he carries out administrative and ceremonial duties for the some 320 undergraduates who live in the house. For example, one of the most important ceremonial duties is the passing out of the Harvard diplomas to each of the graduating seniors in a ritual performed in the courtyard of each house—an event which follows the large commencement gathering in Harvard Yard. The courtyard is packed with fond parents and grandparents watching their adored seniors finish Harvard College.

Since I had had only one year of rest from administration after finishing the chairmanship of the department and was eager to get on with my research and writing, I responded that I was flattered, but wondered if perhaps a later time in my career would not be more appropriate. President Bok said that in his experience, professors served best as masters some years prior to retirement. Then they could finish their masterships and spend the last few years "putting a capstone on their professional careers." I agreed to consider the offer.

I had spent twenty-three years as a nonresident member of the Senior Common Room at Leverett House and had served as a fellow under Master Richard Gill. After we sold our house in Weston, we spent two years as resident associates (renting one of the faculty apartments at the top of the tower) of Mather House under Master Skiddy von Stade and were there when the offer came. I had enjoyed both experiences and had come to have great respect for the role of the Harvard Houses in the educational process. In retrospect, I believe that Skiddy must have passed along my name to the president and dean as a possible candidate for a mastership.

I was also tempted by the offer since it would mean I would be the first anthropologist to serve as a master at Harvard—there being some disagreement as to whether or not Alfred Tozzer had ever actually been offered a mastership. It took me two weeks to persuade Nan, who would become the first comaster at Harvard, as President Bok had just instituted the pattern of formal appointments for the spouses. Nan argued that she did not have a British accent and that we had neither an independent income nor a house in the country, characteristics she associated with previous masters she had known. She finally agreed with some trepidation, but took up the duties enthusiastically and soon came to love the life in Kirkland House. In fact, when I was ready to step down after the eight years we served (1974 to 1982), she would have liked to continue.

Derek Bok had indicated when I was appointed that he hoped very much that the Harvard Chiapas Project would continue during my duty as a master. But as we threw ourselves into the duties of mastership at Kirkland House I soon discovered how time- and energy-consuming the life proves to be. I had thought being a chairman of a department at Harvard was a heavy burden, but I soon learned that the duties and responsibilities of a mastership are many times heavier. Not so much the bureaucratic paper-work (which is heavier for a chairman than for a master), but the sense of heavy responsibility for the decisions one must make. I am referring to those lonely night hours when one suddenly awakens at three to pace the floor and think "My God, did I make the correct decision?"—about, for example, some matter of discipline for a student misdemeanor being considered by the Administrative Board, or about whether your Fellow-ship Committee should have nominated "B," rather than "A," for a prize fellowship.

But since the plans for the 1974 field season were already in place, we went on to Chiapas in June. I was fortunate this season again to have John and Leslie Haviland headquartered at the Harvard Ranch to help with the new undergraduates.

The new graduate student that summer was Richard A. Gonzalez, who had come to Harvard from Stanford where he had performed brilliantly in his undergraduate classes. He was an older student, having worked as a truck driver in California for some years before finishing his A.B. at Stan-ford. Since he planned to work in Chamula I placed him straight away in a household in the ceremonial center. But his first field stay proved to be trau-matic. He had known from his reading and his advance training that beans and tortillas were the standard fare in Chamula households three times a day. What he had not internalized was that the tortillas were used to eat the beans—there were no eating utensils. This, along with no bathrooms and sleeping on the ground, shocked him so profoundly that he never again ventured to spend time in a Chamula household during the months he spent at the Harvard Ranch. Instead, he remained at the ranch and interviewed informants. In spite of his promising beginning, he never finished his Ph.D. requirements at Harvard and has instead pursued another career.

By contrast, the seven undergraduates flourished in Zinacantan and Chamula households. Three worked in Zinacantan, four in Chamula. Samuel M. Anderson, deeply interested in public architecture, did a first-rate study (1974) of the plazas and parks that had been constructed, with the aid of Mexican architects, in the hamlets of Nabenchauk and Nachih and in Zinacantan Center. Paul L. Saffo, who had been a member of my Maya freshman seminar the year before, was placed in the remote ham-let of Saklum (White Earth) where he studied directional orientations and their relationships to astronomical bodies.[21]

Nancy A. Zweng, also a member of my Maya freshman seminar in

1972–73, undertook a fascinating study of the beliefs and practices of the Zinacantecos about the birth of twins. After returning to the field for a second summer, she produced an excellent report, "*Vach' Unen:* A Study of Zinacanteco Twins" (1975), which describes how the difficulties of Zinacanteco life for women virtually preclude taking care of twins, how twins are regarded as witches, and how their birth creates conceptual problems in the culture. While twin births occur rarely, one or both of the twins commonly die as infants. If at least one does not die, it is literally sold to another Zinacanteco or a Ladino family who wishes to purchase it. I shall never forget the shock experienced by Dr. T. Berry Brazelton when he examined and tested a set of twins in a Zinacanteco household. He commented to the mother that the two infants were undernourished and made some recommendations for adding powdered milk to their diet. But when he returned for another visit two weeks later, he found only one nursing child. He questioned the mother about the other twin, fearing it had died. "No," the mother replied with a smile, "we sold it for two hundred pesos to another Zinacanteco family."[22]

Of the four students who worked in Chamula, Denise Z. Field had the most profound field experience. We placed her with Mol Pancho at "the Chamula Bar" in the hamlet of Ichin Ton where she worked with the daughter, Pashku', who is a shaman. Denise focused on the prayers used in ritual, and her brilliant senior thesis, "With a Flower, With a Candle, With a Prayer: An Ethnography of Prayer in Chamula" (1975), is another example of the subtle and sophisticated work that was possible by hardworking undergraduates.[23]

Of the other three students who worked in Chamula, one was Peter J. Haviland, John Haviland's younger brother, who had been a member of my freshman seminar in which he had performed well; he was selected as the fifth freshman to do research on the Chiapas Project. Pete focused on the recent political history of Chamula. Sara J. Lacy elicited a biography of a Chamula woman, and wrote an engaging senior thesis entitled "*Antel:* An Essay" (1976). The third, Marcy S. Richmond, studied the Chamula prisoners who were incarcerated in the San Cristobal jails.[24]

In the late summer I was invited to attend another Wenner-Gren symposium at Burg Wartenstein, on the topic of secular rituals, which was chaired by Max Gluckman, Sally Falk Moore, and Victor Turner. I presented a paper, jointly authored by Suzanne Abel, on the political rituals performed in Mexico (see Vogt and Abel 1977).

Returning to Harvard, we moved into the masters' lodgings of Kirkland House and began a busy round of activities as masters.

1975 TO 1980: CAMBRIDGE AND CHIAPAS

From 1975 through 1980 I focused more on carrying on the mastership duties at Kirkland House and attempting to write more articles and books about the Chiapas research than I did in recruiting large numbers of students for fieldwork. Having had, by 1975, 135 students engaged in field research on the Chiapas Project, I felt I had done my tour of duty in supervising fieldwork and it was time for me to muster what time and energy I could to write more articles and books on the results of our research. During the period, I spent a spring term and four summers in Chiapas, but we had only seven additional students engaged in field research during these six years.

Before I had accepted the mastership at Kirkland House, I had explained to President Bok that the department had agreed to let me take sabbatical leave during the 1975–76 academic year to travel during the fall and to spend the spring term doing research in Chiapas. This request was honored and we left Kirkland House in the competent hands of Dr. and Mrs. Warren Wacker, who served as acting masters for the year.

Jan Rus, who had now had many seasons of fieldwork in Chiapas, was appointed as the field leader. Jan supervised the work of three new students, Victoria Barber, Kelly T. Jensen, and Gilbert V. Marin, in addition to Nancy Zweng, who had returned for a second summer.

Vicki Barber studied markets and wrote an interesting senior thesis, "*Ch'ivit:* Regional Economic Exchange in San Cristobal Las Casas, Mexico" (1977). Kelly Jensen engaged in field research in Chamula hamlets and presented his senior thesis on the Maya farmer, ancient and modern (1976) in which he made some intriguing suggestions about the nature of ancient Maya farming based on his contemporary data from Chiapas. Gilbert Marin collected data on mariachi bands in San Cristobal.

Nan and I began our fall-term travels in Austria, where I attended my third Burg Wartenstein symposium, Long-Term Field Research in Social Anthropology, chaired by George M. Foster, Elizabeth Colson, and Thayer Scudder. I presented a paper entitled "The Harvard Chiapas Project: 1957–1975" (Vogt 1979).

The spring term and summer months were productive ones in Chiapas. With no students to supervise, I found that I had time for both field research and writing. It was also the year that my detailed study of Zinacanteco rituals appeared: *Tortillas for the Gods: A Symbolic Analysis of Zinacanteco Rituals.*

Since 1976 was the year my fourth five-year grant expired at NIMH, I also prepared my report on the research we had accomplished. For the future I decided to apply for a grant from another branch of the National Institutes of Health, the Institute of Alcohol and Drug Abuse, to study one of the most important events to occur in Indian communities in the Highlands of Chiapas. We had begun to observe in both Chamula and Zinacantan a marked decrease in drunkenness during ceremonial events. When we first attended large fiestas in Chamula and Zinacantan in the late 1950s and through the 1960s, we would encounter drunks by the hundreds, including not only men, but often, especially in Chamula, women and children as well.

By the mid-1970s the incidence of drunkenness had decreased markedly in these two Tzotzil communities, and this proved to be a trend that continued through the 1980s. Since these Native Americans appeared to be an exceptional case, in which alcoholism was being brought under control, it seemed important to me to discover more precisely what factors had been involved in this remarkable process. There were several possibilities, such as Mexican government programs against excessive use of alcohol, the strongly antiliquor protestant evangelization in the Highlands of Chiapas, or the realization on the part of increasing numbers of individual Indians that they could not continue to drink to such excess and manage their affairs adequately.

There was an additional factor that intrigued me most of all: the increased pride the Indians felt in being Indians and the consequent improvement in their morale. I hypothesized that the increase in morale was a long-range result of the work of INI and other federal and state agencies that had instituted programs over the years to aid oppressed Indian communities. The programs that were introduced included a spectrum of development projects, ranging from improved breeds of chickens to the training of bilingual Indian teachers (called cultural promoters) for schools. There had been much debate in Mexico and elsewhere about the success or failure of these programs. Clearly, although many of the programs failed or were of only limited success, the long-range effect of INI and its successors conveyed an important message. For the first time, in more than four hundred years of oppression, official agencies of the Mexican government said "We are here to help the Indians." As a result, the Tzotzil-Maya began to acquire a sense of pride in their own identity; they also learned how to become politically effective with government officials, how to borrow funds from banks for economic enterprises, and how to purchase trucks and busses (Vogt 1990).

My new proposal to the NIH was to explore these various factors that appeared to be involved in the decrease in alcoholism. My proposal was not approved, and I decided I had spent so much time and energy already in writing research proposals over the previous twenty years that I would not pursue it further in a formal way. There comes a time when one tires of jumping through the same hoops. Although I have continued to work in Chiapas, I have done the field research at my own expense since the long-range NIMH grant expired in 1976.

We returned to Chiapas in the summer of 1977 and again in 1978 when I supervised the field research of two undergraduates, Alexandra Buresch and Jerome M. Levi. Alexandra's research was focused on an intensive study of the most important ritual plants used in Zinacanteco ceremonies. She added significant information on the importance of color, fragrance, and longevity in the selection of plants used in the ritual life, especially in her senior honors thesis, entitled "The Great Seeing: Red, White, and Black in Zinacantan" (1980).

Jay (as he is called by those who know him) Levi had been visiting Chiapas with his family for many years before he transferred from UCLA to Harvard while he was still an undergraduate in order to work with me. A very adventurous young man, he chose to work in the remote Tzotzil community of Chalchihuitan where he learned to speak passable Tzotzil and collected reams of excellent ethnographic data on the religious and ceremonial life. These data are utilized in two fine articles (Levi 1988, 1989).[25]

Also with us in the field in 1978 were Kazuyasu Ochiai from Tokyo and his wife Ines Sanmiguel from Bogota, Columbia. Kazuyasu was a highly talented graduate of the University of Tokyo who had many skills, including playing tennis, cooking tempura, and playing Japanese music on the recorder. He had also spent some years as a Kabuki actor in Tokyo. When he decided to specialize on Latin America, he joined an archaeological dig in Mexico where he met his former wife, Ines. After doing some anthropological course work in Mexico, Kazuyasu and Ines came to Chiapas to do field research in 1978–79.

The Ochiais selected San Andrés Larrainzar as the site for their work and approached me to see if they could headquarter in San Cristobal at the Harvard Ranch. Here Kazuyasu met Gary Gossen, who invited him to apply for graduate school at the State University of New York at Albany. After course work at Albany, Kazuyasu returned again to work in San Andrés Larrainzar during 1980–81 and in the summer of 1982. I saw a great deal of this "academic grandson," both at the Harvard Ranch where we spent many hours discussing Tzotzil ethnography, and on the tennis courts of San Cristobal in those years after Nan and I had given up smoking and were playing a daily set of tennis (doubles, if possible) to improve our health. We later appointed Kazuyasu and Ines as resident tutors in anthropology in Kirkland House at Harvard where they served dutifully, commuting to Albany from time to time to consult with the anthropology staff there.

Kazuyasu's field research focused on ceremonialism in San Andrés Larrainzar and especially on the rituals, such as the exchange of saints, which establish networks among Tzotzil communities. His thesis for SUNY, Albany, was published in Chiapas under the title of "Cuando los Santos Vienen Marchando: Rituales Publicos Intercomunitarios Tzotziles" (1985).[26]

Two other notable academic grandsons have also done important field research in Chiapas. One was Stuart Plattner, a student of Frank Cancian's from Stanford, who in 1967–68 made a definitive field study and wrote his Ph.D. dissertation, "Peddlers, Pigs, and Profits: Itinerant Trading in Southeast Mexico" (1969), on the regionwide commerce in pigs carried on by merchants from the Barrio of Cuxtitali in San Cristobal Las Casas.[27] Another was Ron Nigh, a student of George Collier's at Stanford, who initiated his field research in Chiapas in 1970. His Ph.D. thesis was on the evolutionary ecology of Maya agriculture with a focus on the varieties of maize grown in the various microniches found in, and on the flanks, of the Chiapas Highlands (Nigh 1976).[28]

In the autumn of 1977 I was thrilled to receive a telephone call from Mexico informing me that I was to receive the Aguila Azteca (Aztec Eagle). This was the highest decoration given foreigners by the Republic of Mexico and had previously been awarded to such luminaries as former Senate

EZV reading his acceptance speech for the Aztec Eagle in Mexico City in 1978. Left to right: EZV, Santiago Roel (foreign minister of Mexico), Nan Vogt, Manuel Velasco Suárez (former governor of Chiapas), Octavio Paz.

majority leader Mike Mansfield and the former ambassador to Mexico, Joseph Jova.

Arrangements were made for me to be decorated by Mexico's minister of foreign affairs in the José López Portillo administration, Licenciado Santiago Roel, at a ceremony in the ministry in Mexico City on 5 January 1978, when Nan and I and the families of three of our four children were returning from the Christmas holidays we had spent at the Harvard Ranch in San Cristobal. I was not only deeply honored by the decoration, which was in the grade of Encomienda (making me what can best be translated as a Knight Commander in the Order of the Aztec Eagle), but also by the presence of a number of distinguished Mexicans. The guests included Octavio Paz, whom I knew well when he was a member of our Senior Common Room at Kirkland House while serving as a visiting professor at Harvard; Manuel Velasco Suárez, the former governor of Chiapas, with whom I had shared a number of experiences in Chiapas, as well as his son Jesus-Augustín Velasco, who had studied at the Fletcher School of Diplomacy at Tufts, and his wife; Licenciado Carlos Bernal, the son of Dr. Ignacio Bernal, who had lived with us in Weston, Massachusetts, in 1967–68; and Manuel Velasco Coelho, the son of my close friend, Don Leopoldo Velasco Robles in San Cristobal, and his wife.

Another exciting telephone call came from Washington in late April in 1978. It was from Professors Ward Goodenough and Fred Eggan informing me that I had just been elected to the National Academy of Sciences, the ultimate honor for a scientist in the United States. I had been a Fellow of the American Academy of Arts and Sciences, located in the Boston area, since 1960. But whereas the American Academy has almost three thousand members, the National Academy of Sciences had a membership of fewer than fifteen hundred. In 1978 the anthropology section had only thirty-seven members, including all the fields of anthropology. I knew how rare it was to be elected and was of course enormously pleased.

With the combination of becoming a Knight Commander in the Order of the Aztec Eagle and an academician in the National Academy of Sciences I felt that the many years of hard work on the Chiapas Project, trying to understand the Tzotzil Maya and how their culture is changing in the modern world, was at last receiving recognition on the national and international scene.

In 1979 the Chiapas Project sponsored one student who had received a grant from the Department of Anthropology to do fieldwork in Zinacantan that summer. He was Stephen L. Roof, who later wrote a senior honors thesis entitled "Cultural Brokers, Factionalism, and Modernization in Zinacantan" (1980).[29]

The last student whose field research I supervised in Chiapas was Cynthia McVay, a talented member of my freshman seminar during 1979–80. The seminar that year was entitled "Cultural Themes in Hispanic Culture: Spain and Mexico," and Cynthia developed a strong interest in the social class system found in Hispanic cultures. When she expressed an interest in undertaking a field study in the city of San Cristobal, she became the sixth freshman to be selected for the Chiapas Project.

McVay knew Spanish well from summers she had spent in Peru, Mexico, and Spain, and she did excellent research on the social class system in San Cristobal, where she not only interviewed and observed people from the various ranks of the society, but also made a detailed study of how the traditional social structure was reflected in the cemetery. The San Cristobal cemetery proved to be a nearly perfect profile of the social class system of the city. The elite are buried in mausoleums in the center, the middle-class graves surround the center, and the working classes are buried in simple graves marked only by small wooden crosses on the peripheries—all reflecting the living city with its elite immediately around the central plaza, its middle class a few blocks away on all sides of the center, and its working classes in the barrios on the edges of the town. Only recently have some of the elite families begun to build houses at the edges of the old city in a pattern that begins to resemble suburban life in the United States. The results of the fieldwork appeared in a joint article entitled "Some Contours of Social Class in a Southern Mexican Town" (McVay and Vogt 1988).[30]

In late August of 1980 I chaired a Burg Wartenstein symposium on prehistoric settlement patterns in honor of my colleague Gordon R. Willey. I had know Gordon well for almost thirty years, and when I discovered in 1978 that there were no plans underway for a festschrift for him, I consulted with a number of his former students and proceeded to organize this symposium sponsored by the Wenner-Gren Foundation.[31]

An interesting spin-off from the Harvard Chiapas Project was organized by Bob Laughlin in 1982 after listening to the comments of our Tzotzil informants following a conference in San Cristobal to celebrate forty years of anthropological research in Chiapas. Our informants were telling us that we anthropologists had aroused their interest and self-consciousness about their own culture, but that while we had presumably made good studies, we had taken our knowledge away with us. They added that the younger generation of Mayas are now widely literate in Spanish, but increasingly ignorant about their own culture, which is rapidly slipping away. The informants expressed a deep desire to at least record their customs on paper before they disappear altogether.

Sponsored in part by Cultural Survival, an organization founded by my Harvard colleague David Maybury-Lewis to help the small-scale non-Western societies of the world, the Chiapas Writers Cooperative, which is officially known as Sna Jtz'ibajom (House of the Writer), was organized by Laughlin. These Tzotzil and Tzeltal writers soon began to write down life histories, folk tales, Mayan myths, native remedies, and other aspects of their culture (Vogt 1985). They used puppets to act out their stories, and more recently have written plays, based on Mayan myths, in which the native actors are costumed and provide magnificent performances. The House of the Writer also offers a literacy program that now has twenty teachers and in the past three years has awarded almost one thousand diplomas to men, women, and children of various Tzotzil communities who have learned to read and write in their mother tongue. Bob Laughlin has reported that the success of this program is an aspect of a native revitalization movement among the Tzotzil and Tzeltal peoples of the Chiapas Highlands.

These native writers have also recorded their observations on Americans and American culture derived from their experiences with anthropologists and others in Chiapas as well as during their travels in the United States (see Haviland 1989; Laughlin 1989).

In a sense the Harvard Chiapas Project has now come full circle. When we began our field research in 1957 we were studying and writing about Tzotzil-Mayan culture to be read in English by our fellow anthropologists in North America and Europe. Now our former informants are studying and writing about American culture to be read in Tzotzil by their fellow Zinacantecos and Chamulas!

12 /
A RETROSPECTIVE VIEW OF THE HARVARD CHIAPAS PROJECT

Without attempting to evaluate the scholarly results of thirty-five years of the Harvard Chiapas Project—these are contained in the existing and ongoing publication of technical books and articles by the members of the project—I now offer a brief retrospective look at what I consider we have accomplished in our field operations with special focus on (a) our strengths and advantages and (b) our weaknesses and difficulties.

STRENGTHS AND ADVANTAGES OF THE PROJECT

The major strengths I perceive were (if I may be permitted some immodesty for the moment) (1) the superb training of our students, (2) the high quality of the ethnography, (3) the first-rate research productivity, and (4) the development of long-term personal and intellectual relationships among the members of the project.

Our training program included the prefield courses in Tzotzil and the seminar on selected problems and methods in Latin American ethnology; the individual placement of students in Indian households in Chiapas; and the field conferences in which students were expected to report on their research progress and be critiqued and advised by both the field leader and their student peers. I believe we produced better-trained students than had previously been the case in Middle American studies. Our students (graduates and undergraduates) could get off the bus in San Cristobal and be doing first-class, productive field ethnography within the first few days of arrival in Chiapas. The arriving students knew Spanish and as much Tzotzil as it was possible to learn in the intensive one-term course that included not only carefully prepared language materials and tapes, but experienced teachers and, whenever possible, a native Tzotzil speaker from Chiapas for part of the term. They had read the published and unpublished ethnographic materials on the Indian and Ladino cultures of Highland Chiapas, and they had at least a preliminary notion of the research problem on which they would be focusing. Finally, when relevant, they brought along aerial photographs of the municipio and hamlets in which they would be working. The students who returned to Chiapas for additional seasons were even better trained and ready to engage in what I consider to have been some of the best ethnographic research in the history of anthropology.

Judging the quality of the ethnographic research an anthropologist does in another culture is always a complicated and somewhat subjective business, but some objective measures can be applied. Knowing the native language, learning and understanding the native patterns of behavior well enough to avoid serious breaches of etiquette, and having two or more observers agree to the basic correctness of ethnographic descriptions are all measures with considerable objectivity. These features of the ethnographic experience are maximized in long-range research projects in which multiple observers cope with understanding and analyzing recurring patterns of behavior in the various domains of the cultures under investigation over many successive years.

What a far cry from the traditional methods of doing ethnography when a single person (or, at most, a married couple) went out to a particular tribe or community, studied it for a year (or two, at the most) and then returned to publish their results. These results were in turn processed into the Human Relations Area Files (and other archives of data) and became the God's Truth about the tribe or community. Often it was years, or decades, later before the field site was revisited, frequently by a different anthropologist, and the result was another celebrated controversy about the nature of the culture.

In our case, copies of the field data were normally deposited in the Harvard Chiapas Project Archives where they were and are available to other members of the project with the understanding, of course, that proper credit be given to the original collector of the data. Each fieldworker also normally circulated manuscripts to other members of the project for comment and criticism in advance of publication. Although I sometimes find it maddening to have to revise an article or a book three or four times in response to the sharp comments from my colleagues and former students, I am convinced the final products are better for it, both ethnographically and analytically (Vogt 1990: 15).

For the most part, our field operations were focused on research in what the late Robert Redfield called "the little community." We were always aware of, and, indeed engaged in some field research on, Ladino culture in San Cristobal and in the various Indian ceremonial centers in which a number of Ladino families lived. We were also aware of the impact of the larger region upon the Indian communities, but the hard focus of the project operations was to understand the culture and the dynamics of change in Zinacantan and Chamula as municipios and of the hamlets within these municipios. Here, I believe, if one takes into consideration the still-unpublished theses and reports, we managed to do a solid and perceptive job of ethnographic reporting and analysis at a level of detail never before reached in Mesoamerican studies.

The research productivity of a project is likewise somewhat subjective in a field like anthropology. One measure might be the number of Ph.D. dissertations (twenty-one) and senior honors theses (thirty-three) to come out of the Chiapas Project. With respect to publication, I have never been one to simply count the number of books and articles published by an anthropologist as an operational measure of his or her productivity. We all know that some articles and some books have a much greater long-range impact on the development of anthropology than do others. Nevertheless, I have always been immensely proud of the publication record of the members of the Harvard Chiapas Project which, for what it is worth, had by 1992 published more than forty books, over 180 articles, and two novels, as well as produced two ethnographic films. For the most part, the books have been published by outstanding university presses, such as Harvard, Stanford, Texas, and Chicago, and the articles have appeared in all the mainline anthropological journals, such as the *American Anthropologist, Man, American Ethnologist, Journal of Anthropological Research,* and *Ethnology* (Vogt 1978).

I suppose another measure of our effectiveness would be the production of professional anthropologists. We provided a field setting and intellectual community for graduate students, as well as many undergraduates, who had already selected anthropology as a career. And, as Dean McGeorge Bundy predicted, we also managed to recruit into anthropology a number of brilliant students who originally had a variety of other careers in mind. I calculate that of the 142 students we had doing field research in Chiapas from 1957 through 1980, 47 are now practicing, professional anthropologists, and another 17 are in closely related fields such as sociology, cognitive psychology, development economics, etc. Further, I believe history will demonstrate that the Chiapas field experience had an important educational impact (international understanding, knowledge of and respect for other cultures, and appreciation of the problems of underdeveloped countries) on the other seventy-eight who have gone on to a variety of careers. That they deeply appreciated the experience has been underscored by letters I have received from them over the years. To quote from two typical examples, Jonathan Hiatt, who was with us in Chiapas in 1968 recently wrote:

> While the quality of my [summer] paper may not make for the best evidence of it, I can assure you that that summer was one of the best of my life. I have absolutely fantastic memories of every aspect of it—the country, the countryside, the work, the food, the parties, the colleagues, and most of all the guidance and hospitality which you and Nan provided. (Personal communication, 30 October 1991)

And Mary Scott, from the 1972 and 1973 summer seasons, wrote: "I don't know if I ever properly thanked you for the enormous differences the Chiapas Project made in my life, but I've had many reasons and occasions to marvel at my own luck in being included in that illustrious and endearing company. Anyway, let me thank you now" (Personal communication, 16 April 1992).

These comments underscore the fourth strength of the project—the enduring personal and intellectual relationships that have developed between fieldworkers of different generations and between anthropologists and informants/consultants, who, in the best of cases, become collaborators. A corollary of these long-term relationships is, of course, the collaboration and academic generosity that has characterized the Harvard Chiapas Project.

WEAKNESSES AND DIFFICULTIES
OF THE PROJECT

The critical weaknesses and difficulties we encountered were (1) paradigm changes in anthropological research, (2) fewer new graduate students in the later stages of the project, (3) the emergence of overly dependent Indian informants, and (4) certain tensions arising from differences of concept and method among members of the project.

One of the weaknesses of the project was that we may not have responded quickly and fundamentally enough to the appearance of different anthropological paradigms during the course of our thirty-five years of research. The principal paradigms I refer to were: (a) the Marxist inspired World-System theories that became all the rage in sociology, and, to some extent, in anthropology in the late 1960s and early 1970s; and (b) the postmodernism paradigm being promoted during the 1980s by the cultural critique school of James Clifford, George Marcus, Michael Fischer, et al.

Among the accompaniments of the counterculture movement, with its intellectual ferment and its student rebellions in Europe and North America in the 1960s and 1970s, was the appearance of a different and quite fashionable paradigm for anthropological research. Converts to this paradigm have leveled a number of criticisms at the work of the Harvard Chiapas Project. For example, Waldemar B.Smith asserted that "society in Chiapas is a stratified regional organization, the basic feature of which, hidden under the colorful veneer of native costume and customs, is a grossly inegalitarian system of social class. The Harvard Chiapas Project has studied the region for almost two decades but has paid little attention to this overarching pattern of class and power" (1977: 23) Hawkins argued that "the Hispanic center of San Cristobal de Las Casas should be studied in relation to Zinacantan, and vice versa. Indeed, the principal criticism one can make of Vogt's impressive opus (1969, 1976) is that it is done without adequate relation to the surrounding Hispanic culture" (1984: 407–8) And Hewitt de Alcantara added that

> during the roughly twenty years covered by the Harvard Chiapas Project . . . the community as [an] object of anthropological interest had experienced a renaissance within an influential sector of American structural-functionalism, precisely at the time when a

number of anthropologists within the functionalist—as well as the cultural ecologist, Marxist, and indigenista—paradigm were seriously questioning the utility of a community-study approach. (1984: 58–59)

These quotes are typical examples of the critiques that faulted the Harvard Chiapas Project for focusing on the Tzotzil-Mayan Indian communities as a unit of study and for ignoring the Hispanic cultural and political presence during the colonial and modern periods as well as the contemporary forces of imperialistic capitalism in southeastern Mexico.

These critiques need to be placed in historical perspective. When my generation was in training in the late 1940s to engage in our first anthropological fieldwork, the focus on "community study" was in full bloom. The emphasis of my professors (Fred Eggan, Robert Redfield, Sol Tax, and W. Lloyd Warner) at the University of Chicago, and of my colleagues in social anthropology (Clyde Kluckhohn and Douglas Oliver) at Harvard was essentially on the study of social and cultural phenomena in a community or tribal unit—the Hopi Tribe of Arizona, the villages of Tepoztlan and Chan Kom in Mexico, the municipality of Panajachel in the Highlands of Guatemala, Yankee City in Massachusetts, the Ramah Navaho, or the Solomon Islanders. Stemming, at least in large part, from the thinking of Radcliffe-Brown and Malinowski, all of these professors and colleagues were in some sense functionalists, or structural-functionalists, as some prefer to label this approach. Earlier generations of anthropologists, we learned in graduate school, thought of culture as "a thing of shreds and patches" as they collected data on particular items like bows and arrows or folktales and studied how they developed or diffused from one tribe to another.

But for my generation the important task of the anthropologist was to engage in field research with a view to understanding the structure and functioning of a whole community or whole tribe—these being the naturally occurring units in which mankind lived out their lives (Redfield 1955). Some careful attention was paid to the history of the community or tribe, especially by scholars like Eggan (1950) but this was secondary to the primary focus on understanding the community or tribe as a contemporary functioning unit.

On the larger theoretical front, most of us had studied Marx in our undergraduate courses. Marx was required reading in Social Sciences I in my college days at the University of Chicago in the 1930s when we debated endlessly with the active members of the Communist Party in our undergraduate councils. The Marxist approach was to be taken into consideration, but hardly regarded seriously as a total explanation of the complex phenomena encountered in the tribes and communities that anthropologists studied.

When I began my anthropological fieldwork I quite understandably focused on communities: the Ramah Navaho, a homesteader community in New Mexico, the municipios (municipalities) of Zinacantan and Chamula in the Highlands of Chiapas. And I recall being particularly impressed with Sol Tax's key article on the municipio as a unit of study in Guatemala (Tax 1937). Even though my colleagues and I were fully aware that each of our communities and tribes were significantly embedded in and related to the larger world, we were occasionally berated in an article whose author thought we should be focusing much more on at least the regional world beyond the local community (e.g., Starr 1954). It was our (largely unstated) view, however, that most anthropologists who wrote such articles had failed as field ethnographers, and that what they had to say was merely a second-class substitute for ethnographic truth of the kind we were getting with intensive fieldwork in communities and tribes.

When I initiated the Harvard Chiapas Project in the Highlands of Chiapas in 1957, my research design was based on the framework of "controlled comparison" set out by Fred Eggan in his classic paper (1954). The Chiapas Highlands contained some thirty-four Tzotzil- and Tzeltal-speaking communities all derived within the past millennia from the proto-Tzotzil-Tzeltal Maya. They shared much in common, but had variations that resulted, I postulated, from differences in their microecological niches, their historical experiences with the Spanish conquerors and their descendants in the colonial and modern period, and their encounters with the contemporary community development programs of the Mexican government, especially on the part of the Instituto Nacional Indigenista (National Indian Institute). My goal was to discover by close comparative study the crucial determinants of the processes of cultural variation and change that had occurred and were continuing among these contemporary Maya Indians in the Highlands of Chiapas.

I believe in retrospect that we never ignored or overlooked the ways in which the municipios of Zinacantan and Chamula we studied were related to or embedded in the larger world of San Cristobal Las Casas (the market town), of Tuxtla Gutierrez (the state capital), of Mexico City (the national capital), or of the imperialistic forces that sweep across the world. How could one ignore the ubiquitous bottles of Coca-Cola and Pepsi-Cola, the General Motors and Ford trucks, or the blaring Panasonic and Sony radios? Rather, we considered it our task to go beyond the easy work of interviewing in Spanish the government officials and business proprietors in Tuxtla Gutierrez and San Cristobal Las Casas, or of reading reports and documents in the provincial or state historical archives, or of socializing with the latest group of visiting Mexican and French Marxist intellectuals in the salons of Na-Bolom. And, in any event, we assumed these were tasks better done by political scientists, historians, economists, or philosophers of science. Our unique anthropological task was to describe, analyze, and understand the inner workings of the "little communities" of Zinacantan and Chamula, including their subsistence systems, their social structures, their ritual life, and their symbol systems. To do this we had to learn Tzotzil as fluently as possible, and we had to utilize the usual battery of field techniques, but especially participant observation of the flow of Indian life and the sustained interviewing of Indian informants.

Now, to be sure, Zinacantan and Chamula are not so little! Zinacantan had a population of eight thousand when we began fieldwork; it has now grown to more than twenty thousand. Chamula was about twenty-thousand strong in 1957, and now has upwards of forty-five thousand within the municipio boundaries, to say nothing of another fifty-five thousand in the outlying colonies established in the recent Chamula diaspora (Gossen 1983). But it was still possible to describe and analyze the social structures and cultures of these two municipios at a reasonably profound level of understanding.

While our focus was explicitly on the local Indian communities, there has been some useful publication from the beginning of the project on the relationships of the Tzotzil Indians to the Ladinos and to the larger world. For example, one of the first pieces of research undertaken by Barbara Metzger in 1960, when she served as my research assistant at Harvard, was to pull together all the available data on the history of Indian-Ladino relations in the Highland of Chiapas (Metzger 1960). Colby (1966) also provides a general summary of ethnic relations in Highland Chiapas, and

Edel (1966) deals with the ejido land reform program in Zinacantan. Frank Cancian's later books (1972, 1992) clearly deal with the larger world in which Zinacanteco maize farmers are involved. We have also had at least thirteen field studies of the Ladino culture and history of San Cristobal, many of them unfortunately still unpublished, but which I have described in earlier chapters.

We have also begun the process of detailed comparative study of Tzozil and Tzeltal communities (Bricker 1973, 1981; Vogt 1973, 1992a, In press; McQuown and Pitt-Rivers 1970), but I do not believe these efforts will be completely successful until we have a larger corpus of solid ethnographic data on more communities than Zinacantan and Chamula.

The new paradigm that influenced the anthropological world in the 1960s and 1970s was clearly anticipated by Eric Wolf in the mid-1950s (see Wolf 1955, 1956, 1957). The new thrust came from such sources as Gunder-Frank (1967) and Wallerstein (1974, 1980) at the world-system level, and the publications of Stavenhagen (1969, 1970), Gonzalez Casanova (1969), Warman (1972, 1980), and Barta (1969, 1974) at the national-regional level in Mexico, and Adams (1970), Waldemar R. Smith (1977), and Carol A. Smith (1978) in Guatemala. All were based on the various brands of Marxist theory that direct attention to the critical role of the infrastructure and apply regional, national, or global analyses to explain what is going on in local rural communities. A balanced treatment of this general shift in paradigms on the Mexican scene is found in Hewitt de Alcantara (1984).

On the Chiapas scene the shift in paradigm influenced one of the University of Chicago students, Salovesh (1979), to urge that we look beyond the municipio to the region as a unit of study, and that we "study up" rather than merely focus on "studying down." He meant by these apt expressions that field ethnographers find it easier to cope with less powerful people in local communities than to study the more powerful economic and political elites of a region or country. Salovesh's interesting point is more applicable to a municipio like Venustiano Carranza, where he did his field research. This municipio has an Indian population that is concentrated in a town center rather than dispersed into a large number of scattered hamlets as is the case in Zinacantan and Chamula. It would actually have been much easier for us to "study up" in San Cristobal Las Casas and Tuxtla Gutierrez using only Spanish than it was for us to "study down," which required mastering Tzotzil and learning how to cope with the rigors of life—fleas, impure drinking water, monotonous food, lack of showers and toilets, sharing one room with large families—in Indian houses in remote mountain villages. I agree with Sherry Ortner's conclusion: "The attempt to view other systems from ground level is the basis, perhaps the only basis, of anthropology's distinctive contribution to the human sciences" (1984: 143).

Even more profoundly influenced by the shift in paradigm were two of our Harvard students: Jan Rus and Robert Wasserstrom. After a preliminary joint article offering a "critical perspective" on the cargo system (Rus and Wasserstrom 1980), Wasserstrom (1983) attempted a Marxist history of central Chiapas that purported to discover not only that the current Indian populations are an oppressed proletariat in the class system, but that such features as the civil-religious hierarchies (or cargo systems) arose during the late nineteenth and early twentieth centuries in response to regional patterns of economic development and demographic change and have no elements that survive from the preconquest period. This latter conclusion is not only demonstrably wrong for the Highlands of Chiapas (Vogt 1983: 103–4), but is also diametrically opposed to what Nancy M. Farriss has discovered in her detailed historical study of the colonial period in Yucatan. Farriss writes: "Most of the formal elements of the contemporary cargo system are colonial adaptations of earlier practices. Its underlying rationale, in which prestige and authority are based on material support of the corporate deity-saints, also has deep roots in the Maya past" (1984: 348).

More recently Frank Cancian (1985) writing on Chiapas has tackled the problem of micro- and macrolevels of analysis in systems of stratification. Cancian has suggested that while a world-system approach is useful in describing and analyzing the broad economic classes that have emerged in the modern world, a microanalysis is equally necessary in order to understand the social rank systems found in local communities. Gary Gossen, in his *Symbol and Meaning Beyond the Closed Community* (Gossen, ed. 1986), has convincingly demonstrated how some of the central features of Tzotzil cosmology are local, regional manifestations of a set of persisting Mesoamerican ideas, while George Collier (1989) shows how variations in the structure of Zinacanteco families reflect the vagaries of employment opportunities for them in southern Mexico.

Some of the most recent ethnographic work in Highland Chiapas combines the insights and approaches of the macro- and microlevels of analysis in highly sophisticated and productive ways. In Chiapas we have, for example, the ecological analysis of George A Collier (1975), which clearly places Zinacantan in a regional context, and the work of Jane F. Collier (1973, 1976), which relates the legal procedures to social and political levels in Zinacantan and in the large Ladino world of Chiapas. An even more recent example is Gossen's study of the Chamula diaspora as the Chamulas have expanded beyond their own municipio and have grown in numbers to more than one hundred thousand; and we have had the recent papers of Haviland (e.g., 1986) in which detailed ethnographic data from a hamlet of Zinacantan is clearly placed in regional and national economic and historical contexts. Indeed, Haviland argues:

> I take as given the general notion that the "cultural life" of peasant Indian communities like Zinacantan is neither autonomous nor insulated, but rather constrained and shaped by the "material" forces of wider Chiapas (and Mexican) economic and political life. . . . To give substance to such a perspective, to breathe into it ethnographic life, however, we must describe how these global or structural interconnections (between regional economic forces, say, and particular local social organization) are realized in detail. I think this is the heart of ethnography: to see how tangible, material forces are transformed, through the mediation of individual choice, consciousness, and understanding. (1986: 4–5)

In sum, I agree that many of the recent macrolevel analyses undertaken by anthropologists have proved to be illuminating for our understanding of the historical and economic forces that have engulfed us all in the contemporary scene. But I would like to make a strong case for the continuation also of the microlevel studies of the little communities of the world and for the kind of fine-grained ethnography that emerges with full control of the indigenous language and the in-depth study of these face-to-face communities in which most humans continue to live.

I make this plea because I hear the drums beating steadily for the macro-level approach, which by now not only deeply impresses our graduate students in social anthropology and ethnology, but also in archaeology. Furthermore, some of the recent articles seem to be reaching the outer limits of credibility. I am thinking, for example, of the recent attempt to relate the whole rise of social anthropology as a discipline directly to the philanthropy of the Rockefellers (Fisher 1986). Or, in archaeology, to the Patterson (1985) attempt to link the "interpretive communities" of American archaeologists to the concerns of national capital and its allies, or to international capital and its allies. The third interpretive community that "has emerged and established a beachhead" being Marxist.

Perhaps the most extreme argument is that of Wilk (1985) who suggests that changing views of the ancient Maya are related to current political trends in the United States, and asserts, for example, that the persisting popularity among archaeologists of my inferences concerning the cargo system among the prehistoric Maya was related to an image of village democracy in the age of the Peace Corps in the 1960s!

Microlevel studies of the small communities are what anthropologists do best, and given the physical and psychological problems of field research in these communities, anthropologists, with their driving curiosity about alien cultures and their deep motivations to escape from their own societies and enter into the life of another culture, are the only scholars who are likely to continue this kind of research in the modern world. Further, these microlevel studies are essential for an understanding of the "inside view," for what is "inside the black boxes," at the local community or tribal level. It could be also argued that most macro studies are better done by professional historians, economists, sociologists, and political scientists who are especially trained to cope with these problems.

If the next generation of Mayanists focuses mainly on the macrolevels of cultural phenomena, we shall no longer have the fine-grained ethnographic research that is exemplified by such Highland Chiapas scholars as Robert Laughlin, whose annotated *Great Tzotzil Dictionary of San Lorenzo Zinacantan* contains more than thirty-five thousand Tzotzil words, took twelve years to elicit, compile, and edit, and is the most complete American Indian language dictionary ever published. These fine-grained ethnographic studies are also exemplified by such Highland Guatemala scholars as John Watanabe, who has done sophisticated macrolevel research on how Santiago Chimaltenango is embedded in the larger world (1984), but whose microlevel ethnographic research on the local cosmology impresses me even more. Had I not insisted that Watanabe spend at least a year learning fluent Mam, we would not have had his recent rigorous demonstration (1983) that the key features of the Mayan worldview of Santiago Chimaltenango in Highland Guatemala are built into the very structure of the Mam language—a discovery of prime significance for Mayan studies, ethnological and archaeological—nor his sophisticated article on souls and social identity (1989) and his recent book (1992).

The postmodernism paradigm grew, in part, out of the interpretive anthropology of Geertz (1973, 1988) and became popular in the 1980s in the theoretical writings of Clifford, Fischer, and Marcus (see especially Clifford and Marcus 1986; Marcus and Fischer 1986; Clifford 1988). Here the view is that anthropologists have been living in a dream world if they think they are writing objective ethnographic descriptions of cultures based on the collection of empirical data by the time-honored methods of participant observation and interviewing. Rather, ethnographic monographs are reports that reflect the time, place, and role of the ethnographer in the unfolding interactions between conquerors and conquered peoples, especially the evolving political and economic relationships between Europeans and the native peoples we study.

Perhaps the three most interesting and sensitive recent treatments of postmodernism to come to my attention have been those of Richard Shweder, Barbara Tedlock, and Richard G. Fox. In his work entitled "Post-Nietzschean Anthropology," Shweder (1991) has argued that there are what he calls "multiple objective worlds" on which hard empirical data can be collected and analyzed.

Barbara Tedlock, in her recent article "Participant Observation to the Observation of Participation: The Emergence of Narrative Ethnography" (1991), makes a plea for the coproduction of ethnographic knowledge with a sensitive, two-way interaction between the the Self and the Other, between the anthropologists and the natives they are studying. In a fundamental way the members of the Harvard Chiapas Project have been engaged in two-way interaction between anthropologists and Tzotzil-Mayas since the beginning of the project. The Harvard Chiapas Project has been teaching Tzotzil-Mayas to read and write in Tzotzil since the early 1960s, and our Tzotzil colleagues have been writing texts both on their own culture and on the culture of the North Americans that they observed on journeys to the United States.

The recent publication of *Recapturing Anthropology* (Fox, ed. 1991) has presented a whole series of cogent papers that place the postmodernism movement in clearheaded perspective and argue persuasively that it is time to get on with the task of doing anthropology.

In my judgment the postmodernism paradigm had less impact on the Harvard Chiapas Project than it did on most other research enterprises in anthropology—in part because of its later arrival on the anthropological scene, in part because our field researchers were less inclined to take it seriously as the pivotal approach to our data. As I review the continuing publications of members of the Harvard Chiapas Project, I note with interest that those who chose to do their Ph.D. fieldwork elsewhere have been somewhat more influenced by postmodernism than have those who continued to work in Chiapas, notably Victoria Bricker, Frank Cancian, George and Jane Collier, Gary Gossen, John Haviland, and Robert Laughlin.

One might wonder if those of us who continue in Chiapas have merely maintained a stubborn mind-set against postmodernism as the pivotal paradigm for ethnography. Or whether, as I believe, our long-range studies with the double-checking of field data over long time periods and among quite disparate observers have convinced us that there is still hope for the writing of objective ethnographies.

A more serious weakness of the project developed in the late 1970s and 1980s: the inability of the project to recruit new graduate students to engage in the field research in Zinacantan, Chamula, and other neighboring Tzotzil municipios. The basic reason for this development is something I should have anticipated, but did not. Each year in my classes and seminars I conveyed to my students the enormous excitement of discovery I had during my early years in Chiapas when we knew next to nothing about the culture and were arriving for the first time in unstudied Indian hamlets. By the time the project research operations in Zinacantan and Chamula had gone on for more than twenty-five years, I began to discover that the best new graduate students readily absorbed my message and then, quite naturally, set out to find new, unstudied communities where they could be pioneers as I had been at the beginning of my project!

In a sense this trend began in the late 1960s when, instead of continuing in Chiapas, Richard and Sally Price decided to do dissertation research among the Saramaka living in the remote rain forests of Surinam, and Renato and Michelle Rosaldo undertook their fieldwork with the headhunting Ilongots in the mountains of Luzon in the Philippines. But the problem was exacerbated by the 1970s after even more research had been done in Chiapas. Two typical examples come to mind from the 1970s.

John M. Watanabe was an outstanding graduate student who had worked with Gary Gossen while an undergraduate at the University of California, Santa Cruz. During his early graduate years at Harvard, he decided to pursue a long-range career in Mayan studies. But rather than accept my invitation to do field research in Chiapas, he decided to work in the Highlands of northwestern Guatemala, where he has learned fluent Mam and has become an internationally known expert on that rugged, beautiful region in the Cuchumatane Highlands.[1] Jerome Levi, another excellent scholar, who transferred from UCLA to study with me, worked in the Tzotzil municipio of Chalchihuitan as an undergraduate and wished to continue in Mesoamerican studies. But he finally chose to work on his own among the Tarahumara of northwestern Mexico, with whom he recently spent almost two years in the field.

I have nothing but admiration for these students, especially since they, in effect, followed in my footsteps. But it does make it tough for a long-term project to recruit able new graduate students who have the same inner motivations and impulses as their teachers—to go out and discover new, if not exactly, virgin, territory for their Ph.D. fieldwork.

To consider overly dependent informants as a project weakness is perhaps too strong a statement. But I have become increasingly concerned about the long-range welfare of some of the Zinacantecos and Chamulas who have worked for the Chiapas Project for more than two decades. The effect of this employment, which has provided them with a reasonably steady income over the years, has been to pull them away from maize farming and other economic pursuits to the point where they no longer have the necessary stamina, knowledge, and skills to make a living in the traditional manner. But to consider this project employment in perspective, I should point out that by 1983 about 50 percent of the Zinacanteco males cultivated no corn and were making their living in a variety of other ways. In the case of the project informants, we have at least provided them with skills and knowledge, notably travel experience in the United States and learning to read and write (including touch-typing on typewriters or personal computers) in Tzotzil, as well being able to serve as experienced informants for other anthropological projects that are initiated in Chiapas.

For some, these skills have been put to good use in their own municipios. Many of them are sought out to write documents for fellow Zinacantecos or Chamulas who need such assistance to borrow money from a bank, to manage time-payments on a new truck, etc. Two of them have served successful terms as presidente municipal: Domingo Pérez Pérez (Little Romin) of Nabenchauk served as presidente municipal of Zinacantan; Mariano López Calixto served as presidente of Chamula. Several others are now working for the Chiapas Writers' Cooperative writing booklets about legends and history in Tzotzil and acting in one-act dramas based on traditional Tzotzil myths.

The family that has been most affected by the presence of the project is that of Romin Teratol, the very first informant we employed full-time, beginning in 1959. Romin, who had disliked maize farming from the beginning, worked for the project for the ensuing eighteen years, until his death in 1976. Now his son, Shun (age thirty), who bore the brunt of the responsibility of supporting his mother and younger siblings after his father died, is a steady member of the Chiapas Writers' Cooperative. All is well, for the time being, as long as the cooperative continues to be supported with sufficient grants and donations from the United States. But should the situation change, Shun would have a difficult time adjusting to farming again, or to a manual labor job that is the fate of most Zinacantecos seeking employment outside the municipio.

Another form of dependence that developed was the perennial pattern of informants requesting loans of money from members of the project. For although the long-range relationships, and especially the compadre connections, we managed to develop with the Zinacantecos and Chamulas led to close rapport that greatly enhanced the quality of the ethnographic data, the multitude and magnitude of accumulated debts became a problem. If a compadre managed to visit us and present a bottle of sugarcane liquor with all the proper etiquette, it was difficult to refuse a loan. At first these loans were minor in amount, compared to our research and fellowship grants, but they increased in magnitude and numbers as the young informants grew older and took more expensive cargo positions in the ceremonial centers, had more more children to support, and aspired to make more expensive purchases, such as chemical sprayers to kill the weeds in their fields or trucks to bring the sacks of maize home from their lowland fields.

We slowly learned more about how to collect these many loans. We discovered that the Indians themselves managed to delay payment of ordinary, small loans by offering cane liquor to their creditors when they encountered them in the market in San Cristobal or at a fiesta in the ceremonial centers, or even on the trail. Indeed, many of the small gatherings of men drinking together in these situations are debtors asking their creditors for more time to repay debts. When a Zinacanteco or Chamula reached a crisis point in his life, such as a forthcoming wedding or a cargo post coming up the following year, then the claim for repayment of loans or asking for new loans could be more insistent, even mandatory. Our fieldworkers adopted the same pattern. For example, one year when Bob Laughlin was leaving Chiapas to return to Washington, he visited all of his debtors in Zinacantan and told them that his airplane ticket home would cost ten thousand pesos and that he needed the money. He managed to collect five thousand pesos from his debtors in less than a week.

But over the long haul many of the debts were never paid, and never will be. I have a lengthy list of debts dating back to 1963, which I have given up trying to collect. For a time, the debtors either served me cane liquor when we met, or tried to avoid me altogether, which was worse, especially when I was eager to talk to with them about other matters of life in Zinacantan. After a time I stopping pressing them about small debts and became more selective about the loans I made. But the requests never ceased, and I guess that we never really solved this debt problem, which is one of the inevitable facets of contact between anthropologists from the developed world working with informants in underdeveloped countries.

On a larger canvas I am often asked about the impact the Harvard Chiapas Project has had on the Tzotzil culture we were studying. Our influence has made itself felt on two levels: the immediate day-to-day relationships with the Maya families and communities and the more indirect effects stemming from our publications.

It is easy to exaggerate our day-to-day influence on the Indian cultures. For although we have been doing fieldwork involving a large number of researchers over the years, the communities we study are relatively large. Even with a field party of a many as fifteen students, we were never so conspicuous in the total Zinacanteco population of eight thousand to twenty thousand or the Chamula population of thirty thousand to one hundred thousand as a single anthropologist is in a tribe of two hundred people in the interior of Brazil. Further, we have never placed more than two fieldworkers in a hamlet, and in these cases the communities have populations of at least fifteen hundred (Vogt 1979: 297). We have had an impact on selected Indian families as I described above. But I doubt that our overall influence on the cultures has been nearly as significant as the countless other forces impinging on the Chiapas Highlands during the last three decades: the rapid increase in population and consequent land shortage, which has led increasing numbers of Zinacantecos and Chamulas to seek a living in ways other than the traditional maize farming; the building of roads, even to remote hamlets, and the startling increase in automobiles owned by Indians; the large number of Mexican government programs to improve life in the native communities, etc. Some members of the project disagree with this assessment. Bob Laughlin has recently argued that "the Harvard Chiapas Project that made a point of treating their Indian 'informants' as individuals worthy of respect and friendship had a greater influence than we would ever imagine" (Personal communication, 1 August 1991).

Our publications have had some effects on the communities, although these effects are also difficult to assess. We have made it a practice to give copies of our publications (especially those that appear in Spanish or have many photographs) to our Tzotzil friends. They spend hours poring over the photographs and read selectively in the texts. Some of the books are proudly kept on household altars and brought out to show visitors. I suppose there is some small Hawthorn effect in this, insofar as it makes the Indians aware that they and their culture are important enough to be studied and written about. Perhaps somewhat more important are effects that stem from the reading of our books by government officials and travelers who come to visit Highland Chiapas. We know that the governors have been personally handed copies of our books. One Chiapas governor promptly gave his copy of my monograph on Zinacantan to the president in Mexico City and wrote me requesting another copy. The governor, Dr. Manuel Velasco Suárez, a well-educated surgeon, read the monograph as well as other project publications. Whether any particular item of government policy was altered by what that governor (or any of the many INI officials who always received our books) read is unclear to me, except for the governor's insistence that government publications using Tzotzil words follow the orthography we were using. There is also some evidence that the establishment of the first radio station in San Cristobal to broadcast in Tzotzil was influenced by our publications. This station might eventually have been established, but I am certain that it was put into operation years earlier than it might have been as a consequence of Gov. Velasco Suárez's reading and acting upon one of the predictions in the final chapter of my monograph (Vogt 1969: 611; Vogt 1979: 299).

Our publications have also had some influence on tourist travel to the Chiapas Highlands, but, judging from the fact that our relatively dry, scientific tracts do not become best-sellers, this impact is probably minuscule compared to the activities of tour companies in the United States, and more especially in France and Germany, which bring tour groups to San Cristobal and bus them out to Chamula and Zinacantan.

On the whole the various members of the Harvard Chiapas Project have gotten along surprisingly well together considering the disparate nature of the group over the years. We have had no celebrated conflicts over whose municipio or hamlet of Indians is whose for the purposes of field research, nor any of the usual fights over the field data we each collected in Chiapas. Many of us believe the liberty afforded students to pursue the line of research they wanted to helped create lifelong friendships, which were not only personally satisfying, but resulted in a frequent sharing and interchange of knowledge.

The main lines of tension we had between members of the project have been twofold: the differences in concept and method between those scholars who are, or hope to be, hardheaded scientists and those who are more humanistic in their operations, and the arguments between the Marxist materialists and the symbolic structuralists.

The contrast between the scientists and the humanists is one between those who develop hypotheses with variables that can be tested empirically with quantitative data and those scholars who proceed with intuitive ideas and models they develop to order the empirical data. This is a well-known contrast in anthropology. I recall Robert Redfield drawing the contrast in his field methods course at the University of Chicago more than fifty years ago. Redfield always argued that it takes both the scientists and the humanists to produce the best anthropological research, and I have always agreed with his views.

To provide some examples from the work of the Chiapas Project, I would contrast the research of Frank Cancian, George Collier, and John Haviland, on the one hand, with the research of Gary Gossen, Renato Rosaldo, and Kazuyasu Ochiai, on the other. The work of the first trio is modeled more on the natural sciences, with a hardheaded approach to data and the use of quantitative information to test the validity of statements. Cancian and Collier utilize a great deal of quantifiable economic and ecological data in their approaches, while Haviland regards the structure of Tzotzil grammar and the utterances in Tzotzil that can be collected and analyzed to be the source of his hard data. The work of the second trio is modeled more on humanistic scholarship in which the investigator collects some data on a certain domain, then creatively comes up with an idea or model that seems to make sense and that provides a guide for the collection of more data. Rather than a focus on economic life, the focus of the latter is more on religion, mythology, cosmology, and worldview. Good examples of Harvard Chiapas Project researchers who nicely combine the two approaches are Victoria Bricker and Bob Laughlin.

These differences in basic concepts and methodology have not led to so much tension that the two types on the Harvard Chiapas Project have had serious difficulties in cooperating or communicating with one another. Rather, the arguments, mainly friendly, express varying modes for reaching ethnographic conclusions.

A more serious source of tension arose between many of the older members of the project and a few of the younger members who were convinced of the validity of a Marxist approach to the Chiapas data and proceeded to write "critical perspectives" on our previous interpretations. Here there was more strain, as these younger members, such as Jan Rus and Robert Wasserstrom, writing from a Marxist perspective that treated culture as an epiphenomenon of the class struggle, considered some of the older scholars to be naively blinded by bourgeois social science to the "realities" of Chiapas history.

By the 1990s, with the astonishing political events and economic collapses in the Marxist-inspired regimes in the USSR and Eastern Europe, this line of tension began to diminish, and, for the most part, the members of the project were back in communication with one another again.

It is interesting that the Harvard Chiapas Project ran through the three decades of change in anthropological theory that were recently described by Sherry Ortner (1984): the 1960s when the major paradigms were symbolic anthropology, structuralism, and cultural ecology; the 1970s with structural Marxism and the political economy (i.e., world-systems analysis) of Wallerstein and Gunder-Frank; and the 1980s with postmodernism and the emphasis on practice (or history).

In retrospect, I believe that our coping with these various intellectual and practical complications that emerged especially in the later phases of the Chiapas Project were in the long run instructive for us all. In any event, they provided illuminating illustrations of some of the major problems faced by cultural anthropology in the past three decades.

13 /
HARVARD FINALE

The 1990s are proving to be a quieter writing and reflective stage of my life as I enjoy retirement but continue to maintain a home on Chauncy Street in Cambridge, a study in the Peabody Museum, and make occasional visits to the Highlands of Chiapas. It is a source of great satisfaction to me that the anthropological work I initiated with the Harvard Chiapas Project continues in the field research of the next generation, notably that of Vicki Bricker, Frank Cancian, George Collier, Gary Gossen, John Haviland, and Robert Laughlin, all of whom have ongoing research underway and books and articles in preparation on the Highlands of Chiapas. Recently I learned that Frank Miller, the first graduate student on the project, plans to return to Chiapas for more field research as well; to say nothing of the recent project of Professor Patricia Greenfield, Dr. Leslie Devereaux, and Carla Childs who are presently studying the next generation of Zinacanteco families they worked with in the mid-1960s.

As I suppose is the case with any research project, there is some unfinished business, even after thirty-five years of fieldwork. We have yet to have a major publication on witchcraft in the Tzotzil area. I have a brief chapter on the subject in my large monograph (Vogt 1969: 406–15), but since Francesco Pellizzi's rich data are still unpublished, too little analysis has been devoted to this important domain in Zinacantan and Chamula. Likewise, we need more publication of the basic ethnographic coverage on Chamula, especially on the rituals of the cargo system and the patterns of shamanism. Even more importantly, I hope in the future there will be more analysis and publication utilizing the method of controlled compari-

367

son in which we examine, for example, kinship structure, cargo systems, shamanistic belief and rituals, in a series of Tzotzil and Tzeltal municipios on which there is beginning to be sufficient ethnographic data.

I am, of course, saddened that the tradition of Mesoamerican studies at Harvard, which Gordon Willey and I carried on for more than four decades, has not continued at the same pace. As of this writing, the vacancy left by Willey in the Bowditch chair has not been filled, nor have any tenured appointments been made in the general field of Mesoamerican ethnography and social anthropology. The focus in this generation of anthropologists at Harvard appears to be on the Old World of Europe, Asia, and Africa, and soon my colleague David Maybury-Lewis will be the only specialist on the New World in a tenured post in anthropology at Harvard.

Perhaps it is fortunate that the thirty-five-year Harvard Chiapas Project has never become a legalized institution at Harvard. I mean by this that I never bothered to request that the faculty of Arts and Sciences, the Department of Anthropology, or the Peabody Museum make the Harvard Chiapas Project into a formalized institution. I simply labeled what I was doing with my various research grants (all of which were administered by either the Laboratory of Social Relations or the Peabody Museum) as the Harvard Chiapas Project.

For some years I used to worry about the project's lack of legal university status. Then I learned that the famous Institute of Social Anthropology (whose name has recently been changed to the Institute of Social and Cultural Anthropology) at Oxford University, initiated by Radcliffe-Brown and later directed by Evans-Pritchard, had no legal status either. All of this was discovered a few years ago when Rodney Needham was appointed to the chair in social anthropology and assumed he would automatically become the director of the institute. When this assumption was challenged by other anthropologists at Oxford, an investigation revealed that the renowned institute had no legal basis at Oxford. It was apparently organized quite informally by Radcliffe-Brown when he was appointed in 1936 and has been in operation ever since.

The fact that the Harvard Chiapas Project also operated informally means that Harvard University has no obligation to try to continue it. With my retirement the project slowly winds down, and the Department of Anthropology and Peabody Museum are free to decide what promising new appointments to make and what innovative research directions to take in the future in Mesoamerica and elsewhere. I recall a remark Dean McGeorge Bundy made one day after being exasperated with the rigidity of Harvard departments. He suggested that *all* Harvard departments be abolished and the members of the faculty of Arts and Sciences be asked to regroup themselves anew. It was a refreshing thought, and reenforced my belief that anthropological research has more vitality when it is built around a set of people who are excited by some basic questions rather than being organized by an institution that can too easily become fossilized.

On 29 April 1989 the Department of Anthropology hosted an elegant black-tie retirement dinner for me in the Massachusetts Room of the Harvard Club of Boston. The guest list included the members of the department and the Peabody Museum and their spouses, all my children and their spouses along with three grandchildren, and thirty of my former students who had worked with me on the Harvard Chiapas Project—some ninety people to wish me well in retirement.

A series of magnificent surprises highlighted the evening. Irven DeVore, chairman of the Department of Anthropology, served as master of ceremonies, and presented a beautiful silver tray engraved with an appreciation for my forty-one years of active duty at Harvard. My four children humorously described how it had been having an anthropologist as a father, and then presented me with a laptop computer to carry on an around-the-world journey Nan and I had planned to celebrate retirement. Then Vicki Bricker and Gary Gossen presented a wonderful festschrift entitled *Ethnographic Encounters in Southern Mesoamerica: Essays in Honor of Evon Zartman Vogt, Jr.* (1989), which they edited and which contained articles by twenty-six of my students and colleagues. How all of them managed to keep the volume a secret from me for over two years, especially with the willing collaboration of my wife, Nan, who wrote one of the articles, still continues to be a source of wonderment.

At the end of the toasts the doors opened between the Massachusetts and Aesculapian Rooms and in marched a Mexican mariachi band (hired by Nan) playing a lively, rhythmic tune. I invited Nan to dance and within minutes all the others had pushed the tables back against the wall and had joined in the joyous dancing. My colleague John Whiting later commented: "They knew the culture of the Harvard Chiapas Project, and they knew what to do. They pushed back the tables and danced to the mariachi band."

Harvard's poet laureate, David McCord, who now lives at the Harvard

Club, heard the music and came to our party. His pronouncement was that "it was the best music he had heard at the Harvard Club." (Whether it was the best music ever played at the Harvard Club of Boston can be disputed, but I'll bet it was the first time that mariachis had been invited to play there.) Shortly thereafter three Mexican couples who were members of the Harvard Law School's Twenty-Fifth Class having a banquet in the Harvard Hall downstairs also heard the mariachis playing and came to the party.

It was for me a peak experience. I was delighted to be with my colleagues and my former students and my family who had shared so much of the Harvard Chiapas Project with me. If I am ever depressed now, all I have to do is look at the handsome, engraved silver tray, read an article or two in my deeply appreciated Festschrift, or write a letter or some field notes on my laptop computer to remember what an extraordinarily rich and exciting life I have lived. My experiences with family and with incredibly talented students and colleagues during my years of field research in the Highlands of Chiapas (and elsewhere) have reached beyond the wildest expectations I held as I left the Vogt Ranch in New Mexico for the University of Chicago some fifty-seven years ago.

NOTES

CHAPTER 2

1. Villa Rojas was born in Merida in 1906 and became a schoolteacher in the Yucatec Maya community of Chan Kom near the famous archaeological site of Chichen Itza, which was being excavated by Dr. Sylvanus G. Morley under the auspices of the Carnegie Institution of Washington. With his interest in the prehistory and culture of the Maya, Villa Rojas became acquainted with Dr. Morley and later, in 1930, with Professor Robert Redfield who had arrived to study the ethnography of the contemporary Yucatec Maya. Villa Rojas worked with Redfield on the Chan Kom study (Redfield and Villa Rojas 1934), and later spent four years (1933–37) studying anthropology with Professors Redfield, A. R. Radcliffe-Brown, and Lloyd Warner at the University of Chicago, where he received his M.A. degree. In 1937 Villa Rojas returned to Mexico to engage in field research in Tusik, a very conservative Maya community deep in the tropical forest of Quintana Roo (1945). In the early 1940s another field trip took him to Highland Chiapas where he lived with his wife in Yochib, a hamlet of the Tzeltal municipio of Oxchuc (1947). This experience of Villa Rojas with both lowland and highland Maya communities was fundamental, and he was unfailingly kind and patient in briefing me about how to do ethnographic research in Chiapas.

CHAPTER 3

1. Frank Miller is now a professor of anthropology at the University of Minnesota, where he has served as chairman of the department as well as the director of the Center for International Studies. He has returned

to Mexico many times for field research, both in Chiapas and in central Mexico where he collected data for his fascinating book *Old Villages and a New Town: Industrialization in Mexico* (1973).

CHAPTER 4

1. For an account of the interesting lives of Frans and Gertrude Blom see Brunhouse 1976.

2. The salt trade is an ancient economic activity for the Zinacantecos who purchase the salt that is extracted from wells in Ixtapa and market it widely in the Chiapas Highlands. Manuel Zabala also published an interesting paper entitled "Instituciones politicas y religiosas de Zinacantan" (1961b). The Zabalas later returned to Colombia.

3. Susan Tax also collected a useful body of data on Zinacanteco weaving (1962) and published an important article (1964) on displacement activity she observed as part of the quality of personal interaction in the Mayan households. Susan returned for an additional field stint in Chiapas during December and January 1959–60, but for a variety of reasons she did not do her doctoral research in Chiapas (Freeman 1989). Instead, she undertook field research in Spain and has now become one of the world authorities on Spanish culture (Freeman 1970, 1979). She is professor of anthropology at the University of Illinois, Chicago Circle.

4. Lore Colby later wrote her Ph.D. thesis, "Zinacantan Tzotzil Sound and Word Structure" (1964), for the Department of Linguistics at Harvard and published an article entitled "Esquema de la morfología Tzotzil" (1966).

5. Nick Colby's publications on Chiapas have also included two papers on education and change (1960b, 1961), as well as two articles on Mesoamerican personality patterns (1964, 1967). Two additional articles on Indian-Ladino relations were coauthored with a sociologist from Harvard, Pierre L. van den Berghe, who worked with Colby in Chiapas (Colby and van den Berghe, 1961a, 1961b). One of the ironies about these early publications on Indian-Ladino relations is that they seem to have been forgotten or ignored by later anthropologists maintaining that the Harvard Chiapas Project studied only local Mayan communities and did not take the larger world of Mexican society and international political and economic networks into account. The Colbys did not continue with field research in Chiapas, but chose instead to undertake work in the Southwest during the

time that Nick was employed by the Museum of New Mexico in Santa Fe, and then, again in collaboration with Pierre van den Berghe in the late 1960s and early 1970s, among the Ixil Maya in northwestern Guatemala. Two significant books have emerged from this Ixil research: Colby and van den Berghe 1969 and Colby and Colby 1981. Nick Colby is now a professor of anthropology at the University of California, Irvine; Pierre van den Berghe, a professor of sociology at the University of Washington.

Chapter 5

1. This collection of folktales and myths provided the basis for Laughlin's excellent Ph.D. thesis, "Through the Looking Glass: Reflections on Zinacantan Courtship and Marriage" (1963). A perfect post as assistant curator in the Smithsonian Institution's Bureau of American Ethnology became available for Laughlin, and he was able to return again and again to field research in Zinacantan where he had become affectionately known as Lol Bik'it Nab (Lawrence Little Lake, from his surname Laughlin). Over the years, he became a full curator at the Smithsonian and has published a really remarkable series of monographs. His dictionary of Tzotzil-Spanish required twelve years of scholarly work; part of the data collection took place in Chiapas, part was done in Santa Fe (where Lore Colby was living at that time and could assist with the work) and in Washington by bringing Zinacanteco informants up from Chiapas for some months at a time and working systematically in the tranquil setting of his offices. With the assistance of John Haviland and my son Eric, who had become skilled on computers, Bob had the dictionary placed in a computer program. *The Great Tzotzil Dictionary of San Lorenzo Zinacantan* was published by Smithsonian Institution Press in 1975. With more than thirty-five thousand Tzotzil words, it is, indeed, the greatest dictionary ever published on an American Indian language. This work had the distinction of winning the Golden Fleece Award from Sen. William Proxmire of Wisconsin, an event mentioned on the front page of the *Wall Street Journal!* More recently Laughlin published *The Great Tzotzil Dictionary of Santo Domingo Zinacantan* (1988), a two-volume work that covers the Tzotzil spoken in Zinacantan toward the end of the sixteenth century, when Santo Domingo, rather than San Lorenzo, was the patron saint. This second dictionary was appropriately dedicated to Senator Proxmire. In between, three additional monographs appeared: *Of Wonders Wild and New: Dreams from Zina-*

cantan (1976), a pioneering collection of dreams from an Indian community in Chiapas; *Of Cabbages and Kings: Tales from Zinacantan* (1977), a full roster of folklore materials with comparative notes; and *Of Shoes and Ships and Sealing Wax: Sundries from Zinacantan* (1980), which contains the only published substantial description of the United States written by Indians from Latin America. Recently published is *The Flowering of Man: A Tzotzil Botany of Zinacantan* (1993) by Dennis E. Breedlove and Robert M. Laughlin, which combines Tzotzil economic botany, ethnoscience, and culture. Together with many articles, these works of Laughlin have added enormously to our corpus of ethnographic data and our understanding of Zinacanteco life. Bob and Mimi Laughlin now own a house in San Cristobal and are able to spend part of every year in Chiapas. I have always admired their decision to continue research in Chiapas after they suffered a terrible family tragedy in 1966. That year the Laughlins had rented an old house in a complex that once functioned as a motel, complete with swimming pool. One afternoon, their two-year old son, Robert Junior, fell into the pool. The maid attending the small boy screamed for help since she could not swim. By the time Mimi Laughlin dove into the pool, dislocating her shoulder in the process, Bobby had drowned. It was the most tragic human accident we suffered during the course of the Chiapas Project.

CHAPTER 6

1. While Jane Fishburne Collier continued with field research in Chiapas, Peggy Reeves Sanday went on to work in other areas, completing her Ph.D. at the University of Pittsburgh and publishing a number of notable books (1981, 1986, 1990).

2. After his senior year at Harvard, Steve Gudeman went to Kings College at Cambridge on a Marshall Fellowship and read social anthropology for his Ph.D., with Sir Edmund Leach as his supervisor. But his early beginnings in anthropology in Chiapas set some of the groundwork for his distinguished books in economic anthropology (1978, 1986; with Alberto Rivera, 1990).

3. Both George and Jane Collier are now professors in the Department of Anthropology at Stanford where George has recently served a term as chairman. Steve Gudeman is a professor of anthropology at the University

of Minnesota, where he has also served as chairman of the department. After a Rhodes Scholarship at Oxford, where he worked with Rodney Needham and received his D.Phil, Jim Fox went to a tenured position in the Institute of Pacific Studies at Australian National University in Canberra. Alice Kasakoff received her Ph.D. at Harvard and is now professor of anthropology at the University of South Carolina. Naomi Quinn, who took her Ph.D. at Stanford, is now professor of anthropology at Duke University, while Martin Silverman, who received his graduate training at the University of Chicago, is now professor of anthropology at the University of British Columbia. Of the three others at the Harvard field station in 1960, Peggy Reeves Sanday is now a professor of anthropology at the University of Pennsylvania; Bill Binderman went on to a notable career in New York City as a lawyer; and Henry York, at last report, was the social sciences librarian at Cleveland State University.

4. I have always been enormously pleased that George and Jane Collier, after spending a year of field research in a Spanish community, decided to return to Chiapas for their Ph.D. research. George's thesis became his first book, *Fields of the Tzotzil: The Ecological Bases of Tradition in Highland Chiapas* (1975), a work that is innovative in both theory and method. Jane's thesis, ultimately presented for her Ph.D. to Tulane University, where George had received a postdoctoral fellowship, became her *Law and Social Change in Zinacantan* (1973), now one of the classic anthropological studies of law-ways. They have both since engaged in additional field research in Spanish communities, but keep returning to Chiapas for long-range fieldwork (see G. Collier 1989; J. Collier 1989) in addition to publishing other books (see G. Collier 1987; J. Collier 1988).

5. Don Bahr is now professor of anthropology at Arizona State University in Tempe and has become a leading authority on Papago Indian culture, especially on shamanism (1974).

6. After his field research in Chiapas, Jack Stauder was ready for more rugged field duty in Africa, this time to the remote Majangir people in southwestern Ethiopia. His thesis became an excellent book (1971). This impressive record led to his being appointed an Instructor in Social Anthropology at Harvard in 1968. He is now a professor in the Department of Sociology and Anthropology at Southeastern Massachusetts University in North Dartmouth.

7. The following year Phil Stubblefield went on to Harvard Medical School and subsequently has became one of the most noted obstetricians in the Boston area.

8. After graduation from Columbia, Harvey Goldberg came to Harvard to do his Ph.D. and is now professor of anthropology at Hebrew University in Tel Aviv.

9. At last report, Jordan Benderly had an important post in the Office of Human Development in the Department of Health and Human Services in Washington, D.C. Of the Harvard students going to field stations in Peru and Ecuador in 1961, all four continued in anthropology. Jane Fearer later undertook graduate work at Oxford under Rodney Needham, and Susanna Ekholm did graduate work in archaeology at Harvard and now does field research in Chiapas. Richard Price and Renato Rosaldo are discussed below.

10. Nick Acheson seriously considered shifting from microbiology to anthropology, but finally went on to his Ph.D. in the former field and is now a professor at McGill University in Montreal.

11. Susan Carey later took her Ph.D. in cognitive psychology at Harvard and is now a professor of psychology at MIT.

12. Matthew Edel later took his Ph.D. in economics and had a distinguished career as professor of economics at Queens College in New York City until his premature death on 5 December 1990.

13. Frank Cancian's classic book (a rewrite of his Ph.D. thesis) *Economics and Prestige in a Maya Community: The Religious Cargo System in Zinacantan* appeared in 1965. Since that time he has published a significant number of articles, including the key article (1967) on cargo systems in the *Handbook of Middle American Indians,* as well as four more books: *Change and Uncertainty in a Peasant Economy* (1972); a volume of his remarkable photographs, *Another Place: Photographs of a Maya Community* (1974); a comparative study entitled *The Innovators's Situation* (1979); and *The Decline of Community in Zinacantan* (1992). Frank continues to do his field research in Zinacantan. He has served as professor of anthropology at Cornell and Stanford, and is now at the University of California, Irvine, where he currently serves as chairman of the department.

14. Francesca Cancian's impressive results appear in a number of articles, notably "Interaction Patterns in Zinacanteco Families" (1964), which was reprinted in Spanish (1966), and her Harvard Ph.D. dissertation (1963).

Franzi turned later to a carefully designed study of norms in Zinacantan; the results appear in *What Are Norms? A Study of Beliefs and Action in a Maya Community* (1975). She went on to serve as a professor of sociology at Stanford, and later moved to the University of California, Irvine, where she has also served as department chairman.

CHAPTER 7

1. Roy D'Andrade is now a professor of anthropology at the University of California, San Diego; Duane Metzger is a professor of anthropology at the University of California, Irvine.

CHAPTER 8

1. Although Linnea Wren did outstanding research in anthropology as an undergraduate and graduated summa cum laude, she finally decided to undertake Ph.D. work in the Department of Fine Arts at Harvard and is now a professor of art history at Gustavus Adolfus College in Minnesota. She has, however, maintained her interest in the Maya and has become a renowned authority on the iconography associated with the ancient Maya ballgame (see, for example, Wren 1989).

2. This volume grew out of a working conference at Harvard University from 10 to 12 May 1969, which I organized and chaired. The purpose of the conference was to exchange information on concepts and methods in the uses of aerial photography in anthropology. The group included Michael D. Coe (Yale) and Elmer Harp, Jr., (Dartmouth), who were working with new uses of aerial photographs in archaeological research; Robert A. Hackenberg (University of Colorado) and Thomas S. Schorr (University of Pittsburgh), who were specializing in novel uses of aerial photographs in the study of cultural ecology. Richard Kroeck, who had been the Itek project engineer, came to the conference, as did Dennis Wood (Clark University), a geographer who had worked with aerial photos in Latin America, and Priscilla Reining (Smithsonian Institution) and Conrad Reining (Catholic University) who had worked with aerial photos on land use and tenure in Tanzania. Other members of the Harvard Chiapas Project attending included Frank Cancian and George Collier (Stanford), Gary H. Gossen (University of California, Santa Cruz), and Richard Price (Johns Hopkins), all of whom had worked intensively with our aerial coverage. The student participants included William B. Fitzhugh, Edward B. Sisson,

and Carolyn Pope Edwards, the latter serving as rapporteur. Unfortunately, Harold C. Conklin (Yale), who was a pioneer in utilizing the new techniques of aerial photogrammetry in Luzon, could not attend as he was away doing field research in the Philippines, but he did contribute an article to the volume.

CHAPTER 9

1. These latter students were Linnea Holmer Wren; David Freidel, who took his Ph.D. in Maya archaeology with Gordon Willey and is now a well-known professor at Southern Methodist University; and Shael Brachman, who did field research in Guatemalan refugee camps in Chiapas in the summer of 1990.

2. After his field experience in Zinacantan, John Early began research among the Mayas in the Highlands of Guatemala and published a basic work entitled *The Demographic Structure and Evolution of a Peasant System: The Guatemalan Population* (1982). He ultimately left the Jesuit Order, married, and took a post at Florida Atlantic University where he served as professor of anthropology and chairman of the department. He is now professor emeritus at the university.

3. The results of Vicki Bricker's important study of ritual humor appeared in her Ph.D. thesis "The Meaning of Laughter in Zinacantan" (1968) and in her book *Ritual Humor in Highland Chiapas* (1973), as well as in various articles. Vicki continued her interests in Chiapas ethnography, but also began to work with the Yucatec Maya in Yucatan. She is the only Mayanist I know who fluently controls two contemporary Mayan languages: Tzotzil and Yucatec. From her work in Yucatan came a brilliant comparative volume, *The Indian Christ, The Indian King* (1981), which is a definitive study of Maya rebellions, and more recently an outstanding *Grammar of Mayan Hieroglyphs* (1986), to say nothing of a remarkable series of articles. Vicki is now professor of anthropology at Tulane University where her husband, Harvey, is also a professor. Her remarkable contributions to anthropology resulted in her being elected to the National Academy of Sciences in 1991.

4. Dan Silver discussed shamanism in Zinacantan in his Ph.D. dissertation and in an article (1966b). In 1967 he collaborated with the medical anthropologist Horacio Fabrega, Jr., who was then a professor of psychia-

try and anthropology at Michigan State University and is now professor of psychiatry in the School of Medicine at the University of Pittsburgh. Dr. Fabrega had come to Chiapas at the invitation of Kim Romney and Duane Metzger to undertake field research in Tenejapa and Zinacantan. This productive collaboration resulted in a key volume on this research, *Illness and Shamanistic Curing in Zinacantan* (1973). In the long run, however, Dan Silver decided that anthropology was not for him. With my friendly support, he applied and was admitted to the Harvard Law School where he finished his law degree and went on to become an eminent international lawyer in Brussels for many years, and now in Washington D.C. In retrospect, it was a tribute to Dan that he accepted the logic in my suggestion that the Sierra Madres of California were higher in elevation than the Highlands of Chiapas and controlled the feelings of original panic he had upon encountering the alien cultural setting of Mexico. I believe he is a superior attorney as a result of his cross-cultural experience in Zinacantan and his combined Ph.D. and LL.B.

5.   Nick Bunnin later undertook graduate work for his doctorate in philosophy at Oxford and now teaches at Essex University in England.

6.   Although tempted by anthropology, Carter Wilson's enduring passion was in writing, and he has become a highly successful novelist. Two of his fascinating books, *Crazy February* (1966) and *A Green Tree and a Dry Tree* (1972), flowed directly from his field experience in Chamula. The reviewer of *Crazy February* for the *American Anthropologist* described it "as a work of art". Carter was also one of the producers (along with Duane Metzger) of a noted ethnographic film on the rituals of the cargoholders in Tenejapa entitled *Appeals to Santiago*. He is now a professor of literature at the University of California, Santa Cruz.

7.   Mary Lowenthal received her Ph.D. in history at Stanford University in 1971 and is now professor of history at San Francisco State University.

8.   James Warfield later served in the Peace Corps in Bolivia and is now a professor of architecture at the University of Illinois.

9.   Nancy Chodorow is now a professor of sociology at the University of California, Berkeley.

10.   Antonio Gilman is now professor of anthropology at California State University, Northridge, and a specialist on the Neolithic and Bronze Age archaeology of Spain and North Africa.

11. Rand Rosenblatt is now a professor of law at Rutgers University Law School. John Strucker took his master's degree at the Harvard School of Education and now teaches in Cambridge.

12. Benedicte Fløystrup is now a science editor at the Getty Museum in California. From this summer came the fourth marriage among Chiapas fieldworkers. Antonio Gilman later married Benedicte Fløystrup, following the precedent set by the Cancians, Colliers, and Bahrs.

13. In 1965 Shelley Zimbalist undertook field research in a community of southern Spain that had been previously studied by the Colliers during their Fulbright year. Following her graduation summa cum laude in English Literature, Shelley started graduate work in anthropology at Harvard and soon afterward married her classmate, Renato Rosaldo. The two of them decided to work in Southeast Asia for their Ph.D. field research and focused on the Ilongot, a head-hunting tribe in the mountains of Luzon in the Philippines. Out of this research (from 1967 to 1969 and in 1974) came a number of significant papers and two brilliant books: *Knowledge and Passion: Ilongot Notions of Self and Social Life* (1980) by Shelley and *Ilongot Headhunting 1883–1974* (1980) by Renato. Shelley and Renato were both appointed to the teaching staff in the Department of Anthropology at Stanford, where they had several happy and productive years together. On a third field trip to the Ilongot country in 1981, Shelley was walking along a precipitous muddy path in a heavy rain with a woman informant when she slipped and fell 150 feet into a roaring mountain stream and was drowned. It was a tragic end for a remarkable person and brilliant scholar. Her premature death will be long mourned by all who knew her. Following Shelley's death, Renato remained at Stanford where he is now a popular professor and chairman of the department of anthropology and author of an interesting new book *Culture and Truth* (1986).

14. A second volume *Symbol and Meaning Beyond the Closed Community* edited by Gary Gossen (1986) extends and refines his approach in innovative ways. Together with many outstanding articles (see especially Gossen 1972, 1975, 1985, 1989), Gary has been another highly productive scholar to emerge from the project and has continued to do field research in Chiapas. Most recently he has been studying the Chamula diaspora (1983). After teaching anthropology at the University of California, Santa Cruz, Gary moved to the State University of New York, Albany, where he has

served as chairman of the Department of Anthropology and director of the Institute for Mesoamerican Studies.

15.   Patrick Menget later joined David Maybury-Lewis's project among the tropical forest tribes of Brazil, on which he wrote his Ph.D. thesis; he is now the head of the department of ethnology in the Faculté des Lettres in Nanterre.

16.   After two summers in Chiapas the Prices decided to branch out on their own and undertook field research for their doctorates among the Saramaka in the tropical forest of Surinam. Rich has published important books on the Saramaka and the Caribbean (1974b, 1976, and 1983), and Sally is noted for her fascinating study of polygyny among the Saramaka (1984). Rich taught anthropology at Yale and later at John Hopkins where he served as chairman of the Department of Anthropology. He and Sally now live on Martinique (where Rich had done field research for his senior honors thesis) and devote their time to research and writing on Caribbean cultures.

17.   Elena Uribe is now the second secretary (covering British domestic affairs, political as well as social) in the Mexican embassy in London.

18.   Roger Dunwell later went to law school and is now an attorney in Port-Au-Prince, Haiti. Todd Rakoff also went on to study law and is now a professor at the Harvard Law School. Barbara Strodt later took her Ph.D. in linguistics at UCLA and now teaches at the University of Puerto Rico. Steve Young is now dean of the Hamline University Law School in St. Paul, Minnesota. For some reason, the 1965 season in Chiapas seemed to attract prelaw students from Harvard!

19.   Gwendoline van den Berghe later undertook graduate work in France and has a Ph.D. from the Sorbonne. Interestingly, her Ph.D. dissertation, based on fieldwork in Lima, Peru, continued a line of research that began with her study of the elite families in San Cristobal. The title: "Contribution a L'etude Social et Culturelle de la Classe Haute Peruvienne" (1970). She is now the secretary general of the *European Journal of Medicine,* published in Paris. Of the eight Harvard students who went to other field stations during the summer of 1965, the only one who continued in anthropology was Julie M. Taylor, who undertook fieldwork in Peru. Following her senior year she traveled to South America on a Fulbright to study a problem I posed for her: Why do Argentines dance the tango, while

Brazilians dance the samba? She collected fascinating data on the tango in Buenos Aires during the summer and has since published articles on both the tango and the samba. Her D.Phil. in anthropology was awarded at Oxford, where Professor Rodney Needham was her supervisor. The thesis, a symbolic analysis of Eva Peron, became the classic book on the subject (1979). She is now a professor of anthropology at Rice University.

CHAPTER 10

1. The *Handbook of Middle American Indians* was a project that had been initiated nearly a decade before when Gordon Willey, serving as chairman of the Committee on Latin American Anthropology of the National Research Council, raised the first funds for the purpose from the National Science Foundation. To plan and supervise the *Handbook,* an editorial advisory board was appointed, including Ignacio Bernal, Howard F. Cline, Gordon F. Ekholm, Norman A. McQuown, Manning Nash, T. Dale Stewart, Evon Z. Vogt, Robert C. West, and Gordon R. Willey. We persuaded Professor Robert Wauchope of Tulane University to serve as the general editor, and appointed members of the advisory board to serve as volume editors. I agreed to edit volumes 7 and 8 on the ethnology of Middle America, another task that absorbed an incredible amount of time over nearly a decade. I received a number of articles for the *Handbook* that were unpublishable in the form they were submitted, and these had to be carefully edited or rewritten. For example, while I received fine articles from Robert M. Laughlin on the Tzotzil-Maya and from Alfonso Villa Rojas on the Tzeltal-Maya, the article by Frans and Gertrude Blom on the Lacandon-Maya was uneven and incoherent; it had to be reworked several times by me and by Mimi Laughlin, who served as my editorial assistant. I had mistakenly assumed from all their work with the Lacandons that the Bloms were the leading experts in the world on the subject. In retrospect, I guess I should have realized that not being professionally trained anthropologists, the Bloms were unlikely to write a coherent and systematic article on Lacandon culture. In the end the article should have been rejected, but for diplomatic reasons we ran it and held our breath, hoping that readers would focus on Trudi's superb photographs and skim over the text, which is the least adequate in the two volumes I edited.

2. After marrying our son Terry and receiving a master's degree in

journalism at Stanford University, Mary Anschuetz lives in San Francisco where she does free-lance writing.

3. John Haviland's revised thesis (1971) became an outstanding book, *Gossip, Reputation, and Knowledge in Zinacantan* (1977). A more recent book, *Sk'op Sotz'leb: El Tzotzil de San Lorenzo Zinacantan*, appeared in Spanish in Mexico in 1981, and there have been many excellent articles emanating from his computer over the years. John was appointed an assistant professor of anthropology at Harvard, where he served from 1971 to 1974 before joining the staff of the Research School of Pacific Studies of Australian National University in Canberra. During his years in Australia, Haviland engaged in fieldwork with an aboriginal tribe, the Guugu Yimidhirr, in northern Australia. In 1986 Haviland joined the staff at Reed College where he is now a professor of linguistics and anthropology.

4. Judy Merkel would have had a brilliant future as an anthropologist, but after earning her bachelor's degree at Harvard, she become a member of the Ananda Marga Cult and is now head of one of the cult centers in Brazil.

5. Ron Trosper is now a professor of forestry at Northern Arizona University, where he serves as director of the first Native American Forestry Program in the United States. The fourth Harvard student, Arden Aibel, collected some interesting data on schools in the Chiapas Highlands, but because of a serious illness left San Cristobal for the United States after only three weeks of field research.

6. Neither Stephanie Krebs nor Rick Shweder continued with research in Chiapas. Krebs later went to Thailand for her dissertation research, which focused on studying and filming nonverbal communication in Bangkok. She continues to do consulting work in Bangkok. Shweder had always been interested in India, where he and his wife, Candy (who served as my administrative assistant in 1968–69) later undertook fieldwork for his thesis under the supervision of Cora DuBois. He is now a professor of human development and psychology with the Committee on Human Development at the University of Chicago and the author of a number of notable books, including *Thinking Through Cultures* (1991).

7. Leslie Haviland returned repeatedly to Chiapas with John and ultimately submitted a distinguished Ph.D. dissertation entitled "The Social Relations of Work in a Peasant Community" (1978) to the Department of

Sociology at Harvard. She is now Leslie Devereaux (having been divorced from John) and is a lecturer in the Department of Anthropology at the Australian National University in Canberra.

8. John Miyamoto is now a professor of psychology at the University of Michigan. Abigail Natelson is currently a noted avant-garde filmmaker in New York.

9. Carolyn Pope (now Carolyn Edwards) later completed her Ph.D. under the supervision of Dr. Beatrice Whiting in the School of Education at Harvard and is now a professor at the University of Kentucky. She is co-author, with Beatrice Whiting, of *Children of Different Worlds* (Edwards 1988); her most recent publication on Zinacantan is "The Transition from Infancy to Early Childhood" (Edwards 1989).

10. Mark Rosenberg went on to take his medical degree at Harvard; he is now the director of the Division of Injury Control at the Centers for Disease Control in Atlanta. From time to time, he still calls me for anthropological guidance; for example, "Where can I get some expert advice as to why the young Shoshone Indians in Wyoming are committing suicide at such high rates?" He recently edited and published a noted book entitled *Violence in America: A Public Health Approach.* Fred Whelan continued in the field of government, completing his Ph.D. at Harvard; he is now a professor of political science at the University of Pittsburgh.

11. After serving as an assistant professor in the Department of Anthropology at Harvard, Felisa Kazen went on to pursue a career in Spanish-speaking television programs in New York.

12. Francesco Pellizzi married an heiress, Philippa de Menil, who spent several seasons with him in Chiapas. Francesco became so interested in the Highlands of Chiapas that he later purchased a ranch house and land on the northeastern outskirts of San Cristobal, to which he still returns from time to time. As a son-in-law in the de Menil family of Houston, Francesco began to assist in the operations of the family foundation, which was especially interested in modern art. As the years elapsed, he became more interested in art and has now become an expert on modern art. With a colleague in France, Francesco founded the very successful art and anthropology journal *Res,* which has published many seminal articles. In 1974 Pellizzi was one of the organizers of an important symposium held in San Cristobal to commemorate the five hundredth anniversary of the

birth of Fray Bartolomé de las Casas, the first Roman Catholic bishop in the Highlands of Chiapas. His stimulating article "Misioneros y Cargos: Notas Sobre Identidad y Aculturación en los Altos de Chiapas" (1981) came out of this Las Casas symposium. In 1977 Francesco generously provided the funds for publishing our useful *Bibliography of the Harvard Chiapas Project*(Vogt 1978b). Francesco continues to live in New York and, although divorced from Philippa, to help advise the de Menil Foundation—all of which has been good for modern art, but I am still awaiting his publication on Zinacanteco witchcraft.

13.   Charles Sabel is now a professor of economics at MIT.

14.   After doing a stint with the Peace Corps in southern Peru, Jan Rus returned to graduate work at Harvard and to Chiapas for further field research. By now, he and his wife Diane, an expert in bilingual education, have had much experience in Chiapas. Jan is working for Instituto Asesoria Antropologica para la Region Maya in San Cristobal and has published a number of interesting articles (including Rus and Wasserstrom 1980). But I am still looking forward to receiving his Ph.D. dissertation on "Great San Juan, Great Patron: The Social History of a Maya Community, 1800–1976."

15.   Carla Childs has also published three sophisticated articles with Greenfield (Childs and Greenfield 1977; Greenfield and Childs 1977; Greenfield and Childs 1980). Their latest scholarly publication, together with Berry Brazelton, "From Birth to Maturity in Zinacantan" (1989) is, in my judgment, among the most brilliant syntheses to emerge from the Harvard Chiapas Project. Carla Childs is now a teacher at the Friends School in Baltimore.

16.   Jonathan Hiatt is now an attorney and serves as general counsel of the Service Employees International Union in Washington, D.C.

17.   Ben Orlove later developed an interest in the same cultural ecological questions in Peru and has published extensively (see, for example, his *Alpacas, Sheep, and Men* 1977). His is another case where early experience on the Chiapas Project helped form his later research interests. He is now professor of environmental studies at the University of California, Davis.

18.   Ira Abrams has continued his work in films, having been the producer and director for "The Three Worlds of Bali" in the Odyssey Series for television in 1981 and one of the cinematographers for "Chiefs and Kings

of Indonesia," which was broadcast in the Explorer series by the Disney Channel in 1983. He is now an associate professor of radio-TV-film at the University of Texas at Austin.

19.   Suzanne Abel later finished her Ph.D. in anthropology at Brown University, specializing in archaeology, and is now the Director of Grace Hudson Museum in Ukiah, California.

20.   Carol Greenhouse later decided to do her Ph.D. fieldwork in a North American community and chose a small Georgia town near Atlanta. The results appeared in her fascinating book, *Praying for Justice* (1986; see also 1989). She is now a professor of anthropology at the University of Indiana.

21.   After this first-rate field research, I was hoping Tim Rush would go on to graduate school in anthropology. But instead he joined the Labor Committee in New York City and pursued quite radical politics. For many years he would talk only about his Labor Committee policies, to the point where it was boring for others. I have now, unfortunately, lost contact with him. I cannot help but believe that the political and intellectual climate of the late 1960s and early 1970s had reenforced an earlier experience Tim Rush once told me about. His family lived near one of the large Rockefeller estates near New York City where he had a job one summer helping mow the lawns. From this background and his later thinking at Harvard must have come his deep sense of injustice about the inequalities of wealth in the contemporary United States.

22.   Lars Smith returned to Chiapas in the summer of 1970 and later undertook field research with the Hadza hunting-and-gathering people of Tanzania for his Ph.D. At last report he was working for an ecology program in Europe.

23.   After serving a few years as an assistant professor of anthropology at Southern Methodist University and later at Columbia University, Rob Wasserstrom left the academic world to work for the World Resources Institute in Washington, D.C., and is now on the staff of a waste disposal firm in Houston.

CHAPTER 11

1.   Because Jeff Howry finished his doctorate at a time when anthropological jobs were at a low ebb in the United States, he did not locate an

academic post, but instead went into the field of energy conservation with a private firm.

2. Priscilla Rachun married Dr. Johannes Linn, an economist with the World Bank, and now lives in Washington, D.C., where she is an anthropologist at the Smithsonian Institution and is rewriting her thesis for publication. Meanwhile, she has published two articles utilizing her Chiapas data (1982, 1989).

3. Following her graduation from Harvard, Lauren Bardrick married; she now pursues a career as an artist.

4. Peter Guarnaccia continued his work in anthropology at the University of Connecticut, where he took his Ph.D., and is now a professor of anthropology at Rutgers. Lisa Wiesner went on to medical school at Case Western Reserve and is now a practicing physician in Connecticut.

5. For graduate work Ken Carson shifted to law school and is now an attorney in the Boston area. Following her graduation from Harvard, Susan Epstein went to medical school and is now a practicing physician in Montana.

6. A later book by Thomas Crump (1981) contains Chiapas data, as do two of his articles (1987, 1989). Crump has gone on to become an expert on Japan where he has done field research, especially on the Japanese emperor (1992a). He also works on numeracy (i.e., the significance of numbers) in various cultures (1990, 1992b). He is now a senior lecturer in cultural anthropology at the University of Amsterdam.

7. Jason Clay later took his Ph.D. in anthropology at Cornell and served as director of research for Cultural Survival in Cambridge, Massachusetts, for many years. He recently founded a non-governmental organization called Rights and Resources, Inc., in Washington, to help save the rain forests of the world. Not surprisingly, Rachel Ritvo later went on to medical school and became a child psychiatrist, now practicing in Maryland. Patricia Lynch did graduate work in anthropology at Cambridge University and is now working for a commercial real estate development company in Washington, D.C. After working with Native American programs in Alaska for four years, Elizabeth Werby is now an attorney specializing in labor and employment law in New York City.

8. Roger Reed went to law school and is now a practicing attorney in McAllen, Texas.

9. Betsy Dodd is now practicing environmental law in San Francisco.

10. After graduation Jane Baird became a journalist specializing in international banking; she is now in Houston. Bill Freeman went on to Harvard Law School and is now an attorney in San Francisco.

11. Eliot Gelwan did not continue with astronomy, but went into medicine and is now a practicing psychiatrist in Cambridge.

12. After taking a Ph.D. in anthropology at Johns Hopkins, Suzanne Siskel became an expert on irrigation systems in Indonesia and is now a program director and the acting head of the Ford Foundation office in Jakarta.

13. Mary Scott later undertook graduate work in Chinese studies at Princeton and now teaches East Asian literature courses at San Francisco State. Along with her husband (who teaches at the University of California, Santa Cruz) she has taken undergraduate students on study trips to China, thereby replicating the experience she had in Chiapas.

14. Marta Turok has become a noted authority on Indian weaving in Mexico and is now engaged in free-lance consulting in Mexico City, where she also serves as president of the Asociación de Artes y Cultura Popular.

15. Donald McVicker is now professor of anthropology at North Central College in Napierville, Illinois.

16. After spending some years in landscape architecture, Thor Anderson decided to return to anthropology and is now studying for his Ph.D. at Berkeley.

17. Tom Paradise is now a land developer in southern California, in a way continuing his Chiapas interests.

18. John Burstein later went on to consulting jobs advising governments on problems of literacy, first in Nepal now in Washington, D.C. His interest in adult education led to research on the Nicaraguan literacy campaign in the early 1980s. He is now working for the Inter-American Foundation in the Washington Office on Latin America.

19. Alaka Wali later took her Ph.D. in anthropology at Columbia, after doing her field research in Panama. She is now professor of anthropology at the University of Maryland, College Park, and author of *Kilowatts and Crisis: Hydroelectric Power and Social Dislocation in Eastern Panama* (1989).

20. After graduation Emily Apter went to Princeton for a Ph.D. in Romance languages and is now a professor in the Department of French

and Comparative Literature at the University of California, Davis. Rowena Frazer later pursued a career related to her anthropological work in Chiapas. She joined the Peace Corps and spent two years in Tonga, where she learned to speak the language fluently. Here she met her husband, a fellow Peace Corps worker, who later became a physician and is now at the School of Public Health at the University of Alabama at Birmingham.

21. Sam Anderson is now an architect in New York City, and specializes in designing public buildings. Paul Saffo is a research fellow and an expert on electronic publishing at the Institute of the Future in Menlo Park, California, and has become an often-quoted authority in the national press on new developments in computers and communication. Paul has a continuing interest in the Maya and currently serves as a member of the board of directors of the Pre-Columbian Art Research Institute directed by Merle Greene Robertson in San Francisco.

22. Nancy Zweng ultimately took a masters in business administration at Stanford and is now a banker in New York City.

23. After Yale Law School, Denise Field became an attorney in Washington, D.C.

24. Pete Haviland later finished his law degree at Stanford and is now an attorney practicing public interest law in Los Angeles. Sara Lacy is now a professor of civil engineering at Tufts University. After finishing law school, Marcy Richmond became an attorney in Boston.

25. After graduating from Harvard, Jay Levi was a Marshall Fellow at Kings College, Cambridge, and then returned to Harvard to complete his Ph.D. He is now teaching anthropology at Carleton College.

26. Kazuyasu Ochiai has also recently published a collection of his articles in *Meanings Performed, Symbols Read* (1989). He now teaches anthropology and Latin American ethnology at Chubu University in Japan.

27. Stuart Plattner went on to become a leading expert on economic anthropology and is now director of the Cultural Anthropology Program of the National Science Foundation in Washington, D.C.

28. Ron Nigh has become a noted specialist on the ecology of Mexico and is now a researcher at the Centro de Ecología at the Universidad Nacional Autónoma de México.

29. After graduation from Harvard, Steve Roof enrolled in the University of Michigan Law School and is now a practicing attorney in Miami.

30. After graduation from Harvard, Cynthia McVay took her MBA at the Wharton School at the University of Pennsylvania and is now with the famous McKinsey consulting firm, handling cases in Latin America.

31. Colleagues and former students of Gordon Willey's who attended and presented papers at this symposium included R.E.W. Adams, Warwick Bray, David A. Freidel, Wolfgang Haberland, Richard M. Leventhal, Joyce Marcus, Michael E. Moseley, Henry B. Nicholson, Donald E. Thompson, William L. Rathje, Jeremy A. Sabloff, and Gair Tourtellot. Others who wrote papers, but could not come to Burg Wartenstein, included Ignacio Bernal, K. C. Chang, Grahame Clark, Olga Linares, and William T. Sanders. The discussion was spirited, and the toasts at the final dinner were particularly poignant because not only was Gordon Willey retiring from teaching at Harvard, but the efficient and engaging Lita Osmundsen was leaving Burg Wartenstein, which had been sold to a private owner. Our symposium (and my fourth international meeting in that magnificent old castle) was the last Wenner-Gren meeting to be held in the Austrian Alps above Gloggnitz. With the skillful assistance of Richard Leventhal, who served as the rapporteur at Burg Wartenstein and also as coeditor, a handsome volume entitled *Prehistoric Settlement Patterns: Essays in Honor of Gordon R. Willey* was published in 1983. Together with a second volume, *Civilization in the Ancient Americas* edited by Richard M. Leventhal and Alan Kolata, the festschrift was presented to Gordon at a black-tie dinner at the Harvard Club of Boston at which I was honored to serve as master of ceremonies.

CHAPTER 12

1. John Watanabe is now a professor of anthropology at Dartmouth.

REFERENCES

Abel, Suzanne
1969   "Patterns of Political Influence—Zinacantan and Chamula." Summer Field Report, Harvard Chiapas Project,
Peabody Museum, Harvard University.

Acheson, Nicholas H.
1962   "The Ethnozoology of the Zinacantecan Indians." Summer
Field Report, Harvard Chiapas Project, Peabody Museum,
Harvard University.

Adair, John, and Evon Z. Vogt
1949   "Navaho and Zuni Veterans: A Study of Contrasting
Modes of Culture Change." *American Anthropologist* 41
(4): 547–61.

Adams, Richard Newbold
1970   *Crucifixion by Power: Essays on Guatemalan National
Social Structure, 1944–1966.* Austin: University of Texas
Press.

Albert, Ethel M.
1956   "The Classification of Values: A Method and Illustration."
American Anthropologist 58(2): 221–48.

Anderson, Samuel M.
1974   "Problems in the Physical Development of Nachih, Nabenchauk, and Zinacantan Center." Summer Field Report,
Harvard Chiapas Project, Peabody Museum, Harvard University.

Anderson, Thor R.

1975   *"Kruston:* A Study of House and Home in a Maya Village." A.B. honors thesis, Harvard University.

1988   "Sacred Games: Ritual Warfare in a Maya Village." 60 Min. Film. University of California, Berkeley.

Anschuetz, Mary H.

1966   "To Be Born in Zinacantan." Summer Field Report, Harvard Chiapas Project, Peabody Museum, Harvard University.

Arbuz, Georges S.

1963   "La Construction de la Guitare et du Violin a Chamula." Summer Field Report, Harvard Chiapas Project, Peabody Museum, Harvard University.

Baca, Joan B.

1974   "A Study in Symbolic Syncretism: The Santoetik of Zinacantan." A.B. honors thesis, Harvard University.

Bahr, Donald M.

1962   "An Exploration of Men's Use and Views of the Physical World in Two Highland Maya Municipios." A.B. honors thesis, Harvard University.

Bahr, Donald M., et al.

1974   *Piman Shamanism and Staying Sickness.* Tucson: University of Arizona Press.

Baird, Jane B.

1970   *"Bankilal and 'Itzinal."* Summer Field Report, Harvard Chiapas Project, Peabody Museum, Harvard University.

Bandelier, Adolf F. A.

1890–1892   "Final Report of Investigations Among the Indians of the Southwest, Carried on Mainly in the Years from 1880 to 1885." 2 vols. Papers of the Archaeological Institute of America, American Series 3 and 4. Cambridge, Mass.

Barber, V. Tonik

1977   *"C'IVIT:* Regional Economic Exchange in San Cristobal Las Casas, Mexico." A.B. honors thesis, Harvard University.

Bardrick, J. Lauren

1970   "Face to Face with the Gods: A Study of Ritual Order and

Holiness in Zinacantan." Summer Field Report, Harvard Chiapas Project, Peabody Museum, Harvard University.

Barta, Roger
1969   (editor) *El Modo de Producción Asiático.* México: Editorial Era.
1974   *Estructura Agrária y Classes Sociales en México.* México: Editorial Era.

Basso, Keith H.
1979   "History of Ethnological Research." Vol. 9 on the *Southwest,* edited by Alfonso Ortiz, *Handbook of North American Indians,* edited by William C. Sturtevant, pp. 14–21. Washington, D.C.: Smithsonian Institution Press.

Bellah, Robert N.
1966   "Religious Systems." *People of Rimrock: A Study of Values in Five Cultures,* edited by Evon Z. Vogt and Ethel M. Albert, pp. 227–64. Cambridge: Harvard University Press.

Benderly, Jordan P.
1961   "The Distribution of Labor in the Production of Panela on a Caña Ranch in Chiapas." Summer Field Report, Harvard Chiapas Project, Peabody Museum, Harvard University.

Berlin, Brent, Dennis E. Breedlove, and Peter H. Raven
1974   *Principles of Tzeltal Plant Classification.* New York: Academic Press.

Blaffer, Sarah C.
1972   *The Black-man of Zinacantan: A Central American Legend.* Austin: University of Texas Press. (Revision of A.B. honors thesis, Harvard University, 1969.)

Blanco, Merida H., and Nancy J. Chodorow
1964   "Children's Work and Obedience in Zinacantan." Summer Field Report, Harvard Chiapas Project, Peabody Museum, Harvard University.

Blom, Frans, and Oliver LaFarge
1926–1927   *Tribes and Temples: A Record of the Expedition to Middle America Conducted by the Tulane University of Louisiana, 1925.* New Orleans: Tulane University Press.

Brazelton, T. Berry
1972   "Implications of Infant Development Among the Maya

Indians of Southern Mexico." *Human Development* 15: 90–111.

1973   "Effect of Maternal Expectations on Early Infant Behavior." *Early Child Development and Care* 2: 259–73.

1974   "Can the Neonate Shape his Environment?" *Infants at Risk*. National Foundation for March of Dimes, pp. 130–40. Intercontinental Medical Book.

1975   "Implications of Infant Development in Mexico and the United States." *Cultural and Social Influences in Infancy and Early Childhood*, edited by P. Liederman and S. Tulkin. New York: Wenner-Gren Foundation for Anthropological Research.

Brazelton, T. Berry, John S. Robey, and George A. Collier

1969   "Infant Development in the Zinacanteco Indians of Southern Mexico." *Pediatrics* 44 (2): 274–93.

Breedlove, Dennis E., and Robert M. Laughlin

1993   *The Flowering of Man: A Tzotzil Botany of Zinacantan*. Smithsonian Contributions to Anthropology 35. Washington, D.C.: Smithsonian Institution Press.

Breton, Alain

1979   *Les Tzeltal de Bachajon*. Nanterre: Laboratoire d'Ethnologie.

Bricker, Victoria R.

1963   "Good Manners in Zinacantan: A Manual on Etiquette for Field Workers." Unpublished ms., Harvard Chiapas Project, Peabody Museum, Harvard University.

1968   "The Meaning of Laughter in Zinacantan: An Analysis of the Humor in a Highland Maya Community." Ph.D. diss., Harvard University.

1973   *Ritual Humor in Highland Chiapas*. Austin: University of Texas Press.

1981   *The Indian Christ, The Indian King: The Historical Substrate of Maya Myth and Ritual*. Austin: University of Texas Press.

1986   *A Grammar of Mayan Hieroglyphics*. Middle American Research Institute, Publication 56. New Orleans: Tulane University.

Bricker, Victoria R., and Gary H. Gossen (editors)

1989   *Ethnographic Encounters in Southern Mesoamerica: Essays in Honor of Evon Z. Vogt, Jr.* Austin: University of Texas Press.

Brunhouse, Robert L.

1976   *Frans Blom, Maya Explorer.* Albuquerque: University of New Mexico Press.

Bullard, William R., Jr.

1960   "Maya Settlement Pattern in Northeastern Peten, Guatemala." *American Antiquity* 25: 355–72.

Bunnin, Nicholas F.

1966   "La Indústria de las Flores en Zinacantan." *Los Zinacantecos: Un Pueblo Tzotzil de los Altos de Chiapas,* edited by Evon Z. Vogt, pp. 208–32. Colección de Antropología Social, vol. 7. México: Instituto Nacional Indigenista.

Bunzel, Ruth L.

1932   "Introduction to Zuni Ceremonialism." *47th Annual Report of the Bureau of American Ethnology for the Years 1929–1930,* pp. 467–44. Washington, D.C.: Smithsonian Institution.

1940   "The Role of Alcoholism in Two Central American Cultures." *Psychiatry* 3 (3): 361–87.

Buresch, Alexandra

1980   "The Great Seeing: Red, White, and Black in Zinacantan." A.B. honors thesis, Harvard University.

Burstein, John N.

1975   "The King Tales in Translation." A.B. honors thesis, Harvard University.

Calnek, Edward E.

1988   *Highland Chiapas Before the Spanish Conquest.* Papers of the New World Archaeological Foundation No. 55. Provo: Brigham Young University.

Cancian, Francesca M.

1963   "Family Interaction in Zinacantan." Ph.D. diss., Harvard University.

1964   "Interaction Patterns in Zinacanteco Families." *American Sociological Review* 29 (4): 540–50.

1966   "Patrones de Interacción en las Familias Zinacantecas." *Los Zinacantecos: Un Pueblo Tzotzil de los Altos de Chiapas,* edited by Evon Z. Vogt, pp. 251–74. Colección de Antropología Social, vol. 7. México: Instituto Nacional Indigenista.

1975   *What Are Norms? A Study of Beliefs and Action in a Maya Community.* Cambridge: Cambridge University Press.

Cancian, Frank

1963   "Economics and Prestige in a Maya Community: A Study of the Religious Cargo System in Zinacantan, Chiapas, Mexico." Ph.D. diss., Harvard University.

1965   *Economics and Prestige in a Maya Community: The Religious Cargo System in Zinacantan.* Stanford: Stanford University Press.

1967   "Political and Religious Organizations." *Social Anthropology of Middle America,* edited by Manning Nash, vol. 6 of *Handbook of Middle American Indians,* edited by Robert Wauchope, pp. 283–98. Austin: University of Texas Press.

1972   *Change and Uncertainty in a Peasant Economy: The Maya Corn Farmers of Zinacantan.* Stanford: Stanford University Press.

1974   *Another Place: Photographs of a Maya Community.* San Francisco: Scrimshaw Press.

1979   *The Innovator's Situation: Upper-Middle-Class Conservatism in Agricultural Communities.* Stanford: Stanford University Press.

1985   "The Boundaries of Rural Stratification Systems." *Micro and Macro Levels of Analysis in Anthropology: Issues in Theory and Research,* edited by Billie R. DeWalt and Pertti J. Pelto. Boulder, Colo.: Westview Press.

1992   *The Decline of Community in Zinacantan: The Economy, Public Life, and Social Stratification, 1950 to 1987.* Stanford: Stanford University Press.

Carey, Susan E.

1962   "Zinacantan's Ladinos." Summer Field Report, Harvard Chiapas Project, Peabody Museum, Harvard University.

Carson, Kenneth L.
1970   "Symbols and Beliefs from Maize Agriculture." Summer
            Field Report, Harvard Chiapas Project, Peabody Museum,
            Harvard University.
Casagrande, Joseph B.
1960   "Report on Visits to Field Sites." Unpublished ms., Harvard
            Chiapas Project, Peabody Museum, Harvard University.
Childs, Carla P.
1970   "Pattern Representation in Zinacantan." A.B. honors
            thesis, Harvard University.
Childs, Carla P., and Patricia M. Greenfield
1977   "Weaving, Color Terms and Pattern Representation: Cul-
            tural Influences and Cognitive Development among the
            Zinacantecos of Southern Mexico." *Inter-American Jour-
            nal of Psychology* 11: 23–48.
Clay, Jason W.
1971   "Final Report on the Paste' Pipeline." Summer Field Re-
            port, Harvard Chiapas Project, Peabody Museum, Har-
            vard University.
Clifford, James
1988   *The Predicament of Culture: Twentieth-Century Ethnog-
            raphy, Literature, and Art.* Cambridge: Harvard Univer-
            sity Press.
Clifford, James, and George Marcus
1986   *Writing Culture.* Berkeley: University of California Press.
Colby, B. N.
1960a   "Ethnic Relations in the Highlands of Chiapas, Mexico."
            Ph.D. diss., Harvard University.
1960b   "Social Relations and Directed Culture Change Among the
            Zinacantan." *Practical Anthropology* 7 (6): 241–50.
1961   "Indian Attitudes Toward Education and Inter-ethnic Con-
            tact in Mexico." *Practical Anthropology* 8 (2): 77–85.
1964   "Elements of a Mesoamerican Personality Pattern." *Actas
            y Memorias del 35th Congreso Internacional de American-
            istas, México 1962*, pp. 125–29.
1966   *Ethnic Relations in the Chiapas Highlands.* Santa Fe: Mu-
            seum of New Mexico Press.

1967   "Psychological Orientations." *Social Anthropology of Middle America,* edited by Manning Nash, vol. 6 of *Handbook of Middle American Indians,* edited by Robert Wauchope, pp. 416–31. Austin: University of Texas Press.

Colby, B. N., and Lore M. Colby

1981   *The Daykeeper: The Life and Discourse of an Ixil Diviner.* Cambridge: Harvard University Press.

Colby, B. N., and Pierre L. van den Berghe

1961a   "Ethnic Relations in Southeastern Mexico." *American Anthropologist* 63 (4): 772–93.

1961b   "Ladino-Indian Relations in the Highlands of Chiapas." *Social Forces* 40 (1): 63–71.

1969   *Ixil Country: A Plural Society in Highland Guatemala.* Berkeley: University of California Press.

Colby, Lore M.

1964   "Zinacantan Tzotzil Sound and Word Structure." Ph.D. diss., Harvard University.

1966   "Esquema de la Morfología Tzotzil." *Los Zinacantecos: Un Pueblo Tzotzil de Los Altos de Chiapas,* edited by Evon Z. Vogt, pp. 373–95. Colección de Antropología Social, vol. 7. México: Instituto Nacional Indigenista.

Collier, George A.

1960   "Zinacantecan Color Categories." Summer Field Report, Harvard Chiapas Project, Peabody Museum, Harvard University.

1963   "Zinacantecan Color Categories." A.B. honors thesis, Harvard University.

1966   "Categorías del Color en Zinacantan." *Los Zinacantecos: Un Pueblo Tzotzil de los Altos de Chiapas,* edited by Evon Z. Vogt, pp. 414–32. Colección de Antropología Social, vol. 7. México: Instituto Nacional Indigenista.

1968   "Land Inheritance and Land Use in a Modern Maya Community." Ph.D. diss., Harvard University.

1969   "Computer Processing of Genealogies and Analysis of Settlement Pattern." *Human Mosaic* 3: 133–41.

1974   "The Impact of Airphoto Technology on the Study of Demography and Ecology in Highland Chiapas." *Aerial*

Photography in Anthropological Field Research, edited by Evon Z. Vogt, pp. 78–93. Cambridge: Harvard University Press.

1975 Fields of the Tzotzil: The Ecological Bases of Tradition in Highland Chiapas. Austin: University of Texas Press.

1987 Socialists of Rural Andalusia. Stanford: Stanford University Press.

1989 "Changing Inequality in Zinacantan: The Generations of 1918 and 1942." Ethnographic Encounters in Southern Mesoamerica: Essays in Honor of Evon Z. Vogt, Jr., edited by Victoria R. Bricker and Gary H. Gossen, pp. 111–24. Austin: University of Texas Press.

Collier, Jane Fishburne

1960 "Some Aspects of the Division of Labor in a Zinacantecan Household." Summer Field Report, Harvard Chiapas Project, Peabody Museum, Harvard University.

1968 Courtship and Marriage in Zinacantan. Middle American Research Institute, publication 25, pp. 139–201. New Orleans: Tulane University. (Revision of A.B. honors thesis, Harvard University, 1962.)

1970 "Zinacanteco Law: A Study of Conflict in a Modern Maya Community." Ph.D. diss., Tulane University.

1973 Law and Social Change in Zinacantan. Stanford: Stanford University Press.

1976 "Political Leadership and Legal Change in Zinacantan." Law and Society Review 11: 131–63.

1988 Marriage and Inequality in Classless Societies. Stanford: Stanford University Press.

1989 "Whodunits and Whydunits: Contrasts Between American and Zinacanteco Stories of Conflict." Ethnographic Encounters in Southern Mesoamerica: Essays in Honor of Evon Z. Vogt, Jr., edited by Victoria R. Bricker and Gary H. Gossen, pp. 143–58. Austin: University of Texas Press.

Crump, Thomas

1977 "Boundaries in the Function of Money: Internal and External Debt in Selected Mexican Communities." Ph.D. diss., University of London.

1981   *The Phenomenon of Money.* London: Routledge and Kegan Paul.

1987   "The Alternative Economy of Alcohol in the Chiapas Highlands." *Constructive Drinking*, edited by Mary Douglas, pp. 239–49. Cambridge: Cambridge University Press.

1989   "Fiscal Systems of Highland Chiapas." *Ethnographic Encounters in Southern Mesoamerica: Essays in Honor of Evon Z. Vogt, Jr.*, edited by Victoria R. Bricker and Gary H. Gossen, pp. 133–42. Austin: University of Texas Press.

1990   *The Anthropology of Numbers.* Cambridge: Cambridge University Press.

1992a   *The Death of an Emperor: Japan at the Crossroads.* Cambridge: Cambridge University Press.

1992b   *The Japanese Numbers Game.* London: Routledge and Kegan Paul.

Cushing, Frank H.

1883   "Zuni Fetishes." *Second Annual Report of the Bureau of American Ethnology for the Years 1880–1881.* Washington, D.C.: Smithsonian Institution.

1896   "Outline of Zuni Creation Myths." *13th Annual Report of the Bureau of American Ethnology for the Years 1891–1892.* Washington, D.C.: Smithsonian Institution.

De Chavigny, Claude

1965   "Les Tisserands dans le Quartier des Mexicanos San Cristobal Las Casas." Summer Field Report, Harvard Chiapas Project, Peabody Museum, Harvard University.

Douglas, Andrew E.

1929   "The Secret of the Southwest Solved by Talkative Tree Rings." *National Geographic Magazine* 56 (6): 736–70.

Dozier, Edward P.

1955   "Forced and Permissive Acculturation." *American Indian* 7: 38–44.

Dunwell, Roger

1965   "Political Factions in Navenchauk." Summer Field Report, Harvard Chiapas Project, Peabody Museum, Harvard University.

Early, John D.

1965   "The Sons of San Lorenzo in Zinacantan." Ph.D. diss.,
        Harvard University.

1966   "El Ritual Zinacanteco en Honor del Senior Esquipu-
        las." *Los Zinacantecos: Un Pueblo Tzotzil de los Altos de
        Chiapas,* edited by Evon Z. Vogt, pp. 337–54. Colección
        de Antropología Social, vol. 7. México: Instituto Nacional
        Indigenista.

1982   *The Demographic Structure and Evolution of a Peasant
        System: The Guatemalan Population.* Gainesville: Univer-
        sity of Florida Presses.

Edel, Matthew D.

1966   "El Ejido en Zinacantan." *Los Zinacantecos: Un Pueblo
        Tzotzil de los Altos de Chiapas,* edited by Evon Z. Vogt, pp.
        163–82. Colección de Antropología Social, vol. 7. México:
        Instituto Nacional Indigenista

Edmonson, Munro S.

1957   *Los Manitos: A Study of Institutional Values.* Middle
        American Research Institute, publication 25, pp. 1–72.
        New Orleans: Tulane University Press.

1971   *The Book of Counsel: The Popul Vuh of the Quiche Maya
        of Guatemala.* Middle American Research Institute, publi-
        cation 35, pp. 1–273. New Orleans: Tulane University.

Edwards, Carolyn Pope

1988   (with Beatrice Blyth Whiting) *Children of Different
        Worlds: The Formation of Social Behavior.* Cambridge:
        Harvard University Press.

1989   "The Transition from Infancy to Early Childhood: A Diffi-
        cult Transition and a Difficult Theory." *Ethnographic En-
        counters in Southern Mesoamerica: Essays in Honor of
        Evon Z. Vogt, Jr.,* edited by Victoria R. Bricker and Gary H.
        Gossen, pp. 167–76. Austin: University of Texas Press.

Eggan, Fred

1950   *Social Organization of the Western Pueblos.* Chicago: Uni-
        versity of Chicago Press.

1954   "Social Anthropology and the Method of Controlled Com-
        parison." *American Anthropologist* 56(5): 743–63.

Epstein, Susan E.
1970   "Civil and Religious Officials in Chamula." Summer Field Report, Harvard Chiapas Project, Peabody Museum, Harvard University.

Fabrega, Horacio, Jr., and Daniel B. Silver
1973   *Illness and Shamanistic Curing in Zinacantan: An Ethnomedical Analysis.* Stanford: Stanford University Press.

Farriss, Nancy M.
1984   *Maya Society Under Colonial Rule: The Collective Enterprise of Survival.* Princeton: Princeton University Press.

Felsteiner, Mary Lowenthal
1963   "The Elite of San Cristobal." Summer Field Report, Harvard Chiapas Project, Peabody Museum, Harvard University.

Fewkes, J. Walter
1896   "The Prehistoric Culture of Tusayan." *American Anthropologist* 9 (5): 151–74.
1900   Tusayan Migration Traditions. *19th Annual Report of the Bureau of American Ethnology for the Years 1897–1898.* Washington: Smithsonian Institution.

Field, Denise Z.
1975   "With a Flower, With a Candle, With a Prayer: An Ethnography of Prayer in Zinacantan." A.B. honors thesis, Harvard University.

Fisher, Donald
1986   "Rockefeller Philanthropy and the Rise of Social Anthropology." *Anthropology Today* 1: 5–8.

Fløystrup, Benedicte
1964   "Settlement Patterns in Zinacantan in Relation to Kinship." Summer Field Report, Harvard Chiapas Project, Peabody Museum, Harvard University.

Fox, Richard G.
1991   *Recapturing Anthropology: Working in the Present.* Santa Fe: School of American Research Press.

Freeman, Susan Tax
1970   *Neighbors: The Social Contract in a Castilian Hamlet.* Chicago: University of Chicago Press.

1979   *The Pasiegos: Spaniards in No Man's Land.* Chicago: University of Chicago Press.

1989   "Notes from the Chiapas Project: Zinacantan, Summer 1959." *Ethnographic Encounters in Southern Mesoamerica: Essays in Honor of Evon Z. Vogt, Jr.,* edited by Victoria R. Bricker and Gary H. Gossen, pp. 89–100. Austin: University of Texas Press.

Freeman, William S.

1972   "Problems and Problem Areas in Zinacanteco Married Life." Summer Field Report, Harvard Chiapas Project, Peabody Museum, Harvard University.

1974   "The Lawyers of Zinacantan." A.B. honors thesis, Harvard University.

Gamio, Manuel

1922   *La Población del Valle de Teotihuacan,* 2 vols. México: Secretaría de Educación Publica.

Geertz, Clifford

1973   *The Interpretation of Cultures.* New York: Basic Books.

1988   *Works and Lives: The Anthropologist as Author.* Stanford: Stanford University Press.

Gelwan, Eliot M.

1972   "Some Considerations of Tzotzil-Tzeltal Ethnoastronomy." Summer Field Report, Harvard Chiapas Project, Peabody Museum, Harvard University.

Gilbert, Gordon A.

1961   "Indian-Ladino Relations in Restaurants in San Cristobal." Summer Field Report, Harvard Chiapas Project, Peabody Museum, Harvard University.

Gilman, Antonio

1964   "Municipio Organization." Summer Field Report, Harvard Chiapas Project, Peabody Museum, Harvard University.

Goldberg, Harvey

1961   "The Coheteros of San Cristobal." Summer Field Report, Harvard Chiapas Project, Peabody Museum, Harvard University.

Gonzalez Casanova, Pablo
  1969   *La Sociología de Explotación.* México: Siglo XXI.
Gossen, Gary H.
  1970   "Time and Space in Chamula Oral Tradition." Ph.D. diss.,
              Harvard University.
  1972   "Temporal and Spatial Equivalents in Chamula Ritual
              Symbolism." *Reader in Comparative Religion: An Anthro-
              pological Approach,* 3d ed., edited by William A. Lessa and
              Evon Z. Vogt, pp. 135–49. New York: Harper and Row.
  1974a   "Another Look at World View: Aerial Photography and
              Chamula Cosmology." *Aerial Photography in Anthropo-
              logical Field Research,* edited by Evon Z. Vogt, pp. 112–22.
              Cambridge: Harvard University Press.
  1974b   *Chamulas in the World of the Sun: Time and Space in
              a Maya Oral Tradition.* Cambridge: Harvard University
              Press.
  1975   "Animal Souls and Human Destiny in Chamula." *Man* 10
              (3): 448–61.
  1983   "Una Diáspora Maya Moderna: Deplazamiento y Persis-
              téncia Cultural de San Juan Chamula, Chiapas." *Meso-
              america* 5: 253–76.
  1985   "Tzotzil Literature." *Handbook of Middle American In-
              dians,* supp. 3, edited by Victoria R. Bricker and Munro S.
              Edmonson, pp. 64–106. Austin: University of Texas Press.
  1986   (editor) *Symbol and Meaning Beyond the Closed Commu-
              nity: Essays in Mesoamerican Ideas.* Institute for Meso-
              american Studies. Albany: Institute for Mesoamerican
              Studies, State University of New York.
  1989   "Life, Death, and Apotheosis of a Chamula Protestant
              Leader: Biography as Social History." *Ethnographic En-
              counters in Southern Mesoamerica: Essays in Honor of
              Evon Z. Vogt, Jr.,* edited by Victoria R. Bricker and Gary H.
              Gossen, pp. 217–30. Austin: University of Texas Press.
Greenfield, Patricia M., T. Berry Brazelton, and Carla P. Childs
  1989   "From Birth to Maturity in Zinacantan: Ontogenesis in
              Cultural Context." *Ethnographic Encounters in Southern
              Mesoamerica: Essays in Honor of Evon Z. Vogt, Jr.,* edited

by Victoria R. Bricker and Gary H. Gossen, pp. 177–216. Austin: University of Texas Press.

Greenfield, Patricia M., and Carla P. Childs

1977   "Understanding Sibling Concepts: A Developmental Study of Kin Terms in Zinacantan." *Cross-Cultural Contributions,* edited by P. Bassen, pp. 335–58. New York: Gardner Press.

1980   "Informal Modes of Learning and Teaching: The Case of Zinacanteco Weaving." *Studies in Cross-Cultural Psychology,* edited by N. Warren, 2: 269–316. New York: Academic Press.

Greenhouse, Carol J.

1970   "Preliminary Work on Liability in Cases of Beating in Zinacantan." Summer Field Report, Harvard Chiapas Project, Peabody Museum, Harvard University.

1971   "Litigant Choice: Non-Secular and Secular Sanctions in Zinacanteco Conflict Resolution." A.B. honors thesis, Harvard University.

1986   *Praying for Justice: Faith, Order, and Community in an American Town.* Ithaca: Cornell University Press.

1989   "Hopeful Masters: Cultural and Legal Pluralism in the United States." *Ethnographic Encounters in Southern Mesoamerica: Essays in Honor of Evon Z. Vogt, Jr.,* edited by Victoria R. Bricker and Gary H. Gossen, pp. 159–66. Austin: University of Texas Press.

Guarnaccia, Peter J.

1970   "Land-holding Patterns in Zinacantan Center." Summer Field Report, Harvard Chiapas Project, Peabody Museum, Harvard University.

1972   "Land and Tortillas: Land Reform in a Maya Indian Village in Chiapas." A.B. honors thesis, Harvard University.

Gudeman, Stephen F.

1961   "Toward a Model of the Highland Maya Economies." A.B. honors thesis, Harvard University.

1978   *The Demise of a Rural Economy.* London: Routledge and Kegan Paul.

1986   *Economics as Culture.* London: Routledge and Kegan Paul.
1990   (with Alberto Rivera) *Conversations in Columbia.* Cambridge: Cambridge University Press.

Guiteras-Holmes, Calixta

1961   *Perils of the Soul: The World View of a Tzotzil Indian.* Glencoe, Ill.: Free Press.

Gunder-Frank, Andre

1967   *Capitalism and Underdevelopment in Latin America.* New York: Monthly Review Press.

Haviland, John B.

1966   "*Vob:* Traditional Music in Zinacantan." Summer Field Report, Harvard Chiapas Project, Peabody Museum, Harvard University.

1977   "Gossip, Gossips, and Gossiping in Zinacantan: *K'al tana mu xpah slo'itael* (Gossip about him will never cease)." Ph.D. diss., Harvard University.

1977   *Gossip, Reputation, and Knowledge in Zinacantan.* Chicago: University of Chicago Press.

1981   *Sk'op Sotz'leb: El Tzotzil de San Lorenzo Zinacantan.* Centro de Estudios Mayas. México: Universidad Nacional Autónoma de México.

1986   "Creating Ritual: Holy Week in the Lake of Thunder." Unpublished ms. Stanford: Center for Advanced Study in the Behavioral Sciences.

1989   "They Had a Very Great Many Photographs." *Ethnographic Encounters in Southern Mesoamerica: Essays in Honor of Evon Z. Vogt, Jr.,* edited by Victoria R. Bricker and Gary H. Gossen, pp. 33–50. Austin: University of Texas Press.

Haviland, Leslie K. M.

1978   "The Social Relations of Work in a Peasant Community." Ph.D. diss., Harvard University.

Hawkins, John

1984   *Inverse Images: The Meaning of Culture, Ethnicity and Family in Postcolonial Guatemala.* Albuquerque: University of New Mexico Press.

Hewitt de Alcantara, Cynthia
1984   *Anthropological Perspectives on Rural Mexico.* London: Routledge and Kegan Paul.
Hiatt, Jonathan P.
1968   "The Social Structure and Politics of Rancho San Nicolas." Summer Field Report, Harvard Chiapas Project, Peabody Museum, Harvard University.
Holland, William R.
1963   *Medicina Maya en los Altos de Chiapas: Un Estudio del Cambio Socio-Cultural.* Colección de Antropología Social, vol. 2. México: Instituto Nacional Indigenista.
Howry, Jeffrey C.
1976   "Fires on the Mountain: Ceramic Traditions and Marketing in the Highlands of Chiapas, Mexico." Ph.D. diss., Harvard University.
Jensen, Kelly T.
1976   "The Maya Farmer, Ancient and Modern." A.B. honors thesis, Harvard University.
Kaplan, Bert
1954   "A Study of Rorschach Responses in Four Cultures." Papers of the Peabody Museum of American Archaeology and Ethnology 42 (2). Cambridge: Harvard University.
Kazen, Felisa M.
1972   "Sociocultural Aspects of Development; A Case Study of the Introduction of a Textile Factory into a Community in Southern Mexico." Ph.D. diss., Harvard University.
Kidder, Alfred V.
1927   "Southwestern Archeological Conference." *Science* 66 (1716): 489–91.
Kluckhohn, Clyde
1951   "Values and Value-Orientations in the Theory of Action." *Toward a General Theory of Action,* edited by Talcott Parsons and Edward A. Shils, pp. 388–433. Cambridge: Harvard University Press.
1952   "Universal Values and Anthropological Relativism." *Modern Education and Human Values.* Pitcairn-Crabbe Foun-

dation Lecture Series, vol. 4, pp. 87–112. Pittsburgh: University of Pittsburgh Press.

1956   "Toward a Comparison of Value-Emphases in Different Cultures." *The State of the Social Sciences,* edited by Leonard D. White, pp. 116–32. Chicago: University of Chicago Press.

1958   "The Scientific Study of Values and Contemporary Civilization." Proceedings of the American Philosophical Society 102: 469–72. Philadelphia, Pennsylvaina.

1959   "The Scientific Study of Values." *Three Lectures.* University of Toronto Installation Lectures. Toronto: University of Toronto Press.

Kluckhohn, Florence, and Fred L. Strodtbeck

1961   *Variations in Value-Orientations: A Theory Tested in Five Cultures.* Evanston, Ill.: Row, Peterson.

Köhler, Ulrich

1977   *Conbilal C'ulelal.* Wiesbadan: Franz Steiner Verlag GMBH.

Krebs, Stephanie L.

1967   "Shunka's Story." 16 mm., 20 min. Harvard Chiapas Project, Peabody Museum, Harvard University.

Lacy, Sara J.

1976   *"Antel:* An Essay." A.B. honors thesis, Harvard University.

Ladd, John

1957   *The Structure of a Moral Code: A Philosophical Analysis of Ethical Discourse Applied to the Ethics of the Navaho Indians.* Cambridge: Harvard University Press.

Landgraf, John L.

1954   *Land-Use in the Ramah Area of New Mexico: An Anthropological Approach.* Papers of the Peabody Museum of American Archaeology and Ethnology 42 (1). Cambridge: Harvard University.

Laughlin, Robert M.

1962   "El Símbolo de la Flor en la Religión de Zinacantan." *Estudios de Cultura Maya* 2: 123–39.

1963   "Through the Looking Glass: Reflections on Zinacantan Courtship and Marriage." Ph.D. diss., Harvard University.

1971 "In the Beginning: A Tale from the Mazatec." *Alcheringa: Ethnopoetics* 2: 37–52.

1975 *The Great Tzotzil Dictionary of San Lorenzo Zinacantan.* Smithsonian Contributions to Anthropology 19. Washington, D.C.: Smithsonian Institution Press.

1976 *Of Wonders Wild and New: Dreams from Zinacantan.* Smithsonian Contributions to Anthropology 22. Washington, D.C.: Smithsonian Institution Press.

1978 *Of Cabbages and Kings: Tales from Zinacantan.* Smithsonian Contributions to Anthropology 23. Washington, D.C.: Smithsonian Institution Press.

1980 *Of Shoes and Ships and Sealing Wax: Sundries from Zinacantan.* Smithsonian Contributions to Anthropology 25. Washington, D.C.: Smithsonian Institution Press.

1988 (with John B. Haviland) *The Great Tzotzil Dictionary of Santo Domingo Zinacantan.* 2 vols. Smithsonian Contributions to Anthropology 31. Washington, D.C.: Smithsonian Institution Press.

1989 "As For Me and the Harvard Chiapas Project." *Ethnographic Encounters in Southern Mesoamerica: Essays in Honor of Evon Z. Vogt, Jr.,* edited by Victoria R. Bricker and Gary H. Gossen, pp. 51–72. Austin: University of Texas Press.

Laughlin, Robert M., and Carol Karasik

1988 *The People of the Bat: Mayan Tales and Dreams from Zinacantan.* Washington, D.C.: Smithsonian Institution Press.

Lessa, William A., and Evon Z. Vogt (editors)

1958 *Reader in Comparative Religion: An Anthropological Approach.* Evanston, Ill.: Row, Peterson.

Levi, Jerome M.

1988 "Myth and History Reconsidered: Archaeological Implications of Tzotzil-Maya Mythology." *American Antiquity* 53 (3): 605–19.

1989 "The Social Ecology of Ethnic Differentiation in the Sierra Tarahumara and Chiapas Highlands." *Ethnographic Encounters in Southern Mesoamerica: Essays in Honor of*

Evon Z. Vogt, Jr., edited by Victoria R. Bricker and Gary H. Gossen, pp. 303–20. Austin: University of Texas Press.

Levine, Susan P.

1968   "A Study of *Barrio* Organization: San Cristobal Las Casas, Chiapas, Mexico." Summer Field Report, Harvard Chiapas Project, Peabody Museum, Harvard University.

Linn, Priscilla Rachun

1977   "The Religious Office Holders in Chamula: A Study of Gods, Ritual, and Sacrifice." 2 vols. D.Phil. diss., Oxford University.

1982   "Chamula Carnival: The "Soul" of Celebration." *Celebration: Studies in Festivity and Ritual,* edited by Victor Turner, 190–98. Washington, D.C.: Smithsonian Institution Press.

1989   "Souls and Selves in Chamula: A Thought on Individuals, Fatalism, and Denial." *Ethnographic Encounters in Southern Mesoamerica: Essays in Honor of Evon Z. Vogt, Jr.,* edited by Victoria R. Bricker and Gary H. Gossen, pp. 251–62. Austin: University of Texas Press.

Locke, Nancy

1964   "A Case Study in Mexican Conservatism: Why the Capital of Chiapas Was Moved from San Cristobal to Tuxtla Gutierrez." A.B. honors thesis, Smith College.

Logan, M. Haven

1966   "The Process of Ladinoization in San Cristobal Las Casas, Mexico." Summer Field Report, Harvard Chiapas Project, Peabody Museum, Harvard University.

Lumholtz, Carl

1902   *Unknown Mexico.* 2 vols. New York: Charles Scribner's Sons.

Lynch, Patrice E.

1971   "Gender Roles in Zinacantan." Summer Field Report, Harvard Chiapas Project, Peabody Museum, Harvard University.

McAllester, David P.

1954   *Enemy Way Music: A Study of Social and Esthetic Values as Seen in Navaho Music.* Papers of the Peabody Museum of

American Archaeology and Ethnology 41 (3). Cambridge: Harvard University.

McCombe, Leonard, Evon Z. Vogt, and Clyde Kluckhohn.
1951   *Navaho Means People*. Cambridge: Harvard University Press.

McFeat, Tom F. S.
1960   "Some Social and Spatial Aspects of Innovation at Zuni." *Anthropológica* 2(1): 18–47.

McQuown, Norman A. and Julian Pitt-Rivers
1970   *Ensayos de Antropología en la Zona Central de Chiapas*. México: Instituto Nacional Indigenista.

McVay, Cynthia, and Evon Z. Vogt
1988   "Some Contours of Social Class in a Southern Mexican Town." *Ethnology* 27 (1): 27–44.

McVicker, Donald E.
1972   "A Preliminary Archaeological Survey of the Municipio of Zinacantan, Chiapas, Mexico." Summer Field Report, Harvard Chiapas Project, Peabody Museum, Harvard University.
1974   "Variation in Protohistoric Maya Settlement Patterns." *American Antiquity* 39 (4): 546–56.

Maduro, Ron
1962   "Schools in San Cristobal Las Casas, Mexico." Summer Field Report, Harvard Chiapas Project, Peabody Museum, Harvard University.

Marcus, George, and Michael Fischer
1986   *Anthropology as Cultural Critique: An Experimental Moment in the Human Sciences*. Chicago: University of Chicago Press.

Menget, Patrick
1968   "Murder and Death in Chamula." *Natural History: Journal of the American Museum of Natural History* 77 (1): 48–57.

Merkel, Judith E.
1967   "Chamula Curing." Summer Field Report, Harvard Chiapas Project, Peabody Museum, Harvard University.

Metzger, Barbara
1960   "Notes on the History of Indian-Ladino Relations in Chiapas." Unpublished ms., Harvard Chiapas Project, Peabody Museum, Harvard University.

Miller, Frank C.
1959   "Social Structure and Medical Change in a Mexican Indian Community." Ph.D. diss., Harvard University.
1960   "The Influence of Decision-Making on the Process of Change: The Case of Yalcuc." *Alpha Kappa Deltan* 21 (1): 29–35.
1964   "Tzotzil Domestic Groups." *Journal of the Royal Anthropological Institute of Great Britain and Ireland* 94 (2): 172–83.
1965   "Cultural Change as Decision-Making: A Tzotzil Example." *Ethnology* 4 (1): 53–66.
1973   *Old Villages and a New Town: Industrialization in Mexico.* Prospect Heights, Ill.: Waveland Press.

Mills, George
1959   *Navaho Art and Culture.* Colorado Springs: Taylor Museum.

Mindeleff, Cosmos
1897   "The Cliff Ruins of Canyon de Chelley, Arizona." *16th Annual Report of the Bureau of American Ethnology for the Years 1894–1895.* Washington, D.C.: Smithsonian Institution.

Mindeleff, Victor
1891   "A Study of Pueblo Architecture in Tusayan and Cibola." *8th Annual Report of the Bureau of American Ethnology for the Years 1886–1887.* Washington, D.C.: Smithsonian Institution.

Miyamoto, John M.
1967   "Ritual Objects: Their Pre-Fiesta Logistics." Summer Field Report, Harvard Chiapas Project, Peabody Museum, Harvard University.
1969   "Cognitive Equivalence in Zinacantan." A.B. honors thesis, Harvard University.

Natelson, Abigail S.
  1967   "Clothing Norms in Zinacantan and Chamula." Summer
            Field Report, Harvard Chiapas Project, Peabody Museum,
            Harvard University.
Nigh, Ronald Byron
  1976   "Evolutionary Ecology of Maya Agriculture in Highland
            Chiapas, Mexico." Ph.D. diss., Stanford University.
Ochiai, Kazuyasu
  1985   *Cuando los Santos Vienen Marchando: Rituales Públicos
            Intercomunitarios Tzotziles.* San Cristobal Las Casas: Uni-
            versidad Autónoma de Chiapas.
  1989   *Meanings Performed, Symbols Read: Anthropological
            Studies in Latin America.* Performance in Culture, no. 5.
            Institute for the Study of Languages and Cultures of Asia
            and Africa. Tokyo: Tokyo University of Foreign Studies.
O'Dea, Thomas F.
  1957   *The Mormons.* Chicago: University of Chicago Press.
Orlove, Benjamin S.
  1977   *Alpacas, Sheep, and Men: The Wool Export Economy
            and Regional Society in Southern Peru.* New York: Aca-
            demic Press.
Ortner, Sherry
  1984   "Theory in Anthropology Since the 1960s." *Comparative
            Studies in Society and History* 26: 126–66.
Paradise, Thomas L.
  1974   "Land Tenure in Peteh." A.B. honors thesis, Harvard Uni-
            versity.
Parsons, Elsie Clews
  1939   *Pueblo Indian Religion.* 2 vols. Chicago: University of Chi-
            cago Press.
Parsons, Talcott, and Edward A. Shils (editors)
  1952   *Toward a General Theory of Action.* Cambridge: Harvard
            University Press.
Patterson, Thomas C.
  1986   "The Last Sixty Years: Toward a Social History of Ameri-
            canist Archaeology in the United States." *American An-
            thropologist* 88(1): 7–26.

Pauker, Guy J.
1966   "Political Structure." *People of Rimrock: A Study of Values in Five Cultures,* edited by Evon Z. Vogt and Ethel M. Albert, pp. 191–226. Cambridge: Harvard University Press.

Pellizzi, Francesco
1972   "Chickens and Other Bipeds: Miscellaneous Notes on the 'Great Vision' Healing Ceremonies." Unpublished ms., Harvard Chiapas Project, Peabody Museum, Harvard University.
1981   "Misioneros y Cargos: Notas Sobre Identidad y Aculturación en los Altos de Chiapas." *America Indígena* 42 (1): 7–33.

Pirrotta, Adelaide
1961   "The Economic Role of Women in San Felipe." Summer Field Report, Harvard Chiapas Project, Peabody Museum, Harvard University.

Plattner, Stuart
1969   "Peddlers, Pigs, and Profits: Itinerant Trading in Southeast Mexico." Ph.D. diss., Stanford University.

Pope, Carolyn C.
1967   "Food for the Soul: Cemeteries in Zinacantan." Summer Field Report, Harvard Chiapas Project, Peabody Museum, Harvard University.
1969   "The Funeral Ceremony in Zinacantan." A.B. honors thesis, Harvard University.

Powell, John Wesley
1891   "Indian Linguistic Families of America North of Mexico." *7th Annual Report of the Bureau of American Ethnology for the Years 1885–1886,* pp. 1–142. Washington, D.C.: Smithsonian Institution.

Pozas, Ricardo
1959   *Chamula: Un Pueblo Indio de Los Altos de Chiapas.* Memorias del Instituto Nacional Indigenista 8. México.

Price, Richard
1965   "Trial Marriage in the Andes." *Ethnology* 4(3): 310–22.

1970 "Aspects of Social Organization in a Maya Hamlet." *Estudios de Cultura Maya*, vol. 8: 297–318. México: Universidad Nacional Autónoma de México.

1974a "Aerial Photography in the Study of Land Use: A Maya Example." *Aerial Photography in Anthropological Field Research*, edited by Evon Z. Vogt, pp. 94–111. Cambridge: Harvard University Press.

1974b *Saramaka Social Structure*. Institute of Caribbean Studies. San Juan: University of Puerto Rico.

1976 *The Guiana Maroons: A Historical and Bibliographical Introduction*. Baltimore: Johns Hopkins University Press.

1983 *First Time: The Historical Vision of an Afro-American People*. Baltimore: Johns Hopkins University Press.

Price, Sally H.

1966 "I Was Pashku and My Husband Was Telesh." *Radcliffe Quarterly* 50: 4–8.

1984 *Co-Wives and Calabashes*. Ann Arbor: University of Michigan Press.

Prokosch, Eric

1969 "Government in Indian Communities in the Chiapas Highland, Mexico." Ph.D. diss., Stanford University

Rakoff, Todd D.

1965 "Time Patterns in Zinacantan." Summer Field Report, Harvard Chiapas Project, Peabody Museum, Harvard University.

Rapoport, Robert N.

1954 *Changing Navaho Religious Values: A Study of Christian Missions to the Rimrock Navaho*. Papers of the Peabody Museum of American Archaeology and Ethnology 41 (2). Cambridge: Harvard University.

Redfield, Robert

1955 *The Little Community: Viewpoints for the Study of a Human Whole*. Chicago: University of Chicago Press.

Redfield, Robert, and Alfonso Villa Rojas

1934 *Chan Kom: A Maya Village*. Chicago: University of Chicago Press.

Reed, Roger H.
1973   "Chamula and the Coffee Plantations of Chiapas." A.B. honors thesis, Harvard University.

Ritvo, Rachel Z.
1972   "Christ and His Brothers as Reflections of the Developing Child." A.B. honors thesis, Harvard University.

Roberts, John M.
1956   *Zuni Daily Life*. Notebook no. 3, Laboratory of Anthropology. Lincoln: University of Nebraska.

Roof, Stephen L.
1980   "Cultural Brokers, Factionalism, and Modernization in Zinacantan." A.B. honors thesis, Harvard University.

Rosaldo, Michelle Zimbalist
1980   *Knowledge and Passion: Ilongot Notions of Self and Social Life*. Cambridge: Cambridge University Press.

Rosaldo, Renato, Jr.
1968   "Metaphors of Hierarchy in a Mayan Ritual." *American Anthropologist* 70 (3): 524–36.
1980   *Ilongot Headhunting 1883–1974*. Stanford: Stanford University Press.
1986   *Culture and Truth: The Making of Social Analysis*. Boston: Beacon Press.

Rosenberg, Mark L.
1967   "Whichdoctor for Zinacantan: The Social Basis for Medical Change." Summer Field Report, Harvard Chiapas Project, Peabody Museum, Harvard University.
1968   "Zinacantan Which Doctor?" *Harvard Medical Alumni Bulletin* 42 (3): 12–16.

Rosenblatt, Rand E.
1964   "Law and Ideology in Chamula." Summer Field Report, Harvard Chiapas Project, Peabody Museum, Harvard University.

Rus, Jan, III
1969   "Pottery Making in Chamula." A.B. honors thesis, Harvard University.

Rus, Jan, III, and Robert F. Wasserstrom
1980   "Civil-Religious Hierarchies in Central Chiapas: A Critical Perspective." *American Ethnologist* 7 (3): 466–78.

Rush, Timothy N.

1969a   "Navenchauk Politics." Summer Field Report, Harvard Chiapas Project, Peabody Museum, Harvard University.

1969b   "Digging for Bells in the Highlands of Chiapas." Summer Field Report, Harvard Chiapas Project, Peabody Museum, Harvard University.

1971   "Navenchauk Disputes: The Social Basis of Factions in a Mexican Indian Village." A.B. honors thesis, Harvard University.

Salovesh, Michael

1979   "Looking Beyond the Municipio in Chiapas: Problems and Prospects in Studying Up." *Currents in Anthropology: Essays in Anthropology in Honor of Sol Tax,* edited by Robert Hinshaw. The Hague: Mouton.

Sanday, Peggy Reeves

1981   *Female Power and Male Dominance.* Cambridge: Cambridge University Press.

1986   *Divine Hunger: Cannibalism as a Cultural System.* Cambridge: Cambridge University Press.

1990   *Fraternity Gang Rape.* New York: New York University Press.

Schneider, David M., and John M. Roberts

1956   *Zuni Kin Terms.* Notebook no. 3, Laboratory of Anthropology. Lincoln: University of Nebraska.

Schroeder, Albert H.

1979   "History of Archaeological Research". Vol. 9 on the *Southwest,* edited by Alfonso Ortiz, *Handbook of North American Indians,* edited by William C. Sturtevant, pp. 5–13. Washington, D.C.: Smithsonian Institution.

Shweder, Richard A.

1972   "Aspects of Cognition in Zinacanteco Shamans: Experimental Results." *Reader in Comparative Religion: An Anthropological Approach,* edited by William A. Lessa and Evon Z. Vogt, pp. 407–12. New York: Harper and Row.

1991   *Thinking Through Cultures.* Cambridge: Harvard University Press.

Silver, Daniel B.

1966a   "Shamanism in Zinacantan." Ph.D. diss., Harvard University.

1966b   "Enfermedad y Curación en Zinacantan." *Los Zinacantecos: Un Pueblo Tzotzil de los Altos de Chiapas,* edited by Evon Z. Vogt, pp. 455–73. Colección de Antropología Social, vol. 7. México: Instituto Nacional Indigenista

Siskel, Suzanne E.

1974   "With the Spirit of a Jaguar: A Study of Shamanism in *Ichin Ton,* Chamula." A.B. honors thesis, Harvard University.

Skinner, G. William

1964   "Marketing and Social Structure in Rural China, Part 1." *Journal of Asian Studies* 24 (1): 363–99.

1965   "Marketing and Social Structure in Rural China, Part 2." *Journal of Asian Studies* 24 (2): 195–228.

Smith, Carol A.

1978   "Beyond Dependency Theory: National and Regional Patterns of Underdevelopment in Guatemala." *American Ethnologist* 5(3): 574–617.

Smith, Lars C.

1970   "Making a Living in *Lomo:* The Consequences of Economic Change in a Maya Community." Summer Field Report, Harvard Chiapas Project, Peabody Museum, Harvard University.

Smith, Waldemar R.

1977   *The Fiesta System and Economic Change.* New York: Columbia University Press.

Smith, Watson, and John M. Roberts

1954   *Zuni Law: A Field of Values.* Papers of the Peabody Museum of American Archaeology and Ethnology 43(1). Cambridge: Harvard University.

Spencer, Katherine

1957   "Mythology and Values: An Analysis of Navaho Chantway Myths." *Journal of American Folklore,* Memoirs 48.

Spicer, Edward H.

1961   *Perspectives in American Indian Culture Change.* Chicago: University of Chicago Press.

Spier, Leslie

1928 Havasupai Ethnography. *Anthropological Papers of the American Museum of Natural History* 29 (3). New York.

Starr, Betty W.

1954 "Levels of Communal Relations." *The American Journal of Sociology* 60: 125–35.

Stauder, Jack R.

1961 "Zinacantecos in Hot Country." Summer Field Report, Harvard Chiapas Project, Peabody Museum, Harvard University.

1971 *The Majangir: Ecology and Society of a Southwest Ethiopian People.* Cambridge: Cambridge University Press.

Stavenhagen, Rodolfo

1969 *Las Clases Sociales en las Sociedades Agrárias.* México: Siglo XXI.

1970 "Classes, Colonialism, and Acculturation: A System of Interethnic Relations in Mesoamerica." *Masses in Latin America,* edited by Irving L. Horowitz. New York: Oxford University Press.

Stevenson, Matilda Coxe

1904 "The Zuni Indians: Their Mythology, Esoteric Fraternities, and Ceremonies." *23d Annual Report of the Bureau of American Ethnology for the Years 1901–1902.* Washington, D.C.: Smithsonian Institution.

Strodt, Barbara S.

1965 "Household Economy in Zinacantan." Summer Field Report, Harvard Chiapas Project, Peabody Museum, Harvard University.

Strucker, John D.

1964 "Ten Days in the INI School in the Paraje of Yalichin, Chamula." Summer Field Report, Harvard Chiapas Project, Peabody Museum, Harvard University.

Stubblefield, Phillip G.

1961 "Medical Beliefs and Practices, and Disease Terminology in a Tzeltal Village." Summer Field Report, Harvard Chiapas Project, Peabody Museum, Harvard University.

Sutton, Ricardo D.
1972   "The Highland Agricultural Situation of Chamula." Summer Field Report, Harvard Chiapas Project, Peabody Museum, Harvard University.

Tax, Sol
1937   "The Municipios of the Midwestern Highlands of Guatemala." *American Anthropologist* 39(3): 423–44.

Tax, Susan
1962   "Weaving in Zinacantan." Summer Field Report, Harvard Chiapas Project, Peabody Museum, Harvard University.
1964   "Displacement Activity in Zinacantan." *America Indígena* 24(2): 111–21.

Taylor, Julie M.
1979   *Eva Peron: The Myths of a Woman.* Chicago: University of Chicago Press.

Tedlock, Barbara
1991   "Participant Observation to the Observation of Participation: The Emergence of Narrative Ethnography." *Journal of Anthropological Research* 47 (1): 69–94.

Telling, Irving
1952   "New Mexican Frontiers: A Social History of the Gallup Area, 1881–1900." Ph.D. diss., Harvard University.
1953   "Ramah, New Mexico, 1876–1900: An Historical Episode with Some Value Analysis." *Utah Historical Quarterly,* (April): 117–36.
1954   "Coolidge and Thoreau: Forgotten Frontier Towns." *New Mexican Historical Review* 29: 210–23.

Thomsen, Evelyn R.
1966   "How to Handle an Earth Lord: An Analysis of the Myths, Prayers, and Rituals which Focus on the Waterholes of Zinacantan." A.B. honors thesis, Vassar College.

Trosper, Ronald L.
1966   "Lending in Apas." Summer Field Report, Harvard Chiapas Project, Peabody Museum, Harvard University.
1967a   "Schools and Schooling in Zinacantan." Summer Field Report, Harvard Chiapas Project, Peabody Museum, Harvard University.

1967b   "Tradition and Economic Growth in Zinacantan: Gradual Change in a Mexican Indian Community." A.B. honors thesis, Harvard University.

Turok, Marta D.

1972   "Handicrafts: A Case Study of Weaving in the Highlands." Summer Field Report, Harvard Chiapas Project, Peabody Museum, Harvard University.

1974   "Symbolic Analysis of Contemporary Mayan Textiles: The Ceremonial *Huipil* from Magdalena, Chiapas, Mexico." Unpublished ms., Harvard Chiapas Project, Peabody Museum, Harvard University.

Untereiner, Wayne W.

1952   "Self and Society: Orientations in Two Cultural Value Systems." Ph.D. diss., Harvard University.

Uribe-Wood, Elena

1979   "Compadrazgo in Apas." Ph.D. diss., Harvard University.

1982   *Compadrazgo en Apas*. México: Instituto Nacional Indigenista.

Van den Berghe, Gwendoline

1965   "Compadrazgo Among the Ladino Population of San Cristobal Las Casas." Summer Field Report, Harvard Chiapas Project, Peabody Museum, Harvard University.

1970   "Contribution a L'Etude Social et Culturelle de las Classe Haute Peruvienne." Ph.D. diss., University of Paris, Faculté des Lettres et Sciences Humaines.

Van den Berghe, Gwendoline, and Pierre E. van den Berghe

1966   "Compadrazgo and Class in Southeastern Mexico." *American Anthropologist* 68 (5): 1236–44.

Villa Rojas, Alfonso

1945   *The Maya of East Central Quintana Roo*. Publication 559. Washington, D.C.: The Carnegie Institution of Washington, publication 559.

1947   "Kinship and Nagualism in a Tzeltal Community, Southeastern Mexico." *American Anthropologist* 49 (4): 578–87.

Vogt, Evon Z.

1947   "Social Stratification in the Rural Middlewest: A Structural Analysis." *Rural Sociology* 12 (4): 364–75.

1949   "Town and Country: The Structure of Rural Life." *Democracy in Jonesville*, edited by W. Lloyd Warner, pp. 236–65. New York: Harpers and Brothers.

1951   *Navaho Veterans: A Study of Changing Values*. Papers of the Peabody Museum of American Archaeology and Ethnology 41(1). Cambridge: Harvard University.

1955a   "Some Aspects of Cora-Huichol Acculturation." *America Indígena* 15 (4): 249–63.

1955b   *Modern Homesteaders: Life in a 20th Century Frontier Community*. Cambridge: Harvard University Press, Belknap Press.

1957   "The Acculturation of the American Indians" *Annals of the American Academy of Political and Social Science*, 311 (May): 137–46.

1961   "Some Aspects of Zinacantan Settlement Patterns and Ceremonial Organization" *Estudios de Cultura Maya* l: 131–45. México: Universidad Nacional Autónoma de México.

1964a   "Ancient Maya Concepts in Contemporary Zinacantan Religion." *Vie Congress International des Sciences Anthropologiques et Ethnologiques*, 2: 497–502, Paris.

1964b   "Some Implications of Zinacantan Social Structure for the Study of the Ancient Maya." *Actas y Memorias del XXXV Congreso Internacional de Americanistas*, 1: 307–19, México.

1964c   "Ancient Maya and Contemporary Tzotzil Cosmology: A Comment on Some Methodological Problems." *American Antiquity* 30 (2): 192–95.

1964d   "The Genetic Model and Maya Cultural Development." *Desarrollo Cultural de los Mayas*, edited by Evon Z. Vogt and Alberto Ruz Lhuiller. Seminario de Cultura Maya, México, pp. 9–48.

1964e   "Summary and Appraisal." *Desarrollo Cultural de los Mayas*, edited by Evon Z. Vogt and Alberto Ruz Lhuiller. Seminario de Cultura Maya, México, pp. 385–403.

1965a   "Ceremonial Organization in Zinacantan." *Ethnology*, 5 (1): 39–52.

1965b   "Structural and Conceptual Replication in Zinacantan Culture." *American Anthropologist* 67 (2): 342–53.

1965c   "Zinacanteco 'Souls'" *Man* 29: 33–35.

1966a   "Ancestor Worship in Zinacantan Religion." *36 Congreso Internacional de Americanistas*, 3 (Sevilla): 281–85.

1966b   "H'iloletik: The Organization and Function of Shamanism in Zinacantan." *Antropología de Mesoamerica*. Homenaje al Ing. Roberto J. Weitlaner, México, pp. 359–69.

1966c   "Some Implications of Weather Modification for the Cultural Patterns of Tribal Societies." *Human Dimensions of Weather Modification*, edited by W. R. Derrick Sewell. University of Chicago Department of Geography Series, paper no. 105, pp. 373–92.

1966d   (editor) *Los Zinacantecos: Un Pueblo Tzotzil de los Altos de Chiapas*, Colección de Antropología Social, vol. 7. México: Instituto Nacional Indigenista.

1967   "Tendéncia de Cambio en las Tierras Altas de Chiapas." *America Indígena* 27 (2): 199–222.

1968a   "Penny Capitalists or Tribal Ritualists?—The Relationship of Market Behavior to Ceremonial Life in a Modern Maya Community." *Proceedings, 8th International Congress of Anthropological and Ethnological Sciences*, 2: 243–44. Tokyo and Kyoto, Japan.

1968b   "Recurrent and Directional Processes in Zinacantan." *Actas y Memorias del 37 Congreso Internacional de Americanistas*, 1: 441–47, Buenos Aires, Argentina.

1969a   (editor) *Ethnology of Middle America*, vols. 7 and 8 of *Handbook of Middle American Indians*, edited by Robert Wauchope. Austin: University of Texas Press.

1969b   *Zinacantan: A Maya Community in the Highlands of Chiapas*. Cambridge: Harvard University Press, Belknap Press.

1970a   "Human Souls and Animal Spirits in Zinacantan." *Echanges et Communications, Melanges Offerts a Claude Levi-Strauss a l'Occasion de son 60eme Anniversaire*, edited by Pierre Maranda and Jean Pouillon, pp. 1148–67. The Hague: Mouton.

1970b   *The Zinacantecos of Mexico: A Modern Maya Way of Life.*
         New York: Holt, Rinehart and Winston.

1971   Addendum to "Summary and Appraisal." *Desarrollo Cultural de los Mayas,* edited by Evon Z. Vogt and Alberto Ruz Lhuiller, 2d edition, pp. 428–47. México: Universidad Nacional Autónoma de México.

1973   "Gods and Politics in Zinacantan and Chamula." *Ethnology* 12 (2): 99–114.

1974   *Aerial Photography in Anthropological Field Research,* edited by Evon Z. Vogt. Cambridge: Harvard University Press.

1976   *Tortillas for the Gods: A Symbolic Analysis of Zinacanteco Rituals.* Cambridge: Harvard University Press.

1977   "On the Symbolic Meaning of Percussion in Zinacanteco Ritual." *Journal of Anthropological Research* 33 (3): 231–44.

1978a   "Town (Cabecera) Planning in the Chiapas Highlands." *Codex Wauchope: A Tribute Roll,* edited by Marco Giardino, Barbara Edmonson, and Winifred Creamer. *Human Mosaic* 12: 65–72. New Orleans: Tulane University.

1978b   *Bibliography of the Harvard Chiapas Project: The First Twenty Years, 1957–1977.* Cambridge: Peabody Museum of Archaeology and Ethnology, Harvard University.

1979   "The Harvard Chiapas Project: 1957–1975." *Long-Term Field Research in Social Anthropology,* edited by George M. Foster, Thayer Scudder, Elizabeth Colson, and Robert V. Kemper, pp. 279–303. New York: Academic Press.

1981   "Some Aspects of the Sacred Geography of Highland Chiapas." *Mesoamerican Sites and World Views,* edited by Elizabeth P. Benson, pp. 119–42. Washington, D.C.: Dumbarton Oaks.

1982   "Tendéncias de Cambio Social y Cultural en los Altos de Chiapas." *America Indígena* 42 (1): 85–98.

1983   "Ancient and Contemporary Maya Settlement Patterns: A New Look from the Chiapas Highlands." *Prehistoric Settlement Patterns: Essays in Honor of Gordon R. Willey,* edited by Evon Z. Vogt and Richard M. Leventhal, pp. 89–114. Albuquerque: University of New Mexico Press.

1985   "The Chiapas Writers' Cooperative." *Cultural Survival Quarterly* 9 (3): 46–48.
1990   *The Zinacantecos of Mexico: A Modern Maya Way of Life.* 2d edition. Ft. Worth: Holt, Rinehart and Winston.
1992a   "Cruces Indias y Bastones de Mando en Mesoamerica." *De Palabra y Obra en el Nuevo Mundo 2: Encuentros Interetnicas,* edited by Manuel Gutierrez Estevez, Miguel Leon-Portilla, Gary H. Gossen, and J. Jorge Klor de Alba, pp. 249–294. Madrid: Siglo XXI de Espana Editores, S.A. Mexico: Siglo XXI Editores.
1992b   "The Persistence of Tradition in Zinacantan." *The Ancient Americas: Art from Sacred Landscapes,* edited by Richard F. Townsend, pp. 61–70. Chicago: The Art Institute of Chicago.
1993   *Tortillas for the Gods: A Symbolic Analysis of Zinacanteco Rituals.* Paperback Edition. Norman: University of Oklahoma Press.
In Press: "On the Application of the Phylogenetic Model to the Maya". *North American Indian Anthropology: Essays on Society and Culture,* edited by Raymond J. DeMallie and Alfonso Ortiz. Norman: University of Oklahoma Press.

Vogt, Evon Z., and Suzanne Abel
1977   "On Political Rituals in Contemporary Mexico." *Secular Ritual,* edited by Sally F. Moore and Barbara G. Myerhoff, pp. 173–88. Amsterdam: Royal Van Gordum Press.
Vogt, Evon Z., and Ethel M. Albert (editors)
1966   *People of Rimrock: A Study of Values in Five Cultures.* Cambridge: Harvard University Press.
Vogt, Evon Z., and Ray Hyman.
1959   *Water Witching U.S.A.* Chicago: University of Chicago Press. 2d edition 1979.
Vogt, Evon Z., and Richard M. Leventhal (editors)
1983   *Prehistoric Settlement Patterns: Essays in Honor of Gordon R. Willey.* Albuquerque: University of New Mexico Press.
Vogt, Evon Z., and Thomas F. O'Dea

1953   "A Comparative Study of the Role of Values in Social Action in Two Southwestern Communities." *American Sociological Review* 18: 645–54.

Vogt, Evon Z., and A. Kimball Romney

1971   "The Use of Aerial Photographic Techniques in Maya Ethnography." *Papers of the VII Congrés International des Sciences Anthropologiques et Ethnologiques,* 11: 156–71. Moscow.

Vogt, Evon Z., and Alberto Ruz Lhuiller (editors)

1964   *Desarrollo Cultural de los Mayas,* México: Seminario de Cultura Maya, Universidad Autónoma de México. (Revised edition 1971)

Vogt, Evon Z., and Catherine C. Vogt

1970   "Levi-Strauss among the Maya." *Man* 5(3): 379–92.

1980   "Pre-Columbian Mayan and Mexican Symbols in Zinacanteco Ritual." *La Antropología Americanista en la Actualidad: Homenaje a Raphael Girard.* 1: 499–523. México: Editores Mexicanos Unidos.

Von Mering, Otto

1956   "Individual and Cultural Patterns of Valuation." Ph.D. diss., Harvard University.

Wali, Alaka

1974   "Dependence and Dominance: The Status of Women in Zinacantan." A.B. honors thesis, Harvard University.

1989   *Kilowatts and Crisis: Hydroelectric Power and Social Dislocation in Eastern Panama.* Boulder, Colo.: Westview Press.

Wallerstein, Immanuel

1974   *The Modern World-System I: Capitalist Agriculture and the Origins of the European World-Economy in the Sixteenth Century.* New York: Academic Press.

1980   *The Modern World-System II: Mercantilism and the Consolidation of the European World-Economy, 1600–1750.* New York: Academic Press.

Warfield, James P.

1966   "La arquitectura en Zinacantan." *Los Zinacantecos: Un Pueblo Tzotzil de Los Altos de Chiapas,* edited by Evon Z.

Vogt, pp. 183–207. Colección de Antropología Social, vol. 7. Mexico: Instituto Nacional Indigenista.

Warman, Arturo
1972   Los Campesinos: Hijos Predilectos del Regime. México: Editorial Nuestro Tiempo.
1980   Ensayos Sobre el Campesino en México. México: Nueva Imagen.

Warshauer, Maxine M.
1969   "Marriage in Chamula." Summer Field Report, Harvard Chiapas Project, Peabody Museum, Harvard University.

Wasserstrom, Robert
1970   "Our Lady of the Salt." A.B. honors thesis, Harvard University.
1977   "White Fathers and Red Souls: Indian-Ladino Relations in Highland Chiapas, 1528–1973." Ph.D. diss., Harvard University.
1983   Class and Society in Central Chiapas. Berkeley: University of California Press.

Watanabe, John M.
1983   "In the World of the Sun: A Cognitive Model of Mayan Cosmology." Man 18 (4): 710–28.
1984   " 'We Who Are Here': The Cultural Conventions of Ethnic Identity in a Guatemala Village, 1937–1980." Ph.D. diss., Harvard University.
1989   "Elusive Essences: Souls and Social Identity in Two Highland Maya Communities." Ethnographic Encounters in Southern Mesoamerica: Essays in Honor of Evon Z. Vogt, Jr., edited by Victoria R. Bricker and Gary H. Gossen, pp. 263–74. Austin: University of Texas Press.
1992   Maya Saints and Souls in a Changing World. Austin: University of Texas Press.

Weathers, Nadine
1947   "Tzotzil Phonemes with Special Reference to Allophones of B." International Journal of American Linguistics 13: 108–11.
1950   "Morphological Analysis of a Tzotzil (Mayan) Text." International Journal of American Linguistics 16: 91–98.

Werby, Elizabeth A.

1971   "Tzotzil Speech and Couplet Pair Formations." Summer Field Report, Harvard Chiapas Project, Peabody Museum, Harvard University.

Whelan, Frederick G.

1967   "The Passing of the Years." Summer Field Report, Harvard Chiapas Project, Peabody Museum, Harvard University.

Whiting, John W. M., Eleanor Hollenberg Chasdi, Helen Faigin Antonovsky, and Barbara Chartier Ayres

1966   "The Learning of Values." *People of Rimrock: A Study of Values in Five Cultures*, edited by Evon Z. Vogt and Ethel M. Albert, pp. 83–125, Cambridge: Harvard University Press.

Wiesner, Lisa

1970   "The Functions of Dreams in Zinacantan." Summer Field Report, Harvard Chiapas Project, Peabody Museum, Harvard University.

Wilk, Richard R.

1985   "The Ancient Maya and the Political Present." *Journal of Anthropological Research* 41: 307–26.

Willey, Gordon R.

1988   *Portraits in American Archaeology: Remembrances of Some Distinguished Americanists.* Albuquerque: University of New Mexico Press.

1989   "Vogt at Harvard." *Ethnographic Encounters in Southern Mesoamerica: Essays in Honor of Evon Z. Vogt, Jr.*, edited by Victoria R. Bricker and Gary H. Gossen, pp. 21–32. Austin: University of Texas Press.

Wilson, G. Carter

1963   "Drinking and Drinking Customs in a Mayan Community." Summer Field Report, Harvard Chiapas Project, Peabody Museum, Harvard University.

1966   *Crazy February: Death and Life in the Mayan Highlands of Mexico.* New York: Lippincott.

1972   *A Green Tree and a Dry Tree.* New York: Macmillan.

Winship, George Parker

1896   "The Coronado Expedition of 1540–1542." *14th Annual*

Report of the Bureau of American Ethnology for the Years 1892–1893. Washington, D.C.: Smithsonian Institution.

Wolf, Eric R.

1955   "Types of Latin American Peasantry: A Preliminary Discussion." *American Anthropologist* 57(3): 452–71.

1956   "Aspects of Group Relations in a Complex Society." *American Anthropologist* 58(6): 1065–78.

1957   "Closed Corporate Communities in Mesoamerica and Java." *Southwestern Journal of Anthropology* 13(1): 1–18.

Wren, Linnea Holmer

1967   "Communications Networks in Zinacantan." Freshman seminar on the Maya, Harvard Chiapas Project, Peabody Museum, Harvard University.

1970   "Aerial Photography: New Perspectives on Anthropological Research." A.B. honors thesis, Harvard University

1974   "Aerial Photography in the Investigation of Settlement and Trail Patterns in Highland Chiapas." *Aerial Photography in Anthropological Field Research*, edited by Evon Z. Vogt, pp. 125–39. Cambridge: Harvard University Press.

1989   "Composition and Content in Maya Sculpture: A Study of Ballgame Scenes at Chichen Itza, Yucatan, Mexico." *Ethnographic Encounters in Southern Mesoamerica: Essays in Honor of Evon Z. Vogt, Jr.*, edited by Victoria R. Bricker and Gary H. Gossen, pp. 287–301. Austin: University of Texas Press.

Young, Allen I.

1962   "Mexico's Federal Corn Warehouses in Highland Chiapas." Summer Field Report, Harvard Chiapas Project, Peabody Museum, Harvard University.

Young, Stephen B.

1965   "Their People's Servants: Political Officials in a Highland Maya Community." Summer Field Report, Harvard Chiapas Project, Peabody Museum, Harvard University.

Zabala, Manuel T.

1961a   "Sistema Economico de la Comunidad de Zinacantan." M.A. thesis, Escuela Nacional de Antropología e Historia. México.

1961b   "Instituciones Politicas y Religiosas de Zinacantan." *Estudios de Cultura Maya* 1: 147–58.

Zimbalist, Michelle

1966   "La Granadilla: Un Modelo de la Estructura Social Zinacanteca." *Los Zinacantecos: Un Pueblo Tzotzil de los Altos de Chiapas,* edited by Evon Z. Vogt, pp. 275–97. Colección de Antropología Social, vol. 7. México: Instituto Nacional Indigenista

Zingg, Robert M.

1938   *Huichols: Primitive Artists.* University of Denver Contributions to Ethnography, no. 1. Denver: University of Denver Press.

Zubin, David A.

1963   "The San Cristobal Corn Market: A Discussion of Vendor-Buyer Interaction." Summer Field Report, Harvard Chiapas Project, Peabody Museum, Harvard University.

Zweng, Nancy A.

1975   "*Vach Unen:* A Study of Zinacanteco Twins." Summer Field Report, Harvard Chiapas Project, Peabody Museum, Harvard University.

APPENDIX 1
PROJECT
FIELDWORKERS:
1957–1980

PROJECT FIELDWORKERS: 1957–1980

(Listed by year of their first field research with the Harvard Chiapas Project)

Year	Name	Present Affiliation or Occupation
1957	Frank C. Miller	Anthropology, University of Minnesota
1958	Benjamin N. Colby	Anthropology, University of California, Irvine
	Lore M. Colby	Linguistics
	Pierre L. van den Berghe	Sociology, University of Washington
1959	Susan Tax Freeman	Anthropology, University of Illinois, Chicago Circle
	Robert M. Laughlin	Anthropology, Smithsonian Institution
	Manuel T. Zabala	Anthropology (Columbia)
1960	William N. Binderman	Attorney, New York City
	Francesca M. Cancian	Sociology, University of California, Irvine
	Frank Cancian	Anthropology, University of California, Irvine
	George A. Collier	Anthropology, Stanford University

	Jane F. Collier	Anthropology, Stanford University
	Stephen F. Gudeman	Anthropology, University of Minnesota
	Duane Metzger	Anthropology, University of California, Irvine
	Peggy Reeves Sanday	Anthropology, University of Pennsylvania
	Henry E. York	Social Sciences Librarian, Cleveland State University
1961	Adelaide Pirrotta Bahr	Anthropology
	Donald M. Bahr	Anthropology, Arizona State University
	Jordan P. Benderly	Government Service, Washington
	Harvey E. Goldberg	Anthropology, Hebrew University (Israel)
	Eric Prokosch	American Friends Service Committee (London)
	Jack R. Stauder	Anthropology, Southeastern Massachusetts University
	Philip G. Stubblefield	Obstetrics, Harvard Medical School
1962	Nicholas A. Acheson	Microbiology, McGill University
	Susan E. Carey	Psychology, Massachusetts Institute of Technology
	Matthew D. Edel	Deceased
	Ronald Maduro	Deceased
	Allen I. Young	Journalism
1963	Georges S. Arbuz	Anthropology (France)
	Victoria Reifler Bricker	Anthropology, Tulane University
	Nicholas F. Bunnin	Philosophy, University of Essex (England)
	John D. Early	Anthropology, Florida Atlantic University
	Nancy L. Ettrick	Geriatrics

	Mary L. Felsteiner	History
	Michelle Zimbalist Rosaldo	Deceased
	Daniel B. Silver	Attorney, Washington
	James P. Warfield	Architecture, University of Illinois
	G. Carter Wilson	Literature, University of California, Santa Cruz
	David A. Zubin	Linguistics
1964	Merida H. Blanco	Anthropology
	Nancy J. Chodorow	Sociology, University of California, Berkeley
	Antonio Gilman	Anthropology, California State University, Northridge
	Benedicta F. Gilman	Editor, Getty Museum
	Rand E. Rosenblatt	Law School, Rutgers University
	John D. Strucker	Teacher, Cambridge, Massachusetts
1965	Claude de Chavigny	Political Science (France)
	Roger M. Dunwell	Attorney (Haiti)
	Gordon A. Gilbert	Teacher, New York City
	Gary H. Gossen	Anthropology, State University of New York, Albany
	Patrick J. Menget	Anthropology, Faculte des Lettres, Nanterre (France)
	Richard S. Price	Anthropology (Martinique)
	Sally H. Price	Anthropology (Martinique)
	Todd D. Rakoff	Harvard Law School
	Renato I. Rosaldo	Anthropology, Stanford University
	Diana M. Scott	Unknown
	Barbara S. Strodt	Teacher, University of Puerto Rico
	Gwendoline van den Berghe	Secretary General, European Journal of Medicine (France)
	Elena Uribe Wood	Diplomat (England)
	Stephen B. Young	Law, Hamline University St. Paul, Minnesota

1966	T. Berry Brazelton	Pediatrics, Harvard Medical School
	John B. Haviland	Anthropology and Linguistics, Reed College
	Lois M. Hinderlie	Unknown
	M. Haven Logan	Unknown
	Judith E. Merkel	Ananda Marga Cult (Brazil)
	John S. Robey	Pediatrics, Harvard Medical School
	Arden Aibel Rothstein	Clinical Psychology
	Ronald L. Trosper	Forestry, Northern Arizona University
	Mary Anschuetz Vogt	Journalism, San Francisco
1967	Carolyn Pope Edwards	Psychological Anthropology, University of Kentucky
	Leslie K. Devereaux	Anthropology, Australian National University
	Stephanie L. Krebs	Consulting, San Francisco
	John M. Miyamoto	Psychology, University of Michigan
	Ana Montes de Gonzalez	Anthropology (Argentina)
	Abigail S. Natelson	Filmmaking, New York City
	Mark L. Rosenberg	Medicine, Centers for Disease Control, Atlanta
	Richard A. Shweder	Anthropology, University of Chicago
	Fred G. Whelan	Political Science, University of Pittsburgh
1968	Maxine Warshauer Baker	Musician
	Carla P. Childs	Teacher, Friends School, Baltimore
	Jonathan P. Hiatt	Attorney, Washington, D.C.
	Felisa M. Kazen	Television, New York City
	Susan Levine Kaplan	Psychology
	Francesco Pellizzi	Anthropology and Art, New York City

	Charles F. Sabel	Economics, Massachusetts Institute of Technology
	Diane L. Rus	Bilingual Education, Los Angeles
	Jan Rus, III	Anthropology
1969	Suzanne Abel	Archaeology
	Ira Abrams	Radio-TV-Film, University of Texas, Austin
	Katherine Brazelton	Musician
	Carol J. Greenhouse	Anthropology, University of Indiana
	Benjamin S. Orlove	Anthropology, University of California, Davis
	Timothy N. Rush	Labor Committee, New York City
	Joshua H. Smith	Researcher, Municipality of Metropolitan Seattle
	Lars C. Smith	Applied Anthropology (Denmark)
	Robert F. Wasserstrom	Waste-disposal,Houston
1970	J. Lauren Bardrick	Artist, Massachusetts
	Kenneth L. Carson	Attorney, Boston
	Susan E. Epstein	Physician, Fort Harrison, Montana
	Patricia M. Greenfield	Psychology, University of California, Los Angeles
	Peter J. Guarnaccia	MedicalAnthropology, Rutgers University
	Jeffrey C. Howry	Applied Anthropology
	Priscilla Rachun Linn	Anthropology, Smithsonian Institution
	Philippa de Menil	Art, New York City
	Elizabeth A. Wiesner	Physician, Branford, Connecticut
1971	Jason W. Clay	Anthropologist, Rights and Resources, Inc.

	Thomas Crump	Anthropology, University of Amsterdam (The Netherlands)
	Patricia E. Lynch	Commercial Real Estate Development, Washington, D.C.
	Roger H. Reed	Attorney, McAllen, Texas
	Rachel Z. Ritvo	Child Psychiatrist, Kensington, Maryland
	Elisabeth A. Werby	Attorney, New York City
	Elizabeth M. Dodd	Attorney, San Francisco
1972	Jane B. Baird	Journalism, Houston
	William S. Freeman	Attorney, San Francisco
	Eliot M. Gelwan	Psychiatrist, Cambridge, Massachusetts
	Donald E. McVicker	Anthropology, North Central College
	Mary E. Scott	Sinologist, San Francisco State University
	Suzanne E. Siskel	Ford Foundation (Indonesia)
	Ricardo D. Sutton	Unknown
	Marta D. Turok	Anthropologist, Asociación de Artes y Cultura Popular (Mexico)
1973	Thor R. Anderson	Anthropology, University of California, Berkeley
	Emily S. Apter	French and Comparative Literature, University of California, Davis
	John N. Burstein	Government Service, Washington
	Rowena I. Frazer	Education
	Thomas L. Paradise	Land Development, Corona, California
	Charles A. Vogt	Environmental Biology (Ecuador)
	Alaka Wali	Anthropology, University of Maryland

1974	Samuel M. Anderson	Architect, New York City
	Denise Z. Field	Attorney, Washington, D.C.
	Richard A. Gonzalez	Unknown
	Peter J. Haviland	Attorney, Los Angeles
	Sara J. Lacy	Engineering, Tufts University
	Marcy S. Richmond	Attorney, Boston
	Paul L. Saffo	Research Fellow, Institute of the Future, Menlo Park, California
	Nancy A. Zweng	Banker, New York City
1975	V. Tonik Barber	Unknown
	Kelly T. Jensen	Computer Firm
	Gilbert V. Marin	Unknown
1976	None	
1977	None	
1978	Alexandra Buresch	Unknown
	Jerome M. Levi	Anthropology, Carleton College
	Kazuyasu Ochiai	Anthropology, Chubu University (Tokyo)
	Ines Sanmiguel	Spanish teacher (London)
1979	Stephen L. Roof	Attorney, Miami
1980	Cynthia McVay	Consultant, McKinsey Company, New York City

APPENDIX 2
FIELD LEADERS:
1957–1980

Field Leaders: 1957–1980

1957 to 1959	Evon Z. Vogt
1960	Duane Metzger
1961	Evon Z. Vogt
1962	Frank Cancian
1963	Evon Z. Vogt
1964	George A. Collier, with G. Carter Wilson as assistant
1965	Evon Z. Vogt, with George A. Collier as assistant
1966	George A. Collier
1967 to 1970	Evon Z. Vogt, with George A. Collier as assistant
1971	John B. Haviland
1972	Priscilla Rachun Linn
1973 and 1974	Evon Z. Vogt
1975	Jan Rus, III
1976 to 1980	Evon Z. Vogt

APPENDIX 3
ADMINISTRATIVE/
RESEARCH
ASSISTANTS

ADMINISTRATIVE/RESEARCH ASSISTANTS

1957–61	Harriet Frazier
1959–60	Barbara Metzger
1961–62	Mary Ascheim
1962–63	Anita Safran
1963–64	Norah Lambelet
1964–66	Gloria Caetano
1966–67	Patricia Balacz de Hume
1966–68	Nora Mascarhenas de Sacerdote
1968–69	Candy Walter Shweder
1969–72	Dolores Vidal
1972–73	Sharon Latterman
1973–75	Suzanne Abel
1975–77	Sara Nordgren

APPENDIX 4
Ph.D. DISSERTATIONS

Ph.D. Dissertations
1959	Frank C. Miller
1960	Benjamin N. Colby
1963	Robert M. Laughlin
1963	Frank Cancian
1963	Francesca M. Cancian
1964	Lore M. Colby
1965	John D. Early
1966	Daniel B. Silver
1968	Victoria R. Bricker
1968	George A. Collier
1969	Eric Prokosch (Stanford)
1970	Jane F. Collier (Tulane)
1970	Gary H. Gossen
1971	John B. Haviland
1972	Felisa M. Kazen
1976	Thomas Crump (London)
1976	Jeffrey C. Howry
1977	Priscilla Rachun Linn (Oxford)
1977	Robert F. Wasserstrom
1978	Leslie K. Haviland
1979	Elena Uribe Wood

APPENDIX 5
SENIOR HONORS
THESES

Senior Honors Theses

1961	Stephen F. Gudeman
1962	Donald M. Bahr
1962	Jane H. Fishburne
1962	Phillip G. Stubblefield
1963	George A. Collier
1964	Nancy Locke (Smith College)
1966	Evelyn R. Thomsen (Vassar College)
1967	Barbara Strodt Lopez
1967	Ronald L. Trosper
1969	Sarah C. Blaffer
1969	Carolyn Pope Edwards
1969	Jan Rus, III
1970	Linnea K. Holmer
1970	John M. Miyamoto
1970	Robert F. Wasserstrom
1971	Carol J. Greenhouse
1971	Timothy N. Rush
1972	Peter J. Guarnaccia
1972	Rachel Z. Ritvo
1973	Roger H. Reed
1974	Joan B. Baca
1974	William S. Freeman
1974	Suzanne E. Siskel
1974	Thomas L. Paradise

441

1974 Alaka Wali
1975 Thor R. Anderson
1975 John N. Burstein
1975 Denise Z. Field
1976 Kelly T. Jensen
1976 Sara J. Lacy
1977 V. Tonik Barber
1980 Alexandra Buresch
1980 Stephen L. Roof

INDEX